# What Others Are Saying

"At a time when the 'star religions' of the ancient Egyptians, Sumerians, and Mayans are coming to light, David's research and insightfulness add a greater depth of understanding to what was known about the sky by the ancient Anasazi and Hopi Indians of the Southwest. In the same brilliant spirit of Robert Bauval and Graham Hancock, David proves again and again the importance of Orion and other constellations to the earliest people on Earth. His book in turn makes a valuable contribution to our spiritual unfolding in modern times." -Page Bryant, author of *Spiritwalking*

"Gary A. David has made a marvelous and insightful contribution to the history of the Hopi Indians with his ongoing research in Arizona. His work is unique and shows the pre-Columbian cross-cultural knowledge, that was shared by the peoples of the world in prehistory, was extant in Arizona with the Hopi."   -Crichton EM Miller, author of *The Golden Thread of Time*

"A truly fascinating reading of Hopi-Egyptian relations. Gary David, a non-Hopi, has put together a significant in-depth research that reflects on some of the Hopis' best-kept knowledge of astronomy and history, known only to a handful of entrusted record keepers of the ancient Hopisinom... a must-read."                    -ros, Hopi village of Munquapi, Third Mesa

"David's work offers an exciting and refreshing new view of history, people and the importance of the stars (star peoples) in the development of their cultures... and now the possibility of reforging the essential connection. This has broad implications."
   -Lane Badger, publisher of *Four Corners* magazine, Sedona, Arizona

"I have examined the Arizona-Orion ground-sky relationship, and I must say that I find this work intriguing. It is worth pursuing to the very end."
                    -Andrew Collins, author of *The Cygnus Mystery*

# The Orion Zone

### Ancient Star Cities
### of the American Southwest

## *Gary A. David*

## Adventures Unlimited Press

**The Orion Zone:**
**Ancient Star Cities**
**of the American Southwest**

**Adventures Unlimited Press**
**P.O. Box 74**
**Kempton, Illinois 60946   USA**
**1-800-718-4514 or 1-815-253-6390**
**www.adventuresunlimitedpress.com**

ISBN 1-931882-65-7

Cover graphic and design by Jack Andrews.
See his excellent Web sites:
http://jackandrewsart.com and http://mysteriousarizona.com

Photographs, maps, and graphics (except Fig. 6) by Gary A. David
Printed in the United States of America

# CONTENTS

# ILLUSTRATIONS

# ACKNOWLEDGMENTS

I wish to thank the following people, who in sundry ways contributed to my understanding of this subject: Jack Andrews, Manoochehr Arian, Steve Bartholomew, Beau Berger, Karen Berggren, T.L. Subash Chandira Bose, Page Bryant, Patrick Conlan, George DeLange, Martin Doutré, Ross Hamilton, Alan Johnson, Amanda Laoupi, Gene D. Matlock, Barry McEwen, Howard Middleton-Jones, Crichton EM Miller, Tom Mills, Rob Milne, Jeff Nisbet, Liz O'Driscoll, Rami Sajdi, Michael Seabrook, Gwynne Spencer, and Ray Urbaniak.

I would like to acknowledge the following publishers, who made articles on or references to *The Orion Zone* available in print or over the Internet: Lane Badger (*Four Corners*), Michael Bourne (www.book-of-thoth.com), David Hatcher Childress (*World Explorer*), Simon Cox (*Duat*, CD-ROM), Gerry (www.farshores.org), Kim Guarnaccia (*Mysteries Magazine*), Graham Hancock (www.grahamhancock.com), Dr. Sri Jagannatha Swami, (www.srilalitha.org), J. Douglas Kenyon (*Atlantis Rising*), Christopher Lock (www.wingmakers.com), Wayne May (*Ancient American*), Hilly Rose (interviews, Sirius Satellite Radio), Preston Peet (*UNDERGROUND! The Disinformation Guide to Ancient Civilizations...*), Alex Sokolowski (www.world-mysteries.com), Greg Taylor and Rick Gned (*Sub Rosa* and www.dailygrail.com), and Gary Vey (www.viewzone.com).

My special thanks go to Rob Milne of South Africa for his great work in compiling the index. His own book *Beyond Orion* will be released by Sabic Publishing in 2007. See his fine Internet site: www.sabic.co.za/robmilne

Finally, I want to thank my wife, Anita S. Descault, who proofread the manuscript and offered many useful, insightful suggestions. Without her support and encouragement, this project would not have been possible.

For additional information and photos, see **The Orion Zone** Web site: www.theorionzone.com
E-mail the author: islandhillsbooks@msn.com.

# Preface

Because of the heterogeneous nature of *The Orion Zone: Ancient Star Cities of the American Southwest*, at least some portion is bound to disturb or displease almost any faction on the intellectual spectrum. Part archaeology, part astronomy, part cultural anthropology, part ethnographic theology, part historical linguistics, part comparative mythology, part metaphysical speculation, pervaded at times with an aura of poetry, the book serves as a point of convergence for a wide variety of disciplines. As the author of such a peculiar ilk of investigative research, I will undoubtedly be perceived in certain quarters as an interloper— the proverbial jack of all fields and master of none. This bias, however, is more the result of the contemporary compartmentalization of epistemology that academia reinforces or the dominance of scientism in the average layperson's world view than it is a valid critique of such a hybrid genre. If the aim is hard science, then one best look elsewhere. Although I have rigorously collected and scrutinized a substantial amount of archaeological and ethnographic evidence to support my book's primary thesis, its ultimate goal is not the advancement of scientific theories or the patient accumulation of data. In fact, the stakes are much higher. The implications found here involve the daunting task of helping to redefine the paradigms and parameters of the cultural evolution and history of our planet.

The discipline closest to the concerns of *The Orion Zone* would probably be the fledgling field of archaeoastronomy. Struggling itself for a reputable niche among archaeologists and astronomers, this field investigates the physical structures, rock art and artifacts of ancient cultures, then speculates on the theories and practices of those people as they gazed upward to the heavens. However, the spirit of this book and that of archaeoastronomy are sometimes not quite simpatico. Perhaps this is the result of an inherent skepticism overarching the field like a cold, blank sky. The proclivity to measure and ratiocinate, quantify and catalogue, gives rise to the notion of the Earth as an outdoor laboratory where sundry hypotheses can be empirically tested —usually with the prospect of a tenured sinecure in the back of the mind— rather than a natural altar upon which hierophanic visions may be received. As John Michell, one of the leading authorities on archaeoastronomy, has written, "Astro-archaeology [an older term for the discipline], therefore, if pursued where it inevitably leads, takes its followers back down to earth and into the realm of spirits and earth energies— losing its academic status and respectability in the process. Spiritual energies are not recognized by archaeological excavators, nor are they much esteemed by modern astronomers! Yet no serious inquiry into the problem of megaliths can avoid the subject of geomancy and the mysterious energies it locates in the landscape."[1] In other words, one will be missing the point if he or she cannot acknowledge such seemingly metaphysical concepts as the mystical energy of ley lines functioning as the terrestrial nervous system of Gaia. Furthermore, in order for the material in my book to make sense one must countenance the possibility of an infusion of spiritual energy flowing from specific stars in the sky to specific points on the earth.

Ultimately, the spirit of this book might best be summed up with the coined word *archaeo-astropoesis*. For the Greeks the word *poesis* (from which the word *poetry* is derived) literally meant "to make" or "to craft" something. Thus, by taking the archaeological and astronomical evidence and intuitively constructing a schema, I may have stumbled across a system that had an incontrovertible meaning for the Ancient Ones. Only the individual can decide for him/herself. To accept the primary theory of my book will take a leap of faith that only poets and mystics are wont to make. Of course, I am not asking readers to leap blindly, but would encourage them instead to bring along the analytical portions of their minds as a compass with which to enter what Joseph Campbell called the "magic ring of myth."[2] It takes even greater courage to penetrate this circle knowing that it was drawn upon the earth by cosmic forces of interstellar space. In the very distant past the seeds of sidereal consciousness spiraled downward to impregnate those creatures emerging from the dust, including *Homo sapiens*, and in so doing shaped their cosmology and basic ontological understanding. "Even though it were possible to resolve all mythology to a basic astral mythology—what the mythological consciousness derives from contemplation of the stars, what it sees in them directly, would still be something radically different from the view they present to empirical observation or the way they figure in theoretical speculation and scientific 'explanations' of natural phenomena."[3] As the philosopher Ernst Cassirer has stated, we must first attempt to grasp the mythical consciousness of our ancestors if we are to conceptualize the spiritual framework and concomitant complexities of their world. At this late stage of civilization this is perhaps a difficult if not insuperable task.

Or perhaps not. The hallmark of a truly advanced civilization might be the ability to fuse mythology and science, to incorporate all the ancient traditions of sacred geometry, astrology, alchemy, etc. within the most contemporary theories or technologies of archaeology, astronomy, and the rest of the modern disciplines, thereby creating or "making" a new synthesis of the religious-intuitive and the rational-empirical.

### A Definition Via Negativa

In trying to show what this book is, I can likewise show what it is *not*. For instance, this book is not specifically about Hopi religion and culture. Where a given Hopi ritual or concept is discussed, it is done so only in the context of what might have held true for the Anasazi. (The connotations of this term will be discussed in Chapter 1.) No secret lore or exclusively esoteric ceremonial details have been revealed in these pages. All the information regarding myths and rituals has been previously published in earlier ethnographic texts. No elders are coming forth to state the ultimate meaning of existence or expound on the prophetic ramifications of what increasingly seems to be the "End Times," or, as the Hopi say, the "Time of the Purification." In the process of writing this book I have merely articulated the idiosyncratic coincidences supported by archaeological or mythological facts and then speculated on the far-reaching consequences of the apparent schema as it emerged. Nevertheless, I regret any offense that either any single Hopi person or the Hopi and other Pueblo people in general may have suffered as a result of a larger readership being exposed to the evidence in this book. Opinions differ on what should or should not be told, but in these chaotic times many Native American elders seem to favor more rather than less disclosure.

Some readers may criticize a few of the book's sources. In particular, Frank Waters' work has drawn considerable fire in recent years, and I am well aware of the controversy. One anthropologist has called *Book of the Hopi* a "notorious confabulation of fact and imagination."[4] Although inaccuracies obviously exist in the ethnographic research of Waters, to summarily reject it might be a case of throwing the proverbial baby out with the bath water. Undoubtedly, Waters in his zeal to impose the universal framework of structuralism upon the heterogeneous Hopi culture unwittingly created a somewhat distorted picture. In the end though, one should ask whether or not his contributions to an understanding of this native group outweigh the misapprehensions caused by the book. In all truth, I believe that one would be disingenuous to respond in the negative.

In addition, certain rumors persists on the un-Hopi (*qahopi*) nature of Waters' primary informant Oswald White Bear Fredericks, focusing on his reputed ostentatious and gasconading manner. However, to discount a serious work such as *Book of the Hopi* solely because of certain culturally incongruent traits of its primary informant would be tantamount to faulting the expertise of a successful Wall Street broker just because he or she may happen to be non-competitive, non-aggressive, and diffident. Adding to the controversy, the popularity of *Book of the Hopi*, published in 1963, unleashed a wave of animosity from the Hopi people that has not receded to this day. The work unfortunately became a convenient paperback guidebook, luring to Hopiland a horde of counterculture seekers of enlightenment whose ethos could not have been further from that of the people they were emulating. Both the libertine lifestyle and psychedelic drugs that these long-haired "pahanas" brought were deeply offensive to the Hopi. Ultimately this intrusion caused misunderstanding and rancor on both sides. In the final analysis, however, I think that Waters wrote a useful book to be approached with caution, not a book to be ignored.

More recently, Thomas E. Mails, former Lutheran minister, talented artist, and prolific writer on Native American culture and religion, has stirred up a similar brouhaha with his books *Hotevilla* and *The Hopi Survival Kit*. He too has been charged with revealing ceremonial secrets and helping to unravel the tightly woven fabric of Hopi society. In many cases, however, the genie had already been let out of the bottle. This was done, for good or for ill, by a number of late nineteenth and early twentieth century ethnographers— men like H. R. Voth, the Mennonite missionary who was accustomed to forcing his way into kiva ceremonies uninvited, or Alexander M. Stephen, who lived on and off with the Hopi for years, producing a massive and richly illustrated journal on Hopi religious practices, but who could still write words such as the following: "They hovered on the boundary of philosophic thought, but they were incapable of pursuing the thread of their investigations, an incompetent reasoning faculty involved (sic) them in a labyrinth of vague and dreamy impressions.... In the *kibu* [kiva] they were content to hide their ignorance in mysticism, and they inculcated their fallacious ideas of nature under this veil."[5] Clearly, the ubiquitous prejudices of one's own era sometimes overshadow the best of intentions.

At least today the majority of the observers of Hopi culture show a more profound respect and even reverence for the object of their inquiry than did their predecessors. Despite this, destabilizing factors persist. A factionalism endemic to many contemporary Indian reservations contributes to the ardor with which certain religious leaders are denounced, including Mails' primary informant the late Dan Evehema.[6] Time and again arises the question of which chief has greater religious authority and power. Add the traditional schism of "hostiles" and "friendlies" perpetuated in part by the B.I.A. (Bureau of Indian Affairs) and the tribal government, and you have a cultural landscape fraught with peril. In the face of all this the only prudent course, it seems, would be to give the benefit of the doubt to those writers who are articulate, sensitive to cultural needs, and genuine in the methods of their research. To give any one source too much credence is foolhardy, but to ignore any substantive research is equally imprudent.

Nonetheless, some people even go so far as to refuse to read some ethnographic literature, especially those examples written earlier. In addition, among certain academic circles the mistrust of the recently transcribed oral tradition vis-à-vis the Anasazi is extreme. Jeffrey S. Dean, a renowned expert from the University of Arizona on dendrochronology, recently stated: "'I don't think the Hopi oral traditions are worth the paper they're written on.'" This comment shows his cleverness but not necessarily his common sense. Dean claims that the two "fault lines" — one being the pueblo abandonment that followed the great drought in the last quarter of thirteenth century and the other the Spanish *entrada* in the mid-sixteenth century— fractured the Hopi culture so badly that it is, for all practical purposes, as far removed from the Anasazi as are contemporary Anglos.[7] Clearly, the evidence shows otherwise. Archived in the Special Collections library at Northern Arizona University is a photograph taken in the early twentieth century of a young Hopi maiden with characteristic butterfly (sometimes misdesignated as squash blossom) hair whorls called *poli'ini* on each side of her head.8 (See Chapter 13.) Depicted in Fig. 1 is a petroglyph with the very same hairstyle carved in about the late thirteenth century. If a simple fashion like this can endure for well over six hundred years, how much more important would be the transmission of myths and legends essential to Hopi cultural identity and beliefs.

Continuity is an important hallmark for the Hopi. This trait allows us to reasonably assume that what is true for these contemporary people was also true for their ancestors, the Anasazi, at least to a degree. Even though cultural variations are inevitable through time, the Hopi more than most have preserved the culture of the Ancient Ones. This sense of continuity is primarily due to their general nature, which is stubbornly and obsessively conservative. (The terms "conservative" and "liberal" as they appear in the modern political context have very little meaning in our discussion. The fact that the Hopi are considered conservative rather than progressive helped them to survive the genocidal tactics used first by the Spanish in the 16th and 17th centuries and then by the Anglos in the 19th and early 20th centuries.)

## *The Upshot*

The *Orion Zone* adds to the mounting evidence gathered worldwide that the Ancients constructed their villages and religious sanctuaries to reflect certain aspects of the stars. One of the first books to illustrate this theory was *The Orion Mystery* by Robert Bauval and Adrian Gilbert. This international bestseller basically notes the spatial correlation of the pyramids at Giza and the constellation Orion. My book acknowledges this research and expands it to include the North American continent. In essence, Orion provided the template by which the Anasazi determined their villages' locations during a migration period lasting centuries. Spiritually mandated

**Fig. 1. Petroglyph of a woman with a maiden whorls hair style, in Hopi also called** nögla, **or "butterfly whorls"**

by a god the Hopi call Masau'u, this "terrestrial Orion" closely mirrors its celestial counterpart, with prehistoric "cities" corresponding to *all* the major stars in the constellation. By its specific orientation the sidereal pattern projected upon the Arizona high desert also encodes various sunrise and sunset points of both summer and winter solstices. Although this configuration extends to a number of contiguous constellations, a central flux of ley line energy occurs along a series of ancient pueblo sites and geoglyphs ranging from southwestern Colorado to the mouth of the Colorado River. This indicates the functional chakra system of Orion as reflected in the transfigured Earth.

By analyzing geodetic alignments of pueblo ruins, photographing rock art, correlating indigenous cultural motifs, and utilizing astronomical computer programs to determine star positions in the ancient past, I explore the fundamental principles and ultimate purposes of the Orion Correlation as manifested in the American Southwest. In doing so, I share participation in an ideological movement that is currently shattering conventional paradigms of human history and evolution. The world suddenly has become far different than previous assumptions about it would ever have admitted. The uniformitarian paradigm of slow, gradual, steady progression from simple, primitive societies to more complex, highly refined civilizations no longer explains the data now coming to light. To account for schemata such as astral-terrestrial correlations, some theorists are beginning to posit both catastrophism and diffusionism as major influences in the development of diverse ancient cultures around the globe. For many people, in fact, the paradigm shift has already occurred.

### *The Outline*

Although I advise against taking the chapters out of sequence, readers will find the book's central thesis in its most concentrated form (viz., the Orion Correlation theory as it is implemented in Arizona) in Chapter 2. The first chapter researches the character of the Anasazi, while Chapter 3 inquires into the mythological significance of Orion according to the various cultures around the world, including the Hopi, who associate the constellation with their god Masau'u.

Chapter 4 describes in greater depth the village and ruin sites corresponding to the belt stars as well as to the shoulders and legs. Chapter 5 deals with the effects on Anasazi culture of both a supernova explosion and a volcanic eruption in the 11th century. It also discusses the Hopi stone tablets and a specific star map/solstice marker petroglyph. Chapter 6 enumerates the Arizona sites correlating to the head and arms of Orion; in addition, the chakra line is talked about in greater detail. Chapter 7 explains the Katsina Phenomenon, especially the celestial beings, while Chapter 8 designates the companion sites to Orion in the Southwest, including Grand Canyon, Chaco Canyon, and Death Valley.

Part II of the book begins with Chapter 9, which delineates the

Hopi-Mesoamerican connection. We follow the chakra line's vector into the South Pacific in Chapter 10, delving into some surprising correspondences to the ancestral Hopi. Chapter 11 investigates the global Orion legacy, focusing upon the Orion Correlation at Giza and Egyptian influences on the ancient peoples of the Colorado Plateau. Chapter 12 involves the Phoenix stargate, the ancient Hohokam, and the Masonic heart of Aztlan. Finally, Chapter 13, the most far-reaching in the book, explores the stunning implications of the Serpent People (i.e., the Knights Templar), Hopi prophecy of the End Times, and the Ant People from Orion.

### *Mea culpa and Pronoun Usage*

The great quantity of statistics in a work such as this makes it especially prone to errors of number, for which I take full responsibility. Errors of interpretation are more egregious, and for these too I must claim culpability. However, during the course of this seven-year project every attempt has been made to clarify concepts and refine the basic theory. One must admit, though, that every speculative book, published or not, is ultimately a work-in-progress, given the persistent influx of new data and hypotheses into the constantly changing intellectual climate. If this book were written five years from now, it might be markedly different in style and/or content. On the whole, *The Orion Zone* unavoidably is a product of the late 20th and early 21st centuries fraught with their millennial fever and Aquarian Age fervor.

Although I have tried to standardize orthography, variant spellings and usages from multiple sources have made this a difficult task. If I have failed at one point or another, I beg the reader's tolerance.

Except for this Preface, which uses the first person singular pronoun due to its more personal nature, the book employs the first person plural. This "we" should be conceptualized as the author and the reader journeying together toward a realization of the book's basic theme, namely the Hermetic maxim: "As Above, so Below."

*The Penguin Dictionary of Astronomy* provides the following rudimentary definition of our primary topic: "**Orion** (The Hunter) A brilliant constellation straddling the celestial equator, widely considered to be the most magnificent and interesting in the sky."[9] To this I heartily agree. A few questions posed by the Biblical author Job are also relevant here at the onset of this book.

> "Canst thou bind the sweet influences of the Pleiades,
>    or loose the bands of Orion?...
> Knowst thou the ordinances of heaven?
> Canst thou set the dominion thereof in the earth?"[10]

The Ancient Ones knew those ordinances well. As we shall see, they did indeed establish the stars' dominion upon the face of the Earth.

# Part I

# Chapter 1
# Leaving Many Footprints
# —the Emergence and Migrations
# Of the Anasazi

"Understanding the creation stories requires that we bend our minds away from the confining concept of linear time and think with the astrophysicists who explain that we are all made of the original stardust."[1]

Gregory Schaaf

"He [the Great Spirit] then gave them instructions according to which they were to migrate for a certain purpose to the four corners of the new land, leaving many footprints, rock writings, and ruins, for in time many would forget that they were all one, united by a single purpose in coming up through the reed."[2]

Dan Katchongva

## *Tracking the Anasazi: An Archaeological Perspective*

Who were the Anasazi, how did they come to inhabit the American Southwest, and why did they leave? These questions are constantly debated among archaeologists and will undoubtedly remain a focus of controversy. Even so, the quintessential Anasazi always seem to hover beyond such academic concerns. Far removed from the exigencies of our modern world, their existence is an enigma we never will fully understand. Despite the limitations of the archaeological perspective, it is nevertheless useful in following the clues these ancient people left behind. Before proceeding though, we should stress that our inquiry emulates the spirit in which most American Indians still track their game, i.e., with respect and reverence for what will provide both physical and spiritual sustenance.

In addition, we need to recognize that the term *Anasazi* is a misnomer. The word derives from the Navajo language and means "ancient ones" or "ancient enemies." Most ethnologists generally accept that the Navajo migrated into Arizona and New Mexico circa A.D. 1500-1600. From the very beginning a strong animosity existed between the long established pueblo people and these newcomers, and the term the former used to describe the latter reflects this. They called the recent arrivals *Tusavuhta*— *tu* meaning "person" and *savuhta* meaning "to pound." This nomadic tribe would capture its enemies and kill them by pounding their heads with a rock or a stone club.[3] For the generally gentle agrarians who had been living here in masonry and adobe "cities" for at least five centuries and in isolated pit houses for even longer, it must have been quite a cultural shock.

The contemporary Hopi *sinom* ("people"), many of whom live on the land in much the same way as their ancestors did, clearly prefer to use the term *Hisatsinom* ("old people" or "ancient ancestors") in referring to the original inhabitants of the land. Speaking the Uto-Aztecan (Shoshonean) language, the Hopi readily identify with these people and the villages they abandoned. The term *Hopi* itself means "people of peace," or more specifically, "those who adhere to the sacred laws." Notwithstanding, the concept of warfare had a small but enduring influence on their seasonal life; thus their pacifism historically was not absolute. While the Hopi traditionally had a disdain for violence and would rarely initiate warfare, they did follow the custom of going on the warpath after the fall harvest to obtain scalps from enemies. Upon returning home, they would frequently perform the Warrior Dance.4

Just as a monolithic representation of an entire culture can be unreliable, so too is the use of a single name to describe a culture. For instance, the Navajo in referring to themselves prefer the term *Diné*, which complicates the matter of mis-designation even further. However, to avoid confusion this book will use the more common terms *Navajo* and *Anasazi* with the full realization that the other terms mentioned are more acceptable to the native groups.

From an archaeological perspective, the Anasazi had a long and dynamic history in the Southwest. The Western Anasazi lived primarily in what is now northeastern Arizona, southern Utah, and southwestern Colorado. The Kayenta Branch of the Western Anasazi was located in Canyon de Chelly and in Tsegi Canyon (where Navajo National Monument is located.) The Mesa Verde Branch inhabited the Four Corners area along the upper San Juan River in southwestern Colorado. Another branch lived along the Little Colorado River drainage and ranged from east-central Arizona in the east to the San Francisco Peaks in the west. The Virgin River Branch existed along that river in southwestern Utah north of the present Lake Mead. At the opposite end of Anasazi domain, the Eastern group was comprised of the Chaco Canyon Branch in northwestern New Mexico and the Rio Grande Branch in central New Mexico. Of course, these classifications are used by archaeologists and not by the native groups themselves. Furthermore, these divisions are not absolutely discrete: architecture, pottery, and other cultural influences of one area sometimes can be found in the area of another.5

In addition, additional native cultures variously known as Sinagua, Hohokam, Mogollon, Salado, Mimbres, Cohonina, Patayan and Fremont have all contributed to the overall characteristics of the region prior to the Spanish *entrada* in A.D. 1540. At that date Francisco Vázquez de Coronado in his frantic but unsuccessful search for the fabled Seven Cities of Cíbola sent out from Hawikuh (near the present Zuni Pueblo) a party led by the senior lieutenant Don Pedro de Tobar into Hopi territory, which he called Tusayan. Another lieutenant named García López de Cárdenas set out northwest with twenty-five horsemen until they unexpectedly reached Grand Canyon, ethnocentrically "discovering" it and nationalistically claiming it for Spain.6 Fortunate because of its remoteness, Hopiland was one of the places in the Southwest least affected by the Spanish presence. But however interesting and important to the development of the Anasazi and their descendants the Hopi, the details of the above mentioned non-Anasazi groups and expeditions of the later historical period are, with a couple exceptions, beyond the scope of this book.

Various changes or developments in the Anasazi culture are marked by a series of chronological periods. Most likely descending from the Paleo-Indian bison and mammoth hunters of the late Pleistocene epoch, the earliest of the Anasazi are called the Basketmakers. As the name implies, this group wove finely crafted, coiled baskets out of split yucca leaves, reed or grass bundles, and apocynum, a plant related to the milkweed. Shaped into trays, shallow bowls or globular jars, the warm yellow or brown colors of these beautiful baskets were accented with red and black dyed willow splints— a precursor to the geometric designs painted on pottery for which the Anasazi are renowned. The people also made large conical water baskets lined with pinyon gum. Provided with a tump strap to go across the forehead, these baskets could carry two to three gallons of water.7. Tightly twined carrying bags and large snare nets made of yucca fiber and human hair were produced as well.

In the Basketmaker II period from A.D. 1-450 (the Basketmaker I period being only theorized but not verified), the people lived in shallow caves or rock shelters, some in which they dug slab-lined storage cysts. Corn and squash grown along alluvial flood plains were the mainstays of their diet. These staples were supplemented by pinyon nuts, acorns, berries, cactus buds, and yucca fruits as well as by sundry seeds, roots and wild greens. They also hunted deer, black bear, mountain sheep, pronghorns, birds, rabbits and other smaller rodents, using curved, wooden throwing sticks or atlatls and darts. Dogs and turkeys were the only domesticated animals; however, they were not used for food. The former were employed as pack animals and for companionship, while the latter were highly prized for their feathers. Clothing consisted of juniper and yucca aprons or breechcloths and fur robes. Durable, square-toed sandals were woven out of yucca fiber. Beautiful necklaces and pendants made of polished bird wing bones, seeds, and various types of stones such as turquoise or red shale exemplify a well-developed aesthetic sensibility. Highly prized olivella or abalone shells traded from the Pacific coast provided additional adornment.

In the Basketmaker III phase (A.D. 450 to 750) the bow and arrow replaced the atlatl, beans were added as an important dietary factor, and scattered pit houses began to be built. These circular structures were dug three to five feet deep and were about eight to twenty-five feet in diameter. Cut down with stone axes, four upright main timbers were imbedded in the floor to support cross-beams upon which rested a cribbed roof made of smaller sticks covered with brush, bark, grass and mud. Banquettes, or earthen benches, stretched around the inner circumference of the pit house, and upright stone slabs sometimes lined the walls. Aligned on a south to north axis along the packed dirt floor were the following: a ventilator shaft with a deflector stone, a fire pit, and a *sipapu,* or small hole symbolically leading to the underworld. (As we shall see, the latter is a crucial concept in the cosmology of the Anasazi.) Entry was by way of a ladder through the smoke hole in the roof. All in all, it was quite a snug refuge, especially in winter. In this phase the earliest pottery also began to be produced— a plain gray ware made by the coil-and-scrape method.

Despite the growing native cultural emphasis on ceramics and the increasingly sedentary lifestyle which that presupposes, archaeologists have deemed the next phase of Anasazi development the Pueblo period, using the Spanish word for the architectural structures of the region. Some archaeologists recognize five requisite "cultural signatures" that separate the Anasazi from other surrounding native groups:

* the kiva— a circular or sometimes rectangular underground structure used for ceremonial and kinship purposes.
* the unit pueblo— a residential structure made of a room block of at least two but sometimes a dozen or more rooms adjacent to a plaza or work space that contains the kiva
* orientation— kivas and unit pueblos that face south or south east
* a gray-and-white pottery decorated with black paint to produce distinctively Anasazi designs as well as a corrugated pottery for utility purposes
* inhumation— bodies with legs tightly flexed against the chest, knees to the chin, and heads often facing east.[8]

In Arizona the Anasazi of the Pueblo I period (A.D. 750-900) experienced minimal change in comparison with the Eastern Anasazi, who underwent a true burgeoning of the pueblo culture. In fact, there is little to distinguish this period from the previous Basketmaker III period. "For reasons we do not yet understand at present, the great Chaco system that swept up so much of the Four Corners region in its religious and organizational embrace left the Hisatsinom [of Arizona] essentially untouched."[9]

It would take until the Pueblo II period (A.D. 900-1100) for the architectural and cultural changes mentioned above to become apparent in this region. In addition to the introduction from Mexico of cotton cultivation as well as the custom of deforming infant skulls by wooden cradle-boards (a cultural tradition that initially caused archaeologists to incorrectly posit the migration of a different racial group into the region), major shifts in religious, political and social organization were taking place. Prior to this period the individual extended family living in a pit house had its own altar shrine and *sipapu* for religious rituals. In the Arizona Pueblo II period these were moved out of the separate dwelling and into the kiva for the common use of the village. At each end of a row of contiguous and aboveground masonry granaries, rectangular jacal (daub-and-wattle) rooms were attached for domiciliary purposes, forming the characteristic U-shaped unit pueblo. Subsurface rooms for the communal grinding of corn were also constructed. In essence, the beginning of the collective life was at hand. "They gathered together in villages and seemed to be approaching urban life, just as the agriculturists did in the Tigris-Euphrates Valley at the beginning of the era of Middle Eastern Civilization."[10]

Pueblo III (A.D. 1100-1300) is considered by many to be the classical period in pueblo development and a virtual florescence of the culture. Perhaps the use of check dams and other improvements in irrigation provided the nutritional boost sufficient for a general increase in population. Along with a rise in numbers, the population density increased as well. Coalescence into larger and larger villages housing thousands of people seemed the trend. "Up to this time the Anasazi had lived in villages totaling no more than a few hundred people, and most settlements had far fewer. Now they began to congregate, answering some call that is a mystery to us. They certainly were a gregarious people and *their villages became cities.* [italics added]"[11] Multi-room, multi-story masonry pueblos exhibiting exquisite architectural styles and craftsmanship were erected. In Chaco Canyon the "great house" later named Pueblo Bonito consisted of a D-shaped pueblo with over 800 terraced rooms, some of which were five stories tall and surrounded by immense plazas. "It has been estimated that it could have sheltered 1200 inhabitants, and it was the largest 'apartment house' in the world until a larger one was erected in New York in 1882."[12] A number of Great Kivas —one nearly sixty feet in diameter— provided areas where a whole community could worship. A system of over 300 miles of ceremonial roads, some of them thirty feet wide, was constructed. Other regions such as Mesa Verde, Canyon de Chelly, and Tsegi Canyon flourished as well. During the same period the Sinagua were building large pueblos near the San Francisco Peaks and in Verde Valley. This was also the time when the first large-scale construction of villages on the Hopi Mesas was achieved. At last the People of Peace had found the Center of the World.

Increased specialization of labor allowed more time for spiritual activities. A complexification of religion and a possible centralization of religious authority developed. However, the pueblos seem to have avoided the type of autocratic priesthood that sometimes arises under similar conditions. Egalitarianism and coöperation, especially in regards to building projects, had apparently reigned. Little evidence of either internecine warfare or what we today call "crime" can be found. During the end of this period the awe-inspiring *katsina* cult took hold and provided a spiritual grounding that remains to this day. (More on this subject in Chapter 7.)

With improvement in the artistic technique of ceramics, the high quality basket making, at which their ancestors had so excelled, began to decline. Finely woven cotton and turkey feather blankets were coveted export products, while items such as copper bells, conch shell trumpets, scarlet and green macaw feathers and even live parrots were imported from Mesoamerica. If not a paradise, it was at the least a communally rich and spiritually fulfilling place to spend what by our standards would be considered a brief lifespan.

Shortly before the end of this period the balance of life changed: the Anasazi diaspora had begun. It was not a mass exodus; instead, various clans gradually drifted away from the once great cities. The Pueblo IV period (A.D. 1300-1540) is seen by some as a regressive phase, though many contemporary native people dispute that claim. "This era marked the period of final unification. Many of the ancient sites were abandoned. The people who built them did not disappear; they moved and regrouped."13 Because the more northern regions of Chaco, Mesa Verde, and Kayenta appear to be most affected, the main vectors of travel were probably east and south. Many Anasazi relocated along the Rio Grande to build the impressive sites of Bandelier, Puyé, Pecos, Kuaua, and later the contemporary pueblos such as Taos, San Juan, Santa Clara,     San Ildefonso, Jemez, Zia, Cochiti, Santo Domingo, San Felipe, Isleta and a few smaller villages. Others settled at Acoma and Zuni farther west. Early in the fourteenth century a large pueblo called Homol'ovi was constructed on the Little Colorado River. Evidence exists that the Anasazi even built villages among the Mogollon communities south of the Colorado Plateau in Arizona.

Archaeologists have proposed many theories to explain this migration, none of which seems totally satisfying. "Tree-ring studies have indicated the occurrence of a prolonged drought in the Four Corners area between A.D. 1276 and 1299. Deforestation, colder temperatures, arroyo entrenchment [accelerated channel erosion], lowered water tables, and shortages of arable land may have been related to the drought. All have been proposed as local causes, at least, for Anasazi dislocation or relocations."14 Further hypotheses include increased pressures from overcrowded living conditions, nutrient depletion of the soil, spread of epidemic diseases, raiding by nomadic Shoshoneans who strayed south from the Great Basin and, most recently, factionalism caused by intratribal warfare. While the drought theory is still the most generally accepted scenario for the migration of this period, some factual inconsistencies exist. "Probably most important is the fact that if the tree-ring analysis is accepted, the Anasazi survived earlier droughts of similar intensity and duration. In some cases the Anasazi who abandoned their San Juan homes moved to areas that modern analysis has shown to have even less rainfall than the region departed, an example being Antelope Mesa [south of Keams Canyon, Arizona]."[15] In support of this, another observer of Hopi culture adds: "...it has been discovered by scientists that during some extended droughts the Hopi did not move at all, and with their dry farming techniques in fact survived remarkably well."[16] With a people such as the Anasazi, who lived as close to the land as they did, certain environmental factors obviously did play some part in a given clan's decision to move or stay. Nevertheless, we must ask whether or not this is the only factor of consideration. Because the Anasazi left no written records, we can only rely on unsubstantiated conjecture, and most archaeologists want to stay out of that arena. Furthermore, archaeologists tend to impose their own particular mind-set upon the objects of their inquiry, attributing rationalistic or pragmatic motives to that which otherwise might be more affected by spiritual or archetypal dimensions.

An oral tradition which has been handed down (and now, at least in part, written down) exists to verify what some contemporary Hopis are saying in contradistinction to the archaeologists, i.e., the migrations were more the result of a spiritual mandate and a covenant with the Creator than either a flight response to environmental hardships or the lure of a better life elsewhere— the "push" and "pull" theories respectively. Because an increasing number of contemporary Hopis are becoming bicultural and are thus articulating within the framework of the Anglo culture their own viewpoints in English, a comprehensive picture of prophecy and destiny superseding environmental factors is emerging. One example of this sort of statement among the many that can be found today is given by Alph H. Secakuku, a member of the Snake Clan who grew up in Shipaulovi on Second Mesa:

> "The Hopi believe their greatest bond is their religion. It has given them the strength to resist external forces and has kept them united for centuries. It has also helped to maintain the *Hopituy* (uniquely Hopi) rapport with their land, which they proudly refer to as *tuuwanasavi*—the spiritual center of the earth. Tuuwanasavi is very special to the Hopi *sinom* (people) because it was established and developed during their migration of the Tuuwaqatsi (earth)."[17]

### Tracking the Anasazi: An Archaeo-psychological Perspective

At times when walking among the thousands of potsherds found in one Anasazi ruin or another, we can easily imagine that "Potterymaker" rather than "Pueblo" might have been a more logical name for this period of development. Viewing some of the whole pots in a museum, we begin to get a inkling of the character of the people who created them. Most famous for their stark black-on-white designs, the Anasazi made pottery in a multitude of shapes: round jars, jars with lids or handles, bowls, jugs, pitchers, mugs, vases, ollas, squash vessels, ladles. The abstract motifs painted on their ceramics are nonpareil: serrate margins, terraced edges, triangles, rectangles, hooks, scrolls, spurs, frets, hourglass figures, checkerboards, parallel lines, hatches. An Escher-esque style of interlocking, abstract patterns together with an elaborate sense of symmetry impart an overall rigorous, balanced, almost classical tone to the art form.

Of course, all these items were ultimately utilitarian in nature. The painted pottery served as eating or drinking vessels, while the gray corrugated ones were used for cooking or storage. In order to produce a pot the wet clay tempered with sand or crushed rock, which prevents cracks in the shaping process, was built up using the coil-and-scrape technique. Polished with a small pebble, coated with a slip of white clay and painted with black pigments of boiled beeweed or iron oxide, the pot was then fired in a low oxygenated kiln to achieve the desired gray and white color.[18] The geometric designs painted on this pottery are not merely decorative. On the contrary, these abstract motifs are incontrovertibly iconographic, i.e., they all represent aspects of the Anasazi world: clouds, rain, lightning, water, river, wind, earth, sky, stars, day and night, the four directions, mountains, house, pueblo, corn, peace, war, death.[19] (This is to say nothing of the obviously representative zoomorphic and anthropomorphic pottery that perhaps reached its zenith with the Mimbres people of western New Mexico.) Developing over a period of fourteen hundred years, this art form is unique to the North American continent. Although putatively derived from central Mexico via the Hohokam and the Mogollon to the south, the pottery in their hands took on a distinctively Anasazi character and undeniably reflects the mind-set of its makers.

Admittedly, archaeo-psychology is difficult to prove and can only be intuited. Who were these people? Why did they produce such transcendentally pure art? What quality of consciousness allowed the creation of this elegant geometric elaboration? Who might have influenced them? A clue to these questions may be found in the theory of the noted anthropologist Ruth Benedict. Using the fashionable Nietzchean dichotomy of her day, she proposes that Native Americans can be divided into two groups: Dionysian and Apollonian. An example of the former would be the Plains Indians, such as the Lakota (Sioux), whose vision quests and self-torturing sun dance rituals were performed to achieve ecstatic results. As further examples of the former she cites such Southwestern tribes as the Pima, who ingest cactus beer, or the Yaqui and others of the Sonoran Desert, who use peyote and jimson weed to create a sort of divine intoxication so that individual visions and dreams received in this state can be accessed by the tribe as a whole. In fact, she claims that Native Americans in general, including those of Mexico, were "...passionately Dionysian. They valued all violent experience, all means by which human beings may break through the usual sensory routine, and to all such experiences they attributed the highest value."[20] On the other hand, the Pueblo people are unequivocally Apollonian. Balance, form, order, tradition, peace— these are key words in the Pueblo lexicon.

As a practical example of the Apollonian principle, the ritual dances that some Anglos have misrepresented as being monotonous are performed to assure that the cosmological balance is not disturbed. Slow and stately, wheeling hour after hour across the plazas of ancient pueblos awash in the primary colors of feathered mask, clan kilt, sash and spruce ruff, the *katsina* dancers press their prayers into the hard packed ground with steps synchronized to the heart beat of a single cottonwood drum. With the clack of deer hooves and sizzle of squash rattles forming a hypnotic aural backdrop, they seek an identification with and participation in the inner workings of the natural world. In fact, during the duration of the dance they lose their human form and actually become the spirits they are representing with their ritual costumes and paraphernalia. In the course of the daylong dance, they help keep the sun-spirit Tawa in his ascribed track in the heavens, help the clouds conceptualized as ancestor spirits to form and the life-bestowing rain to fall. Through the entrancing repetition of dance rhythm and chant a gradual and steadfast accretion of numinous energy peaks at the parabolic apex where the natural and the supernatural merge, and where both are finally subsumed in the sacred order of the universe. According to Benedict:

> "Supernatural power among the Pueblos comes from cult membership, a membership which has been bought and paid for and which involves the learning of verbatim ritual. There is no occasion when they are expected to overpass the boundaries of sobriety either in preparation for membership, or in initiation, or in the subsequent rise, by payment, to the higher grades, or in the exercise of religious prerogatives. They do not seek or value excess.... They have made, in one small but long-established cultural island in North America, a civilization whose forms are dictated by the typical choices of the Apollonian, all of whose delight is in formality and whose way of life is the way of measure and of sobriety."[21]

As with the ritual dances, all the sensations and cognition one experiences when contemplating Anasazi pottery can be summed up by this Apollonian concept. A deep and abiding classicism and a conservatism in the most positive sense of the word were at work in the creation of these artifacts. Here were a people who valued the divine order manifest in the natural world of which they were an integral part. "It is reality the Pueblos are after, so that they are in fact realistic, not idealistic. They are American empiricists, hopeful, reasonable, and hard. Something true and clear, massively unsentimental, runs through all their works, and this is, at bottom, the relationship between men and nature that they embody and reveal."[22] An underlying humility and subservience to the dictates of the cosmological schema are readily apparent. All actions, prayers, and ritual performances attempt to perpetuate this sacred ontological system.

As one of the most respected and prolific early ethnographers of the Hopi, Jesse Walter Fewkes concurs with Benedict regarding the essential distinctive quality of the Hopi vis-à-vis the other tribes of North America, though he sees a kinship of the former with the Maya and Aztecs. "But while this type [the Pueblo people] differed in ancient times from those of Athapascan or Shoshonean aborigines, it bears evidence of a composite nature. It had become so by contributions from many sources, and in turn left its impress on other areas, so that *as a type the Pueblo culture was the only one of its kind in aboriginal America* [italics added]. With strong affinities on all sides it was unique, having nearest kinship with those of Mexico and Central America."[23]

A central question remains, however: In what manner did this placid "cultural island" so unique to our Dionysian continent come to evolve in the way it did? Most likely, neither the archaeological study of potsherds among ruin rubble nor the anthropological conjecture spawned by in-the-field research will provide an adequate answer.

### *Tracking the Anasazi: A Mythological Perspective*

*The primordial age was infused with Tokpela, an immense empty space beyond time or light. All was void existing in the mind of Tawa, the Creator. Because he was lonely he created a nephew called Sótuknang, the Heart of the Sky god, to act as his messenger. Out of this endless space Tawa directed Sótuknang to create the First World. Sótuknang then made the earth, the waters, and the winds. He put them in their proper places and set them in motion. Koyanwuhti, or Spider Grandmother, was there as well. She presided over the mysteries of the Below while Tawa controlled the power of the Above. In addition, there was another being named Masau'u, the spirit of the earth, sometimes referred to as the Great Spirit. Together with Spider Grandmother he would have dominion over the terrestrial realms and the Underworld.*

*Tawa then noticed that there was no life upon the world. He instructed Koyanwuhti to mix some earth with her saliva and make two figurines. She laid a sacred white blanket (the ova cloth) over these two and sang the magic Song of Creation. When she uncovered the figurines, a pair of twins sat up to ask who they were and why they were here. She named the older twin on the right Pokanghoya. His duty was to solidify the mountains and keep them stable. She named the younger twin on the left Polongahoya. His mission was to travel throughout the earth, calling out to everything he saw. In this way all the earth nodes and objects thereupon were tuned to his vibrations, and sound became a way to carry messages. Then Pokanghoya was sent to the north pole and Polongahoya was sent to the south pole, where in unison they would keep the world in balance.*

*Spider Grandmother then created all the plants and animals in the same manner she had created the twins. She spread all these new creatures uniformly over the face of the earth. The land was beautiful and now ready for humans to inhabit it. Again she mixed her saliva with bits of red, white, yellow, and black earth. She placed the* ova *cloth over them and sang the Creation Song. When she withdrew the blanket, four human beings in the image of Sótuknang sat up. They were males and could not yet speak. In the same manner she created four females. Next she called Sótuknang so that he could give all of them the power of speech. To each different color of human being he gave a different language. Finally with an admonition to respect the Creator and keep his teachings, Sótuknang sent them out to live in the spirit of love and happiness on the First World.*24

Thus begins the Anasazi (Hisatsinom)/Hopi cosmogony. The continuation of this epic narrative describes a cyclic pattern of initial joy, harmonious relations, and an existence in accordance with sacred tradition eventually deteriorating into general social and sexual dissipation. The dissension, greed, and corruption of this later phase become so acute that the culture is terminated in mass destruction with only a few survivors given reprieve by a subsequent renewal. Hopi myths claim that they as a people have lived through four different "Worlds," or eras in their development. These Worlds were punctuated by cataclysms specific to each era. (It is interesting to note that these precisely mirror Hesiod's Four Ages of Humankind: Golden, Silver, Bronze, and Iron.) Determined by a process of progressive degeneration, each era, or age, is slightly less hospitable and desirable than the prior one.

The First World, as mentioned above, was called *Tokpela*, or "endless space." Its symbolic mineral is gold, its direction is northwest, and its color is yellow. Described in typically paradisiacal terms, it was a time far in the shamanistic past when humans and animals lived together as one on the Earth Mother and could understand one another even though they all spoke different languages. Then the handsome Káto'ya, "a snake with a big head," along with the mocking bird Mochni began to convince humans of the differences between themselves as well as those between people and animals.25 By their "small talk" (in Hopi, *lavaíhoya*) they slowly drew humankind away from its unity with the natural world and created in human consciousness the first Cartesian schism between subject and object. Increased violence among people led to the destruction of the First World by earthquakes, land mass changes, and fire (volcanism). Nonetheless, a few virtuous people who followed the old laws of the Creator sought refuge in the Ant Kiva until the second era came into being. (See discussion of the Ant People in Chapter 13.)

The Second World was called *Tokpa*, or "dark midnight." Its symbolic mineral was silver, its direction was southwest, and its color was blue. Even though this world was not as pleasant as the first, the people began to show incipient signs of civilization, such as the construction of primitive houses and the creation of tools. Nevertheless, the production of trade goods spawned quarrels and a general feeling of avarice, which ultimately caused the downfall of the Second World. According to the myth, this world was destroyed by a pole shift followed by an Ice Age. It is an acknowledged fact that the earth has undergone a number of shifts in the polar axis during its long geologic history. Much could be said about this, but it will suffice to cite the compelling evidence of the perfectly preserved mammoths found frozen in the ice of northeastern Siberia with grass and leaves still in their stomachs, the species of which only grow over a thousand miles to the south.26 This proves that a pole shift can be a devastatingly rapid event. For the Hopi only the sincere practice of spirituality can insure survival against such catastrophes. Again, the ones who remembered the teachings of the Creator were spared by fleeing to the Ant Kiva.

The Third World was called *Kuskurza*, or "Underworld." Its symbolic mineral is copper, its direction is southeast, and its color is red. This was a time when great cities and trade routes were built, and civilization was vibrant and burgeoning. "The people invented many machines and conveniences of high technology, some of which have not yet been seen in this age. They even had spiritual powers that they used for good."27 This startling description that reverberates with echoes of Atlantis or Mu is corroborated by legends of the *paatuwvota*, or "flying shield." (See p. 161.) In one legend this aerial vehicle is associated with Sótuknang, the sky god who was present at the cosmogenesis. Shortly after an immense flood which destroyed Palatkwapi (variously identified as the red rock country of Verde Valley in Arizona, Casas Grandes in Chihuahua, and Palenque in Chiapas) a brother and sister who were forgotten and left behind by their fleeing parents set out on a journey to find them.

> "It was still daylight in the evening when they decided to make camp and were just about opening their bundle of lunch when they heard a loud roaring noise overhead and they were very much frightened and wondered what it could be. Tiwahongva [the brother] held his sister [Tawiayisnima] tightly to his breast, and behold, someone had descended from the heavens all clothed in a glittering costume of ice that sparkled like silver and his head and face shone like a star. He spoke to them and said, "Do not fear, I am So-tukeu-nangwi, the heavenly God and because of the sympathy I have for you I have come to help you, so come get on this shield (Yo-vota) of mine and let us be on our way."28

He then took them on this flying shield up into the sky so that they could see for many miles around. He fed the hungry children ripe melons and described the type of faith and trust that they must place in him and in his teachings which would come in the form of dreams as the children got older. He set them down a short distance from the village in which their parents had settled, bid them farewell, and ascended into the heavens. Forever grateful to Sótuknang, the brother and sister walked into the village to be reunited with their parents.

Because the Hopi had no such thing as a saucer, they named it after the cultural accouterment which most closely approximates that shape, i.e., the warrior shield. The flying shield appears in more than one myth, and petroglyphic evidence of this tradition also exists. "On Second Mesa near Mishongnovi an ancient petroglyph depicts a dome-shaped object resting on an arrow which represent travel through space, and the head of a Hopi maiden who represents pristine purity. As the Hopis believe that other planets are inhabited, this petroglyph represents a *patuwvota* or a 'flying shield' similar to a 'flying saucer' that came here in the Beginning. So now at the End the sacred ones will arrive from another planet, said to be Venus, by flying saucers. Many Hopi traditionalists recently have reported seeing flying saucers, all piloted by beings they call *kachinas*."[29]

It must be noted here that the previously mentioned "Worlds" were spatially conceptualized as being positioned one on top of the other like houses; thus, a progression from one World to the next would signal a gradual ascent. It is ironic that this cosmological structure is an exact reversal of the Western system, where a spatial rise symbolically represents an increase in perfection. For the Hopi, to go down is, in reality, to go back to the place of former bliss and heightened spiritual attainment.

In addition, the Third World is not only the era prior to the present Fourth World but is also the place where spirits go after death. Known as *Wijima*, this place is the kiva-shaped region (or sometimes a lake) in the Underworld where departed souls go to reside.[30] There exists a poignant story which emphasizes the eschatological link between the Third and Fourth Worlds. Soon after the people had ascended to the Fourth World, the young daughter of a *mongwi* (chief) suddenly died. It was suspected that a sorcerer somehow had accompanied the people to this World. A witch woman then came forth and confessed that she indeed had caused the death of the little girl. Although she was the culprit, she begged to remain in the upper World. In order to stay she claimed that the girl was safe and happy in the Underworld. When the witch woman led the priest over to the kiva opening from which the people had recently come, below in the Third World he saw the spirit of his daughter merrily playing with some other children. He was so overcome with emotion that he allowed the witch woman to remain in the Fourth World, which is why evil thrives today.[31]

As with the previous two Worlds, eventually signs of discord began to become apparent, the agent of which is usually designated as sorcery.

Dan Katchongva, the late Sun Clan leader of Hotevilla, explained this propensity for moral decline as the will of the Creator: "He made our bodies of two principles, good and evil. The left side is good for it contains the heart. The right side is evil for it has no heart. The left side is awkward but wise. The right side is clever and strong, but it lacks wisdom. There would be a constant struggle between the two sides, and by our actions we would have to decide which was stronger, the evil or the good."[32] With the spreading influence of *powakas*, or "sorcerers," in the world, indolence and promiscuity became rampant. Jealousy, envy, adultery, murder, and suicide were increasingly common. Men gambled instead of tending the fields, and women joined the men in the kivas. Consequently, the grinding of corn and other household duties, including the care of children, were neglected.

The Third World was terminated by a deluge, mythological variations of which exist in most cultures around the globe. The few people who still clung to the ways of the Creator escaped the rising waters either by sailing reed boats eastward to dry land or by crawling up through a bamboo reed (in Hopi, *pakave*) that extended to the sky and stuck up into the next world like a kiva ladder. (No native bamboo grows on the Colorado Plateau, but a species reaching a height of fifteen to twenty feet is found in southwestern Arizona.) The Water Clan (in Hopi, Patkinyamu, literally "Dwelling-on-Water," or the Houseboat Clan) from Oraibi on Third Mesa persistently tells the former version of the story.[33] (Read more about this clan in Chapter 10.) Drifting toward the rising sun, the people landed on one "stepping stone" after another. They wanted to stay but were told by Spider Grandmother that these islands were too pleasant and that they must keep moving. (A common theme in Hopi migrations is that places of ease naturally lead to sloth and corruption.) Still they sailed onward, going "uphill" (upstream?) "...traveling, still east and a little north."[34] It is possible that after crossing the Pacific ocean they sailed into the Gulf of California and up the Colorado River.

They finally came to a land that they thought was the Fourth World: "...its shores rose higher and higher into a steep wall of mountains. There seemed no place to land."[35] For ones not accustomed to deep gorges like Grand Canyon, these steep cliffs might indeed seem like mountains. They went both north (Marble Canyon?) and south (the Little Colorado Gorge?) and still they could not find the Place of Emergence. Finally letting their intuition guide them, they emerged upon the sandy shore of the Fourth World. Another tradition especially known in Walpi on First Mesa puts the Sipapuni, or Place of Emergence, near the confluence of the Colorado and Little Colorado Rivers. "One of the springs which feeds the Little Colorado is a present-day Hopi shrine, or *sipapu*. The *sipapu* is about [specific number deleted to preserve its sanctity] kilometers upstream from the Colorado confluence. It is a huge travertine dome, built up from the minerals in the flowing water. The Hopi believe that man emerged into this world through this spring. There are other shrines in the area, along a sacred trail leading down to the Colorado River not far below the confluence. The Hopi, who live about 100 kilometers east of here, make ceremonial journeys to collect salt from near the river."[36]

Because this creation story is an amalgam of legends from the different clans that make up the Hopi and not a unified voice by a single author or even a group of authors with similar perspectives, a number of basic variations exist. One version shows the First World populated by insect-like creatures and the Second World by coyote-like or bear-like creatures having fur, tails, and webbed fingers and possessing a savage, cannibalistic nature. In this version's Third World the people make blankets and unfired pots until Hummingbird sent by Masau'u gives them the fire-drill whereby they can cook food and fire pots. Another variation of the progression from the Third to the Fourth Worlds presents three birds —a swallow (swift), a white dove, and a hawk— subsequently flying up in an attempt to reach the upper world, but each one failing. Finally the cat bird (shrike) wings through the hole and asks of Masau'u permission for the people to live there. In the same version the humble chipmunk plants in turn a sunflower seed, a spruce seed, a pine seed, and a bamboo seed in order to serve as a ladder to the upper world. As mentioned above, it is only the bamboo reed that is tall and straight enough to pierce the sky.[37]

The Four Worlds described heretofore could also conceivably correspond to the four basic archaeological periods: Paleo-Indian, Basketmaker, Classic Pueblo, and, finally, Historic Pueblo. "In the First World they had lived with the animals. In the Second World they had developed handicrafts, homes, and villages. Now in the Third World they multiplied in such numbers and advanced so rapidly that they created big cities, countries, a whole civilization."[38] The Fourth World would correspond to the period extending from the major migrations circa A.D. 1300 through the historic period of Spanish contact up to and including contemporary times. Perhaps the divisions are only coincidental, but the parallels are interesting nonetheless.

The Fourth World was a place of even greater migrational dispersion. It is called *Túwaqachi*, or "world complete," the place where the Hopi now live. Its symbolic mineral is mixed or alloy, its direction is northeast, and its color is white. It is dominated by one of the most complex and enigmatic figures in Hopi mythology: Masau'u. This figure would play a very decisive role in the development and character of the culture. "In the entire pantheon of Hopi mythological figures none is more important than the god Maasaw."[39] (As with most Hopi deities, variant spellings of this figure abound: Maasaw, Másaw, Masauwuh, Masauwu, Maasau'u, Massauu, etc.)

> "So the catbird flew up and passed through the opening in the sky. He passed the place where the hawk had turned back. He went on. He came to a place of sand and mesas. He saw large fires burning alongside gardens of squash,

melons, and corn. Beyond the gardens was a single house made of stone. A person was sitting there, his head down, sleeping. The catbird alighted nearby and waited. The person awoke and raised his head. His eyes were sunken in deeply, there was no hair on his head, and his face was seared by burns and encrusted with dried blood. Across the bridge of his nose and his cheekbones two black lines were painted. Around his neck were two heavy necklaces, one made of four strands of turquoise, the other of bones. The catbird recognized him. He was Masauwu, Spirit of Death, the Owner of Fire and Master of the Upper World, assigned to this place by Tawa because he had no other place for him."[40]

As the above description states, the deity can also take an anthropomorphic form. "Maasaw is both a real person and a manifestation of the Creator."[41] The lengthy quotation above graphically emphasizes the primary quality of Masau'u, i.e., his ostensibly horrific appearance. He wears a mask with large open eye holes and a large mouth. Frequently covered with dried rabbit blood, his head is huge and bald, and his forehead bulges out in a ridge. In one account his head was shaped "...like the biggest squash, and there was no hair on it."[42] His feet are the length of a forearm, and his body is usually described as being a grayish color. This apparently is an essential element, since his name is derived from the Hopi word *maasi*, meaning "gray." In fact, this description from Hopi mythology is uncomfortably close to contemporary images of the race of extraterrestrial Greys.

In addition, the word *masa* means "wing" or "feather," thereby emphasizing his ability of flight. Masau'u also sometimes hermaphroditically wears a tattered woman's dress fastened under the right armpit instead of the customary left. This exemplifies his nature as a "contrary" or trickster figure similar to the Lakota (Sioux) *heyoka*, who dresses and acts the opposite of human expectations and customs. "Halfway to the middle of the mesa they met him [Masau'u], and the sight was so gruesome as to make the eyes strain from the sockets. Had not their hearts been staunch they would have turned back, for he was hideous beyond words. Raw flesh and clots of blood hung all over his body, and his great head was ugly and glaring."[43] In this account the culture hero Tiyo challenges him to a wrestling match and finally overcomes him, after which Masau'u takes off his terrifying mask. He then is seen as a handsome youth, who sits down and graciously smokes a pipe with Tiyo while explaining the extent of his dominion. On the other hand, in his trickster capacity he occasionally is cast in the role of thief, liar, lecher, buffoon, and practical joker.

As his odor of putrefaction suggests, Masau'u is also conceptualized as the god of death and ruler of the Underworld. "The god

16

himself can be introduced as a mythological figure whose primary focus rests in his lively relationship with the realm of death."[44] "Death spirit," "corpse demon," and "mummified corpse" are all phrases formerly used in reference to this dark god. As guardians of the Underworld, members of the elite Kwan (One Horn Society) claim to serve Masau'u. Akin to the Greek god Hermes or the Norse god Odin, he is sometimes known as a psychopomp, traveling between this world and the Underworld. Naturally, a primary attribute is his mercurial character. "He is a worrier and a pacer; constant motion is his nature. He is not a remote deity, he is always around and in the center of things."[45] Paradoxically known as "one who lives unseen," this solitary, austere figure carries only a dibble stick, a canteen of water, and some seeds. In this respect he somewhat resembles the fertility figure readily known in petroglyphs throughout the Southwest as Kokopilau, or Kokopelli, the Humpback Flute Player. In some cases Masau'u holds a cedar bark torch, and his nocturnal presence can be detected by strange fires in the distance, inspiring awe and fear. In this aspect he is strongly connected to the Ko'kop (Fire Clan), which is generally recognized as the most aggressive of the Hopi clans and the one with the largest proportion of sorcerers. In an account previously mentioned he takes on a Promethean role by teaching the

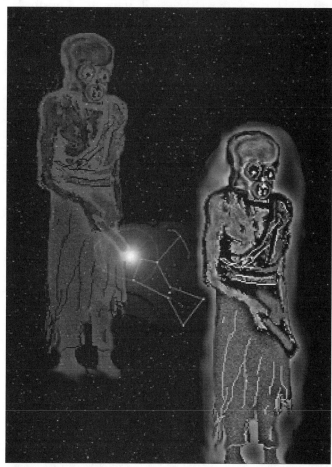

*Fig. 2. Masau'u, Hopi god of death, the Underworld (adapted from Petra Roeckerath—* *see p. 308, n. 18)*

Hopi how to make fire.

In a contradictory aspect he is alternately referred to as the Great Spirit, the Supreme Being, the Holy One, the Purifier, or the Savior of the world. More germane to our discussion, however, is his role as *genius loci*, or tutelary deity of the land. Living at "the backbone of the earth," he is recognized as the god of boundaries or cairns. As protector of his country that is referred to as *mastutskwa,* he is known to make a circuit around the edges of the world. According to the Hopi, Masau'u bequeathed both the *Pötskwani,* or rules for a proper life that form the basic plan still used today, and the deed to the land itself. "Our original Hopi land title was based on permission. We received that permission from Maasaw, the guardian of all land and life [in Hopi, *tuuwaqatsi*] who holds it in trust for the Creator. Thus it is implemented by the forces that create this universe."[46] As they emerged into the Fourth World, the Hopi were appointed as caretakers of physical space, perhaps much in the same way that the Maya of Central America were designated as the caretakers of time.[47] "The traditional Hopi follows the spiritual path that was given to us by Massau'u, the Great Spirit. We made a sacred covenant to follow his life plan at all times, which includes responsibility of taking care of this land and life for his divine purpose."[48]

Living near the Sipapuni, Masau'u was, of course, the first entity encountered upon their emergence. To test the various tribes' wisdom, he laid out different types of corn and had them each choose one. The Navajo quickly chose the long yellow ear. Other tribes such as the Sioux, the Comanches, the Apaches, the Supais, and the Utes greedily chose other colors while the Hopi were left with the smallest blue ear of corn. In reality, this was a test of humility and the ability to face adversity. After all, there was a long journey ahead, and the people were not permitted merely to settle down at that specific place. Masau'u directed them instead to make many migrations throughout the land as a means of marking the boundaries of their territory, thereby sanctifying it. By sinking their spiritual roots into the earth along the way, they would keep the land in balance. They were told to build houses, villages, kivas, and shrines, as well as to make clan markings and other symbols on the rocks (petroglyphs and pictographs). However, they were not to stay too long in any one place. After breaking their pots to serve as a marker of their continuing presence, they were to move on, always searching for the Center of the World, the destination of their journey.

Before leaving on their migrations, Masau'u (together with Spider Grandmother) gave them a set of stone tablets, or *owatutuveni*. These tablets are of utmost importance in both the history and destiny of the Hopi. "We still have the sacred stone tablets given to us by the Spider Woman. This is our title and deed to this world, and it was given to us with the life plan to follow, and with strong instructions and serious warnings."[49] According to one source, two tablets were given. "As the people were about to start forth on their migration, Maasaw entrusted Old Spider

Woman with two stone tablets. Old Spider Woman took the first and drew something on it. With the second she did the same thing. Then she nudged the two tablets in front of her grand-children, who together with Masaw breathed upon them. As a result, her inscriptions were etched into stone. What exactly was drawn on these stones is not known. But their markings are said to describe the land in its entirety. They delineate the dimensions all the way to the sea."50 Clearly this describes a map in stone of the Hopi territory.

A nother source states that the Fire Clan was given a small tablet about four inches square, and the Bear Clan (the primary Hopi clan comprised of spiritual leaders) was given three tablets weighing about eight pounds each. The tablets are inscribed with a number of symbols: star, sun, snake, cloud, corn, bear paw, lightning, swastika, friendship (*nakwách*), and humanoid.51 (See Chapter 5.) In addition, a certain village chief at Oraibi once quite uncharacteristically showed the noted anthropologist Mischa Titiev one of the tablets. "It is a rectangular block of greyish-white, smooth-grained stone, about 16 inches long, 8 inches wide, and one and a half inches thick, splotched here and there with irregular dots which the chief interprets as points of land.... Along the edge representing the east, there is a line of small scratches, interspersed with occasional circles or crosses, which depict the proper Hopi path that the chiefs are supposed to travel."52 Again, this clearly implies a map.

S upposedly the smaller tablet given to the Fire Clan had a corner broken off. This corner was given to the Pahana, the Elder White Brother, who was to migrate toward the rising sun and wait there until he heard the cries of distress from the Younger Brother, or the Hopi themselves. At last he would return, coming to their aid and purifying the land. He would prove his identity by fitting the two pieces of the tablet together. As the contemporary term for "white person," *pahaana* is also archetypally related to the plumed serpent Kukulkán of the Maya, Quetzalcóatl of the Aztecs, and Awanyu of the Tewa. However, some Hopi elders like Dan Katchongva do not believe the Pahana is Caucasian but is instead Hopi. "The stone tablets will be the final acknowledgment of their true identity and brotherhood. Their mother is the Sun Clan. They are children of the sun. So it must be a Hopi who traveled from here to the rising sun and is waiting someplace. Therefore it is only the Hopi that still have this world rotating properly, and it is the Hopi who must be purified if this world is to be saved. No other person anyplace will accomplish this."53 Thus, the Hopi have assumed an immense sacred onus: to keep the whole planet in balance by their life plan and ceremonies. As in the above archaeo-psychological section, again we see the Hopi fulfilling an unique role, in this case unlike that of any other aboriginal people in the entire world. In other words, they must keep the world in balance, or we will all perish.

Clan after clan began the great migration to the four directions represented by the ancient symbol of the swastika. Waters believes that the extent of migration ranged from the Atlantic coast to the Pacific coast and from the Arctic Circle to Tierra del Fuego, but more likely this range is actually much smaller. Certainly the Anasazi traveled from the Colorado River to the Rio Grande, and from a little north of the San Juan River down into Mexico, at least as far south as the lands of the Toltecs and the Maya. Furthermore, the presence of macaw and parrot feathers or even whole birds found in some burial sites around the Colorado Plateau illustrates that the Anasazi had well established trade routes to the south. Regardless of what the farthest limits of actual migration were, the juncture where the two arms of the geo-morphic swastika meet is known as the Center of the World, the Tuuwanasavi, supposedly a spot a few miles from the present village of Oraibi.54 (The full name of the village is Sip Oraibi, "the place where the earth was made solid" or "the place where the roots solidify." The first syllable of the name is similar to the Hopi word for "navel": *sipna'at*.)

In recalling the groundbreaking work of the philosopher of religion Mircea Eliade, we know that the distinction between sacred and profane space was of paramount importance to most aboriginal cultures of the world. "In the realm of sacred space which we are now considering, its most striking manifestation is religious man's will to take a stand at the very heart of the real, at the Center of the World— that is, exactly where the cosmos came into existence and began to spread out toward the four horizons, and where, too, there is the possibility of communication with the gods; in short, precisely where he is *closest to the gods*."55 In order to return to the place of supreme sacrality where contact with the gods is most acute, a long journey spiraling around and back would have to occur. Along with clan markings and footprints carved in stone, the Anasazi would leave spiral petroglyphs to represent their cardinal journey in quest of the terrestrial quincunx.

Centuries passed and the migrations continued. As directed, the people kept leaving their footprints, following celestial omens as they went. In one account the Heart of the Sky god Sótuknang spoke to the people thus: "Now you will separate and go different ways to claim all the earth for the Creator. Each group of you will follow your own star until it stops. There you will settle."56 In another account Masau'u himself talked about a particular guiding star which would serve as a sign that a permanent home was at hand: "Eventually, as you travel along, you'll see a huge star. Where you sight this star, you'll settle permanently at that spot. There you'll found a village and dwell forever. The land where that happens will be yours. No one will compete with you for it."57 In yet another account Spider Grandmother advises the people about to embark upon their hegira: "The stars, the sun, the clouds and fires in the night will show you which directions to take."58 As in the previous account, another of the many versions shows the Hisatsinom pursuing multiple celestial events: "The clans all followed signs on their migration routes, such as a moving star, a constellation, or a light on the horizon. Periodically, they settled down at different spots and built villages. Then according to the signs the time would come to move on, and the villages were abandoned. This is why there are so many ruins throughout the Southwest nowadays."59 After not just forty but perhaps four hundred years in the desert, the Anasazi finally reached their destination. "The Hopis had forgotten about the other tribes by this time and did not know where they were. They were hoping to see the Eastern Star so that they could settle down and not travel any more. Well, finally the Bear Clan did see the Eastern Star..."60

One of the most detailed accounts of the celestial events that directed migration comes from an elder of the Snake Clan:

> "A brilliant star arose in the southeast, which would shine for a while, and then disappear. The old men said, 'Beneath that star there must be people,' so they determined to travel toward it. They cut a staff and set it in the ground and watched till the star reached its top, they started and traveled as long as the star shone; when it disappeared they halted. But the star did not shine every night, for sometimes many years elapsed before it appeared again. When this occurred, our people built homes during their halt; they built both round and square houses, and all the ruins between here and Navajo Mountain mark the places where our people lived. They waited till the star came to the top of the staff again, then they moved on, but many people were left in those houses and they followed afterward at various times. When our people reached Wipho (a spring a few miles north of Walpi) the star disappeared and has never been seen since."61

Some believe that another culturally significant star, namely, the Star of Bethlehem, was the result of a planetary conjunction. "[Astronomical historian David] Hughes cites a triple conjunction (three close visual passes in a row) of Saturn and Jupiter in the constellation Pisces in 7 B.C. and places the birth of the historical Jesus around October of that year."62 Jupiter-Saturn conjunctions occur approximately every twenty years, so this might explain the intermittent appearance of the celestial phenomenon mentioned by the Hopi elder. For instance, a Jupiter-Saturn conjunction occurred during mid-February of A.D. 1107, when the two planets appeared on the southeastern horizon about two hours before sunrise. Another conjunction happened in early September of A.D. 1086. Just after 2:00 a.m. this planetary pair hovered in the southeast, while Orion was rising and Sirius was resting on the eastern horizon. Shortly before sunrise in late October and early November of A.D. 1067, a year after Halley's Comet blazed though (see Chapter 5), a conjunction of Jupiter, Saturn and Venus occurred with the all three orbs positioned within about two degrees of each other. Any one of these three conjunctions (in 1107, 1086, and 1067) may have provided the impetus for a migration that ultimately led to the settling of the Hopi Mesas sometime after A.D. 1100.

Most accounts state that the Anasazi settled at Masipa just beneath the present village of Shongopovi on Second Mesa. Of course, *masipa* is a cognate of Masau'u. They asked the old god who had originally sent them on their way at the beginning of the Fourth World if they could live there with him. Seeing evil in their hearts, he replied: "'It is up to you. I have nothing here. My life is simple. All I have is my planting stick and my corn. If you are willing to live as I do, and follow my instructions, the life plan which I shall give you, you may live here with me, and take care of the land. Then you may live a long, happy, fruitful life.'"63 The Bear Clan then asked him to be their leader but he declined. He saw all the selfish desires they still possessed and told them that the Bear Clan chief would be their leader until such time as they were purified. "'After that I will be the leader, but not before, for I am the first and I shall be the last.' Having left all the instructions with them, he disappeared."64 (The Biblical parallel to Revelation 22:13 —"I am the Alpha and Omega..."— might be the result of either a recent evangelicalism or a deeper archetypal influence, but at this point it is impossible to say which.) The Bear Clan (or father clan) settled there at the southern base of Second Mesa in a village that was later known as Shongopovi. Additional clans such as the Parrot (or mother clan), the Sun, the Badger, the Snake, the Greasewood, the Water, the Fire and a number of others drifted toward the Center of the World from all directions to ask the Bear Clan if they could reside with them. Villages were built both below and on top of the three Mesas. As the pattern of life became more and more routine, the spiritual roots began to solidify. The Hopi were at last fulfilling their destiny established at the beginning of the Fourth World.

### *Tracking the Anasazi: A Footnote*

After consideration of the three perspectives above — archaeological, archaeo-psychological, and mythological— we still are faced with this question: why did the Anasazi (Hisatsinom)/Hopi settle on such a stark and arid landscape? It has been suggested by writers such as Frank Waters that the migrations themselves were a kind of extended sacred rite of purification, and that a migration to an area of relative ease and bounty would have precluded an intimate reliance on the Creator via prayer and ceremony.65 Leslie Marmon Silko, the renowned novelist and poet from Laguna Pueblo, would probably agree:

> "Hopi Pueblo elders have said that the austere and, to some
> eyes, barren plains and hills surrounding their mesa-top
> villages actually help to nurture the spirituality of the Hopi

*way*. The Hopi elders say that the Hopi people might have settled in locations far more lush where daily life would not have been so grueling. But there on the high silent sandstone mesas that overlook the sandy    arid expanses stretching to all horizons, the Hopi elders say the Hopi people must 'live by their prayers' if they are to survive. The Hopi way cherishes the intangible: the riches realized from interaction and interrelationships with all beings above all else. Great abundances of material things, even food, the Hopi elders believe, tend to lure human attention away from what is most valuable and important."[66]

In other words, overabundance sets up conditions allowing for the same lapse of spirituality into materialism that occurred in the previous three Worlds. Of course, the Hopi and their ancestors should be given a great deal of credit for existing and even thriving in such a harsh environment for two thousand years or more. Their ingenuity and fortitude are to be admired. The fact that they are still here after all this time is indisputable proof of their deed to the land. However, as they themselves would undoubtedly admit, this would have been impossible without their unwavering spiritual connection to the Creator. Throughout the long migration period that required the constant building of villages and in some cases cities, they created and maintained a complex cosmological and theological system, ultimately insuring their survival.

In an attempt to find a possible answer to the above question, we can summarize a few hypotheses regarding the Anasazi and their descendants:

1. Among the tribes of the North American continent the Hopi and the other pueblo people are an anomaly.
2. The causes for migration were not simply environmental but instead were primarily spiritual.
3. The most important deity in the Hopi pantheon is Masau'u, the guardian of the Fourth World who possesses absolute sovereignty over the land and its life.
4. The Hopi used a stone map or maps given by Masau'u in consort with Spider Grandmother to guide them in their journeys.
5. They followed certain sidereal signs such as moving stars or constellations to tell them where and when to travel.

Given the crucial role that Masau'u played in the anomalous cultural development of the Anasazi, it would not be unreasonable to posit an even closer interaction than previously acknowledged between the deity and the pueblo people. If we assume this paradigm of intimacy, it seems unlikely that "the Great Spirit" would merely send the people off into the wilderness to let them establish villages wherever they wished. On the contrary, he would exert a more direct and tangible influence upon the geographic location of these Anasazi proto-cities. If this is the case, then we must ask if the stone tablets bequeathed by Masau'u are indeed a predetermined map that specifically instructed the Anasazi on which routes to follow and what places to stop. If they are, we must further ask whether a discernible pattern or dynamic relationship exists between the various Anasazi (Hisatsinom)/Hopi sites scattered across the Arizona and New Mexico. If so, how was it implemented? Is the existence of a transcendent architectonic configuration uniting all the diverse pueblo sites possible? Is there a comprehensive schema superseding the individual characteristics of each ancient "city" on the Colorado Plateau? Finally, did the celestial phenomena that orchestrated the migration take the form of a particular constellation, a conspicuous star, a supernova, a bright comet or some other unidentified object in the night sky? In order to answer these many questions we must make a quantum leap from stardust to blood and back again to star myth resonating at the deepest levels of the human spirit.

In Chapter 2 we shall witness the manifestation of Masau'u's power to establish, whether overtly or covertly, a geodetic configuration of pueblo villages as the reflection of his own celestial image in Orion.

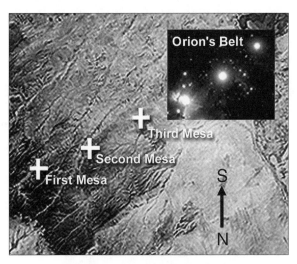

*Diagram 1, a Landsat photo*
*of the three Hopi Mesas in Arizona*
*juxtaposed to the "Zona" of Orion (see pp. 39-40)*

# Chapter 2
# The Sky Over the Hopi Villages

"The night sky over north-eastern Arizona is brilliantly clear, and Orion is a great constellation, only rivaled at this latitude by the Plough turning around the pole star to the north and by Scorpion lying low on the southwesterly horizon; but when Orion is up, it dominates the sky over the Hopi villages, both by its scale and by the magnitude of its individual stars."[1]

Richard Maitland Bradfield

## *Sacred Mountains, Canyons, and Boundary Shrines*

Again we turn to the land: matrix of all life rising from the dark, subterranean reservoir of spirits; focus of all solar, lunar, and stellar energy traversing the cold, fierce distances of cosmic night. After the arduous migration of many centuries and the ultimate establishment of the Center-place they called Tuuwanasavi, the Anasazi must have looked out upon the boundaries of their territory with a sense of relief and newfound security. While the intercardinal directions of the solstice sunrise and sunset points marked the immediate domain of the Anasazi, the living presence of distant mountains verified the harmonic configuration of their sacred cosmology, much as it does today. To the northwest (or more specifically, the north-northwest) the broad, dark dome of Navajo Mountain (10,388 ft.) reposes near the Arizona/Utah border. To the southwest Humphreys Peak (12,633 ft., tallest mountain in Arizona) provides the link to the spirit world as the home of the *katsinam*. Beyond the horizon to the southeast, Baldy Peak (11,403 ft.) in the White Mountains sits on the edge of the Mogollon Rim and guards access from the south. Likewise beyond the horizon to the northeast, Hesperus Mountain (13,232 ft.) presides over the extensive Anasazi ruins of the Mesa Verde region and designates the northern limit. Forming the central point of this quincunx, the three Hopi Mesas extending southwest from the pinyon-juniper woodland of Black Mesa had served as the center of the Anasazi/Hisatsinom world ever since they were settled and pueblo villages were built beginning circa A.D. 1100. The Hopi still see this place as the heart of their cosmos.

Because canyons figure so predominantly in Hopi cosmology, it is possible that the Hisatsinom conceptualized them in the same way as they did mountains, i.e., in a directional sense. If this is true, then the most important canyon would be, of course, the one to the west, Grand Canyon.

The imposing Salt River Canyon would serve as the significant gorge to the south, while Canyon de Chelly in the eastward direction is undoubtedly the most important chasm. Finally, Glen Canyon might serve as the directional canyon to the north. (The latter's magnificence would still be manifest, were not its walls half-submerged by the waters of Lake Powell, which was created by Glen Canyon Dam.) For the Hopi, and presumably their ancestors, canyons generally function as passage ways from this world to the Underworld, and thereby are associated with the spirits that continuously migrate between these two realms, keeping the sacred current in flux.

In addition to the symbolism of both mountains and canyons, a number of boundary shrines marks the perimeter of this ancestral land, or *tutskwa*. In this context a shrine is defined as a portal on the surface of the earth through which a *katsina* may descend to the Underworld or ascend to this one. Characteristically marked by a cairn, a semicircle of stones, or a group of petroglyphs, shrines are frequently overlooked by the uninitiated because of their simple, unelaborated appearance. However, the faithful often leave prayer offerings of cornmeal and feather sticks at these altars in hopes of influencing the spirits who use them. We may recall that the name of the Greek deity Hermes, the archetypal counterpart of Masau'u, literally means "he of the stone heap."[2] Thus the cairns spread throughout Hopiland to mark its borders symbolize the enduring presence and potency of Masau'u. Every person passing by his cairn customarily would add a stone as an offering to the awe-inspiring god.[3] Emphasizing the overall importance of shrines in Hopi society, clan markings are usually found at boundary shrines as well as at pueblo ruins, migration trails, and sources of salt. In addition, eagle shrines signal the potency of that wingéd intercessor of the profane and sacred worlds who acts as a prayer carrier.

Even today pilgrimages are periodically made to the series of boundary shrines that delineate the margins of the Hopi world. The most important shrine, of course, is located at Nuvatuya'ovi, or the San Francisco Peaks. Nah-mee-toka, the easternmost shrine, is located in a red canyon near Lupton, Arizona, not far from the New Mexico border. Another important shrine called Kawestima (Ky-westima) is found on the bottom of Tsegi Canyon at Betatakin Ruin (Navajo National Monument— see Fig. 14, p. 86). The northernmost shrine is located atop Toko'navi, or Black Mountain (Navajo Mountain). The shrine on Bill Williams Mountain west of Flagstaff is called Tusak Choma, while another one located in a marsh near Sedona carries the name Honapa, or Bear Springs. The westernmost shrine, named Po-ta-ve-taka (Potavey'taqa), can be found near the Havasupai Reservation at Point Sublime in Grand Canyon. South of Winslow at Chevelon Cliffs a shrine known as Sak-wai-vai-yu is located on the so-called Apache Trail. Tsi-mun-tu-qui, or Woodruff Butte, a conical hill now desecrated by an open pit gravel mine, is (or was, before it was destroyed) the southernmost shrine of Hopiland.[4] These shrines not only function as a contemporary focus of spiritual energy but also serve as "footprints" that once again reinforce the demarcations of the Anasazi/Hisatsinom realm in much the same way as do the pueblo ruins. At any rate, the Sacred Circle formed by these boundary shrines spins in a vortex fashion like a spiral petroglyph, drawing us inward to encounter cities of stone and adobe constructed long ago with the express purpose of mirroring the stars.

## Orion of the High Desert

To watch Orion ascend from the eastern horizon and assume its dominant winter position at the meridian is a wondrous spectacle. Even more so, it is a startling epiphany to see this constellation rise out of the red dust of the high desert as a stellar configuration of Anasazi cities built from the mid-eleventh to the end of the thirteenth century. The sky looks downward to find its image made manifest in the earth; the earth gazes upward, reflecting on the unification of terrestrial and celestial.

Directing our attention to the three Hopi Mesas at the "Center of the World," we clearly see the close correlation to Orion's belt. (See Diagram1, p. 24 and Diagram 2, p. 28.) Mintaka, a double star and the first of the trinity to peek over the eastern horizon as the constellation rises, corresponds to Oraibi and Hotevilla on Third (or Western) Mesa. The former village is considered the oldest continuously inhabited community on the continent, founded in the early twelfth century. As recently as 1906, the construction of the latter village became a prophetic, albeit traumatic event in Hopi history precipitated by a split between the Progressives and the Traditionalists. (See Chapter 4.) About seven miles to the east, Old Shongopovi (referred to as Masipa in Chapter 1) at the base of Second (or Middle) Mesa is reputed to be the first village established after the Bear Clan migrated into the region circa A.D. 1100. Its celestial counterpart is Alnilam, the middle star of the belt. High on First (or Eastern) Mesa about seven miles farther east perch the adjacent villages of Walpi, Sichomovi, and Hano— the first of which was established before A.D. 1300. They correspond to the triple star Alnitak, rising last of the three stars in the belt.

Nearly due north of Oraibi at a distance of just over fifty-six miles is Betatakin Ruin in Tsegi Canyon, while about four miles beyond is Keet Seel Ruin. Built during the mid-thirteenth century, both of these spectacular cliff dwellings are located within the boundaries of Navajo National Monument. Their sidereal counterpart is the double star Rigel, the left foot or knee of Orion. (We are conceptualizing Orion as viewed from the front.) Due south of Oraibi about fifty-six miles (equidistant to Betatakin in the north) is Homol'ovi Ruins State Park, a group of four Anasazi ruins constructed between the mid-thirteenth and early fourteenth centuries. These represent the irregularly variable star Betelgeuse, the right shoulder of Orion. Nearly forty-seven miles southwest of Oraibi is the

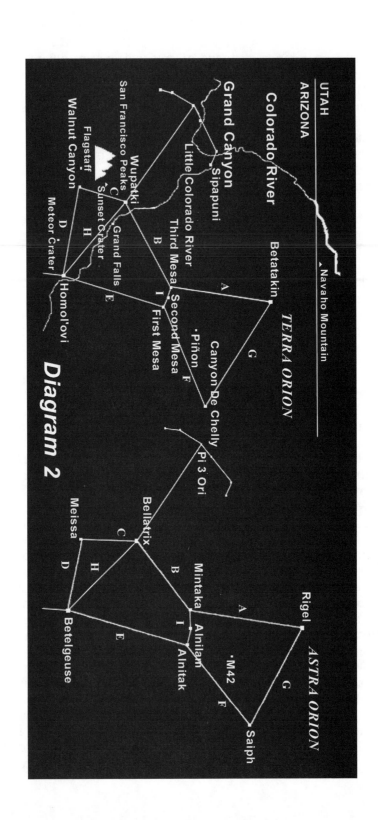

Diagram 2

Sinagua ruin of Wupatki National Monument, along with a few smaller surrounding ruins. Built in the early twelfth century, their celestial correlative is Bellatrix, a slightly variable star forming the left shoulder of Orion. About fifty miles northeast of Walpi is the mouth of Canyon de Chelly, where another national monument is located. In this and its side Canyon del Muerto a number of Anasazi ruins dating from the mid-eleventh century are found. Saiph, the triple star forming the right foot or knee of Orion, corresponds to these ruins, primarily White House, Antelope House, and Mummy Cave. Extending northwest from Wupatki/Bellatrix, Orion's left arm holds a shield over numerous smaller ruins in Grand Canyon National Park, including Tusayan near Desert View on the south rim. Extending southward from Homol'ovi/Betelgeuse, Orion's right arm holds a nodule club above his head. This club stretches across the Mogollon Rim and down past the ruins in the lower Verde Valley region. As a small triangle formed by Meissa at its apex and by Phi 1 and Phi 2 Orionis at its base, the head of Orion correlates to the Sinagua ruins at Walnut Canyon National Monument together with a few smaller ruins in the immediate region.

If we conceptualize Orion not as the rectangle mentioned in the next chapter but as a polygon of seven sides, more specifically an "hourglass" (suggesting Chronos, again discussed in the following chapter) appended to a triangle whose base rests on the constellation's shoulders, the relative proportions of the terrestrial Orion coincide with amazing accuracy. The apparent distances between the stars as we see them in the constellation (as opposed to actual light-year distances) and the distances between these major Hopi villages or Anasazi/Sinagua ruin sites are close enough to suggest that something more than mere coincidence is at work here. For instance, four of the sides of the heptagon (**A.** Betatakin to Oraibi, **B.** Oraibi to Wupatki, **C.** Wupatki to Walnut Canyon, and **F.** Walpi to Canyon de Chelly) are exactly proportional, while the remaining three sides (**D.** Walnut Canyon to Homol'ovi, **E.** Homol'ovi to Walpi, and **G.** Canyon de Chelly back to Betatakin) are slightly stretched in relation to the constellation— from ten miles in the case of **D.** and **E.** to twelve miles in the case of **G.**

This variation could be due either to possible cartographic distortions of the contemporary sky chart in relation to the geographic map or to ancient misperceptions of the proportions of the constellation vis-à-vis the landscape. Given the physical exigencies for building a village, such as springs or rivers, which are not prevalent in the desert anyway, this is a striking correlation, despite these small anomalies in the overall pattern. As John Grigsby says in his discussion of the relationship between the temples of Angkor in Cambodia and the constellation Draco, "If this is a fluke then it's an amazing one.... There is allowance for human error in the transference of the constellation on to a map, and then the transference of the fallible map on to a difficult terrain over hundreds of square kilometers with no method of checking the progress of the site from the air."₅ In this case we are dealing not with Hindu/Buddhist temples but with multiple "star cities" sometimes separated from each other by more than fifty miles. Furthermore, we have suggested that the "map" is actually represented on a number of stone tablets (which will be discussed in greater depth in the Chapter 5), and that this geodetic configuration was influenced or even specifically determined by a divine presence, i.e., Masau'u.

Referring once more to Diagram 2, we also notice the angular correspondences of Orion-on-the-earth to Orion-in-the-sky. Here again the visual reciprocity is startling enough to make one doubt that pure coincidence is responsible. Using Bersoft Image Measurement 1.0 software, however, we can correlate in degrees the precise angles of this pair of digital images seen in the diagram.

| Angle | Degrees | Difference |
|---|---|---|
| **AG** terra | 65.37 | |
| **AG** Orion | 71.19 | 5.82 |
| | | |
| **BC** terra | 132.60 | |
| **BC** Orion | 130.77 | 1.83 |
| | | |
| **CD** terra | 84.31 | |
| **CD** Orion | 100.07 | 15.76 |
| | | |
| **DE** terra | 97.79 | |
| **DE** Orion | 95.65 | 2.14 |
| | | |
| **FG** terra | 56.17 | |
| **FG** Orion | 64.23 | 8.06 |

The closest correlation is between the left and right shoulders (**BC** and **DE** respectively) of the terrestrial and celestial Orions, with only about two degrees difference between the two pairs of angles. In addition, the left and right legs (**AG** and **FG** respectively) are within the limits of recognizable correspondence, with approximately six to eight degrees difference. The only angles that vary considerably are those that represent Orion's head (**CD**), with over fifteen degrees difference between terra firma and the firmament. Given the whole polygonal configuration, however, this discrepancy is not enough rule out a generally close correspondence between Orion above and Orion below.

Another factor that precludes mere chance in this mirroring of sky and earth is the angular positioning of the terrestrial Orion in relation to longitude. As previously mentioned, the Hopi place importance on intercardinal (i.e., northwest, southwest, southeast, and northeast) rather than cardinal directions. Of course, the Anasazi could not make use of the compass but instead relied upon solstice sunrise and sunset points on the horizon for orientation. The Sun Chiefs (in Hopi, *tawa-mongwi*) still perform their observations of the eastern horizon at sunrise from the winter solstice on December 22 (azimuth 120 degrees) through the summer solstice on June 21 (azimuth 60 degrees), when the sun god Tawa is making his northward journey. On the other hand, they study the western horizon at sunset from June 21 (azimuth 300 degrees) through December 22 (azimuth 240 degrees), when he travels south from the vicinity of the Sipapuni (located on the Little Colorado River upstream from its confluence with the Colorado River) to the San Francisco Peaks in the southwest.6 (Azimuth is the angular distance measured in degrees clockwise from the north on the arc of the horizon.) A few days before and after each solstice Tawa seems to stop and rest (the term *solstice* literally meaning "the sun to stand still") in his winter or summer *Tawaki*, or "house." In fact, the winter Soyal ceremony is performed in part to encourage the sun to reverse his direction and return to Hopiland instead of continuing south and eventually disappearing altogether.

A t any rate, the key solstice points on the horizon that we designate by the azimuthal degrees of 60, 120, 240, and 300 (at this specific latitude, that is) recur in the relative positioning of the Anasazi sky cities. (See Diagram 3, p. 32.) For instance, if we stand on the edge of Third Mesa near the village of Oraibi on the winter solstice, we can watch the sun set at exactly 240 degrees on the horizon, directly in line with the ruins of Wupatki almost fifty miles away. The sun disappears over Humphreys Peak, where the major shrine of the *katsinam* is located. Incidentally, if this line between Oraibi and the San Francisco Peaks is extended southwest, it intersects the small pueblo called King's Ruin in Big Chino Valley, a stop-off point on the major trade route from the Colorado River.7 If the line is extended farther southwest, it intersects the mouth of Bill Williams River on the Colorado. Conversely, if we stand at Wupatki on the summer solstice, we can see the sun rise directly over Oraibi on Third Mesa at 60 degrees on the horizon. On that same day the sun would set at 300 degrees, to which the left arm of the terrestrial Orion points. In addition, from Oraibi the summer solstice sun sets at 300 degrees, twelve degrees north of the Sipapuni on the Little Colorado River, the "Place of Emergence" of the Hopi from the Third to the Fourth Worlds.

After going east, if we were to perch on the edge of Canyon de Chelly and instead of looking downward gaze southwest at the winter solstice sunset, the solar disk on the horizon would appear about five degrees south of the First Mesa village of Walpi. If this line were extended farther southwest beyond the horizon, it would intersect both Sunset Crater and Humphreys Peak. Again, the reciprocal angular relationship between

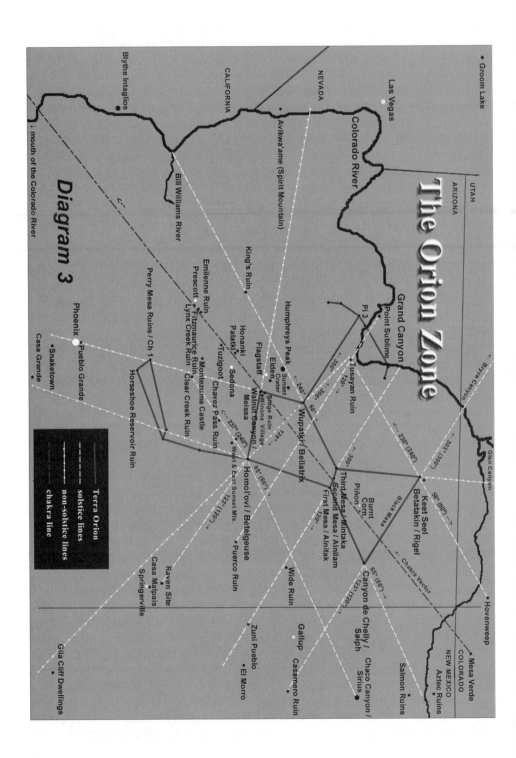

# The Orion Zone

## Diagram 3

Legend:
- ———— Terra Orion (solstice lines)
- – – – – non-solstice lines
- ········ chakra line

Groom Lake

Las Vegas

NEVADA

CALIFORNIA

Colorado River

Blythe Intaglios

← mouth of the Colorado River

Avikwa'ame (Spirit Mountain)

Bill Williams River

King's Ruin

Perry Mesa Ruins / Ch 1

Emilenne Ruin

Prescott

Fitzmaurice Ruin

Lynx Creek Ruin

Phoenix

Pueblo Grande

Casa Grande

Snaketown

Horseshoe Reservoir Ruin

Humphreys Peak

Honanki

Palatki

Tuzigoot

Montezuma Castle

Clear Creek Ruin

Sedona

Chavez Pass Ruin

Flagstaff

Elden

Sunset Crater

Bridge Ruin

Winona Village

Walnut Canyon

Meissa

Wupatki / Bellatrix

West & East Sunset Mts.

Homol'ovi / Betelgeuse

Puerco Ruin

UTAH

ARIZONA

Grand Canyon

Point Sublime

Pi 3

Tusayan Ruin

Third Mesa / Mintaka

Second Mesa / Alnilam

First Mesa / Alnitak

Burnt Corn

Piñon

Wide Ruin

Black Mesa

Glen Canyon

Keet Seel

Betatakin / Rigel

Canyon de Chelly / Saiph

Gallup

Casamero Ruin

Zuni Pueblo

El Morro

Raven Site

Casa Malpais

Springerville

Gila Cliff Dwellings

COLORADO

NEW MEXICO

Mesa Verde

Aztec Ruins

Salmon Ruins

Chaco Canyon / Sirius

Hovenweep

Blythe Canyon

Chakra Vector

240°

308°

300°

720°

60°

128°

237° (240°)

65° (60°)

123° (120°)

120°

300°

58° (60°)

123° (120°)

65° (60°)

305° (305°)

305° (300°)

238° (240°)

the two pueblo sites remains, so from Walpi at summer solstice sunrise the sun would appear to rise from Canyon de Chelly fifty miles away. A northeastward extension of this 65 degree line would eventually reach a point in New Mexico near Salmon Ruin and Aztec Ruin.[8] In addition, a winter solstice sunrise line (120 degrees) drawn from Walpi past Wide Ruin traverses the Zuni Pueblo (a tribe culturally though not linguistically related to the Hopi) and ends just south of El Morro National Monument.[9]

Standing during winter solstice sunrise on the edge of Tsegi Canyon where Betatakin and Keet Seel Ruins are located, we could look southeast along the edge of Black Mesa and watch the sun come up over Canyon de Chelly and Canyon del Muerto. In fact, the sun would be at 120 degrees on the horizon directly over Antelope House Ruin in the latter canyon. An extension of the same line into New Mexico would intersect Casamero Ruin.[10] Later on that first day of winter from the same spot at Tsegi Canyon we could see the sun set at 240 degrees azimuth over Grand Canyon near Tusayan Ruin more than eighty miles to the southwest. From Tsegi a summer solstice sunrise line of 60 degrees would intersect Hovenweep National Monument in southeastern Utah, well known for the archaeoastronomical precision of its solstice and equinox markers. Again from Tsegi a sunset line of 300 degrees would cross Bryce Canyon National Park and Paunsaugunt Plateau, where nearly one hundred and fifty small Anasazi and Fremont ruins have been identified.[11]

If we travel one hundred and twelve miles almost due south of Tsegi Canyon to stand at Homol'ovi, the summer solstice sunset would appear eight degrees south of Wupatki, which is fifty miles to the northwest. This line (designated as **H** in Diagram 2, p. 28) between Homol'ovi and Wupatki passes between Grand Falls, an impressive cataract along the Little Colorado River, and Roden Crater, a volcanic cinder cone that artist James Turrell has turned into an immense earth sculpture, to finally end at Tusayan Ruin on the south rim of Grand Canyon. Again, from the reciprocal village of Wupatki the winter solstice sun would rise just north of Homol'ovi, which is at 128 azimuthal degrees in relation to the former site. This Wupatki-Homol'ovi line extended southeast would pass just south of Casa Malpais Ruin and end less than ten miles south of Gila Cliff Dwellings.[12]

From Homol'ovi a winter solstice sunrise line (120 degrees) would pass seven degrees north of Casa Malpais [13] and three degrees north of Raven Site Ruin [14], both north of the town of Springerville. From Homol'ovi at winter solstice sundown (240 degrees), the sun passes through East and West Sunset Mountains, the gateway to the Mogollon Rim. This close solstice line (237 degrees) from Homol'ovi proceeds past the early fourteenth century, thousand-room Chavez Pass Ruin on Anderson Mesa (in Hopi, Nuvakwewtaqa, "mesa wearing a snow belt")[15] and continues along the Palatkwapi Trail down to the Verde Valley, ending near Clear Creek Ruin. If we extend a close summer solstice sunrise line

(65 degrees) from Homol'ovi into New Mexico, we intersect the vicinity of Chaco Canyon, perhaps the jewel of all the Anasazi sites in the Southwest. In this astral-terrestrial pattern Chaco corresponds to Sirius, the brightest star in the heavens located in Canis Major. (This will be discussed further in Chapter 8.)

Thus, in this schema each village is connected to at least one other by a solstice sunrise or sunset point on the horizon. This interrelationship provided a psychological link between one's own village and the people in one's "sister" village miles away. Moreover, it reinforced the divinely ordered coördinates of the various sky cities come down to earth. Not only did Masau'u/Orion speak in a geodetic language that connected the Above with the Below, but also Tawa verified this configuration by his solar measurements along the curving rim of the *tutskwa*, or sacred earth.

In addition to the solstice alignments, a number of intriguing non-solstice lines exists to corroborate the pattern as a whole. As heretofore stated, an extension of the solstice line between Oraibi and Wupatki (the belt and left shoulder of the terrestrial Orion respectively) would ultimately end on the Colorado River at the point where a major trail east toward Anasazi territory began. Similarly, if the non-solstice line between Walpi and Homol'ovi (the belt and the right shoulder respectively) were extended, it would intersect the wrist of the constellation and terminate within five miles of the important Hohokam ruin site and astronomical observatory of Casa Grande Ruins National Monument, near the Gila River one hundred and fifty miles away. We have also already discussed the extension of the Walpi-Canyon de Chelly solstice line (Orion's right leg) ending up at the Salmon Ruins and Aztec Ruins area. An extension of the Oraibi-Betatakin non-solstice line (Orion's left leg) would bring us to Glen Canyon National Recreation Area. Ruefully, hundreds or perhaps even thousands of small Anasazi ruins were submerged by the construction of the Glen Canyon Dam in 1963, and the few that remain can only be reached by boat.

Another alignment of ancient pueblo sites forms the grand chakra system of Orion and indicates the direction of the flow of spiritual energy. (See the section entitled "The Head of Orion" in Chapter 6 for a fuller discussion of chakras.) Drawing a line southwest from Shongopovi/Alnilam, we pass less than five miles southeast of Roden Crater and Grand Falls, both mentioned above. Continuing southwest the line runs by Ridge Ruin 16, through Winona Village 17, and into the forehead of Orion, viz., Walnut Canyon National Monument, a mid-twelfth century Sinagua ruin located in the foothills of the San Francisco Peaks. If the line is extended farther still, it intersects the red rock country of Sedona with its electromagnetic vortices, passing the small but gorgeously located ruin and pictograph site of Palatki, "Red House," as well as the larger Honanki, "Bear House." In the Verde Valley the newly energized vector directly transits Tuzigoot National Monument, a major thirteenth century Sinagua ruin of over one hundred rooms perched on a hilltop for the probable purpose of stellar observation. (The ruins in both Walnut Canyon and the Verde Valley will be fully discussed in Chapter 6.) The line traverses the Black Hills of Arizona, goes by the newly excavated Emilienne Ruin [18] in Lonesome Valley, intersects the Fitzmaurice Ruin [19] located upon a ridge on the south bank of Lynx Creek in Prescott Valley, continues through the small Lynx Creek Ruin at the northern base of the Bradshaw Mountains, treks across the northern limits of the Sonoran desert, passes near the Arizona geoglyphs[20] and ultimately reaches a point just north of the mouth of the Colorado River, perhaps the place where the ancients migrating on reed rafts from the Third World to the Fourth entered the territory. (See Chapter 1.) If we were to extend this line in the other direction from Shongopovi, it would travel northeast across Black Mesa, passing just southeast of Four Corners to finally end up at the major Anasazi sites of Mesa Verde National Park in southwestern Colorado.

In this series of villages we have eleven both major and minor Anasazi or Sinagua ruins and one Hopi pueblo perfectly aligned over a distance of over 275 miles within the framework of the tellurian Orion. The probability that these are randomly distributed is highly unlikely and increases the possibility that Masau'u (or some other agent perceived as being divine) directed their positioning.

At this point the question might arise: Why is the template of Orion placed upon the earth at the specific angle relative to longitude that we find it? The "chakra" line mentioned above, which runs in part from Shongopovi/Alnilam (the belt of Orion) to Walnut Canyon/Meissa (the head of Orion) is 231 degrees azimuth in relation to Shongopovi. The azimuthal direction of southwest is 225 degrees. Thus, the axis for the terrestrial Orion is within six degrees of northeast/southwest. If we stood at Shongopovi shortly after midnight nine centuries ago on the winter solstice and looked southwest, we would find the middle star of Orion's belt hovering directly above the *southwest* horizon at an altitude of about 38 degrees. Specifically, at 1:15 a.m. on December 22, A.D. 1100, Alnilam is at 231 degrees azimuth. [21] In other words, gazing from the central star of the earthbound belt of Orion toward its head located in the foothills of the San Francisco Peaks where the *katsinam* live, we would see the celestial constellation precisely mirror the angle of the terrestrial configuration.

One might also question the significance of this precise time when the middle star in Orion's belt is at 231 degrees. At the very moment we are watching this sidereal spectacle, "one of the most sacred ceremonies"[22] of the Hopi known as the Soyal (also discussed in the following chapter) is taking place down in the kiva. Just past his meridian Orion can be clearly seen through the hatchway. This is the time "when Hotomkam begins to hang down in the sky." Now a powerful, barefooted figure descends the kiva ladder. He is painted with white dots resembling stars on his arms, legs, chest, and back. He carries a crook on which is tied an ear of black corn, Masau'u's corn signifying the Above. One account identifies him as Muy'ingwa, the deity of germination we will mention in Chapter 3 in connection with Masau'u.23 Another calls him "Star man," ostensibly because of his headdress made of four white corn leaves representing a four-pointed star, perhaps Aldebaran in the Hyades.24 At any rate, this person takes a hoop covered with buckskin and begins to dance. His "sun shield" fringed with red horsehair is about a foot across with a dozen or so eagle feathers tied to its circumference. Its lower hemisphere is painted blue, its upper right quadrant is red, and its upper left quadrant is yellow. Two horizontal black lines for the eyes and a small downward pointing triangle for the mouth are painted on the lower half of this face of Tawa. Alexander Stephen, who witnessed the ritual at Walpi in 1891, remarked that the Star Priest stamps upon the *sipapu* (the hole in the floor of the kiva that links it to the Underworld) as a signal to start the most important portion of the ceremony.25 *This occurs just after 1:00 a.m.*, the time on this date in the year A.D. 1100 (the approximate onset of settlement on the Hopi Mesas) when Orion was at 231 degrees azimuth.

As the dance rhythm crescendos, the "Star man" begins to twirl the sun hoop very fast in clockwise rotation around the intercardinal points between two lines of Singers, one at the north and the other at the south. With "mad oscillations" (to quote A.M. Stephen) he is attempting to turn back the sun from its southward journey. "All these dances, songs, and spinning of the sun are timed by the changing positions of the three stars, Hotomkam, overhead. Now is the time this must be done, before the sun rises and takes up his journey."26 If this were merely a solar ritual, one would assume that it would take place at sunrise. On the contrary, the sidereal position of Orion must reflect the terrestrial positioning of the constellation, which only occurs after the former has passed its meridian, i.e., "...when Hotomkam begins to hang down in the sky." Prior to dawn runners are sent out to the shrines of *both* Masau'u (Orion) and Tawa (the sun) in order to deposit *pahos* (feather sticks), prayer offerings to the two gods whose complex interaction helps assure the seasons' cyclic return, keeping the world in balance for yet another year.

In addition to the solstice lines, the celestial phenomenon of lunar standstill further substantiates the specific orientation of the Orion template upon the Arizona desert. Similar to the annual cycle of the sun, the moon in its monthly cycle rises and sets at different points on the horizon. However, the moon also has a longer cycle —18.6 years, to be exact— when its rising and setting points reach extremes on the horizon. At this time in the so-called major lunar standstill cycle the moon rises and sets 6.1 degrees north and south of the positions of the rising and setting of the summer and winter solstice suns.27 For instance, in A.D. 1500 at 36 degrees North Latitude the moon at its extreme north excursion rose at

54°02' azimuth and set at 305°58'. At its extreme southern excursion the moon rose at 126°45' and set at 233°15'.28 A computer program to determine lunar standstill set for 35.48 degrees latitude (Shongopovi, Arizona) at A.D. 1100 (approximate settlement date) retrieved nearly the same results: 54.6 degrees, 305.0 degrees, 126.0 degrees, and 233.0 degrees.29

Surely the Anasazi recognized that at certain times the moon rises and sets farther north and south than does the sun at its most extreme points, and this fact must have caused consternation or even awe. Indeed, we have evidence that major lunar standstills were ritually incorporated into the architectural axes of some of the pueblos at Chaco Canyon 30, as well as into the design of the Sun Dagger petroglyph on Fajada Butte.31 In addition, an outlier of Chaco Canyon known as Chimney Rock Pueblo in southern Colorado was specifically oriented to take into account this phenomenon. Only at the northern extreme of this eighteen-and-a-half year cycle would the moon rise between two great pinnacles of rock beneath which the pueblo was built.

> "The most important astronomical event visible from the town may have been the spectacle of the full moon rising between the chimneys near the time of winter solstice.... The full moon always rises at sunset. When it rose between the double spires above the snow-covered landscape, colored red from the glow of the sunset, the moon must have appeared huge and brilliant. The sight of the moon rising between the chimneys ranks as one of the dramatic events in the heavens. Our Anasazi predecessors could not help but have been impressed."32

Witnessing a variation of the same phenomenon from the Hopi Second Mesa (the middle star in the terrestrial belt of Orion), they may have been equally impressed by the rising moon over the snow-dusted foothills of the San Francisco Peaks nearly seventy miles away— the place where the pueblos in Walnut Canyon (the heard of Orion) are located. For instance, on December 21st of A.D. 1112 the sun set as usual at about 5:00 p.m. at its farthest point south on the western horizon, i.e., 240 degrees. Forty-five minutes later the slender sliver of a waxing moon hung on the same horizon at 233 degrees azimuth— even farther south than the sun had set. This must have given sky watchers cause for some concern.

As previously stated, the chakra line from Shongopovi to Walnut Canyon is 231 degrees azimuth, two degrees less than the setting of the moon at its southern extreme. Going the opposite direction, the line from Shongopovi to Mesa Verde is at 51 degrees azimuth, three degrees less than the rising moon at its northern extreme. The left-to-right-shoulder line from Wupatki to Homol'ovi (**H** in Diagram 2) crosses the chakra line to form a Latin cross. (Also see Diagram 3.) The azimuth of this line is 128 degrees, less than a two degrees difference from the rising moon at its southern extreme (126°45'). Going in the opposite direction, i.e., from Homol'ovi to Wupatki, we find an azimuth of 308 degrees, less than a three degrees difference from the setting moon at its northern extreme (305°58'). These discrepancies may be the result of the astronomical phenomenon that causes the moon to appear larger on the horizon than when its altitude is greater. When the moon is high in the sky it takes up about one-half of one degree (as does the sun, coincidentally), but because of atmospheric conditions it might appear twice its actual size or more as it rises or sets. "A number of factors, such as parallax and atmospheric refraction, can shift and broaden the range of azimuth where risings and settings of the solstice suns and the standstill moons appear on the horizon."[33] The huge appearance of the moon on the horizon could plausibly account for the two to three degrees difference between the lunar standstill points and the azimuths of both the chakra line and the perpendicular **Line H**. If this is the case, not only is Terra Orion positioned via a variety of solstice lines, but it is also affixed to the landscape seemingly in accordance with the moon's most extreme positions on the horizon.

Given that the head of the celestial constellation points north throughout the night, one might question why the terrestrial Orion is oriented toward the south. An answer to this can be found in the schema of Hopi cosmology we will discuss again in Chapter 3. The subterranean realm of ancestral spirits is putatively an exact replica of the pueblo world of physical beings, except in reverse.

> "While the winter fields lay fallow, residents of the underworld were said to be cultivating and harvesting crops. The harvest obtained in the underworld, good or bad, would be duplicated in this world during the fall months. Similarly, while the Hopi were celebrating the summer solstice with a relatively meager ceremony, the elaborate winter solstice rituals were underway in the underworld, and while *Soyal*, the Hopi winter solstice festival, was in full swing, denizens of the underworld were holding the celebration of summer. Thus, the upper and lower worlds were mirror images of each other."[34]

When the Anasazi gazed into the heavens, they were not looking at an extension of the physical world as we perceive it today but were witnessing a manifestation of the spirit world. Much like the Egyptian Duat, the Hopi Underworld encompasses the skies as well as the region beneath the surface of the earth. This is apparent in the dichotomous existence of ancestor spirits who live in the subterranean realm but periodically return to their earthly villages as clouds bringing the blessing of rain. Even though the eastern and western domains ruled by Tawa remain constant, the directions of north and south, controlled by the Elder and Younger Warrior Twins respectively, are reversed. Thus the right hand holding the nodule club is in the east and the left hand holding the shield is in the west, similar to the star chart. However, the head is pointed roughly southward instead of northward. This inversion is completely consistent with Hopi cosmology because the terrestrial configuration is seen as a reversal of the spirit world, of which the sky is merely another dimension. Another explanation for the change of directions is the possibility that the pole shift which destroyed the Hopis' Second World reversed the position of the constellation in its mundane manifestation.

When looking up at Orion on a midwinter night, we can imagine that our perspectives have switched and that we are suspended high above the land, gazing from the northeast to the southwest toward the sacred *katsina* peaks and the head of the celestial Masau'u suffused in the evergreen forests of the Milky Way.

## *The Celestial Cities of Arizona*

Considered as a gestalt, these "celestial cities" built by the Hopi and their ancestors the Hisatsinom/Anasazi form a geodetic configuration intentionally constructed to mirror the primary stars of the constellation Orion. Even if we acknowledge the impressive ability of the Anasazi/Hisatsinom to track the sun and stars across the sky, the question remains moot as to whether or not they were totally aware that their villages were the terrestrial reflection of the stars. Ultimately, the schema was ordained by Masau'u, to whom they deferred all authority and puissance. This god of earth and death was there in the beginning when the people emerged from the Underworld; at a distance he accompanied them on their migrations, and he was found to be living at the Center-place during the time the various clans reconverged. Today we recognize that this pattern of pueblo villages traced upon the earth corresponds to the constellation of paramount ritualistic importance for these people, but we have little success in making sense of this anomaly by using mainstream archaeological paradigms. We could chalk up this whole complex of interrelated coördinates to mere coincidence, but when one coincidence is heaped upon another in a series, we reach the point where we have to admit the probability of synchronicity ("*meaningful* coincidence," as psychologist C.G. Jung defined the term), though we may not be able to explain the spiritual mechanism used to accomplish this New World doctrine of signatures. What we can confirm, however, is that over a period of almost two-and-a-half centuries a terrestrial analogue to Orion took shape on the high deserts of Arizona.

As the American poet Walt Whitman states, "All the greatness of any land, at any time, lies folded in its names."35 If we look at the name Arizona, the first phrase that comes to mind is "arid zone," which is a possible derivation for this term of uncertain source. Some claim that the state was named after a Tohono O'odham (Papago) word "Aleh-zon," referring to a small spring eighty-five miles south of Tucson just on the other side of the Mexican border near the village of Banera.36 Looking deeper, however, we find other layers of meaning more relevant to our discussion. According to the Oxford English Dictionary, a 1599 reference for the word "zone" from T. Hill's *Schoole of Skil* has the following meaning: "The constellation named Zone or the gyrdle of Orion." In other words, a constellation within the larger constellation, or his belt. Following Aristotle's usage, the Latin poet Ovid refers to "Zona" specifically as the three central stars of Orion.37 Considering the prefix Ari-, we readily think of Ariel, the powerful spirit of air and earth in Shakespeare's play *The Tempest*. In the Old Testament book of Isaiah, Ari-el is an appellation for the city of Jerusalem and literally means "Lion of God." In Ezekiel the word refers to the "Hearth of God," or the altar upon which burnt offerings were made.38 Thus, in the name *Arizona* is hidden the fiery belt of Orion emblazoned upon the sacred navel of the world, in this case the three Hopi Mesas located on the high desert of the southwestern United States.

An alternate meaning of our suffix "zona" is herpes zoster, or shingles, a viral infection of the skin that causes blisters. Again we must decide whether it is merely coincidence or a case of synchronicity in considering that one of the characteristics of Masau'u, the chief god of the Hopi and deific representation of the constellation Orion, was the presence on his body of pus-filled ulcers called *masna'paliwta*, which he could also use as a weapon, causing them to form on other people.39 This aspect of Masau'u is also reminiscent of the Aztec legend of the birth of the Fifth Sun (corresponding to the Hopi Fourth World). Nanahuatzin, the bubonic god covered with pustules, stood before a sacred fire next to Tecciztecal, the handsome, greedy and arrogant god (perhaps a correlative to the Hopi sky god Sótuknang). One or the other of these gods would sacrifice itself to the intense flames in order to start the present epoch. At the last moment Tecciztecal balked, but Nanahuatzin had the courage to hurl himself into the fire, thereby kindling the new age.40 We must remember, of course, that the Hisatsinom/Hopi traded not only goods but also gods and legends with Mesoamerica.

Contained in this semantic and mythic evidence is a case where synchronicity as defined by Jung converges with the concept of Hopi prophecy. (Entire volumes have been written about the latter; therefore, we will only touch upon this topic briefly in the last chapter.) Here we have a situation where Masau'u/Orion, who was present when the Hopi emerged to this current Fourth World and who to a great extent determined the parameters by which the Hopi culture developed, is in some manner connected to the designation of the territory of Arizona in the mid-19th century. This falls under Jung's third category of synchronicity: "The coincidence of a psychic state with a corresponding, not yet existent future event that is distant in time and can likewise only be verified afterward." (The other two categories are the following: 1. a psychic state that simultaneously coincides with an external, objective event with no discernible causal connection involved, and 2. a psychic state that coincides with an external event outside the observer's field of perception.)[41] In this situation we are dealing with an initial psychic state dominated by the deity Masau'u and separated from a future event, i.e., the naming of Arizona, by a period of perhaps a thousand years. Hopi prophecy is accustomed to such vast amounts of time, even though it does not quantify them in the way to which European culture is wont. The above-mentioned synchronicities are not specifically designated by Hopi prophecy, but after considering similar types of predictions we can put them in the same class. For instance, the Hopi had prognosticated horseless wagons riding on black ribbons and cobwebs strung across their land (telephone and electric power lines) long before these things actually appeared. Other prophecies foretold of vehicles that would travel roads in the sky and a "gourd of ashes" (the latter determined by Hopi elders ex post facto to be the atomic bomb) that would fall upon the earth.[42] So maybe a link between the primary Hopi god and the Anglo-bestowed name of the state in which the former people have always lived and performed elaborate sacred rites in order to keep the whole world in balance is not so far-fetched after all.

The fact that the Hopi have one of the most complex ritualistic systems of theology on the planet is perhaps due in part to the very culture characteristic responsible for Orion's terrestrial analogue being so long hidden. Whereas the Great Plains tribes such as the Lakota (Sioux) directly confronted the exploitive powers spurred on by the doctrine of Manifest Destiny and Western imperialism, in part because the former were geographically in the immediate path of frontier expansion, historically the Hopi have used for the most part avoidance and passive resistance as a means of physical and spiritual survival. For instance, even today when visiting the Hopi reservation, one finds that the people are always demurely courteous and in general friendly, yet some frequently turn evasive when asked about the location or time of a particular *katsina* dance. Many villages allow non-Indian visitors while others do not, and the schedule of dances is never known beforehand or published in the reservation newspaper (nor should they be). Of course, no photography, video taping, audio taping, nor even sketching and note taking are permitted at any of the plaza dances. This is all an attempt to preserve their religion from the onslaught of the encroaching outside world. And this other world had always been "outside" the concerns of the Hopi and very far away, at least until recently. This is one of the benefits of living "in the middle of nowhere," as some uninformed and condescending tourists like to put it, who themselves are hopelessly deracinated beyond the comprehension of most Hopi, whose ancestral lines reach back many centuries or perhaps even thousands of years at a single spot upon the earth.

A specific example of the ability to obfuscate for the grander purpose of cultural preservation might be found in a question posed by a Navajo person to Leigh Jenkins (also known as Leigh J. Kuwanwisiwma), the director of that very tribal office, in a recent panel discussion on the Anasazi. Drawing on his own memory and background in the region, this Navajo states: "I've heard stories about the different villages, about the First and Second Mesa villages representing the different portions of the body of an Indian who was lying east to west. You know, I remember that story very vaguely even from the time I was a small child. And I wonder if there is any significance to that story from your own teachings and learnings from your fathers." The Hopi disjointedly and somewhat bluntly replies that he is unaware of any such legends relating to "...whether or not there's any symbolism of the Hopi villages, or the mesas, representing a view of either a male... or the human race being represented in that fashion..."[43] This "no-comment" sort of response might actually be the truth, i.e., he really has no knowledge of such a configuration. This is totally possible, given the nature of the heterogeneous clan system of the Hopi, where certain mythological data would be available to a given clan while other information would not be. However, notice that the questioner did not mention that a "male" figure was imposed upon the land, but merely that of "an Indian"— who could be either male or female. Perhaps this is only an example of the sexism inherent in both Indian and non-Indian contemporary cultures, or possibly Mr. Jenkins divulged a bit more than he intended to. In addition, the questioner did not mention "the human race," but the body of a single Indian, which only confuses matters further. Maybe this unexpected question made it difficult for the cultural preservation officer to gracefully sidestep the issue. Maybe Mr. Jenkins' reticence was the result of the historic antagonism between Navajo and Hopi. Maybe the hour was late and everyone was tired. At any rate, we are left with yet another mystery waiting to be solved: the apparent anthropomorphic figure delineated by a pattern of ancestral "sky cities" spread across the high desert.

When we survey the four sites in Arizona that comprise the shoulders and legs of the terrestrial Orion, we notice that each village or village group corresponds to the four classical elements. As John Anthony West states, "The four terms needed to account for matter are the famous four elements— which are not, as modern science believes, a primitive attempt to account for the mysteries of the material universe, but rather a precise and sophisticated means of describing the inherent nature of matter."[44] Thus, we are dealing not with an inchoate form of chemistry but instead with a complex metaphysics. In terms of our discussion the village of Betatakin/Rigel corresponds to fire, and indeed the Fire Clan was its builder. In addition, the red color of Tsegi Canyon suggests this caustic element. Wupatki/Bellatrix is associated with air, with its adjacent blowhole feature and its subterranean labyrinth of air passages whose purview is the wind god Yopontsa. Homol'ovi has always been a refuge in time of drought, and it is the only site in the complex that is close to a continually flowing source of water, the Little Colorado River. Lastly, Canyon de Chelly was known to its Anasazi inhabitants as "the place of Loose Sand," thereby suggesting the element crucial to agriculture: earth. However, if we follow this alchemical schema to its end, we find the quincunx at the heart of this quaternity to be ether, which correlates to the Hopi Mesas/Orion's belt, the Center-place. The ancients believed that this most sacred medium filled the upper regions of space and was the essence of the gods as well as the home for departed souls.

If we recall the hourglass outline of tellurian Orion discussed earlier in this chapter, a little modification of this form will produce the ancient petroglyph for war, i.e., two opposing triangles, the apexes of which are touching.45 Also conceptualized as two arrow points facing each other, this shape (whose center focuses upon Shongopovi, the first village settled on the Mesas) is symbolic of Masau'u, once thought of as primarily the god of war and death as well as of the earth. The northern "arrowhead, " which is formed by Black Mesa, is higher in elevation than the southern "arrowhead" near the Little Colorado River. The northern edge of Black Mesa is over 7,000 feet whereas the riparian region to the south is generally about 5,000 feet. However, the two ruin sites comprising the angles at the base of the northern triangle are located in canyons; thus, they may be considered as being feminine in character. The sites making up the base of the southern triangle are located on low hill tops and may be seen as being masculine. Here we see yet another manifestation of the Hisatsinom/Hopi system of duality in this north-south polarity. An example of an east-west polarity can be seen when we recognize that traditionally the Two Horn Society protected the Northeast and the Southeast while the more important One Horn Society was guardian of the Northwest (the Sipapuni) and Southwest (the San Francisco Peaks).46

When Orion begins to rise out of the landscape of the Southwest, many questions regarding ancient cultural influences and stellar events also arise. The rest of this book will try to address these questions.

# Chapter 3
# Orion Rising In the Dark Crystal

"The stars were a deific reflection of terrestrial activity,
for they returned in sequence, either with the seasons
or according to esoteric mathematical formulae. The sky was a palace
and a kingdom where deities acted out eternal roles. It was also a dark
crystal in which Earth's landscapes revealed their essence."[1]
Richard Grossinger

## The Presence of the Gods

Shortly after the monsoons arrive on the Colorado Plateau and the *katsinam* depart for their home on the San Francisco Peaks, one of the most impressive yet enigmatic constellations becomes an abiding presence in the night sky. An hour before the sun in early July and three hours before by late July, Orion rises due east to repose for a few seemingly eternal moments on the horizon.[2] The readily identifiable "belt" hovers vertically above the dark silhouette of the sleeping land. Equidistant on either side of this stellar trinity in a line parallel to the horizon, the prominent blue-white Rigel and the reddish Betelgeuse grace the pre-dawn hours with a solemn beauty. Slightly above Orion, the constellation Taurus with its fiery garnet Aldebaran is held aloft like a guardian scepter. Higher still the Pleiades plant their clustered seeds of light in the celestial loam. An extension of the upper horn of the Hyades connects to Elnath in the inverted pentagonal constellation Auriga, its conspicuous star Capella burning a few degrees to the north. Meanwhile Auriga's apex points downward toward the Twins Castor and Pollux in the constellation Gemini, which also rests on the horizon. These constellations along with Procyon and Sirius (the latter the most brilliant star in the sky rising directly below Orion's belt about two hours afterwards) form the Winter Hexagon and will continue to dominate the heavens during the coming colder months. However, for the Anasazi the influence of these stars is not merely aesthetic. Instead the presence of the gods inherent in complementary worlds of earth and sky is making itself known to the faithful who offer prayer feathers and cornmeal in order to perpetuate this sacred cycle.

## The Legacy of Orion

If one reviews Orion's influence throughout a number of cultures, a composite picture begins to emerge: Hunter, Warrior, Hero, Giant. Probably derived from the Akkadian *Uru-anna*, his name means "the Light of Heaven" and originally referred to the sun.3 In Greek mythology Orion was the handsome giant and quintessential hunter from Boeotia who fell in love with Merope, daughter of Oenopion, king of Chios, which is located off the Ionion coast. After Orion had ridded this island of wild beasts, Oenopion still refused to grant his daughter's hand in marriage; consequently, Orion raped her. As punishment the king with the help of Dionysus made Orion drunk and put out his eyes as he slumbered. Left blinded upon the shore, he consulted an oracle that advised him to seek the sun's rays in order to regain his vision. With Cedalion, the son of Hephaetus, as his guide, Orion journeyed toward the east and slept with Eos, or Dawn, whereupon Helios restored his sight.

This mythological connection to the sun finds an astronomical interpretation in the heliacal rising of the constellation. Orion's communion with the sun at the beginning of summer follows his absence from the night sky, or "blindness," for a few months out of every year. After the summer solstice he again is able to look down upon the earth until spring, at which time the cycle of his mythical loss of sight is replayed. Curiously, the object of his affection, Merope, in an alternate myth was known as one of the Pleiades, who was turned into a dove along with her sisters and placed in the heavens when Orion tried to ravish them. According to the Greeks, the death of Orion had astronomical ramifications as well. In one version Artemis sent a scorpion to bite him after he yet again tried to commit rape, this time against the goddess herself. The animosity between Scorpius and Orion is represented by their placement at opposite ends of the ecliptic, one constellation never being visible when the other is in view.4

In the Middle East Orion was known to the Hebrews as *cesîl*, and his terrestrial counterpart was Nimrod, the mighty hunter whose Mesopotamian empire included the city of Babel.5   In Arabia he was recognized as Al Jabbar, the Giant. In China he together with Taurus represented the White Tiger. In India he was Praja-pati, the master of created beings, taking the form of the stag Mriga. Pursuing his own daughter Rohini who assumed the form of a doe (Aldebaran), he was shot by a hunter (Sirius) who was trying to avenge this incestuous impulse. The belt represents the arrow still sticking in the stag's body. In Egypt Orion was seen as the soul of Osiris, who communed with his son, the solar deity Horus. (Chapter 11 describes the Egyptian connection.) In Ireland Orion was referred to as Caomai, the Armed King. In Scandinavian mythology his belt was known as Frigge's (or Freya's) distaff. This fertility goddess was Mother Earth herself, whose axis was conceptualized as a spinning wheel.6

In the Western Hemisphere the Maya of eastern Chiapas believed that the three stars of the belt represented a turtle. An eighth century A.D.

mural at Bonampak depicts this celestial amphibian swimming across the base of a vaulted ceiling.7 According to Fray Bernadino de Sahagún's *Florentine Codex: General history of the things of New Spain*, the Aztecs named these stars Mamalhuaztli, the "little sticks" or the Fire Drill.8 Indeed, the constellation rising due east described in the beginning of this chapter does resemble the perpendicular sticks used to start fires and could conceivably spark the sun into fiery being, if one were metonymically inclined. The Lakota (Sioux) of the northern plains of North America also have a complex structure of ritual and myth in this regard. In particular, their system links the stars of Orion to specific sites in the Black Hills of South Dakota. The belt represents the backbone of a huge buffalo called *tayamni*, "the first born of the three relations." Rigel and Betelgeuse form the ribs, while the Pleiades serve as the head and Sirius the tail of this stellar bison.9 Here as in many native cultures, the archetypal theme of sacred earth mirroring sacred sky recurs.

In the Southwest the Navajo (Diné) call Orion *'Átsé'etsózi*, or the First Slim One. Frequently connected with agriculture, the constellation by its absence delineates the duration of the planting season, setting upon its beginning at twilight in late April or early May and reappearing at dawn in late June after which no planting should occur.10 The Tewa, who settled primarily along the Rio Grande in New Mexico but some of whom also migrated to the village of Hano on the First Mesa of the Hopis, see Orion as the sagacious warrior Long Sash. (The sword hanging from the belt is conceptualized instead as a clan kilt.) According to the story, he led the people on a long journey, traveling the Endless Trail (Milky Way), then stopping at the Place of Decision (Castor and Pollux) and the Place of Doubt (the constellation Cancer) before reaching the Middle Place.11 In this case the terrestrial migration myth described in Chapter 1 is put in the context of the complementary schema of earth and sky, with stars conceived of as resting places on a celestial cartography.

The Hopi term for Orion is *Hotòmqam*, which literally means "to string up" or "trey." This might be a reference to the belt, but it also suggests Orion's three major stars: Rigel, Alnilam (the middle star of the belt) and Betelgeuse.12 Alexander M. Stephen, the late 19th century ethnographer who lived periodically among the Hopi over a span of twelve years, transcribes the term as Hotûmkono, "strung together (as beads on a string)," or Wutom'kamü and Wutom'kami. During the important winter solstice ceremony known as Soyal, Stephen observed a wooden star effigy ten inches long and two inches wide in the front portion of a war chief's altar. Represented by imbedded bits of white shell and abalone, Orion appeared in the middle of the staff and the Pleiades were at the tip of the flat oval end. During the germination ceremony of Powamu in February, Stephen noticed on the walls of the Chief Kiva a number of four-pointed stars in the pattern of both Orion and the Pleiades. They were painted in white with black outlines and accompanied by a crescent moon and perhaps the morning star.13

These two constellations serve as the primary indicators for a precise timing of nocturnal Hisatsinom/Hopi ceremonies. For instance, in addition to consulting the position of Orion during the August Flute Ceremony, the late September or early October Márawu (Mamzranti) women's ceremony, and the above-mentioned Soyal ceremony, the Hopi watch through the kiva hatchway for the constellation to reach its meridian during the Wúwutcim ceremony in the Sparrow Hawk Moon of November. More than an initiation involving the symbolic death of adolescent males and their subsequent rebirth as mature men into the various ritual societies, this New Fire Ceremony is a re-establishment of the connection between the living and the dead. At the time when the central star of Orion's belt is directly above the fire burning down in the kiva, a Two Horn priest recounts the Emergence legend in which Masau'u played a crucial role and reminds the participants of the long journey their ancestors made from the tripartite Underworld up to the present existence. Two fires ignited by rotating drills and kept going by pieces of coal obtained from Black Mesa represent the sun's gift to Masau'u, who in turn redirects Tawa's warmth and light to the earth for the benefit of all its creatures, including humankind.14 As noted in Chapter 1, Masau'u himself bequeathed fire and taught its uses to the Anasazi in the beginning times. At one point in the Wúwutcim ritual, men with large four-pointed stars on their foreheads descend the kiva ladder along with Masau'u, whose face and neck is coated an ashen gray. (Stephen reports that the face and body of the god are a shiny black, associating him with coal. In this context Masau'u is also related to the warrior-like Chakwaina Katsina, who appears with a dark face rather than the god's more commonly described gray color. 15) It is to the deity Masau'u that pine needles set ablaze by the "new fire" are sacrificed.

## The Legacy of Masau'u

Whereas Orion on the horizon resembles the fire spindle and flat board or possibly the pump drill used to make holes in beads (hence an association to the Hopi term *Hotòmqam* previously cited), Orion rising in the dark crystal of midnight displays a more anthropomorphic presentation. Extending from Orion's right shoulder formed by Betelgeuse, a nodule club reaches into the center of the Milky Way above his head. Orion's face is represented by a small triangle with Meissa at its apex and Phi 1 and Phi 2 Orionis at its base. Projecting from his left shoulder created by Bellatrix, a curved warrior shield or perhaps a bow points west. Strung together from the stars Alnitak, Alnilam, and Mintaka, his shimmering belt at this time is aligned in a nearly east-west direction. The brilliant left foot Rigel and the paler right foot Saiph are firmly planted in the heavens, ready for action. Considering this celestial figure, one might find it ironic that the "People of Peace" associate the stars in general and Orion in particular with the concept of war.16

Although no apparent direct evidence from Hopi mythology or linguistics exists to link Wutom'kamü (Orion) with Masau'u, god of war and death, circumstantial evidence indicates a close connection. (See Fig. 2, p. 17.) Perhaps this paucity of information is the result of a taboo against openly speaking about the darker aspects of Masau'u. At any rate, from 12:00 to 1:00 a.m. during the fourth night of the nine-day Wúwutcim ceremony, the esoteric portion of which is briefly described above, Orion stands at about 50 degrees above the southern horizon. According to Titiev, an understanding of this ritual over which Orion presides is essential in grasping Hopi religion as a whole.

> "Let us recall that on the fourth day of the proceedings, visitors are barred from the pueblo and all the trails are closed. This is a night of mystery and terror. People are forced to remain indoors and are forbidden even to glance outside, and patrols of Kwans [the Agave, or One Horn, Society] and Horns [the Al, or Two Horn Society] rush madly through the village, constantly challenging each other and maintaining a dreadful din. Concurrently, in the kivas underground, a most esoteric and awe-inspiring ritual is being performed which no white observer has ever glimpsed."17

All the roads leading to the village have been closed with lines of cornmeal by the fierce and autonomous Kwan Society, the only exception being the road from the northwest where the Maski, or House of the Dead, is located and up which the spirits may proceed. This, of course, is also the direction of Grand Canyon, the place of the initial Emergence and the home of ancestor spirits. Around sundown great quantities of food had been set out on the western side of the village of Oraibi for the visiting spirits to consume. (In reality, the spirits can only feast upon the steam and aroma of food, not the food itself. This custom is reminiscent of *El Dia de los Muertos*, or "the Day of the Dead," also held in November in Mexico.) Just at the time when Orion is assuming his annual reigning presence at the crest of the constellation's parabolic journey across the night, the spirits throng the village and enter the kivas with which they were connected while still alive. Thus, in the pandemonium that results from the mingling of the living and the dead, Orion looks down in the dead of night from his most commanding position in the firmament, observing the ceremony expressly dedicated to Masau'u, the god who can only walk nocturnally upon the face of the earth.

In addition to his sovereignty of the Underworld, Masau'u is the overseer and steward of this world. "The vast expanses of this land are, of

course, quite insignificant to Maasaw. Because he is endowed with gre.
than human powers, he can traverse the entire earth before mornin,
arrives."18 What better way to express Orion's movement from the eastern
to the western horizon during the course of the night? When he wanders
about his domain, Masau'u as "owner of fire" sometimes places
smoldering embers in his eyes and mouth but never gets burned. Perhaps
this represents the cold stellar fire to which Orion is impervious as he
blazes through the long winter nights. Masau'u is also frequently seen with
a streak of black hematite painted from the bridge of his nose down each
cheek. This is possibly a reference to the forked constellation Taurus,
which is adjacent to Orion. Masau'u's habit of wearing strands of turquoise
beads might also relate to the meaning of *Hotòmqam* mentioned above.19
Recalling the Tewa legend of Long Sash, we discover further that Orion
was identified as a *kalehtaka*, or war chief, and his belt was a *to'zriki*, or
bandoleer.20 If Orion is truly synonymous with Masau'u, then this warrior's
garment would be worn contrary to the usual way. Indeed, we see the belt
tilting somewhat upward toward the left shoulder, instead of being fastened
to the customary right shoulder.

The scholar of Hopi culture Richard Maitland Bradfield, whose work
is especially relevant to our discussion, describes how various
phratries, or clan groupings, relate to the stars and the concept of war.
In particular, one of the clan names for the Reed-Greasewood-Bow phratry
(whose *wuya*, or clan totem, is Pokanghoya, the elder Warrior Twin) proves
to be *sho'hü* (*sohu*), the Hopi term for stars, which literally means 'all of
them.' "On this ground it seems a reasonable guess that the stars (*sho'hü*),
which figure among the clan names of this phratry grouping, are not the
stars in general, but refer specifically to the stars of the Orion constellation,
'all of them', and perhaps also to the Pleiades."21 Hence the Hopi focal
point in the firmament is undoubtedly Orion. In addition, the Reed Clan is
associated with Sótuknang, the Heart of the Sky god, whose bloody eye is
apparently formed by Aldebaran in the constellation Taurus. Furthermore,
this clan is tied closely in a ritual and conceptual sense to the Ko'kop-
Coyote phratry, whose *wuya* is none other than Masau'u. Additional folk
tales relating how Masau'u lifted the sky on his shoulders because the
"ceiling" of this world was too low 22, or how Coyote foolishly scattered
the stars across the sky and ruined its symmetry 23, only reinforce the
gestalt of the sidereal/mortuary correlation. In order to avoid becoming
mired in the staggering complexities of the Hopi clan and phratry systems,
it would not be unreasonable at this point to readily assume a direct
relationship between the fiery outlines of Orion and the militaristic aspects
of Masau'u who presides over the groups directing the New Fire
Ceremony.

However, before moving on we should discuss what is perhaps the
most compelling link between Orion and Masau'u, i.e., the morphology of
the former. There is nothing more numinous than this great rectangular

constellation hovering over the high desert landscape dusted with freshly fallen snow. Perhaps it is the clarity of atmosphere or the low latitude that accentuates the emotional impact of perceiving this luminous quadrilateral arcing slowly across the southern quadrant. Gemini is too elongated and Hercules too irregular, but Orion is the perfect rectangle, not only by virtue of its symmetry but also because of its sheer brilliance.

*Fig. 3. The central figure possibly represents Masau'u. Both this and the one on the left are assuming the "prayer stance." Note the central figure's rectangular body, the lower portion of which may denote the Milky Way. To the right are "crows feet," which symbolize warfare, another purview of Masau'u. Petroglyph located in the vicinity of Homol'ovi, Arizona.*

A frequent motif of rock art throughout the Southwest, the rectangle or square is representative of geographic place or land. Particularly when used with clan symbols, it can also mean "house" or "pueblo." In this respect James Cunkle calls it "the 'property' icon."[24] This latter meaning probably came into use after the round pit house construction was abandoned and rectangular-roomed or square-roomed pueblos began to be built. In addition to rectangular plazas where the *katsina* cult could expand its public rituals, kivas became primarily rectangular instead of round, especially in the vicinity of the three Hopi Mesas. The rectangle was also used to depict both a particular shrine house and the *Sipapuni*, or Place of Emergence.[25] As mentioned above, the

50

concepts of land, house, and primordial emergence were all inextricably linked with the primary function of Masau'u as proprietor of the earth. We remember as well that Masau'u's gift of the *owatutuveni*, or stone tablets upon which the Hopi land was delineated, were in the shape of rectangles. Furthermore, a great number of anthropomorphic petroglyphs and pictographs scattered across the Southwest use a rectangle to form the torso of the figure. These depictions frequently assume the so-called "prayer stance." In this position the legs and upraised arms extend horizontally from the corners of the torso, while each limb makes a right angle at its joint. Without a doubt the rectilinear sky deity Orion came down to earth in order to inhabit the rocks and proclaim the extent of his dominion.

## The Legacy of Saturn

A few points to emphasize the archetypal resonance of Orion/Masau'u are in order here. The quadrilateral has a relatively consistent significance throughout many cultures. In Sumer it meant "garden," in Egypt "house," in China "enclosure," and in Aztec Mexico it designated "place"[26]— all variations on the theme of earth. Of course, the ancients did not conceptualize the earth as actually quadrangular but instead recognized the vernal and autumnal equinoxes together with the summer and winter solstices as forming this geometric figure. Author Francis Huxley states that Saturnus, the Roman god of earth and patron of agriculture, is directly related to the celestial body of Orion. He goes on to say that "Saturn is in fact associated with the square or cube, as can be seen from Kepler's diagram, in which he assigned a different Platonic solid to each of the five planets, and boxed one within the other."[27] Thus both Saturnus and Masau'u share an affinity for this geometric figure which represents earth.

The Roman god's Greek counterpart is the Titan Kronos. The deity's orthographic variant *chronos*, or time, literally means "to grind." In this connection we are reminded of the rectangular corn grinding bins with their manos and metates (in Hopi, called *mata* and *matahki* respectively) used by the Hisatsinom women. In order to achieve an increasingly finer meal, these were sometimes placed (for instance, at the Betatakin Ruin in northern Arizona; Fig. 4) adjacent to each other in row of three, similar to the belt of Orion. To cite a further example of this Saturnus/Chronos/Orion

*Fig. 4. Grinding bins, Betatakin Ruin*

association, the constellation was known in India not only as Praja-pati, as mentioned earlier in this chapter, but also as Kal-Purush, or the "Time-Man."[28]

The Hopi Soyal discussed above is synchronized during the day by the sun and during the night by Orion. Although this ceremony is much more sedate than the Roman Saturnalia with its legendary license and master/slave role reversal, they both occur near the winter solstice, they both are highly communal in nature, and they both seek to promote purification and fertility. The first portion of the Soyal involves the purifying acts of brewing war medicine and making *pahos*, or prayer sticks. In a similar regard Sir James Frazier remarks that Saturnalia "...was originally celebrated as a sort of public purification at the end of the old year or the beginning of a new one..."[29] The fertility aspect of the Soyal becomes apparent in the latter part of the ceremony when the Mastop, or Death Fly Katsina, who wears Orion's belt or perhaps the Hyades of the constellation Taurus painted in white on both sides of his black mask, rushes into a crowd of females and simulates copulation. (This *katsina* will be discussed in greater depth in Chapter 7.) Another *katsina* connected with both fertility and death is the Masau'u Katsina. Unlike the sort of three dimensional doll, or *tihu*, that represents most *katsinam*, this flat, significantly rectangular figure is crudely carved out of a cottonwood root and painted with the fingertip instead of a brush. Commonly given out to both married women and adolescent or small girls, the doll is culturally distinct from effigies of Masau'u the deity, which are rare and more or less taboo.[30]

In addition to controlling the temporal cycles of sowing and reaping in his capacity as the lord of the world and of time, Saturnus can also be compared to Masau'u as the god of metamorphosis. Assisted by Hopi individual and collective acts of prayer, Masau'u directs the natural processes whereby whatever is shadowy, insubstantial, ethereal, mental, emotional, psychological, or non-corporeal is ultimately manifested. In other words, he brings "such stuff as dreams are made on" from its subjective realm into the objective world of sensation and perception. Because he acts as divine catalyst, the state in which human striving and hope mingle with the larger notion of a prophetic future flows constantly into an opposite state in which the achievement and fulfillment of the present give way to historical facts or events. The types of transformation Masau'u oversees are as follows: 1. physical metamorphosis (combustion of flammable material and its reduction to ashes), 2. physiological metamorphosis (plant germination and growth), and 3. social metamorphosis (birth, initiation into religious societies, marriage, and death).[31] His domain includes the four directions upon the surface plane of the earth (with the Hopi Mesas as center) as well as the vertical dipole linking the netherworld (below Grand Canyon) and the vault of heaven (Orion at meridian).

As linguist Benjamin Lee Whorf notes, stars belong to the category of latency, i.e., the yet unmanifested (or subjective). However, their shifting positions in the night sky synchronize the already manifested (or objective) ceremonies of the Hopi calendar. As a result, humans can tap into the numinous forces of creation. Orion, the sidereal reflection of tellurian Masau'u (whose Roman brother is Saturnus), acts as a transducer of unmanifest energy, ushering it into the reality of being, much like a crystal's prism turns invisible white light into the colors of the visible spectrum. Incidentally, in Hopi mythology the symbolic color for the direction of the zenith, Orion's purview, is "black," while the symbolic color for the nadir, Masau'u's purview, is "all colors." Using this dialectic, we can see that black at one pole and all colors (produced by white) at the other are merely opposite dimensions of the same Orion/Masau'u (Saturnus) axis.

Turning to Western astrology and medieval alchemy, we see that the planet Saturn possesses traits similar to those of Masau'u. Its ideographic symbol is the cross of matter connected to the crescent of spirit or consciousness. Of course, the cross is merely an altered form of the quadrilateral. Although Saturn is associated with the metal lead and the color gray, the god nonetheless reigned over the Golden Age. In this respect he is akin to Masau'u's role as one of the primordial deities. (The other four Hopi cosmogonic gods are: Tawa, the sun; Koyanwuti, Spider Grandmother; Sótuknang, the Heart of the Sky god; and the dyad of Pokanghoya and Polongahoya, the Twin Warriors. See the section in Chapter 1 called "Tracking the Anasazi: A Mythological Perspective.") Above all Saturn is the master of the material realm with its concomitant variety of forms and structures. Under Saturn even the ego or self is subsumed in the demands and challenges of the physical plane. "The planet fundamentally charts whatever remains in consciousness as real beyond or through the focus of any particular form of interruption or superficial alteration in the self or its affairs. Thus it rules the support gained from land or exceptionally fixed possessions."[32] This is completely consistent with Masau'u's role as benefactor of the Hopi world kept in balance by their ceremonial calendar. As stern taskmaster, disciplinarian, and ruler of the mundane, Saturn is characterized by his lugubrious and dour nature. Sluggish, cold and gloomy, this god also epitomizes rigid, authoritarian patriarchalism. Known traditionally as "the dreaded great malefic" and thus related to the fallen archangel Satan, it is the planet of limitations or boundaries, hardships, and delays. Displaying the darker side of his agrarian providence, he becomes the Grim Reaper. The word for Saturday, the Jewish sabbath, is derived from Saturn; hence Saturn was known as "the star of Israel," symbolizing the tribulations of the Hebrews and their Exodus in the desert. According to the Sabians, this heavenly body was "the black star," thought to be made of black stone or lead.[33]

In a more positive sense Saturn represents practical economy, frugality, patience, and the fulfillment of one's duties and responsibilities.34 This is very much in keeping with the essentially Spartan character of the Hopi people, which was paradigmatically forged to a large extent by Masau'u. Saturn is furthermore identified as the planet that controls karmic dispensation, a concept that somewhat resembles on an individual level the communal tradition of Hopi prophecy and destiny extending even to the fate of whole world. As Lord of Time, Saturn controls spiritual causation in much the same way that Masau'u acts as the sovereign judge of both lower and upper worlds, not only deciding the ultimate fate of individual spirits who come before him in the nether realm but also presiding over the absolute purification of the Fourth World at its final hour.

In esoteric astrology Saturn rules Capricorn in the zodiac and basically reflects the characteristics of that sign.35 It comes as no surprise then that the most important phase of the aforementioned Soyal ceremony in which Masau'u plays a key role takes place on the winter solstice when the sun traditionally entered Capricorn (before the precession of the equinoxes altered the position of the constellation relative to the sun.) In addition, esoteric astrology formerly identified the sign of Scorpio with Mars, the planet of struggle and warfare, which are also hallmarks of Masau'u. As we have seen, the Wúwutcim, or New Fire Ceremony performed to rekindle the powers of the Tawa, occurs just after the sun traditionally entered Scorpio. However, the rulership of Scorpio shifted from Mars to Pluto after the discovery of the latter. Of course, this outer planet is the Lord of Death and the Underworld, precisely the purview of Masau'u. It is ironic —or even synchronistic!— that one of the first serious studies of Mars as well as the discovery of Pluto should take place, at Lowell Observatory in the San Francisco Peaks, the home of the *katsinam* located in the territory over which Masau'u reigns.36

Besides mentioning Orion-cum-Masau'u as a synchronizer, A. M. Stephen has also noted a solar marker on the western horizon for the New Fire Ceremony. From the rooftop of the Bear Clan's house in the village of Walpi on First Mesa, a *tawa-mongwi*, or Sun Chief, could observe the sun setting over the San Francisco Peaks during this ceremony. Stephen states that on November 24, 1891, the sun set between the notch made by Fremont and Agassiz Peaks. In that year the Wúwutcim ran from November 10th through the 18th. This means that during those days the sun would be slightly north of Stephen's mark on the horizon, placing it approximately over Humphreys Peak, highest point in Arizona. Thus at the New Fire Ceremony Tawa's own fire signals to the *katsinam* who reside on the pine covered mountains in the southwest to get ready for their return to the Hopi Mesas after the winter solstice.37

In addition to this solar/terrestrial synchronization, the Wúwutcim occurs in early November possibly for the purpose of coinciding with the Taurid meteor shower. The Taurid meteor stream passes through the Earth's orbit twice a year and lasts about twelve days in each passage.

Between November 3rd through November 15th (peaking on November 9th) and June 24th through July 6th (peaking on June 30th) a substantial number of shooting stars blaze through the Earth's atmosphere. This natural phenomenon is named after the constellation Taurus, from which the meteors seem to emanate. Because the June passage occurs during the day, it is usually invisible to the naked eye; only at the November passage can it be readily seen at night. As a torus (i.e., a donut-shaped tube) thirty million kilometers wide, this stream is thought to contain not only meteors but asteroids and comets, including Comet Encke, which itself is five kilometers across.38 This poses a substantial threat, especially if we remember that the asteroid which smashed into the northern tip of the Yucatan peninsula sixty-five million years ago to cause the extinction of the dinosaurs along with about ninety percent of all life on earth is estimated to have been only about twice the size of Encke, or ten kilometers in diameter.

Unlike other meteor showers such as the Leonids, the Perseids, or the Andromedids, the Taurids therefore have a potentially devastating effect that could reach a planetary scale. Especially dangerous is the June crossing. On the evening of June 25th, 1178 A.D. a monk at Canterbury, England witnessed a fragment strike the moon, spewing fire and sparks to create what was later known as the Giordano Bruno crater. On this day sunset was at approximately 8:15 p.m. and moonset was not until about 12:30 a.m. on the 26th. The precise time, of course, was not recorded, but if this medieval monk observed this collision between 9:30 p.m. and 12:30 a.m., then the ancient Hopis in the Southwest could possibly have also seen it, since moonrise in Arizona was at 2:30 p.m. (9:30 p.m. in England). An impact of this magnitude might have been visible upon the face of the rising moon even during the day. Another cataclysmic June event occurred in Tunguska, Siberia on the peak date of the 30th in 1908, when a bolide estimated to be seventy meters wide caused an airburst which flattened more than 2,000 square kilometers of forest.39 The November passage, however, can be equally dramatic though not as destructive, at least so far. On the night of November 12th, 1833 a "Storm of Stars" was observed by most of the United States and recorded in practically all of the Native American Winter Counts.40

The significance of the Hopi New Fire Ceremony occurring during this biannual meteor storm is increased by the fact that the ritual is led by the Al, or Two Horn Society, whose symbolic representation is found in Aries, the constellation in the zodiac adjacent to Taurus. This sacred group wears ram horns on their heads and is said to possess knowledge of this world (the Fourth), the Underworld (the Third), and the two previous worlds (the First and the Second). (Taurus possibly represents the ritual artifact used by the Two Horn Society called a *mongko*. For a full discussion of this, see Chapter 8.)

Shortly after midnight on the early November nights of the

ceremony the Hyades of Taurus are passing the meridian due south, and the spirits of the dead throng the villages. A few hours later, life and death, Tawa and Taurus, are poised in opposition. In other words, at 7:00 a.m. (at least in A.D. 1100, when the Hopi Mesas were settled) the sun is a little over one degree below the eastern horizon while Aldebaran, the red major star of Taurus, is a little over one degree above the western horizon. Furthermore, as we shall find in the next section of this chapter, the meteorically active months of November and June have a specific association for the Hopi. Briefly stated, when the Hopi are performing the Wúwutcim in November, the ancestor spirits in the Underworld are celebrating the summer solstice, another sort of fire when the sun's strength is greatest. Taurus also figures as a major presence in the early morning sky in June. For instance, in A.D. 1100 the Hyades rose one hour before the sun early in the month and two hours before the sun by the solstice. In light of these facts we might conclude that the New Fire Ceremony, symbolically involved with death and initiatory rebirth, is biannually synchronized (via both versions of the ritual— terrestrial and subterranean) to the potentially destructive igniting of the sky by this "sidereal storm" that issues out of the constellation Taurus.

In the above discussion we have detailed the close relationship between the Roman god Saturnus, whose celestial manifestation was Orion, and Masau'u, the chief purveyor of Hopi cultural beliefs and values. In addition, we have seen how the adjacent constellation of Taurus is ceremonially synchronized and symbolically linked to the Orion/Masau'u complex of death. Before we proceed with a closer examination of the star cities of the Anasazi in the next chapter, a brief review of the Hopi concept of a dual universe would be beneficial.

### The Legacy of Correlation

Hopi cosmology is permeated with the notion of dualism. However, it is not the sort of dualism that our culture frequently conceptualizes, i.e., the Manichaean struggle between two opposing forces. The Hopi universe might be better described as correlative dichotomy, much like the Chinese yin-yang symbol in which each side mutually nestles into the other, forming a reciprocally flowing whole. This correlation is most graphically demonstrated by the movement of astronomical bodies. For instance, when the sun reaches his eastern house and starts to rise over the land of the Hopi, he has just entered his western house in the Underworld and has begun to set. In essence, the two worlds, each shaped like a hemisphere, share the same circular horizon, which at the moment of sunrise or sunset simultaneously bisects the disk of the sun in each converse dimension. After sundown in the upper world, Tawa continues onward in the lower world, arcing across its sky to create the chthonic day. He ferries himself westward until he reaches the western house (the upper world's eastern house), thus completing one round in the ceaseless rhythm that these elegantly complementary realms perpetuate.

Similarly, when the sun arrives at his winter house in the southeast during the winter solstice sunrise, he leaves his summer house in the Underworld, located at the northwest point of the summer solstice sunset. Thus day and night, summer and winter, are mirror images of each other. In fact, the upper pueblo world and the lower pueblo world are thought to be exact replicas of each other, except that in the latter a person possesses a *hik'si*, or a breath-body, instead of a physical body. In this regard, one might theorize why the Anasazi broke so much pottery upon permanently departing a particular pueblo (other than to leave a marker of their territory), i.e., they wanted to release the spirit-forms of the ceramics so that the dead could use them in the Underworld. According to Titiev, this schema of correlation "...provides a basis for synchronous, co-operative activities between the inhabitants of the two realms."[41]

A further correlation exists between the cycles of astronomical bodies and the cycles of birth and death. When a person is born in this upper world, he or she dies in the lower world. When an individual lives out a life on this upper plane and finally expires, he or she is being born into the society of the subterranean world, ready to mature there and eventually assume its responsibilities. Thus life and death are not distinct levels of existence, but merely changes in status within a perpetually recurring cycle that the Hopi perceive as offering a type of immortality. The question of individuality probably troubles a Western (European) sensibility more than a Hopi one, since each *katsina*, or ancestral spirit, supposedly has no particular identity other than that of a tribal one. Here is another example of the Native American propensity to place the value of the whole group above that of any discrete member of the group.

In addition to the culturally unifying and psychologically edifying ramifications of Hopi eschatology, the Hopi calendar assumes that the lower world of the dead is one season ahead of the upper world. Technically, the Hopi recognize only two seasons: winter extending from November until May, and summer extending from June until October. The names of five out of the seven winter months are identical to the five summer months. More specifically, the following months share the same names: November and June, December and July, January and August, February and September, March and October.[42] Consequently, in November when the people of the upper world are performing the New Fire Ceremony, the spirits in the nether realm are celebrating the summer solstice, the time when the sun's fire is most acute. During the Soyal ceremony in December, the first *katsinam* begin to arrive for their half-year residence, but down below during the spirit world's Niman, or Going Home Ceremony in July, those same *katsinam* are in the process of departing. The prayer sticks made at Soyal will be used in the upcoming Niman, which in the Underworld is already in progress. The February

Powamu, or germination ceremony, proceeds in the upper world with the knowledge that the lower world is currently celebrating September Lakon, or harvest ceremony. In terms of Whorf's linguistic work 43, this cosmographic system puts the subterranean world in the category of the future, or the unmanifest subjective, even though the spirits of ancestors were once physical beings and therefore related to the objective realm of the past. As a result the future potentiality of these relatives dwelling in the netherworld intermingles with the emotional participation of those living above (e.g., their hopes for rain or their desire for a good harvest) to produce the overall sense of "religious and magical awesomeness" inherent in an intimate connection between the living and the dead.

However, the dualistic division of the Hopi calendar still leaves the months during the latter part of Hopi winter unaccounted for. More specifically, April and May are the only two months that have separate names and which do not participate in this cyclic structure. The April "windbreak" moon and the May "waiting" moon are typically dry months in the high desert. Even though various public *katsina* dances are held in the village plazas during this time, none of the major ceremonies of the Hopi calendar take place. This is apparently a time when thoughts about the Underworld are suspended. Instead, the terrestrial realm takes precedence, and as a result considerable agricultural activity occurs. In April when the fruit trees are beginning to bud, fields are prepared for the year's upcoming planting, windbreaks for seedlings are constructed, and early sweet corn is planted in sheltered areas. Beans, pumpkins, squash, watermelons, and muskmelons are planted next in early May. This is also the time when eaglets are collected and adopted into clan families in anticipation of the raptors' ritual sacrifice in July.44 The "waiting" of this month is for the eventual return of warmer weather and the planting of the main corn crop, which takes place from May 21 until the summer solstice.45

During the latter part of April, all of May and June, and about half of July, Orion's influence is significant by virtue of either its departure or its total absence from the sky. At present Rigel is approximately 15 degrees above the western horizon on April 20 at 8:00 p.m., an hour after sunset, and by 9:15 in the evening it is just touching the horizon. Orion is last seen on the western horizon in early May, and by mid-May it is blotted out altogether in the sun's glare, which is called its heliacal setting. (The Hopi supposedly watch this constellation in May as an omen for a long and therefore a good summer.46) After that it will not reappear until about July 21st, its heliacal rising in the east, as mentioned at the beginning of this chapter in connection with the restoration of the Greek Orion's vision. However, some nine centuries earlier when the first villages on the Hopi Mesas were being settled, Rigel touched the western horizon on April 20 at 8:00 p.m., again an hour after sunset, and by early May achieved its heliacal setting. At this same time (i.e., circa A.D. 1100) it was not seen again until about the second week of July, its heliacal rising coinciding with the annual arrival of the monsoons.

But what is the meaning of all these star positions? If the Hisatsinom and Hopi planting schedules coincide (which is likely, given the pervasive conservatism of the latter), then sweet corn, whose symbolic direction is designated as Below, was planted by the Anasazi in late April when Orion was departing for his two-month sojourn in the Underworld. The importance of sweet corn is reflected primarily in its customary harvest at the Niman ceremony and its use as a gift from the Hemis Katsinam to the children. The remainder of the corn was planted from late May until the summer solstice when Orion was inhabiting his subterranean abode. Possibly his influence causes the spirits of the corn to rise from the Underworld and enter into the sown seeds, acting as a catalyst for germination, or perhaps another god acts in consort with Masau'u/Orion to achieve this process. Muy'ingwa, the god of germination, is also associated with the Underworld, but like Masau'u, he too possesses a celestial nature, in this case as the chief of clouds. (When discussing the Hopi pantheon, we may use strict nomenclature only in a tentative way.) This dual nature makes sense, since the ancestor spirits who live in the Underworld also take the form of clouds and return to the aboveground villages as rain. Scholar John D. Loftin argues that the reciprocal relationship between the two gods involves a cycle in which Muy'ingwa controls the metamorphosis from death to life and Masau'u controls the metamorphosis from life to death.47 At any rate, Orion is planted in the Underworld at the same time as all the various types of corn, thereby assuring their germination and quickening growth during the lengthening days of the year.

During this part of the seasonal cycle a minor agricultural rite of planting is performed in the fields. This is actually a sort of native Passion play "...in which Masau'u strikes down his challengers and strips them of their clothes, until in the end he also falls down as if dead. Then he rises to accept prayers and gifts. On one level this is a mime depicting the life cycle of the corn plant; the ear is stripped from the plant, the cob is stripped of its seeds, and some of these are buried —it was his clothes, the 'killing and burying of Masau'u'— but he, as a corn symbol, rises again and accepts the thanks of the people."48 Thus, Masau'u/Orion functions as not only as symbol of resurrection to be imitated by the farmers, thereby assisting the forces of nature, but also as a manifestation of the corn itself, which is planted in the spring and returns after a few months to provide the people with its bounty.

Domesticated in Mesoamerica circa 5000 B.C., corn is undoubtedly the most sacred and ritualized of all Hopi foodstuffs. The symbolic color directions for each type of corn are as follows: yellow for northwest, blue for southwest, red for southeast, and white for northeast. This encompasses the terrestrial (horizontal) plane of Masau'u's domain. In addition, black (or purple) corn, known as *kokoma*, or Masau'u's corn, symbolically representing the direction of Above, is also planted at this time.[49] When Masau'u's dark corn of the zenith is brought down and placed in the dark earth together with Orion, then, as we previously noted, no major ceremonies can be held. The resumption of the ceremonial cycle will have to wait until Orion once again rises in the east just before dawn, at the time when the ripening sweet corn is reaching its full maturity.

We have seen here a direct relationship between the perceived absence of Orion and the vernal sowing of corn. The ancient Hopi's placement of seeds in the soil at the very time Orion in the chthonic realm is urging the life force forward and upward into the light must have seemed to them a cosmically ordained synergy. Fettered by the paradigms of science, we moderns rarely have the opportunity to witness a synchronistic magic of such magnitude.

As demonstrated in this chapter, Orion, chief constellation of the sky, and Masau'u, major god of the earth and the Underworld, are merely two dimensions of the same archetypal complex. In the next chapter we will describe in greater detail each of the major villages that comprise the terrestrial Orion and how they correspond to the heavens.

# Chapter 4
# The Cosmo-magical Cities
# Of the Anasazi

"The organization of the ceremonial centers appears to have been inspired by a way of thinking that has been called 'cosmo-magical,' in which builders perceived a relationship between the celestial order above them and the biological rhythms of life. The two realms were seen as parallel in structure and synchronized in time. The cosmic city was aligned with the cosmos. Its streets and structures were often carefully oriented to the cardinal directions. The pattern of life within the city in its festivals and celebrations resonated with the sun, moon, planets, and stars."[1]

J. McKim Malville

### *The Hopi Mesas: Alnilam, Mintaka, Alnitak (Orion's Belt)*

Tuuwanasavi, the center of the Hopi universe, is comprised of the First Mesa, Second Mesa, and Third Mesa— non-native designations indicating the direction of entry from east to west into the territory by the Spanish or Anglos, and not rank of importance. This area corresponds to the three stars in the belt of Orion, which is the visual focus and spiritual heart of the constellation. (See Diagram 1, p. 24.) Frequently described as fingers extended southwest from Black Mesa, the Mesas more accurately function as natural ziggurats, lifting the supplicant even closer to the celestial forces that must be appeased in order to gain the blessing of rainfall. "Once we see the mesas as more than simply man-chosen but almost literally man-constructed —at the very least, man-finished, as the Hopi see them— their true scale in Hopi culture opens to our understanding. We remember moreover that there is no semantic distinction for the Hopi between the works of nature and those of mankind. Hence the collaboration of the mesas is between commensurable beings. The Hopi are one with the rock."[2] Thus, the "choosing" and "finishing" of the Mesas in the Anasazi/Hisatsinom migration saga are tantamount in cultural importance to the construction in Mesoamerica of such great pyramids as those at Teotihuacán, Chichén Itzá, Palenque, or Tikal.

One of the concepts that accompanied the Spanish conquest of the New World was the Gran Chichimeca (literally, "Sons of the Dog" or "nomad"), the northern place where barbarian outlanders lived.[3] This negative attitude was perhaps influenced by the Toltecs vis-à-vis their indigenous neighbors to the north. Even so, we should not look upon the construction of pueblos on the mesa tops located at the *axis mundi* of the

61

Anasazi world as any lesser accomplishment. Whether it be a geologic structure (such as a mountain or mesa) or a human-made one (such as a ziggurat, pyramid, or earth mound), the function is still the same: to provide a link between heaven and earth. New Age writer Page Bryant has even suggested that these sacred spots scattered across the globe are in reality what she terms "beacon vortexes," or two-way conduits for cosmic energy flowing between the sidereal and terrestrial realms. In essence, they are can be conceptualized as *"celestial* ley lines." "This constant reciprocal and cyclic activity joins Earth not only with other planets, stars, and galaxies, but with the entire universe. In short, celestial leys form a sort of cosmic network that links all celestial bodies together."[4] To analogize in computerese, these celestial ley lines download epiphanic visions and archetypal information to the Earth while at the same time providing upload links to the U.W.W. (Universe Wide Web). Furthermore, these lines interconnect with Gaia's network of terrestrial leys, or in Hopi terms, Spider Grandmother's web of interrelated strands, which facilitates psychic communication between distant points on the Earth, or, specifically in terms of our discussion, between the Anasazi sky cities.

The simple act of climbing a mountain, a mesa, or their human-made equivalent —not for the purpose of conquest but for spiritual enlightenment— has been a cross-cultural constant throughout history. "Ascending it is equivalent to an ecstatic journey to the center of the world; reaching the highest terrace, the pilgrim experiences a break-through from plane to plane; he enters a 'pure region' transcending the profane world."[5] In this case, however, we are talking about a non-ecstatic, sedentary people who have taken up residence in this high *sanctum sanctorum*, performing ceremonies for nearly a millennium that in effect have assured the balance and continued existence of the entire world.

At the center of the quadrilateral which forms the tellurian constellation of Orion are located three contemporary Hopi villages upon each of the three Mesas, with two more villages located below, and a number of ruins scattered both on top and at the base of the Mesas. Here we see some of the continent's oldest remaining structures in which life gained a foothold and in many cases even thrived. The heart of Hopiland is anything but a paradise, with the nearest perpetually flowing stream, the Little Colorado River, about forty miles away. Despite the few springs located at the base of the Mesas and the periodic run-off in the washes, this region can seem starkly barren and unappealing, especially if one has just come from the San Francisco Peaks or the White Mountains. The novelist D.H. Lawrence percipiently though petulantly captures this sense of arid desolation in his August, 1924 description of a Snake Dance: "The Hopis are Pueblo Indians, village Indians, so their reservation is not large [compared to the Navajo Reservation, that is]. It consists of a square track of greyish, unappetising desert, out of which rise three tall arid mesas, broken off in ragged, pallid rock. On the top of the mesas perch the ragged, broken, greyish pueblos, identical with the mesas on which they stand."₆ The adjectival repetition stresses an oppressive feeling of benumbing monotony and blind endurance that perhaps is more a European than an indigenous reaction to the place. Unaccustomed to the jumble of wan or ocher talus and tawny sand, the common tourist scrambling across the southern spurs of the three dry mesa tops baked by the high desert sun is prone to a characteristic faintness or vertigo. This subjective state is sometimes misapprehended, only to be projected upon the scene and misrepresented as the same sort of forlorn squalor by which primitive people historically were stereotyped— again, the Gran Chichimeca syndrome.

On the other hand, an exhilaration unequaled by almost any in the world can be experienced by perching as if in an eagle's aerie on the edge of a sheer mesa rising six hundred feet. If one gazes south upon the vast, clean spaces scoured by wind and time, dark volcanic cones and buttes rise like solitary sentinels upon the southern horizon. Indeed, the center of the traditional Hisatsinom country is one of the most isolated places on earth, far from the main historic westward trails or the Santa Fe railroad line. "Being out here in such a desolate place they thought that they would be safe from other people, who would not think that they had anything worth taking."₇ This in part has assured the physical and ritualistic survival of the Hopi, who have one of the most elaborate ceremonial cycles on the planet and, causally, one least affected by the doctrine of Manifest Destiny and the modern religion of "Progress at any price."₈ Suspended above a treeless landscape colored only by creosote bushes and sagebrush, heaped clouds pure as Hopi cotton form a long parade of spirit-ancestors. Ever shifting in a distance incomprehensibly vast, they make their trek across a pristine arc of blue whose motion imitates the most intimate rhythms of breath. As one stands there in reverent silence as others have done for centuries, something opens inside oneself— perhaps a window to an immense spiritual dimension where men and women once acted with both poise and humility to the adversities posed by their fiercely beautiful home. Then the sun sets, and three stars in a line slowly rise through this window of eternal wonder to balance the complementary realms of sky and earth.

The first area of the Hopis' central territory to be settled is Second Mesa, whose stellar correlative is Alnilam (Epsilon Orionis), the central star in the belt, both in terms of position and of ritualistic importance. For instance, in the "fire drill" configuration of the constellation, it serves as the pivotal star between Betelgeuse and Rigel. Indeed, if one draws a line from Homol'ovi/Betelgeuse to Betatakin/Rigel and then another line from Wupatki/Bellatrix to Canyon de Chelly/Saiph, the point of intersection is very close to the southern tip of Second Mesa where we find the first village that the Hisatsinom established, which terrestrially mirrors Alnilam. Literally named "a Belt of Pearls," this bright white supergiant is

1,600 light-years away and has a magnitude of 1.70.₉ According to Hopi myth, the powerful Bear Clan following lights in the sky eventually established a village called Masipa at the base of Second Mesa. (See Chapter 1.) Archaeologists believe this occurred sometime after A.D. 1100. The village was renamed Shongopovi (Shong-O-po-vee), or "place by the spring where the tall reeds grow," and it became a "mother village."₁₀ After the Pueblo Revolt of 1680 when the San Bartolomo mission built about fifty years before was destroyed, Shongopovi moved to the mesa top, where it exists today as a ceremonial focal point utilizing five detached kivas.₁₁ Beside the main kiva located in the central plaza is a "pyramidally massed central house." One author believes that despite its asymmetrical shape and its function as a dwelling, this construction was influenced by Mesoamerican pyramids.₁₂

On an eastern spur of Second Mesa are located the villages of Mishongnovi (Mih-SHONG-no-vee), or "place of the black man," and Shipaulovi (Shih-PAW-lo-vee), or "mosquitoes." The former was established about A.D. 1250 by the somewhat darker skinned Crow Clan who migrated from the San Francisco Peaks area. They are the guardians of the shrine and burial ground at Corn Rock, a bifurcated sandstone upthrust at the south end of the mesa. (Fig. 5) Highest of the pueblos with a small enclosed plaza area, Shipaulovi was established about A.D. 1700

*Fig. 5. Mishongnovi on Second Mesa with Corn Rock center-right.*
*Second Mesa corresponds to Alnilam in Arizona's Orion Correlation.*

by a group from the Homol'ovi region in order to protect the Tuuwanasavi against reprisals from the Spanish due to the Pueblo Revolt twenty years earlier.13

Shortly after the establishment of the first settlement of Shongopovi, a split between Yohoya, the *kikmongwi*, or village chief, and his brother Masito caused the establishment of Oraibi (O-RYE-bee) on Third Mesa. Apparently the latter was ostracized because of gluttony during a time of food scarcity, indolence, or adulterous behavior with the former's wife— all traditional taboos in Hopi society. Under construction possibly by A.D. 1120, Oraibi, or "place of the rock called Orai (Round Rock)," as stated above, has been continuously inhabited longer than any community on the North American continent. Even today in the plaza while watching *katsina* dances carrying forth rituals that go back centuries, one sees well maintained houses of traditional masonry architecture juxtaposed to modern cinder block constructions which in turn are adjacent to abandoned buildings falling into ruin. Oraibi was once one of the largest pueblos in the Southwest, containing more residents than the rest of the Hopi villages combined. It consists of seven irregular rows of parallel room blocks, some four stories high and facing southeast.14 The lanes between the structures open to the far horizons, allowing for observation of the sacred "sun watcher" points as well as of a greater span of night sky. We sense a looser, less constricted architectural paradigm than the tight, closed plazas of Mishongnovi or Shipaulovi.15 Perhaps this earlier construction was less concerned with defense and more open to the expanses of the cosmos.

The corresponding sidereal coördinate to the Third Mesa is Mintaka (Delta Orionis), the western star in the belt and thus the first one to rise above the horizon. (Some also say that Oraibi was the first of the Hopi villages to be settled.) At a distance of 1,500 light-years, Mintaka has a magnitude of 2.20.16 Its status as an "eclipsing binary" star is symbolically related to a crucial event in recent Hopi history which was formerly prophesied by native elders. During the late nineteenth and early twentieth centuries, friction had been mounting between the Traditionalists, who wanted to preserve Hopi rituals and customs, and the Progressives, who were willing to accept the technology and the belief system of modern society. Finally on September 8th, 1906 (the year of the San Francisco earthquake), a confrontation occurred between Yukioma of the Fire Clan (the so-called Hostiles) and Tawakwaptewa of the Bear Clan (the so-called Friendlies). Although the threat of violence was in the air, the two settled their differences in a customarily peaceful Hopi way by engaging in a pushing match. After a great struggle, Yukioma and his Traditionalists lost and consequently moved a few miles northwest on Third Mesa to build the village of Hotevilla (HOHT-vi-lah), or "skinned back."17 Though it might seem inconsequential, this conflict shook the conservative ritualistic system to its core, dividing families and cutting across various religious societies in the process. As a result, the religious power of the centuries-old Oraibi waned after this schism. On the other hand, the ceremonies of Hotevilla became stronger, thereby "eclipsing" the former village.

The architectural structure of Hotevilla embodies its recently entrusted ritualistic role.

> "All paths within the village are linked to all the directions and to sacred places of spiritual power; for the delivery and receiving of prayers. Therefore the village is a shrine itself, a special holy place, identical to the Bahanna's [White] church. This includes the layout of the village; clan duties; and kivas where the chief important duties and symbols are placed and planted, and then blessed with certain powers to maintain the balance and directions for humans in relationship between heavenly and earthly forces of nature, complete with ceremonials and the ritual cycle."[18]

The link between the sacred Above and the sacred Below is further underscored by the paramount location of Oraibi, Hotevilla and its smaller splinter-village of Bacabi (BAH-ka-vee), or "place of the jointed reed," the latter established in the fall of 1907 a mile southeast of Hotevilla. Mintaka lies almost precisely on the celestial equator, thereby bisecting the constellation.[19] This stresses both in a physical and a spiritual sense the centrality of the three Hopi Mesas forming the belt of the terrestrial Orion, whose feet rest in the two distinct canyons of Tsegi and de Chelly, whose legs and thighs form Black Mesa, and whose shoulders touch the two low hill-top ruins of Wupatki and Homol'ovi. (See descriptions below.) More specifically, the proximity of Oraibi/Mintaka to the celestial equator gives this location a particularly sacred significance.

The final medial location we shall discuss is First Mesa with its corresponding star Alnitak (Zeta Orionis), whose magnitude is 1.79 and whose distance is 1,600 light-years— virtually the same as Alnilam.[20] Literally meaning "the Girdle," Alnitak is the eastern star of the belt and the last of the three to rise. Indeed, the villages of First Mesa were the last to be settled. The initial villages were established in the late 13th century below First Mesa on the lower terraces. These villages include Koechaptevela (KOE-chahp-teh-veh-lah), or "Ash Mound," established by the Snake and Bear Clans or possibly the Reed Clan; Pakatkomo (Pah-KAHT-ko-mo), built by the Water and Sand Clans after they migrated north from the Homol'ovi area; and Sikyatki (sik-YAHT-kee), settled by the Coyote Clan.[21] The designation of Ash Mound metaphorically mirrors the especially nebulous region around Alnitak in the same way that the Pleiades are known to the Hopi as *Tsöötsöqam*, a cognate of which means "die down to ashes." As a constellation to the west of Orion, this is consistent with Masau'u's role as god of fire.

After the Pueblo Revolt of 1680, three villages were established on the mesa top: Hano (HAH-no), Sichomovi (see-CHO-mo-vee), and Walpi (WAHL-pi). These villages correspond to Alnitak's classification as a triple star.[22] Hano was built by a group of Tewa from the Rio Grande area who even today retains both its non-Hopi language and its skill at making pottery. A one-story pueblo with an open plaza, Sichomovi is the middle village between the former and Walpi. In 1870 when the explorer and ethnographer J.W. Powell came through this region which he called Tusayan, he estimated the population of Hano to be about 75, that of Sichomovi to be 100, and that of Walpi to be 150. "Walpi, Sichumovi, and Hano are three little towns on one butte, with but little space between them; the stretch from town to town is hardly large enough for a game of ball. The top of the butte is of naked rock, and it rises from 300 to 400 feet above the sand plains below by a precipitous cliff on every side. To reach it from below, it must be climbed by niches and stairways in the rock."[23]

*Fig. 6. Walpi on First Mesa (photo by Ansel Adams,*
*U.S. National Archives and Records Administration)*

As Powell suggests, the narrow mesa provides a breathtaking location for a pueblo, and Walpi is perhaps the most dramatically situated of all the Hopi villages. Literally meaning "the place of the gap," this pueblo of over one hundred rooms is perched on the extreme tip of the

67

mesa.24 Along the northwestern side runs a trail the length of the village, and on the southeastern side are located five kivas carved eight to ten feet into the stone, a small plaza, and Snake Rock, a natural monolith about ten feet high which is frequently seen in early photographs of the biennial snake dance (held in August during odd-numbered years.) A narrow strip of stone no wider than fifteen feet separates Sichomovi and Walpi, providing, as Powell also notes, an easily defensible site. However, the strategy for the location of Walpi upon this finger of rock pointing directly toward the home of the *katsinam* in the San Francisco Peaks at 240 degrees (the azimuthal position of the winter solstice sunset) is not primarily military but spiritual. "So all is directed high in space as in an arrow flight toward Walpi, which is thus doubly made to stand out as a solid pyramidal object [again the Mesoamerican influence] before the sacred landscape forms far off on the horizon. It is a construction that is somehow worked out between three villages to allow them to interact with each other in order to act out, focus, and control the sacred drama of the landscape in which they are set."25

We are standing behind the last high house in Walpi, the Bear Clan house. At the edge of this sheer butte we gaze southwest toward the sacred snow peaks— the dual panorama of hot bleached sand and cobalt blue sky extending farther than we can imagine. Here on this flat rock heaving itself heavenward, we receive the subtle yet undeniable impression of walking the deck of some grand barge bound for a distant continent of spirits. Or perhaps we are floating in a dream dirigible made of pale sandstone, drifting above the desert ocean in league with cloud spume and *katsina* feathers. The sun rolls over the edge of the world and is gone. While the night shifts its shadow onto the cooling earth, we see our life as but a gleam on the rising belt of Orion— a luminous prayer in the ear of Masau'u, who eternally answers us with his warm words of rain.

### *Canyon de Chelly National Monument: Saiph (Orion's Right Foot)*

A pair of small creeks flows westward from the Chuska Range that straddles the Arizona-New Mexico border northwest to southeast. Gradually eroding the downward slope of the Defiance Plateau, they have created two of the most magnificent gorges in the Southwest: Canyon de Chelly (duh-SHAY-ee), a Spanish corruption of the Navajo word *tségi,* or "rock canyon" (thus our unintentional tautology), and Canyon del Muerto, which in Spanish means "Canyon of Death." The former is cut by Chinle (CHIN-lee) Creek, while its tributary is carved by Tsaile (SAY-lee) Creek, which flows from the northeast and meets the main canyon almost four miles east of its mouth. Driving north across the monocline, we might have missed Canyon de Chelly altogether, had we traversed near the mouth, since its cliffs there reach a height of only about thirty feet. However, toward its opposite end toward the east near the pinnacle of Spider Rock, the canyon is close to twelve hundred feet deep.

**Fig. 7. White House Ruin, Canyon de Chelly National Monument**

Standing on the southern edge of Canyon de Chelly across from White House Ruin (a quarter of the way up its twenty-seven mile length), we can clearly see how the sky and the canyon are inseparably linked. Cumulous clouds drift overhead, suspended in a sea of pure blue air. Stopping long enough to watch them float like vaporous jellyfish in the cerulean depths, we begin to breathe with long, slow rhythms only the spirits know. These ancestor clouds appear to us mutable and fluid, which paradoxically is their only constant. Here at the rim, perspective is reversed: looking down into the canyon is like gazing into the vault of the heavens. The perpetually eroding Rorschach shapes of cloud shadows crawl red walls of sensuously curving sandstone. Shifting across the polished surface of smooth rock, they mirror the graceful motility of water or the time-lapse of a solar eclipse. Orange, black, and cinnabar streaks of manganese oxide stretching downward from the rim give the canyon walls their characteristic "desert varnish," resembling spontaneous strokes of an artist's brush which in reality have taken millions of years to create. Along the shallow, braided stream immigrant tamarisk and Russian olive trees intermingle with native Fremont cottonwood and coyote willow. From far below the lone tinkle of a bell and a few plaintive bleatings announce a flock of Navajo sheep, drifting like the billowing clouds past fields of corn and peach trees or an occasional hogan.

Sit on the flat bottom of this chasm at White House Ruin, and a

69

*Fig. 8. Antelope House, Canyon del Muerto (car and person, lower left)*

*Fig. 9. Mummy Cave Ruin, Canyon del Muerto*

sheer wall rising eight hundred feet or more meets the perpendicular plane of clouds scraping across the rim. As you listen to the gentle rustle of cottonwood leaves and the gurgle of the creek, it is hard to imagine that 230 million years ago a Sahara-like desert covered this region. Hundreds of feet thick, red sand dunes formed by prevailing north winds were eventually petrified into the cross-bedded formations you see now. 30 million years later these frozen swirls began to be covered by the more irregular Shinarump conglomerate, a twenty to sixty feet thick layer that forms the contemporary rim. Indeed the canyon can be a dizzying and breathtaking experience, both in terms of space and of time.

Equally dizzying is our gaze into the night sky. Much as we might have easily missed the mouth of Canyon de Chelly in our journey across the land of the Ancient Ones, we also might initially fail to perceive this canyon's corresponding triple star Saiph (Kappa Orionis), since it is fainter than most of the major stars in the constellation. Some cultures do not even include it when configuring Orion. This supergiant has a magnitude of 2.06 (close to that of Oraibi/Mintaka), but it is 2,100 light-years away, the most distant star in the constellation.[26] Indeed, in the mid-11th century from the major urban center of Chaco Canyon the "backwater" of Canyon de Chelly must have seemed distant. Vincent Scully has referred to them as "country houses," romantically projecting the sense of a rural hideaway.[27]

The Hopi name for Canyon de Chelly is Suyátupovi, "the Place of Loose Sand," or "Where the Soil is Soft." It played a key role in the early migration period, especially for the Flute Clan, but possibly for the Snake Clan, the Sun Clan, and the Fire Clan as well.[28] Traveling from the impressively large —but oppressively dry— ceremonial city in Chaco Canyon, this must have seemed like an oasis, a rustic sanctuary along the hard route the Anasazi/Hisatsinom were destined to trace. "During their journey they followed a light in the sky, and whenever it disappeared they settled down to wait for its return. In their songs, they refer to one of their stopping places, Canyon de Chelly, as 'the place of running water.' While living there, the Hopi saw a light in the west. Again they moved toward it, stopping several times before ending up at Walpi on First Mesa."[29] Again recall the solstitial line linking the two places: the winter sunset point from Canyon de Chelly and the summer sunrise point from Walpi.

We can imagine strains of the sacred flute echoing against the canyon walls, engendering fertility in both humans and maize. The Anasazi had lived, reproduced, and grown crops in this canyon since at least A.D. 300 and probably earlier. However, not until the mid-11th century would they aggregate in large numbers. Six miles up Canyon de Chelly one hundred or more people once lived at White House Ruin, which took its name from the white stucco plastered on one of the upper rooms. (Fig. 7, p. 69) Showing a Chacoan influence in style, the construction began about A.D. 1060 and was finished by 1275. The lower level on the bottom of the canyon contained approximately sixty rooms and two or three circular kivas, while the upper level beneath a small stone alcove thirty-five feet above the canyon floor had from ten to twenty rooms. Archaeologists believe that upper level was connected to the lower level by a four story structure, but water erosion has damaged much of the latter.30

Four miles northeast from the junction of Canyons de Chelly and del Muerto up the latter canyon, Antelope House (named for Navajo pictographs made in the early 1800s) began construction circa A.D. 1140. (Fig. 8, p. 70) Done in the somewhat less sophisticated Kayenta style, this multi-storied pueblo had ninety-one rooms as well as two to three large kivas and a number of smaller ones. About A.D. 1200 a circular plaza was added between the two separate room blocks. One observer believes that this reflects a moiety system (characteristic of the later Rio Grande pueblos), where two different phratries used the central plaza.31

Named for the two naturally desiccated Anasazis found at the site, Mummy Cave Ruin is located in del Muerto twelve miles from the junction of the canyons. (Fig. 9, p. 70) It contained seventy to eighty rooms plus three circular kivas sixteen feet in diameter constructed in the Mesa Verde style beneath two arching rock overhangs.32 A three-story square tower built on the ledge between the two alcoves has been tree-ring dated at A.D. 1284. An additional structure included a rectangular, roofless great kiva twenty to thirty feet across. Resembling the Fire Temple in Fewkes Canyon at Mesa Verde, this kiva suggests that its builders migrated from the San Juan region in the north.33

At the height of their populations the two canyons probably had a total of no more than eight hundred people. Both canyons were completely abandoned by A.D. 1300, the cause of which archaeologists are wont to incessantly debate. As was mentioned in Chapter 1, the perennial mystery of the "disappearance" during this period of the Anasazi from sites throughout the Southwest is usually explained in pragmatic terms— primarily drought or warfare. Interestingly enough, while most archaeologists posit either environmental or social adversity as the major cause of migration, Hopi legends in general stress an overabundance and luxury ultimately leading to social degradation as the prime motivating factor in their movement. In other words, 'Life is too easy here, so it's time to move on.' But scientists discount the idea that the Anasazi migrated because of certain celestial events as so much primitive *myth*— the term being synonymous with "untruth." However, if we take these ubiquitous references in Hopi legends seriously, then we are presented with an even greater mystery: What astronomical phenomena caused the Anasazi/Hisatsinom to migrate? We shall address this question in the next chapter; but first, three more sites comprising the Arizona Orion need to be discussed.

## *Wupatki National Monument: Bellatrix (Orion's Left Shoulder)*

The ruins of Wupatki (Woo-PAHT-Kee) National Monument lie on the margin between stark red Moencopi sandstone and black basaltic cinders expelled from Sunset Crater (in Hopi, Palotsmo, or "Red Hill") thirteen miles to the south. The eruption that began in the fall of A.D. 1064 and continued for the next few years might have triggered a land rush to the region in the late eleventh and early twelve centuries. An 800 square mile layer of ash and "black sand" was discharged from the 1,000 feet high volcanic cone. It is thought that the ejectamenta added trace minerals to the soil and created a moisture-retaining mulch, which aided the process of dry farming.34 (More on the volcanic eruption in the next chapter.) Although an 11,000 year old Clovis spear point has been found here, and a number of small pit houses from Basketmaker and Pueblo I periods are scattered throughout this prehistoric frontier, population traditionally had been minimal until the eruption of the volcano.

Afterwards Wupatki became a crucial agrarian sanctuary and trading hub in a harshly beautiful land. "This seems a most unlikely locale to nurture a human population estimated at over four thousand."35 In the 1970s about 800 archaeological sites were thought to be located within the monument's fifty-six square miles; twenty years later that estimate had jumped to over 2,700.36 Looking across this wide and windy vista, one is surprised by the viability of the region to support so many people. Near the main ruin at an elevation of 4,800 feet, one notices such low, scrubby vegetation as saltbush, rabbitbrush, and ephedra (Mormon tea). Not much more than a few scraggly juniper trees grow from between red rectangular sandstone slabs broken off and scattered across the dry landscape. To the east the colors of the escarpments forming the Painted Desert, which is washed out at midday, bleed vibrant shades of vermilion and indigo at sunset. To the south pyramidal spatter cones and lava fields rise dark, rugged, and at some points nearly impassable. To the west the isolated tableland called Antelope Prairie is covered with sparse grass or hardy juniper, while the broad Big Hawk Valley extends along the monument's western border. Although some scientists claim that the ash-mulch theory is the most credible one to explain migration, others hypothesize that the population influx was more the result of increased rainfall between A.D. 1050-1130.37 Regardless of which is correct, this landscape would have challenged the survival skills of even the most stalwart native person.

Archaeologists have aptly named the primary group of people who once lived here the Northern Sinagua, which is Spanish for "without water." (This is opposed to the Southern Sinagua, who lived below, or south, of the Mogollon Rim.) Indeed, the main ruin of Wupatki is about six miles west of the nearest permanent source of water, the Little Colorado River. In addition to those of the Sinagua, artifacts and architectures have been found that relate to a variety of cultures, including the Anasazi from the north, the Hohokam from the south, the Mogollon from the southeast, and the Cohonina branch of the Hakataya from the west.38 It was a true "melting pot," both in terms of the people who emigrated from other regions and of the trade goods imported from as far south as Mexico and as far west as the Pacific coast.39 In fact, Museum of Northern Arizona archaeologist David R. Wilcox believes that Wupatki served as a "geographic gateway" or nexus between the Hohokam to the south and the Chaco Canyon Anasazi to the east.40 Consequently, the Northern Sinagua, it seems, became inveterate traders *par excellence*. "The Sinagua thus served as important middlemen or brokers of a wide variety of trade items, facilitating the flow of both utilitarian and exotic 'prestige' goods between the southern and northern Southwest."41 The variety of goods that flooded into the area included black-on-white ceramics from the Anasazi to the north, red-on-buff ceramics from the Hohokam to the south (as well as macaws from the jungles of Mexico farther south), shells from the Pacific and Gulf of California to the west and southwest, and turquoise from the Cerrillos area near present-day Santa Fe, New Mexico to the east.

*Wupatki* is the Hopi word for "tall house," but it also means "something long ago that has been cut or divided." In addition, an alternate meaning for *Wupatki* is "great rain cloud ruins," apparently referring to the monsoon deluges that occur only in July and August.42 In fact, the word *wupaki* (without the "t") is the word for "tall house." The Hopi adjective for "tall," or "large," is *wuko*.43 The word *pa'tki* means "water house," whose source is either from clouds or from springs and cisterns.44 Thus, a combination of the two words signifies "big water house."

Once the largest building for fifty miles around, the four-story pueblo 345 feet long and 140 feet wide 45 consisted of about two hundred rooms, half of which have been excavated. Unlike the ruins tucked beneath rock shelters in places like Canyon de Chelly or Betatakin, these structures were fully exposed to the elements. Constructed on a long outcrop of red sandstone that is oriented on a nearly north-south axis at the head of a shallow canyon, Wupatki at its peak sheltered approximately 150-200 people.46 Terraced rooms extend downward to the east and south, while those built upon the outcrop are integrated with the sandstone boulders as deftly as any architecture designed by Frank Lloyd Wright. A number of characteristics specifically indicate an Anasazi influence: coursed masonry with a minimum of mortar, T-shaped windows, above-floor ventilators, upright draft deflectors, and stone-lined fire pits.47 The walls are generally six feet high, with no external doorways at ground level.

The main construction period extended from A.D. 1120 to 1210, although tree-ring dates as early as 1106 and as late as 1220 have been found.48 (The trees used as roof beams were ponderosa pine logs hauled from the San Francisco Peaks miles away.) By 1225 some clans had begun to leave Wupatki and by the mid-thirteenth century the whole area was virtually abandoned, perhaps in part due to nutrient depletion of the soil or the fact that the volcanic eruptions of Sunset Crater which had occurred periodically for almost two hundred years had finally ceased.49 Many of these Sinagua moved south to both Walnut Canyon (the head of Orion) and the Verde Valley (the extension of Orion's "chakra line"), either to be assimilated into preexistent sites such as Tuzigoot or to establish new sites such as Montezuma Castle, Sacred Mountain, and Clear Creek Ruin. Some of the Sinagua also moved southeast to the Homol'ovi region or northeast to the Hopi Mesas.

*Fig. 10. Wupatki Ruin, Wupatki National Monument*

Of course, the above is an archaeological scenario. The contemporary Hopi do not recognize the term Sinagua but instead suggest that various clans of the Hisatsinom settled at Wupatki. "A group of the Water Clan families went toward the west and a little to the north, following the river [the Little Colorado]. In time they passed through Neuvatikyao, now called the San Francisco Mountains, and there turned north. A little beyond the tall peaks they came to a place called Wupatki, where already there was a settlement of Hopis, and there they remained."50 The people already located there were probably the Bear Clan, who reputedly founded Wupatki.51 After their desertion of the pueblo, the Parrot Clan (second in importance to the Bear Clan) supposedly reinhabited it for a time.52 Three miles east of Wupatki, the small, three-story pueblo called Wukoki (Woo-KOH-kee), or "big house," was supposedly the stopping off point for some of the Snake Clan on its way south from its old home at

Toko'navi, or Navajo Mountain.53 This is partially verified by the substantial amount of Kayenta Anasazi pottery found near the site.54 (The customary style of Sinagua ceramics is undecorated brownware, influenced by the Mogollon culture to the southeast.55) Contemporary members of various clans from the Hopi Mesas such as Snake, Bear, Water, Greasewood, Katsina and others periodically return to perform ceremonies and reconnect with the spirits of their ancestors who, 750 years later, still act as guardians of the old houses.

At the head of the shallow arroyo above Wupatki is a small but significant petroglyph. The general area is comprised of mostly red Moencopi sandstone and has little of the dark patination suitable for incising; thus, few rock carvings are found in the immediate area of the pueblo. However, not far from one of the few kivas at Wupatki we find a spiral snake petroglyph about six inches in diameter facing north. This could either represent the presence of water —indeed, a dried-up spring is located behind the pueblo to the west— or the influence of the Snake Clan, or both.

If we stand at this petroglyph and look northward, the round ceremonial plaza, or "amphitheater," and the ball court a bit farther north together form a straight line. Approximately thirty feet east of the pueblo, the former structure is forty-eight feet in diameter with an additional continuous bench one-and-a-half feet wide and two feet high. Since it lacks a *sipapu* and post holes to support a roof, the structure was probably not a Great Kiva but instead some sort of communal area.56 However, its round form is unlike the rectangular plazas associated with Hopi architecture and has some additional features that suggest that it possibly functioned as an astronomical observatory as well as a dance plaza. For instance, it has only one door, which faces northeast— more specifically at 60 degrees azimuth, where the sun rises on the summer solstice. Above this communal area at 240 degrees, where the sun sets on the winter solstice, a curious upright post extends about two feet from the unexcavated portion of the west side of the rectangular plaza north of the main room block. Was this some sort of marker that the sun would seem rest upon if one were standing in the center of the "observatory" at sundown on the first day of winter, or is this just a coincidence? Because of the deteriorated condition of the ruin, it is difficult to confirm either way. At 300 degrees azimuth on the first day of summer the sun sets directly above the "sheep herder's room" at the north end of the pueblo. Was this three-story room also an observation point? Other rooms in the pueblo also seem to have astronomical configurations. The room on the northwest side of the main room block, which is partially formed by natural sandstone boulders, appears to have windows that face both the winter solstice sunrise (120 degrees azimuth) and the summer solstice sunset (300 degrees azimuth.)

North of the ceremonial plaza we find the northernmost ball court on the North American continent and the only masonry structure of its kind in the Southwest. It reflects the influence of the Hohokam to the south, or perhaps even that of the Aztec and Maya cultures. Aligned on the traditional north-south axis with entryways on both ends, this ovoid construction is formed by two crescent-shaped embankments about five feet high and twenty feet across at the widest portion of each. The

*Fig. 11. Ball court, north end of Wupatki Ruin*

playing area is approximately ninety-three feet long and forty-eight feet wide, the latter measurement being the same as the round plaza. The eastern and western crescents possibly represent the waxing and waning moons respectively. They might also signify the two horns of the plumed serpent Palulukang, a universal symbol of water throughout North and Central America, with the main part of the pueblo forming the snake's body. In addition, these crescents are similar in shape and relative positioning to those found on a pictograph at Betatakin Ruin. (See the section in this chapter on Navajo National Monument.)

To the southeast not far from the ball court we find what is called a blowhole (again at 120 degrees azimuth in relation to the former.) On a hot summer day this geological feature must have provided a refreshing and relaxing interlude between segments of the game. As a link to the cavernous depths of the Underworld, it blows out a cool breeze when the air pressure above ground is lower than that below, whereas it sucks in warm air when the conditions are the reverse. "In the hot desert summer, the air generally enters the blowholes during the late-night and early-morning hours. The air that comes out so strongly in the hot afternoons is therefore pleasantly cool, which may explain the concentration of the ruins of Indian dwellings around the blowholes."57 The soothing quality of this air, which is emitted from the blowhole sometimes at more than thirty m.p.h., is due to the increased amount of negatively charged ions and the measurably higher though nontoxic radioactivity. Many contemporary tourists are happy to encounter this natural "air conditioner" after a walk in high desert, where the mid-summer temperatures can reach over one hundred degrees.

The blowhole near the ball court at Wupatki is merely one of a number of interconnected, labyrinthine passageways in a subterranean cavern system which has a total volume of over seven billion cubic feet and even causes a slight but measurable decrease in gravity. Other blowholes found at various points in the vicinity include one along the western border of the monument, one west of Sunset Crater, one southwest of the San Francisco Peaks, one near Mormon Lake, one near Meteor Crater, and one near Sedona almost fifty miles away. The Hopi believe that the wind god Yopontsa lives in an "earth crack" in the black rock at the base of Sunset Crater, and *pahos* offerings are left there to diminish the strong, almost incessant winds, especially during the "Whispering Month" of March.58

On Antelope Prairie about six miles west of Wupatki, Citadel Ruin is situated just north of a what is known as a "sinkhole," a depression in the Kaibab limestone five hundred feet in diameter and one hundred and twenty five feet deep. Contrary to the ruin's name, no evidence of warfare exists. The supposedly "defensive" location could be more the result of its function as an astronomical observatory, and line-of-sight can be established with eight other smaller pueblos in the area. Construction took place at Citadel from the late twelfth to the early thirteenth centuries, and the structure probably had about fifty rooms.59 Made with red sandstone slabs and black volcanic chunks held together with a substantial quantity of mortar, the walls of the pueblo conform to the outer edge of the butte, thereby giving them a wavy appearance. The corners of the pueblo are oriented on northeast-southwest and northwest-southeast axes. On the northeast (60 degrees azimuth) and southwest (240 degrees) corners, turret-like extensions about four feet across suggest observation points for the summer solstice sunrise and the winter solstice sunset respectively. On the northwest corner (300 degrees azimuth) there is a pentagon-shaped room with the base about six feet long and the sides on the average of ten feet long. At the apex of the pentagon the remains of what looks like an observation window face directly toward the summer solstice sunset. To the southeast the remaining corner has a curved wall about thirty-five feet long that once possibly contained a window facing 120 degrees, or the winter solstice sunrise. Below Citadel Ruin is a ten to fifteen room, finely built coursed masonry structure called Nahakihu, or "house standing alone." One-third of the broken pottery found at this site originated from the Prescott area nearly ninety miles away.60

Located due north a little over a mile from the Citadel on a narrow arroyo called Box Canyon (another volcanic fault line known as an "earth crack") is a well-constructed, slab masonry pueblo that rose only two stories high and contained only nine rooms. Tree-ring dated at A.D. 1192 61, Lomoki (Lo-MO-ki), or "Beautiful House," is a rectangular structure oriented along a 60-240 degree azimuthal axis, with the windows on the narrow ends positioned toward summer solstice sunrise and winter solstice sunset vantage points. In addition, a number of windows along the length of the building face the winter solstice sunrise and summer solstice sunset points, 120 and 300 degrees respectively.

It is clear from the above discussion of the various architectural orientations at Wupatki National Monument that the sunrise and sunset points of the summer and winter solstices were very important to the ancient people, much more so than the cardinal directions. Furthermore, the conscious positioning of their houses reflect these key sacred "houses" on the horizon, imbued as they were with a spiritual significance our profane, technological culture can scarcely comprehend.

Wupatki's starry correlation is Bellatrix (Gamma Orionis), known to the Old World as the Roarer, in particular referring to a lion or less frequently a camel. The significance of this designation becomes apparent when we realize that Bellatrix is the first star of the constellation to rise above the horizon, thus heralding its arrival the way a beast announces its presence.[62] More specifically, Bellatrix (which forms the left shoulder of Orion) and Meissa (which forms the head) rise in a straight line parallel to the horizon. Thus, the head of the tellurian Orion which thrusts into the forested region of the *katsina* peaks (the Milky Way) together with the body's traditionally sacred left side (as opposed to the profane right side) are the first to be seen as Orion/Masau'u makes his appearance. Also known as the Amazon Star, Bellatrix is a slightly variable blue star 470 light-years away with a magnitude of 1.64.[63] The female emphasis is significant if we recall that the Parrot Clan, especially important at Wupatki, was known as the mother clan, whereas the Bear Clan was the father clan. Although the latter was the putative founder of Wutpatki, perhaps the Parrot Clan finally gained ascendancy, which is why it inhabited the pueblo for a time after other clans had migrated elsewhere circa the mid-thirteenth century. The left arm of Orion extends from Wupatki/Bellatrix to Pi 3 Orionis (see Chapter 6) in the middle of the "shield," terrestrially located near Point Sublime in Grand Canyon, the great Sipapuni, origin of all life and location of the three previous worlds for the ancient people. (Diagram 3, p. 32.)

Leaving Wupatki National Monument, we notice one final astronomical orientation. Due east of what was once a four-story tower at the south end of the main pueblo, we see two buttes on the horizon almost fifty miles away: Montezuma's Chair and Giant's Chair. These sites about twenty-five miles due south of Shongopovi are places where the Hopi currently gather sacrificial eagles used in their ceremonial cycle.[64] Although the buttes fancifully could take the shape of wings, they more closely resemble horns rising from the high desert. We have already discussed the role of the Two Horn Society in the Wúwutcim held in November. However, within the matrix of mythological associations these buttes could also represent the horns of Palulukang, the plumed water serpent. Standing in the tower at Wupatki on the vernal equinox at sunrise, sky watchers would have witnessed the deity Tawa ascend from between these two horns.

Because of its ever-present winds, March is known as the Whispering Noises Moon. Early in this same month the Hopi, undoubtedly carrying forth the tradition of their ancestors the Hisatsinom, perform

Pa'lülükonti (the Water Serpent Dance). Generally held at night, this ceremony includes dipping the tails and horned heads of serpent effigies into the pool of a nearby village spring.65 At one point the participants blow upon the surface of the water with gourd "...trumpets by which the roars of the serpent are imitated."66 At the culmination of the ritual the serpent effigies dart out like puppets from behind a screen to accept a plaque heaped with cornmeal offered by Hahai'i Wuhti, the mother of all the *katsinam*, also known as Pour Water Woman.67 Uncustomarily talkative for a *katsina* and as energetic as the wind during this month 68, she (in truth, impersonated by a man) also offers her breasts to be symbolically suckled by the serpents.

The Water Serpent Dance ushers in the month where the strongest breezes persist. Wupatki, whose shape, as we have suggested, could be seen as a horned serpent, is the closest major ruin to Sunset Crater, home of the wind god Yopontsa. Representative of the Snake Clan, the serpent petroglyph found near the pueblo's only kivas further reinforces the associative aspect of water. According to the Skyglobe computer program, from A.D. 1106 (the first tree-ring date for Wupatki) until A.D. 1250 (the date when the pueblo was abandoned) the sun rose at approximately 6:25 a.m. on March 21st at 86.5 degrees azimuth. About four hours later at 10:30 a.m. Bellatrix rose at 84 degrees, a discrepancy of two-and-a-half degrees. Of course, Orion blotted out by the sun is invisible at this time, but Bellatrix, the "Amazon star" that "roars" the approaching ascendancy of this constellation, rises at nearly the same point on the horizon at any time, and the sky watchers would have been familiar with this. Thus, the sidereal correlative of the female-dominated pueblo Wupatki rises at nearly the same place on the horizon as does the male sun on the vernal equinox, i.e., between the horns of the great terrestrial water snake which rests on the horizon directly east of the "big water house." Although the four serpent effigies in the Water Serpent Dance are identified as a male, a female, and two children, the snake itself is generally recognized as a feminine force in the Hopi mythological matrix. The interaction of dry wind in the middle of the annual *katsina* cycle and monsoon rains arriving to the grateful relief of the people at its end in July is animated by the pueblo Wupatki, whose serpentine head rests at one of the blowhole openings of Yopontsa, and whose sunrise equinoctial orientation links it with the horned buttes of Palulukang fifty miles away.

### Homol'ovi State Park: Betelgeuse (Orion's Right Shoulder)

Homol'ovi (Hoe-MOL-oh-vee) in Hopi means "place of the little hills." To the untrained, contemporary eye gazing across the wind-swept high desert covered with saltbush, greasewood and sagebrush, this desolate place has not much to offer. The low red mesas scattered over the landscape are made of finely grained Moencopi sandstone. Rough gray ridges of Shinarump conglomerate also rise, topped with chert cobble, chunks of petrified wood, and quartzite— not much of an attraction for the casual tourist. (In fact, at the time of this writing a bill pending in the legislature proposes to close the State park due to its low profitability.) Many people accustomed to the lush green of the eastern U.S. rush past along the interstate with hardly a second look.

However, for the Anasazi/Hisatsinom this region was a bonanza, though the source of wealth was not gold or silver but water. The Little Colorado River (in Hopi, *Paayu*, which literally means "river") snakes northwest across Arizona on its way from the White Mountains in the east to merge with the Colorado River at Grand Canyon in the west, creating wide, loamy floodplains in the process. Though suitable to nourish the traditional New World triad of corn, beans, and squash, one crop in particular thrived in the sandy soil: at this place cotton indeed was king. The Hopi still utilize the cultivated plant for sacred ritual articles such as clan kilts or bridal shawls as well as for everyday wear, and it was probably the same in earlier times.

The Anasazi/Hisatsinom established extensive trade routes to accommodate this export. Ranging from the Hopi Mesas in the north to the Salt and Gila Rivers in the south, and from the Rio Grande in the east to the San Francisco Peaks in the west, a plenitude of trade goods arrived, including ceramics, obsidian for projectile points, shells from the Gulf of California, and even such exotic items as copper bells and macaws from Mexico.[69] Pottery was especially coveted by the people at Homol'ovi because of the local dearth of wood required in the firing process.

Plagued by alternating periods of flooding and droughts, Homol'ovi must have been a challenging place to live but apparently worth the effort. Perhaps it was partially the grand vistas: to the west the San Francisco Peaks spread their dark mass on the horizon, home of the sacred *katsinam*; to the southwest the twin Sunset Mountains provide a gateway to the Mogollon Rim and the Palatkwapi Trail which links the Anasazi/Hisatsimom territory to Verde Valley, the region once inhabited by the Sinagua; and to the north the volcanic upthrusts of the Hopi Butte district are reminders of kin located a bit farther north at the Tuuwanasavi, the Center of the World.

Four major ruin sites and a few outlying sites exist in the vicinity of Homol'ovi. On the east side of the Little Colorado River we find Homol'ovi I and II; on the west side of the river are Homol'ovi III and IV, all settled at slightly different periods. Homol'ovi IV, a 150 room masonry pueblo built in a stepwise manner on the east and south sides of a small butte as well as on its top, was settled in A.D. 1260 by immigrants from the Hopi Mesa region.[70] It was occupied only for a period of twenty years, which might have been the result of an influx of clans moving from the south to build some of the other sites at Homol'ovi.[71] (Fig. 12, p. 82)

A half-mile south and nearer to the river, Homol'ovi III was a fifty-room pueblo with three rectangular kivas and one masonry great kiva built in A.D. 1280 at about the time of the abandonment of Homol'ovi IV. Because of the style of ceramics found —black-and-white painted on red ware— plus the larger room construction of masonry and puddled adobe 72, archaeologists hypothesize that the builders of this pueblo were Mogollons who migrated from the Silver Creek region of eastern Arizona near the contemporary towns of Snowflake and Showlow. As with Homol'ovi IV, this pueblo's lifespan was brief; it was abandoned in the early 1300s due to the extensive flooding which followed the Great Drought of 1276-1299, the earlier event perhaps partially causing the migration to Homol'ovi III in the first place.

On the eastern side of the Little Colorado River the comparatively large, 900 room pueblo of Homol'ovi I was begun in 1280 at about the same time as Homol'ovi III and perhaps assimilated some of the people from the abandoned Homol'ovi IV. Some portions of Homol'ovi I were two stories high, and the pueblo also contained a number of open plazas and kivas. One of the latter measuring fourteen feet wide and twenty feet long was paved with flagstones and had a stone bench on the south end with a number of loom holes on the east and west sides. This highly stratified pueblo that used a variety of masonry and adobe construction styles suggests much renovation during its relatively long history. It was abandoned in circa A.D. 1390 after a period of massive flooding.

About three-and-a-half miles north on a low knoll rests Homol'ovi II, the largest ruin in the area with over 1,200 rooms, forty kivas, three large plazas, and a ramada three hundred feet long on the south side. Beginning construction in A.D. 1330, it gradually became the focal point of the trade network in the region. This pueblo was also the center of the *katsina* cult that developed in the late thirteenth century. (More on *katsinam* in Chapter 7.) In addition to numerous representations of these spirit beings on ceramic bowls and petroglyphs, two beautifully painted murals were found on the walls of two separate kivas at Homol'ovi II: one depicts the San Francisco Peaks where the *katsinam* live, while the other shows two *katsina* dancers with cotton kilts. Homol'ovi II was abandoned at about the same time as Homol'ovi I near the end of the fourteenth century.

*Fig. 12. Homol'ovi IV, Homol'ovi State Park*

The sidereal point corresponding to Homol'ovi is Betelgeuse (Alpha Orionis), known as "the Right Shoulder of the Giant."[73] Because of its golden orange or deep topaz hue, this variable red supergiant has also been called "The Martial Star," reflecting the red color of the Moencopi sandstone in the region of Homol'ovi. Betelgeuse is the second brightest star in Orion and the eleventh brightest in the whole sky with a primary magnitude of 0.7. and a distance of 520 light-years. However, due to its "irregularly pulsating" nature, the range of magnitude can vary from between 0.2 (making it slightly brighter than Rigel) and 1.2 (about the magnitude of Bellatrix). Betelgeuse is also one of the largest known stellar objects, having a diameter equal to the orbit of Mars at its smallest and the orbit of Jupiter at its largest.[74] Like this incredibly luminous star, Homol'ovi certainly has had a variable history, enduring pulsations of flood and drought, construction and abandonment. And like this ruddy sidereal presence, the main pueblo here was once one of the largest and most impressive in the region. However, today not much more than low foundations remain of the walls, their crumbling bases strewn with thousands upon thousands of multi-hued potsherds.

Homol'ovi was one of the last stops on the long migration of the Anasazi/Hisatsinom toward their ultimate goal of Sichtilkwi, or Flower Mound, at the Center-place (specifically, near Walpi.) The people who had traveled from Palatkwapi in order to settle along the Little Colorado River include the Water Clan (Patki), the Sand Clan, the Sun Clan, the Tobacco Clan, the Rabbit Clan and a few others.[75] Palatkwapi (briefly mentioned in Chapter 1), the mystical red city located perhaps as far south as Mexico, was destroyed by a great flood. We probably will never know its precise location; nevertheless, we do know that most of the people who lived at Homol'ovi migrated from the south. We immediately think of the red rock country around Sedona in the Verde Valley, where rest such Sinagua ruins as Palatki and Honanki, Tuzigoot, Montezuma Castle, and Clear Creek. (See Chapter 6.) The heretofore mentioned "chakra line" of the terrestrial Orion intersects this region. The 145 mile long Palatkwapi Trail ascends east from the Verde Valley to the Mogollon Rim via the rough volcanic malpais rock in Rattlesnake Canyon, across the pine-studded plateau where Stoneman Lake and Long Lake are located, through Chavez Pass near the large ruin of Nuvakwewtaqa on Anderson Mesa, and down Jacks Canyon going through Sunset Pass ultimately to arrive at Homol'ovi.[76] From their red city in the south to their new home on the Little Colorado, this is the route that some of the clans followed in their journey to fulfill prophecy. Perhaps Homol'ovi's corresponding star Betelgeuse symbolically reflects the very color that these people brought with them in their memory and their hearts.

### Navajo National Monument: Rigel (Orion's Left Foot)

Located about twenty miles from the Utah-Arizona border and north of Black Mesa, northeast of White Mesa, southeast of Navajo Mountain, and southwest of Monument Valley, Tsegi Canyon (Fig. 13, p. 85) cutting through the Shonto Plateau contains two of the major Anasazi ruins in the Southwest: Betatakin and Keet Seel. (As we recall, *tségi* is the Navajo word for "rock canyon"— thus another unwitting Anglo tautology.) Looking down from the rim at Betatakin tucked beneath a grand alcove of red sandstone, one is startled by the rectilinear buildings nestled among a profusion of swirling lines and arches formed by the huge rock masses. Tiny rectangular windows project the inky silence of seven centuries, as mote after dust mote falls unnoticed inside the structures dwarfed by their natural setting. After the abandonment of these pueblos, it seems as if time itself had simply stopped.

At its peak Betatakin (Be-TAH-tah-kin, Fig. 14, p. 86), the Navajo term for "ledge house," once sheltered about 125 Kayenta Anasazi within its 135 rooms. The construction is generally cruder than the Chaco or Mesa Verde styles, using a substantial quantity of mortar to make the stones adhere. The sloping floor of the alcove forced its builders to "glue" the foundations of the pueblo in place with mud. Betatakin contains only one kiva— more correctly termed a *kihu*, since it is above ground.[77] Rectangularly shaped like most of the contemporary kivas in Hopiland, this double-walled, core-filled masonry structure was equipped with the standard fire pit and air deflector, but instead of a shaft for air circulation a door was used. In addition, four loom-anchor holes were found in the floor, suggesting ceremonial activities of the typically male-oriented religious societies. (In Hopi culture the men are the weavers; the women are the potters.)

On the eastern side of the pueblo the natural spring created a cool oasis that offered an excellent source for water, while down below on the bottom of the canyon Gambel oak, aspen, boxelder, and Douglas fir trees provided firewood and building material. Fortunately, tree-ring dating gives us a very accurate picture of the site's construction. The first few people inhabited it in circa A.D. 1250, with more families moving in about 1267. A large number of timbers were cut and stockpiled in 1269 and again in 1272, suggesting conscious planning for future development of the area. Then in 1275 a large group of people moved in and used the stockpiled timbers for the major construction work, which continued until 1286. Similar to many other Anasazi sites, Betatakin was abandoned by 1300.

Eight miles north of Betatakin is Keet Seel (sometimes written Kiet Siel), which in Navajo means "broken pieces of pottery." As is frequently mentioned, this ruin is one of the largest cliff dwellings in Arizona and one of the best preserved in the Southwest. It had 160 rooms and supported a peak population of perhaps 150 people. About twenty-five room clusters have survived the centuries, each cluster usually containing one habitation

**Fig. 13. Tsegi Canyon, Navajo National Monument**

room, from one to four storage rooms (frequently with jacal walls), a number of granaries, and a few grinding rooms all facing an open courtyard where public ceremonies undoubtedly were held. Four round kivas (sans pilasters) have also been discovered, as well as a keyhole-shaped kiva approximately thirteen feet in diameter.[78] The 340 feet long pueblo was accessed via hand and toeholds carved into the rock. Another interesting feature is a retaining wall 180 feet long and over ten feet high in places. Used to level the alcove floor and provide space for three "streets" parallel to the edge of the cliff, this wall required the movement of literally tons of dirt and rubble from the canyon floor with nothing more than woven baskets held by tump straps.[79]

Whereas Betatakin appears to have been both settled and abandoned as a cohesive community, Keet Seel grew one family at a time and was deserted in the same manner. Although pottery and tree-ring evidence of habitation as early as A.D. 950 exists, construction of the extant pueblo using reused timbers from the original structures started about 1250. However, the bulk of the building process occurred in 1272, suggesting that one or more clans joined the original group. Before these Anasazi migrated elsewhere, they sealed many of the doorways, perhaps with the hope of one day returning. As with Betatakin, Keet Seel was a "ghost town" by the year 1300.

Impressive as they are, the buildings at Navajo National Monument are not the primary reason for the sense of awe that the place engenders.

Instead, the alcoves themselves evoke an architectural grandeur similar to the great cathedrals of the world. Briefly at sunset these unearthly rainbows of orange, pink and violet stone can glow almost as vibrantly as neon before turning to evening shades of blue and gray. However, one cannot merely gaze down from the rim and still get a true feeling for the immensity and magic these spans of rock create. Instead one must stand below at the base of the ruins and look upward.

*Fig. 14. Betatakin Ruin, Navajo National Monument*

In particular the archway over Betatakin ruin seems to be the focus of sacrality for the entire Tsegi Canyon— so perfect in form are the alcove's dizzying dimensions. Like a vast amphitheater the rock shelter marked with characteristic "desert varnish" rises 450 feet, more than half the height of the canyon itself. A common phenomenon in the Southwest, this sort of alcove is created when falling water issuing from a spring erodes the sandstone eon after eon until it hits a harder layer, whereupon it starts flowing horizontally to create the floor of the shelter, in this case almost 375 feet wide.[80]

The Anasazi were perhaps the first people on the North American continent to employ this unique geologic form for passive solar heating. The cliffside dwellings were built not primarily for defensive purposes, as some archeologists theorize, but for utilization of southern exposure and avoidance of both the harsh northwesterly winds on the mesa tops and the colder air along the canyon floor.[81] This perch above the canyon bottom also allowed for the conservation of precious arable land.

More than mere protection from the elements or expansion of available farm land though, the alcove at Betatakin served a sacred astronomical function as well. In reality, it framed the celestial gods in their seasonal cycle of arrival and departure. Because of its orientation facing due south, this proto-planetarium creates a terrestrial orifice leading to the southern portion of the sky. If one is sitting in the ruin's only kiva and facing south, the sun, moon, and stars (in particular the constellations Orion and Taurus) rise from the left side and set on the right side of this stone arc.

Aided by a pocket transit, author and neurobiologist William H. Calvin discovered "...an interesting ledge in the overhang, which forms a notch..."[82] He determined this corner-shaped notch to be 139.5 degrees azimuth (the angular distance going clockwise from the north) and 17.5 degrees altitude (the angular distance measured vertically above the horizon.) A check of the Skyglobe computer program indicates that the sun was at those exact coordinates at 9:35 a.m. —about two hours after sunrise from the rim of the canyon— on December 21st from A.D. 1250-1300 (the period of inhabitancy at Betatakin). Inside the canyon sunrise comes later, so on the shortest day of the year Tawa's appearance would have been framed by the corner notch. After dawn a few days past the winter solstice Calvin further verified this from the rim of the canyon by his observation of the shadow falling across Betatakin. He noticed that the shadow of the corner notch passed directly inside the rectangular kiva; thus, from the kiva the sun would appear to be resting in the notch before making its low arc across the southern portion of the sky.[83]

The celestial correlative of the two ruins in Tsegi Canyon is Rigel (Beta Orionis), a very young supergiant binary star. Blue-white in color, it is the brightest sidereal point in the constellation and the seventh brightest in the entire sky with a magnitude of 0.34. From the Arabic its name means "Left Leg of the Giant," and it is about 900 light-years away. Its bluish companion star has a magnitude of 6.7.[84] The geomantic perfection of Betatakin and Keet Seel rivals the luminosity of Rigel and its double. In fact, these pueblos demonstrated an ideological approach to living in nature which was very different from that of the great urban center constructed two-and-a-half centuries earlier at Chaco Canyon (represented by Sirius, the brightest star in the heavens—see Chapter 8).

Vincent Scully in his brilliant book on pueblo architecture suggests that the "abstractly shaped and heroic form" of the Great Kiva, such as the one at Casa Rinconada in Chaco Canyon (see Fig. 43, p. 175 of the present book), gave way to the more communal open plaza. The latter allowed for a clearer relationship to land forms such as sacred mountains. It also provided a better view of astronomical phenomena such as the passage of sun and moon along seasonal paths or the movement of planets and zodiac constellations along the ecliptic as well as the arc of Orion across the southern sky in winter. Likewise the unnatural (or perhaps bow-shaped—

thus man-made) D-shaped Pueblo Bonito in Chaco would historically revert to the more humble cliff dwellings in which the canyon itself again became the primary source of sacred power, much as it was for the earlier Basketmaker culture of the Anasazi. In essence, we find the first "back to Earth" (and sky!) movement on the North American continent.

> "Contact with the earth had to be renewed; it was perhaps mankind's first wholly conscious attempt to reach back out, or down, to mother earth in this area—his first major philosophical leap, or regression, not to separate himself from nature but to attempt a firmer grip on more of it.... The cavern, not the Great House, is now, or perhaps we should say once more, the primary physical and psychological protector of human beings. The majestic caves at Kayenta have special powers along those lines. They create enormously monumental volumes of space and suggest figural images at tremendous scale as well. It would be hard to believe that they were not sought out largely for their ritual power."[85]

Ritual indeed, but as we have seen, the canyons were also implemented as markers for solar and stellar transits, especially at Betatakin. The Hopi name for the ruins in Navajo National Monument is Kawestima (Kah-WEHST-ih-mah), or "North Village" because it is due north of Shongopovi. Settled one hundred and fifty years after the first villages on the Hopi Mesas were established, Kawestima was home to primarily the Fire (Ko'kop) Clan but also to the Snake Clan, Horn (Flute) Clan, and the Spider Clan. In addition to their founding of the Warrior Society called Motswimi, the members of the Fire Clan were the first to emerge from the Underworld but declined a leadership role because they wanted to stay by themselves. They are considered to be the most aggressive of all the Hopi clans with ties to both the Warrior Twins and the death god Masau'u. By a majority of the "People of Peace" they are known as "the redheads"— coincidentally, the same term that the Aztecs used to designate their enemies.[86]

An interesting pictograph (Fig. 15, p. 89) reputedly painted by the Fire Clan on the eastern wall of the Betatakin alcove shows in a negative image an anthropomorphic figure inside the perimeter of a war shield. The figure is in the customary "prayer stance" mentioned in Chapter 3, and there is one handprint below each of its elbows. Although it is difficult to determine because of the eroded condition of the pictograph, especially its bottom half, both handprints apparently depict the left hand. Traditionally the left hand was used for ritual purposes, such as cornmeal or prayer feather offerings, while the right was the more profane "food hand," used primarily for eating.[87] In addition, two arcs flank each side of the upright

**Fig. 15. Pictographs of zoomorph, handprints and Masau'u/Orion,
Betatakin Ruin, Navajo National Monument**

body. Outside of the shield to its upper left are located two pairs of handprints —left *and* right, one pair on top of the other. These are probably the signatures of the two artists who created the image, not for self-expression in our contemporary aesthetic sense but to signify their supplication of the god.

Although the author Frank Waters claims that this pictograph (greatly distorted in his book) portrays "Taknokwunu, the spirit who controls the weather,"₈₈ a number of Hopi elders have expressed their belief that it represents Masau'u, the important totemic entity of the Fire Clan.₈₉ Because of the pictograph's bodily stance, i.e., upraised arms, and its location on the alcove's eastern side whence arises various major constellations, it very possibly could represent Masau'u/Orion. Perhaps the two arcs on each side of the body signify not rainbows as Waters says but opposite horizons between which Orion hovers in both his celestial journey across the winter sky and his enduring terrestrial configuration upon the Colorado Plateau.

In the next chapter we shall talk about both the celestial and the terrestrial events of the 11th century, which apparently had a profound effect on the process of Hisatsinom migration and shaped the cultural milieu as a whole. We shall also discuss the Hopi stone tablets and examine a petroglyph star map in terms of the terrene Orion.

# Chapter 5
# Windows Onto the Cosmos

"Many people in the Native American Southwest conceive of themselves quite literally as the offspring of a fecund Mother Earth and a potent Father Sun. For these people, the sky is not something impossibly remote from the earth. Rather, it is part of a unified and inspiring whole—both a window onto the cosmos and an instrument for understanding and measuring its rhythms."[1]

Ron McCoy

### *Supernova, A.D. 1054 (and Other Celestial Phenomena of the mid-11th Century)*

*It has been fourteen days since the sun god Tawa reached his summer house at dusk in the northwest. Already the warm, wet winds have begun to churn up heavy clouds from the low desert beyond the Mogollon Rim, bringing the ancestral promise of rain to the Colorado Plateau. At Homol'ovi, the Place of the Low Hills, a small hamlet of pit houses sleeps in pre-dawn stillness upon the eastern shore of Paayu (the Little Colorado). This river flows across northern Arizona into Suukotupqa (Grand Canyon), that great Sipapuni whence the people emerged from the previous world. Unlike the sacred city of Hopqöy far to the east in Chaco Canyon, no great villages stand here yet. Only a generation or so ago, work had been started on a hilltop settlement to the south in Palatkwapi (Tuzigoot in Verde Valley), while over one hundred miles to the northeast a cliff dwelling in Suyátupovi (Canyon de Chelly) is now under construction. It will be another fifty or so journeys of the sun along the horizon to the south and back before the initial Hopi village of Shongopovi on Second Mesa is settled.*

*The Sun Chief rises about two hours before dawn to make his morning prayers and cornmeal offerings. Walking stiffly through cool shadows, he climbs the highest hill, unaware that three centuries hence a large pueblo populated by some of his progeny will stand on this exact spot. He is accustomed to coming here early each day because it offers an unobstructed view of the landscape. It is his duty to keep track of the rising and setting of Tawa against certain reference points on the horizon, as well as the positions of the various star people for the timing of sacred rituals. As he finishes his chant, he opens his eyes and gasps in astonishment. Just above the eastern horizon near Wuyok sho'hu (Aldebaran in the constellation Taurus), he sees a star he had never noticed before. It hangs diagonally above the crescent moon Mu-yao. In the gradually reddening light before sunrise, his heart begins to race. This is the brightest star he has ever seen! —brighter even than Ponótsona (Sirius), who in another month will begin to rise with Wutom' kamu (Orion) shortly before Tawa. Even after sunrise, this star does not fade like the other star people, but remains to burn a reddish-white path before the sun. He must go down to tell the Bear Clan elders about this strange event. Prayers to Sótuknang and Masau'u must be performed, so the meaning of this new light will be made clear. This may be the beginning of the fulfillment of the ancient prophecies!*

What this early astronomer-priest had witnessed was the catastrophic birth of a supernova that became visible on the North American continent on the early morning of July 5th, 1054 A.D. A supernova is in actuality the violent *death* of a star, in this case one that is perhaps eight to ten times as massive as our sun. At the end of its life cycle this type of stellar object suddenly collapses to a sphere no more than twenty miles in diameter. The resulting nuclear reaction causes a tremendous explosion, releasing more energy in a few moments than the luminosity of an entire galaxy. Short of the Big Bang which scientists say created the universe, there is no event more violent. The material ejected from this explosion became known as the Crab Nebula, a cloudy mass of tangled filaments that has spread over a volume approximately ten light-years in diameter. In fact, it is still expanding. Located 6,300 light-years away and visually adjacent to Zeta Tauri in the constellation Taurus, this supernova is also known as M-1, the first object in Charles Messier's catalogue. Today one remnant of the explosion that is not visible to the naked eye is a neutron star. Similar to the beam of a lighthouse striking the earth, this so-called pulsar rotates thirty times per second and produces x-ray and radio emission, spewing electrons into space at nearly the speed of light.[2]

On the evening of July 4th the supernova was visible in the eastern sky over China. In the Annals of the Sung Dynasty this new object was referred to as a "guest star," an omen signifying either disaster or triumph. "T'ien-kuan" was the name that the Chinese called the vicinity between the horns of Taurus (i.e., Zeta Tauri [3] and Elnath, the latter shared by both Taurus and Auriga—see Fig. 27, p. 121). They considered this to be the "Gate of Heaven" through which the guest star was ushered.[4] Two accounts from China and Japan independently state that the 1054 supernova burned at high noon on Earth, stayed visible during daylight hours for twenty-three consecutive days, and remained in the night sky for almost two years. The magnitude of the supernova is estimated to have been —5, about six times as bright as Venus.[5] Chinese astronomers also describe the star as having pointed rays in all four directions and being a reddish-white in color. Ibn Butlan, a Christian medical doctor traveling through the Near East at the time, noted in his journal that the star coincided with epidemic plagues which killed thousands in both Constantinople and Cairo.₆

Although European records are strangely absent ₇, in the Western Hemisphere numerous American Indian tribes recorded this unique event. The Anasazi of Chaco Canyon created one of the most impressive, a pictograph painted in reddish-brown hematite on the ceiling of a shallow sandstone shelter near a pueblo called Peñasco Blanco. The panel contains three images: a large ten-rayed star, directly to the north of this a crescent moon with cusps pointed westward, and directly to the east of the moon at

**Fig. 16. Supernova pictograph, Chaco Canyon, New Mexico**

a right angle to the star a left handprint. South of this grouping below on the vertical cliff that runs north-south is an additional image of three concentric rings and a central dot. According to the SkyGlobe computer program, on July 5, 1054 exactly an hour before sunrise at 4:00 a.m. the belt of Orion rested vertically on the eastern horizon. The supernova and the waning crescent moon, located south to north respectively, were two to three degrees apart, with the ecliptic running exactly between the two. Both were sixteen degrees above the horizon. Five degrees above the moon was Elnath, one corner of the pentagon-shaped constellation Auriga. The sun in conjunction with Mars was about eleven degrees below the horizon.

Thus, an Anasazi resting his or her back against the vertical wall would look out at the eastern sky and see the same relationship between star and crescent moon that now appears upon the ceiling of the rock shelter. (From the rim of the canyon about seventy-five feet directly above the shallow cave, a completely unobstructed view of the eastern horizon can be obtained.₈) As mentioned in the previous chapter, in a ritual context the left hand called *hya'kyauna* is considered to be sacred, as opposed to the profane right hand.₉ Because it has five major stars and mirrors the pentagonal morphology of the hand, the constellation Auriga appearing above the moon at the time of this celestial event might also be symbolically connected to the handprint. The Hopi term *Soomalatsi*, or "star finger," refers to "...a constellation which is bright in the western sky during the winter; it seems to be pointing fingers in all directions."₁₀ Most likely this is a reference to Auriga. At any rate, the position of the handprint is significant. Astronomer Michael Zeilik of the University of New Mexico discovered that the middle finger of this handprint points to the exact place on the horizon where the supernova rose on the morning of July 5, 1054.

As previously stated, on the vertical wall are three concentric circles surrounding a dot, frequently interpreted as a sun sign. "According to the interpretation by modern Pueblo informants, the three circles represent the rays of the Sun Father and the central dot his umbilicus, from which his power emanates."[11] However, this image may alternately represent a so-called "footprint" of Masau'u, alerting the observer in the shallow cave to his ominous presence.[12] Although a sun chief (*tawa-mongwi*) might have also watched the stars, another person, perhaps of the Masau'u Clan, might have better served this function. Masau'u is the proverbial "night owl," so one who was accustomed to staying up late might have actually witnessed the supernova. (Another interpretation of the concentric circles stems from the faint red streak trailing off to the right of the circles. Some say this is the tail of Halley's Comet, which appeared in 1066. See below for further discussion.)

It is interesting to note that at 3:00 a.m. Orion was below the horizon, with Mintaka, the first star in the belt still to rise, at about minus nine degrees. If we assume that the crack between the vertical back wall and the horizontal ceiling of the cave represents the horizon, then the star-crescent combination on the ceiling and the concentric circles on the vertical wall are in a directly proportional relationship to the star chart at this moment, with the star-crescent about five to six degrees above the horizon and Masau'u/Orion (represented by the circles) yet to rise. Orion was azimuthally south of the star-crescent, as were the circles, whereas the sun below the horizon was located north, which leads us to believe that the former is the correct representation. If this pictograph accurately illustrates the proportional coördinates of the celestial bodies when first perceived, and we accept that the circles represent the footprint of Masau'u/Orion, then we can put the arrival of the supernova at roughly 3:00 a.m. on July 5th.

Some of the first images of a star in conjunction with a crescent moon, the latter relatively rare in rock art of the Southwest, were found in 1955 by William C. Miller in northern Arizona. On White Mesa he discovered a pictograph with a circle overlapping the lower cusp of a crescent moon (an impossible astronomical phenomenon). In Navajo Canyon he came across a petroglyph with a crescent moon above a circle (the star). (Fig. 17) "...[E]arly on the morning of July 5, before dawn, the crescent moon stood just two degrees north of the supernova, making a

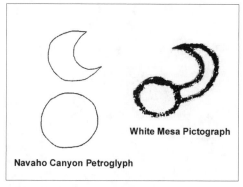

White Mesa Pictograph

Navaho Canyon Petroglyph

*Fig. 17. Rock art of 1054 supernova*

configuration of spectacular beauty; this supernova was probably the brightest object other than the sun ever to have appeared in the sky in the memory of man..."13 Because of its brilliance and longevity, the supernova must have been readily seen throughout the American West. By the late 1970s at least nineteen other candidates for representations were found 14, including rock art sites at the Village of the Great Kivas, San Cristobal, and Scholle (Abó Monument), all in New Mexico; Breckenridge, Texas; Capitol Reef National Park in Utah; and Baja California.15 Two pictograph sites are even located at Fern Cave and Symbol Bridge in Lava Beds National Monument in northern California.16 Dated from A.D. 1000-1070, an exquisite Mimbres ceramic bowl thought to represent this celestial event has also been unearthed. It is painted black on white slip with a crescent-shaped rabbit above a dot surrounded by a circle that radiates twenty-three lines— the number of days the supernova was seen during daylight hours.17

Another possible supernova representation (Fig. 18) was found by the present author at Homol'ovi State Park near Winslow, Arizona. (According to our hypothesis, this site corresponds to Betelgeuse. See Chapter 4.) On a south-facing, vertical slab five-and-a-half feet high and four feet wide is a deeply incised crescent moon four-and-a-half inches across with cusps facing westward (similar to the crescent moon pictograph in Chaco Canyon.). About six inches above and a couple inches to the left of the moon is a much fainter equilateral cross representing a star. The crescent looks as if it was pecked into the rock more recently, while the star is pecked near the top of the slab and is consequently more eroded. However, an employee of Homol'ovi State Park, a Hopi man from Third Mesa who shall remain anonymous for reasons of privacy, believes that the moon was *re*-incised, either by the Hopi or by a non-Indian, while the original star figure remained untouched.

*Fig. 18. Supernova petroglyph*

According to archaeoastronomer John C. Brandt, "The presence of three crescents [referring to the Lava Beds National Monument site] is remarkable, for crescents are quite rare: there are probably only thirty or forty 'respectable' crescents reported in the entire rock-art literature."[18] However, the present author discovered at least two additional crescent petroglyphs at Homol'ovi as well as a crescent pictograph at Palatki Ruin in the Verde Valley, contradicting the reputed rarity of this image in rock art of the Southwest. One of the crescents at Homol'ovi was found adjacent to three equilateral crosses (stars) on a very large, nearly horizontal slab that was carved with many other petroglyphs, while another was incised next to a circle on the side of a low butte. All these are "respectable candidates" for the 1054 supernova and deserve further study. The proliferation of Masau'u iconography at Homol'ovi in consort with the unusually large number of crescents is also noteworthy, since it was Masau'u/Orion who accompanied the "guest star" through the stargate near Zeta Tauri.

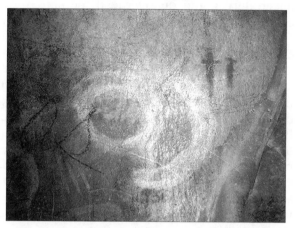

*Fig. 19. Pictograph at Palatki Ruin, northern Arizona. White (kaolin) star on left and crescent moon on right with red (hematite) "daggers" and crude modern graffiti.*

The latter half of the 11th century must have been a tumultuous time for the Anasazi. In Hopi cosmology the stars are frequently perceived in the context of warfare, and for their ancestors it was probably no different. To see a star of this magnitude suddenly erupt in the night sky must have been the cause of great concern and debate within the kivas. The supernova might even have catalyzed the final series of migrations that lead to the formation of the settlements on the three Mesas at Tuuwanasavi, the Center of the World. "I have known at least one Hopi to speculate that perhaps that was the star that told the first arriving bands that they had finally reached the place where they should permanently settle."[19]

Mythological narratives are full of references to various celestial bodies that initiated migrations and guided the people toward their geographic destiny. Even though the grand city in Chaco Canyon to the east was perhaps reaching its architectural and cultural zenith during this period, in the Arizona region the pit house was still the major form of domicile. "Sometimes they stopped for a year or more to plant and harvest some of the corn they carried with them. They would make homes by digging holes in the ground and roofing them with brush and poles— which people now describe as 'pit houses.' Then the star which was guiding them moved on, and they packed up again to follow it. The remains of these pit houses and the rock writings they made on their way are the 'flags' and 'footprints' marking their long journey."[20] (See Chapter 1.) Other similar references in the transcribed literature abound. "People had journeyed from one place to another, built villages, abandoned them and gone on, following the instructions of their wise men and the signs that appeared in the sky."[21] Indeed, during this period some of the first true pueblo villages in the region were constructed. With all this sidereal uncertainty going on overhead, perhaps the Anasazi felt safer in more centrally located villages as opposed to smaller structures widely scattered across the landscape. "Following prophecies and signs in the sky, still other clans or parts of clan came together where the Bear Clan had settled."[22]

Finally the centuries-long migration began to wind down, and the last clans migrated northward. "...one night there was a bright shooting star in the northeastern sky, and it was taken as a sign that the migration should be resumed."[23] These clans came up to Chavez Pass, then to Homol'ovi, living for a time at each place, and arrived at last on the Hopi Mesas. Even though the preceding quotation refers a celestial event in the northeast rather than the southeast where the supernova was, suggesting instead a comet or meteorite, we recall that Masau'u was frequently connected with such latter phenomena as well. "He assumes the form of a fireball, and what we often mistake for a falling star or comet is really Maasaw going by."[24]

A mere decade after the supernova faded from the skies, a major comet did indeed blaze across the night. Comets often portend death and destruction, and this one was no different, at least for Anglo-Saxon Great Britain, since the year was 1066 and the comet's name was Halley. It appeared in April of that year, the same time that the Anasazi "emperor" of warfare and death, Masau'u/Orion, is making his annual departure for the Underworld. On October 14th (a few days before the annual Orionids meteor shower generated by debris from Halley's Comet), King Harold was slain and his forces defeated at Hastings by William, duke of Normandy. Halley's Comet was impressive enough in Europe to be embroidered on the Bayeux Tapestry underneath a group of awe-struck observers pointing to it as the Latin inscription in translation reads, "These marvel at the star."[25] However, this comet and comets in general are not heavily depicted in rock art of the Southwest— at least, we have not yet found much evidence of such celestial phenomena. The Kawaiisu, a native group similar to the Chemehuevi who lived west or southwest of Hopi territory in the eastern Mohave Desert and along the Colorado River and who share the same Shoshonean language group as the Hopi, referred to a comet with its trailing tail as a "White Coyote."[26] This designation recalls Masau'u's role as trickster and his strong connection to that animal.

In addition to the supernova in Taurus and Halley's Comet, two solar eclipses occurred in North America during the latter half of the 11th century: one at about 5:00 p.m. on March 7th, 1076, a decade after the comet, and the other at about 4:00 p.m. on July 11th, 1097, about the time that the first settlements were established on the Hopi Mesas. "These astronomical events may have influenced spiritual societies and ceremonies, such as Soyal, based on solar cycles. Solar and lunar cycles are important indicators in Pueblo culture, signaling the time for planting and harvesting crops, as wells as other activities."27 As we have seen, both solar and stellar positionings are crucial to the synchronization of the ceremonial cycle. To have the above-mentioned sidereal anomalies followed within one generation by even a temporary blotting out of the face of Tawa, one of the Hisatsinom's paramount deities, must have been highly disturbing. Naturally gregarious in contradistinction to some of the more nomadic tribes, the pueblo people would have sought spiritual protection and psychological comfort in numbers. As a response to all these supernatural changes in the sky, they would have coalesced even more assiduously. The last half of the 11th century, at least in Arizona, marks the transition from a highly dispersed pit house culture to a true pueblo culture, fulfilling the Life Plan laid down by Masau'u in the beginning times.

### *Sunset Crater, A.D. 1064*

The quintessential theme of this book could probably be summed up by the pithy Hermetic epigram: "As Above, so Below." In the preceding section of this chapter we examined some of the celestial phenomena that may have shaped the path of migration and altered the direction of cultural evolution. In this section we shall look at a terrestrial event that had an undeniable effect on the Anasazi/Hisatsinom of the 11th century.

Sometime in the fall of 1064, perhaps during the gloomy Wúwutcim, or New Fire Ceremony, a previously dormant volcano northeast of the San Francisco Peaks began to send up great plumes of dark smoke and ashes. The earth began to quake and black cinders rained down upon the few pit houses in the region. However, it was more like the volcano that slowly came to life in 1943 near the village of Paracutín in Michoacán, Mexico than the swift explosion of Pompeii. This gradual eruption fortunately gave residents ample warning to remove their possessions, and some even had time to take out the precious, labor-intensive roof beams and floor posts from their domiciles.28 After a few weeks or months of rumbling, the volcano finally burst forth in a river of basaltic lava from the eastern side of its base, unleashing the fury of one of nature's most devastating forces.

This so-called Kana-a flow was followed over a century later, in 1180, by another major eruption called the Bonito flow. However, from the first of these more recent volcanic activities in 1064 until the mid-1200s when most of the venting ceased, black cinders and spheroid "bombs" together with steam and volcanic gases were sporadically released, while a blanket of ash covering an area of about 800 square miles was created. Cut by fissures, fumaroles, ice caves, xenoliths, and squeeze-ups, a black and forbidding landscape composed of both the more jagged "aa" lava and the smoother "pahoehoe" took shape. As a result of all this volcanism, a perfectly symmetrical cinder cone gradually rose to a height one thousand feet. Today we call this geologic wonder Sunset Crater, so named because of the red and yellow cinders made of oxidized iron and sulfur particles ejected during the final stage of the volcano's life. These glow in the setting sun and give the cone the illusion of transparency, allowing us to fancifully look into the volcano and see its seething lava.29

The Hopi refer to Sunset Crater by the name Palotsmo, or Red Hill, while the area of cinder cones formed far in the geologic past and situated east and north of the San Francisco Peaks is humorously called Löhavutsotsmo, or Testicle Hills. A few legends describe the creation of Sunset Crater, always in terms of its destructive aspects. For instance, because of Pivanhonkapi's social corruption and immorality in the customary Hopi fashion (i.e., failure to perform ceremonies as well as uncontrolled gambling, promiscuity, and brawling, etc.), this village on Third Mesa near Oraibi was destroyed by a rain of volcanic embers and ashes ejected from Sunset Crater almost sixty miles away.30

In another long and complex myth a handsome Ka'nas Katsina from the San Francisco Peaks marries a maiden from Mishongnovi. Meanwhile a group of sorcerers (crassly called the Turds) decides that one of them should impersonate the *katsina* while he is absent from the village. In this guise the chosen sorcerer seduces the *katsina*'s wife and sleeps with her. Despite this act of unavoidable adultery caused by trickery, the Ka'nas nonetheless jealously ignites a fire near the mountains, which somehow gets out of control and burns into the ground where live the "relatives of Maasaw" who tend the subterranean fires. The two fires merge, and a volcanic eruption occurs which threatens to destroy Mishongnovi. At the last moment the *katsina* takes pity on the people and summons the wind god Yopontsa living at the base of Sunset Crater to help him blow back the flames from the path of the village.31

Of course, the myth is out of sync with the chronology established by archaeology, since it says that the volcanic eruption supposedly occurred after Mishongnovi was settled, not before. Nevertheless, this does not invalidate the abiding psychic impression that the event had upon the Hopi and surrounding people. Imagine witnessing the exhalation of black smoke and rumblings on the distant southwestern horizon, while a strange fire from the bowels of the earth eerily tints the clouds a reddish-orange. An eruption of the magnitude of Mount St. Helens would have caused massive devastation in the immediate area with the continued fallout of ash from the volcano diminishing the sunlight for an extended period. As discussed in the previous chapter in the section about Wupatki, on the positive side this ash deposition supposedly formed a nutrient-rich mulch for agriculture and created a land rush to the region. However, in recent years some archaeologists have stated that this theory exaggerates the population influx to the Sunset Crater region.32 Certainly the Hopi myths do not point to any such migration. If anything, the myths of the eruption suggest a movement ultimately away from the region of the San Francisco Peaks and toward the Tuuwanasavi, where most of the Hopi now live.

On the other hand, if the active volcano did not cause a major increase in habitation of the region, it might have at least been the destination for religious pilgrimages. "It is not far-fetched to speculate that the people also attributed to the erupting volcano incredible supernatural power. People flocked to the area, we suspect, to propitiate the power to which they attributed the eruption, and perhaps to absorb some of it. We note that quests to places of power in order to pray, meditate, and seek visions are common in many Native American religions, and the roots of this practice were probably prehistorical."33 As we noted about Wupatki in the previous chapter, many trade goods, especially ceramics, were imported into the region. Given the paucity of natural resources around Sunset Crater, one wonders what was offered in return. Perhaps an Anasazi from the north would trade her prize black-on-white water jar in order to worship at the foot of the hill of fire. Perhaps a Hohokam from the south brought a basket full of shells or a live macaw for the chance to be in close proximity to the fiery juggernaut. In return, he might have been welcome to play a game at the local ball court, which, despite the spectacular backdrop of smoke and rumbling, would give him a familiar sense of home.

The disruption in the sky in 1054 and the eruption on the earth a decade latter, reinforced by the arrival of the comet in 1066 and followed by the solar eclipses later in the century, all must have made a profound cultural impact on a people trying to live in accordance with the laws of Masau'u. The combination of a "sky volcano" and an "earth supernova" together with the other celestial anomalies set in motion the final series of migrations in which the configuration of Orion etched into the high desert would achieve its ultimate expression. By the beginning of the 12th century the villages as we know them today were being born while the terrestrial coördinates of the Fourth World became fixed vis-à-vis the template of Masau'u/Orion.

### The Stone Tablets of Techqua Ikachi

In Chapter 1 we introduced the concept of the stone tablets, or *owatutuveni*, and discussed their role in the initial migration of the Anasazi/Hisatsinom. Furthermore, we established that these tablets, which Masau'u and Spider Grandmother bestowed to the people à la Moses, functioned as both a deed to the land and a map. In his 1972 monograph Dan Katchongva emphasized an additional cultural significance: "Before the first people had begun their migrations the people named Hopi were given a set of stone tablets. Into these tablets the Great

Spirit inscribed the *laws* [italics added] by which the Hopi were to travel and live the good way of life, the peaceful way. They also contain a warning that the Hopi must beware, for in time they would be influenced by wicked people to forsake the life plan of Maasau'u."34 The Hopi phrase *Techqua Ikachi* (the title of a newsletter published from 1975-1986 by various Hopi elders 35) literally means "land and life"— two concepts inseparable in the Hopi mind. Simply stated, the land itself cannot be abstractly divorced from the human, animal and plant life that depends on it for survival. In our contemporary ecological age, this might seem obvious, but the Hopi have maintained a lifestyle in accordance with this philosophy for over a millennium. They were apparently guided by these stone tablets —both in a literal sense of direction and through divine principles— to live in a sacred manner upon the land with its concomitant life.

Although nearly all Hopi informants and mythological sources mention them at one time or another, reputedly only one of these stone tablets was witnessed by just two white people: ethnologist Mischa Titiev sometime between 1932 and 1934, and writer Frank Waters in 1960. The extremely sacred nature of these artifacts probably precluded most incidents of such casual exposure. Waters states that at the beginning of the Fourth World three tablets were given to the Bear Clan and a smaller one with its corner broken off to the Fire Clan. According to prophecy, the latter tablet would be matched with its other broken part brought by Pahana at the End Times. Waters relied upon the description of his informant for this Fire Clan tablet and the first two Bear Clan tablets, whereas he actually saw both sides of the third Bear Clan tablet.36 (Again, see Chapter 1.) [*Nota bene*: drawings of the second and third Bear Clan tablets described below can be found in Frank Waters' popular *Book of the Hopi*, Penguin Books, 1987, p. 32 and p. 33.]

On the obverse side of the third Bear Clan tablet was a rectangle with double borders representing the land over which Masau'u presided, surrounded by six naked male figures thought to be either leaders of the most important clans or priests who conduct the Soyal ceremony.37 As noted in Chapter 3, this geometric form is symbolic of Masau'u/Orion in particular and land in general.

On the reverse side was a variety of iconography, which Titiev enumerates (even though he unfortunately reproduces only the observe side):

> "One surface is covered with miscellaneous symbols, including a row of eight little scratches, said to stand for the eight-day period during which the Soyal is observed; clouds and lightning emblems in a random arrangement; an unidentified Katcina figure; two or three sets of bear claws; an old age crook; a poorly executed serpent, said to represent the Little Colorado river; and eight circles

arranged in parallel rows, which the chief explains as thunder (?) because the sound of a thunder clap is like that of a number of objects being struck in succession."38

The crook does not appear on Waters' version of the tablet, unless it can be construed as the bending leaves of either of the two corn plants inscribed on the surface. The "Katcina" figure (again in duplicate) looks more like a Masau'u representation with its white body and round head devoid of facial features, especially the example of the smooth, brown sandstone boundary marker that A.M. Stephen found between Shongopovi and Oraibi.39 However, since the cloud-and-lightning image is located directly above this figure, it might conceivably represent the O'mau (Cloud) Katsina.40

Both Waters and Titiev remark that the snake is emblematic of the rivers that mark the boundaries of Hopi territory. If the snake on the back of the tablet is indeed the Little Colorado, then we can orient some of the other images in relation to it. This snake is located at the bottom of the tablet above the four pairs of "little scratches," which might also depict water signs; therefore, this would represent the west.

Two bear claws are located in the northwest corner of the tablet, signaling the direction from which this clan came to settle the Tuuwanasavi. (As with the figure of Masau'u/Orion, here we find a reversal of the north-south axis. The bear is traditionally associated with the intercardinal direction of southwest.)

Arranged vertically in the center of the tablet are Titiev's "eight circles," the thunder interpretation of which he seems to doubt. However, in the Waters' version of the tablet there are five *nakwách* (friendship) symbols in a row, which are known to alternately represent water.41

Extending vertically from top to bottom parallel to this row off to the right (south) are the following: a sun symbol, a star symbol, two concentric circles, another star symbol, and another sun symbol that is near the snake. If we orient these images in relation to the snake/river, the two sun symbols could represent the eastern (sunrise) and western (sunset) houses of Tawa respectively. In between these two solar emblems are three images that might delineate the three Hopi Mesas and simultaneously the three stars in the belt of Orion.

If this is the case, the top equilateral cross correlates to Walpi/Alnitak, while the bottom one represents Oraibi/Mintaka. In the middle are the two concentric circles, which correspond to Shongopovi/Alnilam, both the first village established and the mother village. As previously mentioned, concentric circles can also be conceived of as Masau'u's footprints. (If we recall, the original name for Old Shongopovi was Masipa.) We find represented here the very center of the Center-place, the *sanctum sanctorum*, thereby augmenting its significance. Even though such discussions as the meaning of aboriginal iconography are highly speculative, on the reverse side of this third Bear Clan tablet we seem to have an actual cartographic representation of *Techqua Ikachi.*

The second Bear Clan tablet could possibly be a map as well, though this is less certain due to the fact that it was merely described by the informant White Bear Fredericks and not witnessed by Waters himself. On the front of this tablet is a hoop formed by two snakes which Waters says are the Rio Grande and the Colorado River, roughly conforming to the eastern and western boundaries of the Hisatsinom territory. At the center is a large cornstalk with three other cornstalks within the serpentine circle. Also depicted are side-view silhouettes of five animals: a deer, a mountain sheep, and possibly three canines. On the other hand, the Hopi totemic correlatives for the intercardinal directions are as follows: a deer for the northwest, a mountain sheep for the southwest, a gray wolf for the southeast, and a wildcat (bobcat) for the northeast.42 (The discrepancy between this symbology and that found on the tablet is plausibly the result of a faulty description of the latter.) On the outside of the hoop are four figures, one located in each corner and each figure with one outstretched arm. Waters believes these represent "...religious leaders holding and claiming the land for their people..."43

On the back of this tablet is simply a large figure standing with knees slightly flexed and arms hanging to each side. If we accept that these double-sided tablets reflect the duality inherent in the Hopi cosmology, then we can easily imagine this figure to be Masau'u/Orion in his dark Underworld domain (which, as previously stated, includes the sky), while on the opposite side is the animal and vegetable world shared with humans and drenched with the life-giving sunlight of Tawa. Thus, the tablets function not only as a title to the land, a map, and a pictorial exemplar for the life plan of Masau'u but also as an *imago mundi*, a "window onto the cosmos" whereby the ancient people of Arizona could conceptualize their mysterious and sometimes volatile world.

### Carving the Cosmos: A Solstice Marker and Star Map In Stone At Homol'ovi, Arizona

Across ocher and salmon colored sandstone a shadow crawls like a shallow pool of water flowing in slow motion. Its fuzzy penumbra gradually slides over the spiral petroglyph pecked into smooth rock. We know this movement is the result of the greater spinning of our planet in relation to a stationary sun. For the Hisatsinom, on the other hand, shadows were animate beings whose movements reflected those of the Underworld spirits. The Pueblo people conceived the spirit world as being coterminous with the chthonic zone of the previous Third World, accessed primarily through the Sipapuni at the bottom of Grand Canyon just east of the confluence of the Colorado and the Little Colorado Rivers. The duality of light and dark, day and night, summer and winter, etc. inherent in the

Hisatsinom cosmology was infused with an animism that allowed the great sun god Tawa to interact with the lesser dusky revenants who periodically return from the subterranean realms via the various manifestations of the Sipapuni. For us the importance of such a natural phenomenon is mostly esthetic, exemplified by lavish Sierra Club photography that depicts shadows playing across sensuously curving sandstone sunlit in stark, vibrant colors. For the Ancient Ones, however, shadows were supernatural 'shades' imbued with a mysterious vitalism that imparted not only beauty in the eye of beholder but awe as well.

> "The play of sunlight and shadow along a wall in a room or across a landscape may deeply interest or even visually thrill us, but for a people who live by the sun and depend heavily on it for knowing the seasons, the day, or the time, the interaction of light and shadow takes on a much deeper meaning. For them, displays of light and shadow may extend into the realm of the sacred; they constitute a sacred appearance, or hierophany (from the Greek words *hieros*, 'sacred,' and *phaino*, 'to reveal or make appear.'"[44]

We can imagine the members of the first village settled at Homol'ovi (see previous chapter) gathering before dawn on the summer solstice in an alcove-like enclosure of rock not far from their pueblo. Here they await the sacred interplay of shadow and sunlight. The main panel, which faces eastward, is created by a vertical sandstone fault about twenty-five feet long and fifteen feet high. It is capped by an overhanging slab that extends horizontally about four feet to the east. Approximately ten feet to the east is a round-topped boulder that forms the inner east wall of the enclosure and casts a curved shadow upon the main panel. Open to the south but blocked to the north by broken chunks of rock heaped higher than their heads, this enclosure protects the observers who sit cross-legged and close together on the ground, gazing in rapt attention at the primary grouping of petroglyphs on the main panel. (Fig. 20, p. 104)

On the left (south) side of this panel near the bottom are clan markings (not seen in photo). These include a bear print, a human left handprint, possibly a badger claw (all arranged horizontally), and a snake glyph looping horizontally above these. Just to the right of this grouping is a long, abraded line (possibly symbolizing migration) curving upward and to the right, finally ending in a spiral comprised of four revolutions. Near the bottom of the panel immediately to the right of this "trail" is a somewhat circular "corral" that contains a zoomorph in profile. Its head faces obliquely upward and to the right. In between the trail and the left side of the corral is a vertical zigzag snake, while on the right side is a pair of similar zigzag snakes, all of which have recently been defaced. Slightly above and a few inches to the right of the spiral is a glyph depicting some sort of V-shaped "artifact" pointed downward. To the right of this we find a large equilateral cross formed by an oblique axis we shall call the "plumed serpent," carved from the top left to the lower right of the panel. A "vertical axis" bisects the oblique line and extends downward to nearly the same height as the bottom of the corral, ending in a cupule about an inch in diameter. To the far right (or north) at the same height that the two axes of the cross intersect, there is a petroglyph of an antelope— a pronghorn in profile with its head facing toward the left. Viewed as a composite, these petroglyphs are about eight feet long.

*Fig. 20. Solstice marker and star map petroglyph, Homol'ovi State Park*

The sun priest's low, plaintive chant mingles with pungent smoke of juniper leaves smoldering on a chill desert wind. At about 5:15 a.m. the upper arc of the sun's disk flows like molten gold over the edge of the world. Within a few moments orange sunlight bathes the top of the main panel, while the eastern wall of the enclosure begins to cast a gently arcing, horizontal shadow. Soon this shadow-being starts to crawl down the panel, passing consecutively through a number of petroglyphs: the head of the plumed serpent, the center of the spiral, the V-shaped artifact, the intersection of the cross, the antelope, the corral, and the clan petroglyphs on the far left. One section on this generally horizontal shadow has two right angle jogs that first nestle the plumed serpent's head as they pass through and then follow the slight curve on the upper portion of the vertical axis.

This progression has already taken over an hour when the shadow finally touches both the cupule at the bottom of the cross's vertical axis and the beginning of the trail at the lower left. The horizontal shadow continues downward for another half hour, after which it finally leaves the panel altogether. Chants to both Tawa and the chthonic spirits accompany this "sacred appearance," as an aura of the miraculous pervades the gradually warming air of morning.

Just as this shadow creature is departing, another one formed by the overhanging slab begins to proceed down a yet unmentioned pair of vertical rows of dots which are located at the very top right of the panel. Each row contains either twenty or twenty-one pecked dots, but erosion now makes it impossible to determine the exact number. Because of the irregularities on the edge of this horizontal slab, its adumbration has a number of bumps and notches that interact with specific petroglyphs during the various stages of the spectacle. In comparison with the former shadow discussed, this one will create a dynamic synergy of sunlight and shade that staggers the mind. Not unlike a written account of the movements in a ballet or —more germane to our discussion— the ritual acts of a *katsina* dance, any description of this presentation is bound to fall short of its actual intricacy and sanctity. In other words, the play's the thing.

For about an hour and forty-five minutes the "large bulge" on the right side of the shadow cast by the rock overhang has been inching down the two vertical parallel rows of dots. At 8:45 a.m. as it reaches the bottom of these rows, the "small bulge" is poised directly above the antelope, the "nipple" rests above the vertical axis, and the "large notch" hovers above the head of the plumed serpent. (Fig. 21, p. 106)

Nearly an hour later the horizontal portion of the shadow to the right of the large notch bisects the antelope, while the horizontal portion to the left bisects the V-shaped artifact. At this point the notch itself is lodged on top of the vertical axis.

After five minutes this same horizontal section to the right reaches the feet of the antelope, while the horizontal section to the left touches the lower tip of the artifact. Simultaneously, the lower left side of the notch is almost at the center of the cross. In addition, a smaller notch that has formed to the left of the larger one is lodged between the artifact and the spiral. Furthermore, the curving shadow to the left of this smaller notch grazes the upper part of the spiral.

In seven minutes the left side of the shadow reaches the center of the spiral, and the large notch begins traveling down the lower part of the oblique plumed serpent.

Approximately twenty minutes later this notch reaches the end of the serpent, while the left side of the shadow touches the outer left curve of the spiral, where it will remain for nearly two more hours. (Fig. 22, p.

107)

As the small notch begins traveling down the bottom part of the vertical axis, the left side of the large notch touches a small cupule located at the tail of the serpent. (It is now 10:40 a.m. As the reader may have noticed, the sun's ascension causes the shadow to move generally from the upper left to the lower right of the panel.) After about another half hour, the horizontal lower edge of the whole shadow has moved off the panel, though its left side still rests on the left side of the spiral.

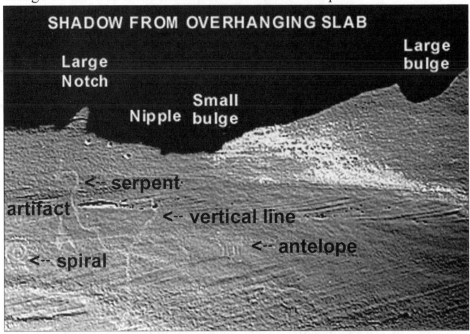

*Fig. 21. Shadow cast by overhanging ledge. Large bulge far right at end of two vertical rows of dots (not shown). Small bulge above antelope. Nipple above vertical line. Large notch on left above the head of serpent.*

Around noon the shadow that has obscured the spiral since about 10:00 a.m. begins to move again, back through its rings toward the right. Thus far, we have been dealing primarily with shadow against stone. Now another element enters into the play. Near the top left side of the whole shadow, a triangle of light forms. A few minutes after noon this triangle begins to move downward toward the spiral. At about 12:30 p.m. this triangle splits into two smaller triangles of light. When these lights pass directly into the center of the spiral, however, they merge. (Fig. 23, p. 107) This one triangle proceeds downward and passes out of the spiral, where it again splits into two smaller triangles of light. The left side of the whole shadow will soon be passing through the corral, the only time it will be obscured.

Thus far we have been witnessing an unequivocal hierophany. For approximately seven and a half hours we have seen the worlds of shadow and sunlight interact with amazing complexity, evoking beyond a doubt the discernible presence of the divine. But while the bottom of the shadow touches the bottom of the corral, and with most of the main panel no longer illuminated, something startling occurs. Just when we think that the sacred show is over, the light leaves the main panel and leaps across to the smaller panel opposite it, i.e., the inner east wall of the rock enclosure. A crescent of light with down-turned cusps hovers over the petroglyph representing an artifact comprised of four crescents arranged on a vertical shaft. At its top is a small circle, and just beneath that is a crescent with up-turned cusps that mirrors the crescent of sunlight with breathtaking congruence. The lower three carved crescents have down-turned cusps.

This artifact is located directly across from the V-shaped artifact on the main panel. To the right of the former artifact is a zoomorph that is also directly across from the one inside the corral on the main panel. To the right and a few feet below this animal on the smaller panel is a "double rainbow" with a dot in the middle, which is across from the clan markings on the main panel.

**Fig. 22. Left side of shadow rests on left side of spiral. Large notch reaches tail of serpent at lower right.**

At about 1:00 p.m. when the sunlight has left the main panel altogether, a serrated shaft of light on the smaller panel advances from the lower left toward the double rainbow on the lower right. It ultimately reaches the dot at the center, as the whole panel is bathed in the luminous power of Tawa. Between the droning chants of the sun priest and his offerings of cornmeal and paho feathers, he has been explaining to the people of the village the subtle ritual performed jointly by the sun god

**Fig. 23. Triangle of light moves downward through center of spiral.**

and the Underworld spirit shadows. Now on this longest day of the year when Tawa again begins his southward journey along the sunrise and sunset horizons, the balance of the world is once more restored. (For more photographs of this petroglyph panel at Homol'ovi, see the article "Carving the Cosmos" archived at The Orion Zone Web site, www.theorionzone.com.)

But what is the significance of all this iconography vis-à-vis the interplay of dark and light? Let us discuss the discrete elements of this configuration of rock art, looking at the cultural symbology of each separate petroglyph.

When first viewing this group of petroglyphs, the eye is immediately and instinctively drawn toward the spiral, which is the latter's primary function. This inward swirling form creates the illusion of three-dimensional space into which the perceiver's eye is pulled, whirling toward the mysterious and transcendental realms of the spiral's eye. Some believe that the spiral represents the shaman's tunnel or portal though which spirit journeys are made. "The most frequent use of the spiral was to illustrate emergence or vortex travel from one level of existence to another."[45] In the context of Pueblo culture this would signify the passage via the Sipapuni between the Third and the Fourth World.

It is easy to imagine why the spiral would also be associated with whirlpools in water and whirlwinds in air. Polly Schaafsma, an expert in the field of rock art, has given a number of interpretations for this ubiquitous petroglyph of the Southwest: "...it may symbolize water or wind, or have an association with the sun, especially if the rock art is positioned so that it interacts with a beam or shaft of light. To modern Hopis and Zunis the spiral represents migrations."[46]

This latter comment is especially true if the end of the spiral is extended into a "trail," which is precisely the case of the spiral at Homol'ovi we have discussed. This is connected to a very long, curving path that terminates at a number of clan petroglyphs, in particular the Bear, the Snake, and perhaps the Badger. The loops of the spiral are also thought to represent the number of rounds or *pásos* made in ancient migrations to each of the four directions.[47]

One interpretation closely associates this petroglyph with a primary Hopi deity: "...counter clockwise spirals are reported to symbolize the 'path of Masau (Maasaw) bringing rain' and 'members of Chief Kiva form (a) spiral at Winter Solstice'."[48] (We may recall Masau'u's role in the Soyal ceremony of December.) One source geographically particularizes the symbology of the spiral by relating it directly to the Sipapuni in Grand Canyon and the Hopi salt gathering ceremony performed there. "'Close to this deposit [of salt] the river forms a series of eddies which is supposed to mark one of the entrances to the house of *Masau*, and in these eddies the *Hopitus*, when they go there to gather salt, toss their breath-feathers and [corn] meal offerings to *Masau*.'"[49] In this context the spiral/whirlpool is known as "the gate of *Masau*'s house." This is an important element in constructing the stone "map," the solstitial aspects of which are described in detail above.

Another element crucial to our conceptualization of this Homol'ovi petroglyph grouping as a cartographic representation is the large equilateral cross to the right of the spiral. Small equilateral crosses represent stars, but this larger one could be construed as a modified swastika, a common symbol in Anasazi, Sinagua and Mogollon iconography for the land, especially the center of the land. (This image is far older than the Nazi regime and has a sacred rather than a malevolent connotation.) "We can now see that the complete pattern formed by the migrations was a great cross whose center, Túwanasavi [Center of the Universe], lay in what is now the Hopi country in the southwestern part of the United States, and whose arms extended to the four directional *pásos.*"50

One intriguing variation of the Homol'ovi cross can be found in its oblique axis, which we have labeled the "plumed serpent." As we have seen in our discussion of the stone tablets earlier in this chapter, snake iconography represents rivers in particular and water in general— perhaps in part because the reptilian resembles the riparian morphologically. "The snake's undulations also suggest the pattern of lightning, and the snake strikes swiftly, as lightning strikes."51 If the Anasazi/Hisatsinom were lucky (or more correctly, punctilious in regard to their ceremonial cycle), lightning was accompanied by copious amounts of rain. As the northern equivalent of the Aztec god Quetzalcóatl or the Mayan god Kukulkán, the plumed (or horned) serpent, called Palulukang by the Hopi, acts as a guardian of underground springs.52 Furthermore, it serves as a universal provider, offering its bounty in a land of scarcity. "It is a great crested serpent with mammae, which are the source of the blood of all the animals and of all the waters of the land."53 This hybrid creature unites the three planes of subterranean, terrestrial, and celestial by its corresponding characteristics of reptile, mammal, and bird. Especially in the desert the serpent symbolizes liquid life itself, either as an indispensable potable substance (i.e., the primordial milk of existence) or as a vital fluid flowing through the veins of all beasts.

If we orient the elements of the Homol'ovi petroglyph to various geographical and human-made features of the landscape, a precise map of the southwestern edge of the Colorado Plateau begins to take shape. The center of the equilateral cross, of course, corresponds to Tuuwanasavi, the "Center of the World," or the Hopi Mesas. At the upper end of the vertical axis is a natural hole in the rock over which a somewhat eroded but recognizable small equilateral cross has been abraded. This correlates to the ruins of Betatakin and Keet Seel in Tsegi Canyon due north of the Hopi Mesas. Approximately the same number of inches below the intersection point, just to the right of the vertical axis, is a faint mark in the rock that represents Homol'ovi itself. If the Hopi Mesas were indeed first settled circa A.D. 1100, then the Hisatsinom living at this spot where the petroglyph is located would have certainly recognized the well established Center-place off to the north, since this first settlement at Homol'ovi is dated A.D. 1260. As previously noted, Betatakin and Homol'ovi are equidistant on this north-south axis and were built at about the same time.

As we have shown, the oblique axis of the petroglyph forming a plumed serpent represents water, specifically the Little Colorado River that snakes from the southeast to the northwest and joins the Colorado River at Grand Canyon. To the right on the lower portion of the oblique axis is an incised mark in the rock just above the extended length of the serpent. This represents the Canyon de Chelly pueblos, the construction of which began in A.D. 1060 between the supernova explosion and the eruption of Sunset Crater. The tip of the serpent's tail might correspond to the ruins at Casa Malpais and Raven Site in the southeast near the source of the Little Colorado. To the left on the upper portion of the oblique axis midway between the intersection and the serpent's head is a right angle turn that represents the Wupatki pueblos, built in the first few decades of the twelfth century just after the Hopi Mesas were initially settled. The construction of pueblos at both the Mesas and Wupatki directly followed the series of astronomical anomalies in the latter half of the eleventh discussed early in this chapter. The serpent's head could be linked with the smaller ruins in Glen Canyon along the Colorado River north of Grand Canyon. As an extension of the spiral, the "trail" roughly follows the geographic arcing of the Colorado River as it flows downstream, terminating at a number of clan petroglyphs, in particular the Bear Clan and the Snake Clan. As we have seen in Chapter 1, the migration from the Third to the Fourth World entailed the use of bamboo rafts to escape a tremendous flood. Some believe that the Hisatsinom traveled upstream and through Grand Canyon to arrive at the Sipapuni, where they emerged to seek their final destination upon the Colorado Plateau.

Consistent with this book's primary theme, the configuration of pueblo villages is an analogue to the celestial plane, and the stone map at Homol'ovi seems to bear this out. To the northeast Canyon de Chelly was settled first in A.D. 1060, and its correlative star Saiph has a magnitude of 2.2.54 (Although Burnham has 2.06 for Saiph, considerable variation occurs, depending on the source.) The three Hopi Mesas were next settled, with Shongopovi on Second Mesa established circa A.D. 1100 and Oraibi on Third Mesa shortly thereafter. (Some versions, however, state that the villages were constructed in reverse order.) Shongopovi's corresponding star is Alnilam with a magnitude of 1.7, while Oraibi's is Mintaka with a magnitude of 2.2. Walpi supposedly was settled in the late 1200s, but the village of Koechaptevela preceded the existence of the former village, so its date of origin may have coincided with those of Shongopovi and Oraibi. At any rate, the correlative star of First Mesa is Alnitak with a magnitude of 1.79, approximately that of Alnilam. To the southwest Wupatki was established about A.D. 1120, and its sidereal twin is Bellatrix, which has a magnitude of 1.64. Thus, we can perceive the northeast-southwest axis as part of the oblique line of the petroglyph. To the south of the Hopi Mesas, Homol'ovi IV was established in A.D. 1260, with its sidereal companion being Betelgeuse, whose magnitude is 0.7. (However, because it is a variable star it sometimes appears as bright as Rigel.) To the north is Betatakin, built in A.D. 1260 as well. Its correlative is Rigel with a magnitude of 0.34. Now we can also perceive the north-south axis as part of the vertical line of the petroglyph.

The reader may have noticed a proportional relationship between the age of the pueblo villages and the magnitude of each village's corresponding star. Specifically, we find that the relative age of a given ruin or extant village is for the most part in inverse proportion to the magnitude of its sidereal correlative. In other words, the older the village the dimmer the star. (We must remember that a lower magnitude number signifies a greater sidereal brilliance.) To recapitulate, the oldest villages like those in Canyon de Chelly have the dimmest stars (i.e., Saiph), while the youngest villages like those at Homol'ovi and Tsegi Canyon have the brightest stars (i.e., Betelgeuse and Rigel respectively). Again we must decide whether or not this coincidence is "meaningful." Perhaps it is indeed another part of the elegant pattern in which the terrestrial mirrors the celestial.

We have seen how the large equilateral cross of the Homol'ovi petroglyph represents both the Hopi Mesa villages at the Center-place and the ruins sites at Tsegi Canyon, Wupatki, Homol'ovi, and Canyon de Chelly. This Anasazi swastika symbolizing the land also mirrors the sky, specifically the constellation Orion. (Fig. 24 and Fig. 25, p. 113) The oblique line forming a plumed serpent corresponds to the Little Colorado River, which flows into Grand Canyon. We have also established that the spiral glyph signifies the gate through which Masau'u descends to his house located just east of the two great rivers' convergence. This is the grand Sipapuni, whence the people emerged onto the Fourth World where they now live. On a personal level this is also the passageway through which the spirit will descend on its afterlife journey.

Equidistant between the plumed serpent and the spiral is an image we have not yet discussed. A V-shaped artifact points downward, enigmatically radiating its stellar power. If we look at a sky chart in the region of Orion, we notice that the V-shaped Hyades of the constellation Taurus lies adjacent to Orion in the same relative positioning we find on the panel. (A more detailed discussion of Taurus vis-à-vis Grand Canyon, and a related ritual artifact used by the Hopi will be given in Chapter 8.) Briefly mentioned in Chapter 3, the relationship between Taurus, in particular the fiery red star Aldebaran, and Sótuknang, the Heart of the Sky god, is an enduring theme in Hopi mythology.

Thus, on this one petroglyph panel at Homol'ovi we unequivocally find elements that iconographically link both the celestial and the terrestrial. "On a balance between these two forces, the forces of the sky (or the Above) represented by Sho'tukünuñwa [Sótuknang], and those of the Below represented by Pa'lülükoñ [Palulukang], the Hopi universe rests. Symbolically, the two elements are brought into contact in the making of medicine water [during the Snake Ceremony in August], where the ray of sunlight flashed into the bowl signifies the Above, and the water itself, the Below."55

In addition to the petroglyphic constellations of Orion and Taurus, to the left of the V-shaped glyph is located the spiral, which on the sky chart corresponds perfectly to the Pleiades, known to the Hopi as either *Tsöötsöqam* or *Sootuvìipi*.56 Here we have three glyphs in a row corresponding directly to the configuration of three major constellations. However, the correlative factors do not stop here. To the right of the large equilateral cross of Orion is the glyph of the antelope. Looking to the sky chart in the same relative position, we find the brightest star in the heavens, Sirius in Canis Major. "'Now,' the chief continues, 'another star appears in the southeast, Ponóchona [The One That Sucks From the Belly]. This is the star that controls the life of all beings in the animal kingdom. Its appearance completes the harmonious pattern of the Creator, who ordained that man should live in harmony with all the animals on this world.'"57 We should note here that in Hopi cosmology the intercardinal direction of southeast is totemically represented by the antelope.58 East of First Mesa nearly 140 miles are the ruins of a grand ceremonial city in Chaco Canyon, which is represented in a proportional distance on the Homol'ovi petroglyph by this appropriate zoomorph. (See Chapter 8 for a thorough discussion of Sirius/Chaco Canyon.)

Still other constellations may possibly be portrayed on this petroglyphic star map. Just below a gentle curve in the vertical line are two abraded marks, one on each side. This line continues downward until it terminates in an abraded mark made inside a natural cupule. A few inches to the right is another slightly larger natural cupule. Looking at the sky chart, we find this corresponds to the rectangular constellation Gemini. The upper pair of marks represents Alhena and Mu Gemini, while the lower pair Pollux and Castor, known to the Hopi as *Naanatupkom*, or "the Brothers."59 Perhaps it is merely a coincidence, but a natural groove in the panel cuts horizontally just below Betelgeuse and above Alhena. Terrestrially this could correspond to the Mogollon Rim cutting across the middle of Arizona, while celestially this might signify the Milky Way, which the Hopi call *Soomalatsi*. In addition, the tip of the plumed serpent's tail which we said plausibly represents the region the Hopi deem Weenima 60 (the ruins at Casa Malpais and Raven Site) may very well correspond to the constellation Canis Minor with its bright star Procyon, known to the Hopi as Taláwsohu, or "Star Before the Light."61

Again consulting the sky chart, we find one more constellation represented on the Homol'ovi petroglyph. The aforementioned corral at

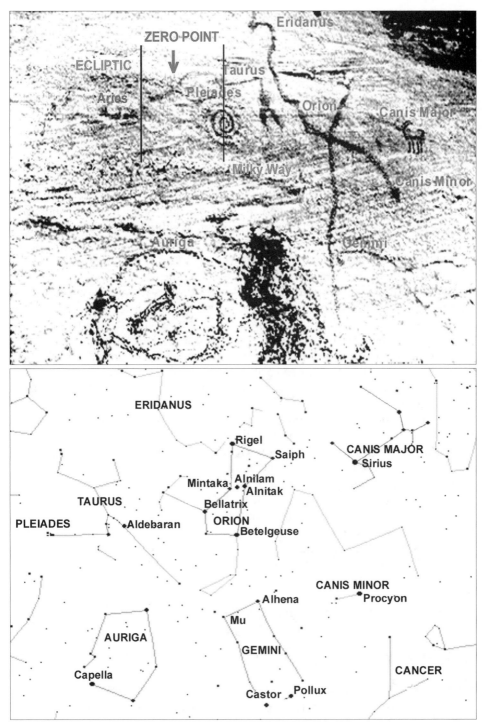

*Fig. 24 and Fig. 25. Sky chart inverted 180 degrees.*

113

first glance appears rather circular, but on closer examination we find that it looks five-sided. The Anasazi/Hisatsinom had no technical difficulty incising a perfect circle in stone, if that is what they intended. The deliberately pentagonal figure, then, very likely corresponds to Auriga. More recently the zoomorph inside the corral has been badly defaced, so it is difficult to determine its species. Nevertheless, it quite possibly is a mountain goat or mountain sheep. Having the exact magnitude of Rigel, the brightest star in this constellation is Capella, which means "little she-goat."[62] The zoomorph inside the corral could indeed be a mountain goat or a mountain sheep, the latter of which is the Hopi totemic symbol for the southwest— the direction where the terrestrial Auriga could possibly be located in our constellatory schema.

We have already discussed the vertical zigzag snakes on either side of the corral, which are stylistically different than the undulating horizontal snake off to the left near the clan glyphs. The zigzag snakes appear to be more recently incised because the re-patinization is not as pronounced as it is on the rest of the petroglyph. In addition, these too have been badly defaced. Initially one is enraged at such wanton destruction of rock art, but since these zigzag elements do not seem to fit either the conceptual configuration as we have described it or the style of the rest of the petroglyph panel, perhaps this was an intentional defacement. Possibly some modern Hopi tried to erase the negative spiritual effect of such spurious graffiti made in more recent times, probably by a non-Indian. As with most rock art, a mysterious conundrum supersedes any such speculations.

To sum up the elements of this earth/star map and solstice marker petroglyph in terms of the supernal dimension, we have found on the panel all the constellations of the Winter Hexagon: Orion, Taurus, the Pleiades, Auriga, Gemini, Canis Minor and Canis Major. In terms of the tellurian dimension, represented by the large equilateral cross are the villages of the Hopi Mesas as well as the ruins located at Navajo National Monument, Wupatki National Monument, Homol'ovi State Park, and Canyon de Chelly National Monument. What we have called the plumed serpent represents the Little Colorado River and the on the left side of the panel the V-shaped artifact corresponds to all the smaller ruins in Grand Canyon. On the right side of the panel the antelope signifies the magnificent Anasazi/Hisatsinom ruins in Chaco Canyon. The spiral corresponds to the Hisatsinom's Place of Emergence in Grand Canyon, while its extension represents the Colorado River flowing southward.

### Hamlet's Mill In Arizona

When simultaneously dealing with these reciprocal dimensions of supernal and tellurian, we sometimes confuse uranography with geography and vice versa. Such is the beauty of this elegant schema. Students of mythology frequently try to find specific terrestrial locations for various myths, and sometimes they do, as in the case of the German archaeologist Heinrich Schliemann unearthing the city of Troy at Hisarlik in modern-day Turkey. On the other hand, Giorgio de Santillana and Hertha von Dechend, co-authors of the masterful and scholarly *Hamlet's Mill*, steer us in the opposite direction, i.e., skyward. They contend that a number of consistent mythological motifs from places as diverse as Iceland, Finland, Polynesia, India and Iran correspond to various celestial phenomena, in particular the precession of the equinoxes. Using the Icelandic version of the legend as one variant of the famous Hamlet figure, they summarize their theory.

> "Amlodhi was identified, in the crude and vivid imagery of the Norse, by the ownership of a fabled mill which, in his own time, ground out peace and plenty. Later, in decaying times, it ground out salt, and now finally, having landed at the bottom of the sea, it is grinding rock and sand, creating a vast whirlpool, the Maelstrom (i.e., the grinding stream, from the verb *mala*, "to grind), which is supposed to be a way to the land of the dead. This imagery stands, as the evidence develops, for an astronomical process, the secular shifting of the sun through the signs of the zodiac which determines world-ages, each numbering thousands of years. Each age brings a World Era, a Twilight of the Gods. Great structures collapse; pillars topple which supported the great fabric; floods and cataclyms herald the shaping of the new world."[63]

In the context of our star map petroglyph at Homol'ovi, this all seems vaguely familiar. In lieu of the marine location found in many of the mythic renditions, our desert "mill" located at the bottom of Grand Canyon is represented by the spiral or whirlpool. Also known as the gate of Masau'u, it leads to the land of the dead. The Lord of the Mill in one variation is Saturn/Kronos [64], whom we determined in Chapter 3 was none other than the Hopi god of the Underworld. The direction of the mill was generally thought to be northwest, "...where... Kronos-Saturn is supposed to sleep in his golden cave notwithstanding the blunt statement (by Homer) that Kronos was hurled down into deepest Tartaros."[65] At this point we probably don't need to be reminded that the Sipapuni is located northwest of the Hopi Mesas.

In the variegated terms of the mythological logic so assiduously explicated in *Hamlet's Mill*, the friction caused by the turning of the quern also produces fire at the *axis mundi*.[66] Masau'u, earth god of fire, is translated into Orion of the (eastern) Horizon, which, as we saw in Chapter 3 of our book, resembles the fire-drill or fire sticks sparking the sun god Tawa into his daily existence during the end of the annual ceremonial cycle in July. Although the Hopi Tuuwanasavi is not directly coextensive with the whirlpool of Grand Canyon, it is contiguous, and, given the wide range of Anasazi/Hisatsinom migrations, close enough to be conceptualized as part of the Center-place.

The recurrent image of salt in the so-called mythological "implex" described by Santillana and Dechend corresponds to the destination of the salt collecting expeditions made by the Hopi and presumably by their ancestors as well. In fact, the Hopi term for Grand Canyon is Oentupqa, or Salt Canyon. This theme is related to the image of the "Saltwater-Tree" of the Cuna Indians who live in Panama as well as on the San Blas Islands, and whose ancestors conceivably had trade relations with the Anasazi/Hisatsinom. "God's whirlpool" is located beneath this tree, which, when chopped down by Tapir (a sun god somewhat resembling Quetzalcóatl), unleashes a great flood to form the world's oceans.67 As we recall from Chapter 1, a mighty deluge caused the destruction of the Hopi Third World.

According to the co-authors, the devastation of the World Tree or world pillar celestially correlates to the gradual shifting —one degree every seventy-two years— of the vernal equinox sunrise point from one zodiacal constellation to the preceding one (hence the *precession* of the equinoxes), occurring once every 2,160 years and completing the full cycle once every 25,920 years. Instead of an actual tree, which is not a very potent image in the cosmology of desert dwellers, a hollow bamboo reed through which the virtuous people emerged from the lower Third to the upper Fourth World finally comes crashing down (or is cut down), leaving the wicked either imprisoned inside it or stranded below in the nether realm.

The Norse version of the tale has an additional element found on our star petroglyph. Corresponding to the whirlpool spiral, Hvergelmir, whose name literally means "bubbling or roaring cauldron," is the source and subsequent destination of all the earth's waters. It lies beneath the third root of the World Tree, an ash named Yggdrasil. This root extends into Niflheim, the dark abode of the Underworld, and is gnawed upon by Nídhögg, a flying dragon who also slowly devours the bodies of the dead.68 As we have stated, the plumed serpent is represented by an oblique line on the Homol'ovi petroglyph. If we conflate Palulukang and Masau'u/Orion, contained therein are the vitalizing force of water and the mortuary aspect of a subterranean denizen, both of which we find in the figure of Nídhögg. Incidentally, the harts nibbling on the shoots of Yggdrasil could plausibly correspond to the zoomorphs on the petroglyph panel.

In discussing this star map vis-à-vis contemporary notions of cartography, we must remember that the former is conceptual rather than proportionally representational. Archaic societies were not interested in producing scale maps of either the earth or the sky. For a rendering of mythic symbology in rock art it was sufficient to contain merely the essential elements, as does the petroglyph at Homol'ovi.

> "That there is a whirlpool in the sky is well known; it is
> most probably the essential one, and it is precisely placed.
> It is a group of stars so named (*zalos*) at the foot of Orion,
> close to Rigel (beta Orionis, Rigel being the Arabic word
> for 'foot'), the degree of which was called 'death,'
> according to Hermes Trismegistos, whereas the Maori
> claim outright that Rigel marked the way to Hades (Castor
> indicating the primordial homeland). Antiochus the
> astrologer enumerates the whirl among the stars as Taurus.
> Franz Boll takes sharp exception to the adequacy of his
> description, but he concludes that the *zalos* must, indeed, be
> Eridanus 'which flows from the foot of Orion.'"[69]

The spiral of our star petroglyph is probably closer to the left
shoulder of Orion than the left foot, but the significance of the icon still
remains. The Greek word *zalos* may be related to a combination of the
intensive *za-* and the eleventh letter of the Greek alphabet *lambda*, which
is V-shaped— thus indicating Taurus and the V-shaped artifact. The great
sage Hermes Trismegistus (whose Egyptian name was Thoth) states that
the stars near Rigel signify death, and this is borne out in
Anasazi/Hisatsinom cosmology by the glyphic depiction of Grand Canyon,
the great Sipapuni. The name Eridanus literally means "the river," and head
of the plumed serpent could indeed represent the upper Colorado River.
The plume on the snake's head extended vertically for a few feet could
possibly even correspond to the Green River which flows from the north to
join the Colorado River in Utah.

   Santillana and Dechend also discuss in sidereal terms the Platonic
cosmology found in the *Timaeus*. "When the Timaean Demiurge had
constructed the 'frame,' *skambha* [Sanskrit word for *axis mundi*], ruled by
equator and ecliptic—called by Plato 'the Same' and 'the Different'—
which represent an X (spell it Khi, write it X ) and when he had regulated
the orbits of the planets according to harmonic proportions, he made
'souls.'"[70] In other words, "the frame" is the point where the celestial
equator crosses the ecliptic. Called by astronomers the First Point of Aries,
this juncture where the sun crosses the equator in its northward journey
marks zero point in the measurement of right ascension, which can be
conceptualized as celestial longitude. In addition to the swastika's
representation of land on the star petroglyph, another smaller crossed
incision on the panel might jointly refer to this astronomical decussation.

   To the left of the spiral is a horizontal mark. (See Fig. 24, p. 113.)
Due to its proportional relationship to the spiral (the Pleiades) and the other
constellations, this could very well represent the constellation Aries. In
addition, the long abraded line starts at the lower left of the panel and arcs

upward above Aries to end in the spiral. This line, which we previously said was symbolic of an ancestral migrational path, might also be conceptualized as the ecliptic. The line ends at the spiral of the Pleiades, whereas the ecliptic itself passes within only four degrees or so of the constellation. On the petroglyph panel an additional line had been carved from the notched end on the left of the horizontal extension of Taurus, arcing downward to join the right side of the horizontal line of Aries. This line intersects the abraded line (ecliptic) at a little more than half the distance between Taurus and Aries.

Did the Ancient Ones who carved this petroglyph panel mean to point to this specific spot on ecliptic as a time marker? If so, they were indicating a date of approximately 1000 B.C. These petroglyphs were probably incised about the time that the nearby village (known today as Homol'ovi IV) was established, circa 1260 A.D. Why, then, would this rock art refer to a date twenty-two centuries earlier? Were the petroglyph makers in actuality putting a copyright date, so to speak, on their creation? This sort of artistic individuality, of course, probably did not exist, but the petroglyph carvers may have wanted to indicate this approximate date for astrospiritual purposes.

During this same period about three millennia ago, the Hopi language gradually distinguished itself from the other members of its Uto-Aztecan family. "The linguistic evidence indicates that the forebears of the Hopi separated from their Numic congeners, and 'came out' of the Great Basin around 1000 B.C..."[71] This date is squarely at the center of the Age of Aries. Were the carvers of this cosmology trying to tell their descendants (as well as us) the time frame of their arrival in this region of northern Arizona?

Rock art has been dated with only minimal success, using cultural style or degree of patination as guides. (Patination is the relative weathering and oxidation of a stone surface that makes it appear darker than underlying surfaces that have not been exposed or carved into.) However, if we do indeed have a sidereal map that shows the ecliptic with an "X marking the spot" of the precession of the equinoxes during that era, then the petroglyph panel can be confidently dated within a span of no more than about 500 years. Looking at a star chart for sunrise of the vernal equinox in 1000 B.C. (Fig. 26, p. 120), notice the apparent distance (not the actual light-year distance) between Xi or Omi in Taurus (both magnitude 3.8) and Hamal in Aries (2.0 —the smaller the number, the greater the magnitude). This is proportional to the distance between the leftward extension of the Taurean V-shaped artifact and the right side of the Ariean horizontal petroglyph. Furthermore, the distance between the two stars in Taurus and the zero point (the ecliptic crossing the celestial equator) as well as the distance between Hamal in Aries and the zero point are both proportional to the corresponding carvings on the petroglyph panel. (Compare Fig. 26 with Fig. 24, p. 113.)

We stated in the previous section of this chapter that at sunrise the eastern wall of the enclosure starts to cast a gently arcing, horizontal shadow upon the petroglyph panel. At the point where it crosses the ecliptic line, this shadow may represent the celestial equator. Specifically, the right side of a slight convex bump in the shadow occurs precisely at the spot where the ecliptic crosses the dividing line carved between Taurus and Aries. If this shadow can indeed be construed as representing the celestial equator, then the Ancients had a firmer grasp of celestial mechanics than heretofore suspected. This presupposes that so-called "primitive" humans knew that the earth was a sphere, as some independent researchers have suggested.[72]

As heretofore stated, the celestial equator now passes very near Mintaka (one of three stars in Orion's belt, terrestrially corresponding to Oraibi), while the ecliptic always passes through Gemini, just above the right hand of Orion and between the horns of Taurus. The point at which the celestial equator presently crosses the ecliptic is located between Pisces and Aquarius— hence we are entering the celebrated "Age of Aquarius." However, about 6,500 years ago the fiducial point of the vernal equinox was located between Gemini and Taurus above Orion's upraised weapon with the Milky Way passing directly through it. (Fig. 27, p. 121)

For the Anasazi/Hisatsinom this date, archaeologically speaking, places it squarely in the middle of the Archaic period. For the Hopi this may correspond to the First World, the pristine era just after the cosmogony. For classical writers it was the Golden Age. The early 5th century A.D. Latin grammarian and philosopher Macrobius states that during this age, souls ascended through the "Gate of Capricorn" and descended to be reborn through the "Gate of Cancer."[73] Because of the precession of the equinoxes caused by the slight wobble of the Earth's axis, the former gate is currently located between Scorpius and Sagittarius on one end of the Milky Way (the southern stargate near the galactic center), while the latter gate is found between Taurus and Gemini on the opposite end (the northern stargate near the galactic anticenter). (See Gary A. David's article "The Dual Stargates of Egyptian Cosmology," *Duat*, Issue 1, CD-ROM, Sept.2002. Now published at the following Web site: <www.theorionzone.com/egyptian_stargates.htm>.)

In terms of our star petroglyph the forked icon represents Taurus (recalling the Chinese "Gate of Heaven" mentioned earlier in this chapter), located terrestrially in Grand Canyon, which, as we have stated, is an important pathway for the *katsinam* or spirits in their afterlife journey. Thus, in 4500 B.C. the place where the celestial equator crosses the ecliptic was at the heart of the galactic plane. This "stargate," so to speak, functioned as an inter-dimensional portal through which souls could pass into this life.

A source much earlier than Macrobius reverses the two stargates. The *Prasna Upanishad*, a Vedic text written sometime between 900 B.C.

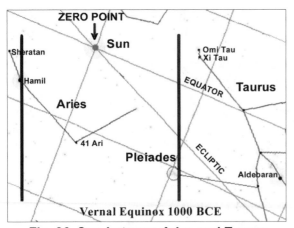

**Fig. 26. Sun between Aries and Taurus**

and 600 B.C. but obviously hearkening back to a far earlier age, describes two celestial paths: "Prana [primal energy, symbolized by the sun] and Rayi [form-giving substance, symbolized by the moon] divide the year. Two are the paths of the sun— two are the paths that men travel after death. These are the southern and the northern."[74] The solar and lunar references are obviously symbolic, perhaps alchemically so, since the points on the horizon at which the sun and moon rise and set are both north *and* south of the equinox points during various times of the year. Those seeking either progeny or reincarnation on the earth piously travel Rayi, the southern way, the lunar path of the fathers or ancestors. Those seeking to transcend the cycle of birth and death and achieve a place of rest beyond fear chose Prana, the northern way, the solar path of abstinence, faith, and knowledge, whence no return is possible. Here we find a celestial orientation that is the opposite of the skies today. In other words, this Sanskrit text deems the southern stargate as Taurus-Gemini and the northern stargate as Sagittarius-Scorpius. While the psychospiritual functions remain the same as in the Macrobius description, the directional positions of these constellations along the Milky Way fit a sky chart corresponding to at least 10,500 B.C. or earlier— halfway around the 26,000 year precessional cycle.

In his recent book *Signs in the Sky* Adrian Gilbert interprets these stargates from a Biblical perspective. Specifically, Genesis 28:12 briefly relates to Jacob's dream of a great ladder: "And he dreamed, and behold a ladder was set up on earth, and the top of it reached to heaven: and behold the angels of God ascending and descending on it." In Verses 17 and 18 of the same chapter, Jacob with some trepidation erects a pillar from the stones he had used as a pillow, calling the place Bethel, or the "house of God," and "the gate of heaven." Gilbert makes the connection: "If we equate Jacob with Orion and his ladder with the Milky Way, then it would appear that this 'gate of heaven' is the same star-gate that Macrobius describes as being at the crossroads of the latter with the ecliptic. We have, therefore, the image of Jacob seeing the angels passing through the star-gate which lies at the top of the ladder of the Milky Way." This association is reinforced by the notion that Orion's belt has also been known traditionally as Jacob's staff, i.e., his phallus.[75]

Gilbert further cites Matthew 16:19 where Christ gives to Simon Peter the "keys of the kingdom of heaven" and appoints him its gate-keeper. "Using a different but related metaphor, Peter also was to become the door-keeper of heaven, as he was to be given the keys to the gates of Hades. In church art and statues of St. Peter he is usually shown holding the keys: one gold and the other silver, suggesting two different gates."[76] The reference to the two most precious metals corroborates the solar/lunar symbology found in the Hindu version. These portals to the afterlife were obviously important

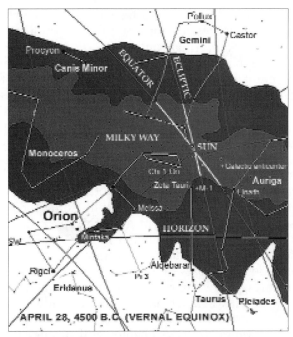

**Fig. 27. Northern stargate located where the celestial equator crosses the ecliptic in the middle of the galactic plane. This is near the galactic anticenter (R.A. 5h 46m, Dec. +28° 56'), to which Orion's right hand points.**

components in the cosmologies of many diverse cultures around the globe.

We have shown that the Homol'ovi petroglyph panel is a multifunctional device using natural and man-made elements to produce a dramatic interplay of light and shadow. Manifesting a stunning complexity and beauty, this example of rock art carved probably in the late thirteenth century serves as both a terrestrial cartography associated with the migrations of various clans and a sky chart establishing the template of Orion and other constellations upon the earth. In addition, it is a highly accurate solstice marker announcing the longest day of the year when the sun god Tawa reaches his summer house on the northeastern horizon. The purpose of the two parallel rows of dots at the top right of the main panel is yet undetermined, but they may prove to have some supernal function, perhaps lunar.

For us securely ensconced in the secular world of rationalism, scientific empiricism, and technological gadgetry, the earth/star map and solstice marker is a mute mystery whose deeper implications have been irretrievably lost in the intervening seven hundred years of cultural and psychological dislocations. Beyond the academic speculations it engenders, this rock surface provides a dream screen upon which we project our desires for a unified cosmology complete with its holistic framework of ritual and myth. For its makers, on the other hand, the petroglyph panel was undoubtedly a manifestation of the numinous forces inherent in a vital and vibrant world where the membrane between the physical and the spiritual was as diaphanous as a breath.

Archaeological evidence shows that the average life expectancy of an Anasazi (at least in Chaco Canyon) was a mere twenty-seven years, and only five to fifteen percent lived to age fifty.[77] On the other hand, we contemporaries are allotted our three score and ten, which will no doubt soon be extended by a welter of wonder drugs, nanotechnology, and genetic manipulation. Do we not, therefore, look back through the distorted lens of temporal chauvinism with some measure of pity for the brief life span of these so-called primitive people? In an age of chaos when "Things fall apart; the centre cannot hold..." and the world appears to be on the brink of an absolute holocaust, are we not the ones who should be pitied instead? The carved rock at Homol'ovi remains stoically silent— the enduring recurring rhythms of sunlight and shadow its only refrain

This chapter has tried to provide a number of windows onto the Anasazi world via the many permutations of the celestial-terrestrial connection. The next chapter will discuss the villages that comprise the head and upper limbs of Orion as well the grand chakra system that channels ley energy across the landscape. In addition, we will consider our ancient schema of Orion superimposed upon the high desert in terms of the implications it could have for one of the most high-tech, scientific areas of research being done today, viz., SETI, or the search for extra-terrestrial intelligence.

# Chapter 6
# The Architecture Of Existence

"The palpable presence of religion covered and enclosed each village like an invisible dome. I could sense it when entering and leaving. It eventually came to me that the Hopi village was like a cathedral—the architecture was invisible but it was there nevertheless. White Americans and Europeans expressed their religion in their churches, temples, and cathedrals, the Hopi in *their very existence.*" 1

Edward T. Hall

## *The Testament to Humility*

What is true for the Hopi was true for their ancient ancestors. Perhaps few other peoples on the planet today could warrant a statement of such conviction. Certainly no other aboriginal group on the North American continent has preserved its rituals, customs, and myths in the degree to which the Hopi have done. A complex and elegant architecture of existence persists, a living testament passed down through the ages in a form the Ancient Ones would probably have no trouble recognizing. The actual physical structures both in contemporary Hopi villages and in the prehistoric ruins of their forebears are consistent with the builders' basic character, i.e., gracefully modest and understated. With the exception of the grand city in Chaco Canyon (discussed in Chapter 8), the intricacy is one of spirit, not of stone and mortar.

The splendor of great temples and the grandeur of exquisitely carved pyramids such as those found in Mesoamerica are not apparent here. In fact, this was the key to survival, viz., the minimization of material culture. By living in humble stone and adobe villages tucked away in deep canyons or atop high mesas, the Hisatsinom/Hopi for the most part were simply overlooked by the exterminating forces that swept across the New World. Unlike the fabulous material riches of the Aztec empire, especially its treasures of gold and precious jewels, the wealth of the Hisatsinom living far to the north in what the Spanish called the Gran Chichimeca (see Chapter 4) lay in the many permutations of their ceremonial cycle. The cathartic chaos of the New Fire initiation into manhood, the noble responsibility of the winter solstice ritual, the diligent construction of prayer feathers and perpetual oblation of cornmeal, the bean sprouting ceremony and the chastisement of the children as a rite of passage into adolescence, the intriguing puppet drama to propitiate the plumed serpent, the elaborate and unearthly dances of the *katsinam*, the chthonic strangeness of the Snake Dance, the joyful women's celebration of the autumn harvest festivals— all these and much more comprised an architecture tantamount to any tangible edifices a culture might erect. Even today this architecture of existence is still standing.

## The Head of Orion: Walnut Canyon/Meissa and Other Ruins

The terrestrial template of Hisatsinom/Hopi villages geospatially arranged to mirror Orion and other constellations is one more aspect of this spiritual architecture. Emerging from a plethora of proto-Hopi cultural and religious concepts, the schema we have described is part and parcel of a gestalt that is more enduring and perhaps more imposing than any tangible archaeological evidence could ever be. In Chapter 4 we discussed the pueblo sites that correlate to Orion's belt as well as to his shoulders and lower limbs. In this section we shall inquire about the head of Orion manifested on the tellurian plane in the region of the sacred San Francisco Peaks.

As home to the *katsinam* from about mid-July until the winter solstice, these mountains offer a cool green refuge from the arid adversities of the high desert. Their subalpine succor ranges northwest to southeast via the Mogollon Rim which cuts an evergreen swath across the present state of Arizona, extending through the White Mountains and into the Mogollon Mountains of western New Mexico. As we see by the diagram of the terrestrial Orion, the constellation is lodged in this coniferous haven in much the same manner as is the celestial Orion with his head in the starry clouds of the Milky Way. As he strides the night sky, his crown is infused with sidereal glory while his image on the Earth is bathed in an aura of these intercessory spirits that ceaselessly aid the Hisatsinom/Hopi. Or again: "As Above, so Below."

If we recall from Chapter 2, a line which forms part of a grand chakra 2 system can be drawn from Shongopovi/Alnilam to the ruins at Walnut Canyon/Meissa and beyond. This provides an inseparable link and a conduit of mutually flowing pranic energy from the Hopi Mesas to the evergreens forests of the San Francisco Peaks and back. More specifically, Walnut Canyon symbolizes the Third Eye, or pineal gland (etymologically derived from the Latin word *pinus*, or "pine cone"), of Orion. Esoterically, the Third Eye, i.e., the sixth chakra, relates to what is termed the *celestial body*. "It is the world or body which holds our individual future and it is also our access to that future. The term 'celestial' derived from antiquity where it was believed that the future existed in space and that one day each of us would die and become a 'star,' thus returning to the divine celestial Light from which we had come."[3] Hence, this particular region in the San Francisco Peaks has a direct sidereal connection because of the specific chraka associated to it. (The other "bodies" —namely the physical, emotional, mental, astral, and ethereal— are associated with the first through the fifth chakras respectively.)

The collateral montane ruins of Elden Pueblo and Turkey Hill Pueblo to the west along with the heretofore mentioned Ridge Ruin and Winona Village to the east plausibly form the terrestrial constellation's left and right physical eyes. In addition, both the dormant volcano at Sunset Crater located to the left (viz., west) side of Orion's head and impact site at Meteor Crater to the right (viz., east) side of his head help create the aureole of Orion. This nimbus is infused with a natural dynamism the autochthons more correctly had designated as divine, or in Hopi, *a'ni himu*, which literally means "very something" or "Mighty Something"— an incomprehensible mystery resonating autonomously yet anonymously at the heart of the cosmos.[4]

*Fig. 28. Cliff dwellings at Walnut Canyon east of Flagstaff, Arizona*

Named for the Arizona black walnut trees found at the bottom of the 400 feet deep gorge, Walnut Canyon National Monument contains about 300 rooms in eighty-seven clusters built between circa A.D. 1125 and 1250. Many of these are small cliff dwellings tucked like swallows' nests beneath horizontal limestone overhangs, while a few domiciles and seasonally inhabited, agrarian field houses rest on both canyon rims. The structures at Walnut Canyon were built at about the same time as the ruins at Wupatki farther north by people of the same group, what archaeologists call the Northern Sinagua. Constructed of limestone slabs and mud mortar, these recessed rooms provided a cozy refuge for a number of extended families— perhaps as many as 600 people altogether. Above the diminutive doorways (some T-shaped) near the tops of the walls, small holes vented smoke, though the soot of innumerable fires still stains the low ceilings. Despite decimation in the late 19th and early 20th centuries by illegal pot hunters who even dynamited some of the walls, the ruins have yielded many artifacts for study, including whole ceramic vessels, potsherds, textiles, baskets, sandals, cordage, and tools made of stone, bone, and wood. One supposedly ceremonial cave even contained wooden wands and prayer sticks. The human connection to this far-off world becomes especially poignant when one enters one of these tight living spaces to discover actual impressions in the warm, golden colored mortar of the hands —probably those of women— that shaped the walls.5 Like most of the ruins in this area, Walnut Canyon was deserted by A.D. 1300.

A great variety of tree species can be found within this narrow chasm, including ponderosa and pinyon pine, juniper, Douglas fir, aspens, box elder, locust, dogwood, and, of course, black walnut. Undoubtedly, yucca fruits, elderberries, serviceberries, currants, wild grapes, lambsquarters, and wild lettuce supplemented the traditional native triad of corn, beans, and squash. Providing another source of protein and adding variation to the diet, mammals such as bighorn sheep, deer, squirrels, rabbits, and packrats were hunted along this bountiful defile. In the drowsy afternoon sunshine turkey vultures riding the updrafts make great sweeping arcs above the canyon, just as they did when the Hisatsinom lived here, while the descending warble of a canyon wren blesses the stillness. At certain times of the year this must have been an immensely satisfying place to live.

Although the ruins themselves are not particularly grand in a comparative sense, the location definitely is. Sinuously cutting through Kaibab limestone and Coconino sandstone, the canyon's original oxbow channel, at one time or another in the geologic past, was diverted in alternate directions by earthquake action. The result was a series of "islands" in the middle of the canyon floor, dramatically towering hoodoo columns of rock which offered niches for domestic habitation on the ledges along their sheer cliff sides as well as spaces for a somewhat more enigmatic purpose on their tops.

Five so-called "forts" are positioned along the twenty-mile length of Walnut Canyon, though First Fort and Fifth Fort lie outside the boundary of the monument. Generally, these forts consist of several rooms of dry-laid limestone built on large island prominences with compound walls outlining some of the steep escarpments. Second Fort, which rests on a triangular island at the southeast boundary of the monument, has one limestone rubble room on top and four or five other rooms on the southeast side. A wall curves around the southeast part of the point some ten to fifteen feet away from the rooms. Particularly significant is the pair of "defensive" walls running the length of a saddle that connects this island to the north rim of the canyon. "These contain several enormous, shaped limestone blocks quarried from the surrounding area. The west wall, the best preserved, measure 36 meters long by 2.5 meters high and one meter thick."[6] From a photograph of the connecting wall on the west side, one perfectly rectangular foundation block appears to be thirty-six inches long and sixteen inches high. "It would have been a tremendous construction project with machinery let alone with hand labor used in the past."[7] At the western end of the monument Fourth Fort consists of five aboveground masonry structures and one limestone-lined pit house. This "fort" also has a wall connecting it with the north rim of the canyon. The wall is more than three feet high and three feet wide, and extends over sixty-five feet in length.

The apparent focus of the canyon, however, was Third Fort, which now lies unexcavated above the asphalt "Island Trail" looping from the monument headquarters past eight clusters of restored cliff dwellings. Third Island has the largest concentration of rooms and has access to the majority of canyon sites. Directly across from it on the north rim are large field houses and multi-room dwelling sites which may have served as distribution centers for goods coming in and out of the canyon.[8] Located on top of the island, Third Fort consists of about five rooms, some built with wing walls along the edge of the cliff side. On the central part of the island's western edge a "community room," measuring nearly fifteen by twenty feet, was probably used for ceremonial rituals and astronomical observation. Because the corners of this room are directly oriented north/south and east/west, any windows in the northwest and southwest walls would have given a good view of the summer and winter solstice sunsets respectively. Another slightly smaller room on the southeastern tip of the island would have afforded views of the summer and winter solstice sunrises. A cairn on the northwestern tip of the island may have also served some astronomical function.[9]

The nature writer Scott Thybony has called the structures found on top of these islands in Walnut Canyon "warless forts."[10] Indeed, there is little evidence of any active warfare in the region, as shown by the condition of local burial sites.[11] Although the forts may have provided some defensive protection, their primary *raison d'être* was clearly otherwise. "Some have suggested that rather than being used for defensive or warfare-related functions, the forts served as communal storehouses for food and other commodities, the residences of elite families or individuals, or as astronomical observatories."[12] As to the storage of provisions and trade goods hypothesis, the transportation of both the food grown mainly on the rims of the canyon and the goods arriving at the same place would have been a superfluous and arduous labor. In particular, this would have entailed carrying the articles down from the rim, across the saddle, and up to the tops of these lofty islands in the middle of the canyon. If raiding was not a problem, why go to such trouble? As to the idea of providing prehistoric penthouses for the elite, no archaeological or anthropological evidence from either the Sinagua or the Hopi exists to show any significant sociopolitical hierarchy, at least any that would warrant such exclusionary structures. This leaves the *astronomical* hypothesis, which for ancient cultures always simultaneously meant *ceremonial*.

The ledges on the flanks of these islands in Walnut Canyon have little space for ritual dancing, etc., much less than even the narrow First Mesa of the Hopi and barely enough for domestic dwellings. Hence, the only available open space near enough to the domiciles would be on top. The islands settled at about the same time as the Hopi Mesas serve a similar function, i.e., as ziggurats to both physically and spiritually exalt those ancient worshippers of the empyrean wonders. Here in the forehead of the terrestrial Orion, "a node in a minor chain of sites"[13] extending in an arc through the evergreen region from Ridge Ruin through Walnut Canyon to Elden Pueblo, Tawa and Masau'u/Orion along with other prime constellations such as Taurus, the Pleiades, and Canis Major could be tracked as they traversed the heavens. Unlike most of today's astronomical endeavors, this would have been a form of supplication.

The sidereal correlative to Walnut Canyon is the double star Meissa (Lambda Orionis). Its magnitude is 3.40 and its distance is 1,800 light-years.[14] Its name meaning "white spot" or "shining"[15], Meissa is the center of an expanding spherical nebula, which gives it a somewhat misty appearance. This star also forms the apex of a small triangle whose base is formed by Phi 1 and Phi 2, the former possibly corresponding to Ridge Ruin and the latter to Winona Village. (Diagram 3, p. 32. Cf. an alternative correlation: Phi 1 and Phi 2 = Elden/Turkey Hill [16] and Ridge/Winona.)

Six miles north-northwest of Walnut Canyon is Elden Pueblo, constructed by the Sinagua in circa A.D. 1100 over an earlier pit house village. Situated in a ponderosa pine forest near a permanent spring, this one and two-story pueblo contained from sixty to seventy rooms made of small sandstone and basalt boulders. Other features include four separate smaller room blocks and plastered storage bins or roasting pits. Three cemeteries near the ruin were found to contain about 130 individuals, while burial goods included turquoise ear rings, incised shell bracelets, a sandstone nose plug, and a carved bone hair pin. One of the most significant structures is a community room similar in function to the one at Third Fort in Walnut Canyon. Adjacent to the domestic rooms, this room measuring thirty by thirty-six feet contains a stone bench two-and-a-half feet high and two feet wide on all four perimeter walls, a slab-lined ventilator shaft, a fire pit, and loom anchor holes. At the southwest corner is a large round boulder about two feet across located on the bench. This may have served as a marker for the summer solstice sunrise, whose rays could have streamed through a small window near the opposite corner, bathing the boulder in sunlight, though this is hypothetical because the pueblo walls are only partially reconstructed.17

*Fig. 29. Elden Pueblo near Flagstaff, Arizona. Note boulder in far corner.*

The Hopi name for this site is Pasiwvi, which means "the place of coming together" or "the meeting place." (A cognate of this name is the word *pasiwna*, which means "worship." This says something about the nature of Hisatsinom/Hopi religion, i.e., that worship was/is a communal activity.) Located at the eastern base of the eponymous mountain (which the Hopi call Hovi'itstuyqa, or "Buttocks-sticking-out promontory")18, Elden Pueblo was the original home of a number of clans, including Badger, Water, Snake, and Antelope. Famous for their healing powers and knowledge of herbal medicines, members of Honani, or the Badger Clan, lived with the Katsina Clan for a time at the sacred Nuvatukya'ovi (San Francisco Peaks) before resettling at Tuuwanasavi (the Center-place). In fact, the former clan is ritually associated with the spruce trees found in abundance on those mountains. Quite significantly, spruce boughs are used in many *katsina* dances as a powerful magnet for rain. John Lansa of the Badger Clan at Oraibi discusses the significance of this tree: "Picking them up gently after they are cut, we put our arms around them and take them to our bosoms for we know that we are bringing their *kachina* spirits into our village, and the *kachinas* who participate in the ceremony are the spirits who bring rain. For you must know that the spruce tree has a magnetic power upon which the clouds rest. Salavi [the spruce] is the *chochokpi* [throne] for the clouds."[19]

Thus, the Coming-Together-Place of worship rests in the head of Orion, whose evergreen hair glistening with rain is refulgent with the halo formed by *katsina* spirits. Enveloping the constellation's triangular head (the apex of which is Walnut Canyon/Meissa), the San Francisco Peaks are themselves a throne, lifted up higher than anywhere else in the surrounding terrain, seemingly a part of the Milky Way. Mirroring the function of Walnut Canyon's Third Fort, they served perhaps as a grand mastaba to raise the devout toward their origin and source of being in the heavens. It is interesting to note that the two stars forming the base of the triangle, Phi 1 and Phi 2 Orionis, "...constituted the Euphratean lunar station **Mas-tab-ba-tur-tur**, the Little Twins..."[20] Hence, Orion's head in the mountains is uplifted toward its celestial counterpart in the Milky Way. In the context of our schema this reinforces the concept that a natural mastaba (sharing the same prefix as the Hopi god Masau'u) or ziggurat can provide spiritual benefits no less efficacious than a human-made one. In addition, it is interesting to note how the San Francisco Peaks from a certain angle can even resemble the three major pyramids on the Giza Plateau in Egypt (see Fig. 47, p. 249), which themselves have been found to be constellatory paradigms and interstellar links. In fact, the Egyptian Orion Correlation was main reason for the genesis of this book.

The *katsina* peaks were obviously a source of great "medicine power" and the repository for an unutterable numinosity. With the wind god Yopontsa howling all around them, the snow-capped peaks are still an awesome presence (in the original, non-jargonized sense of the adjective). After the tumultuous volcanic eruption of Sunset Crater in the mid-eleventh century, the region must have attained legendary status, becoming the spiritual focus for the whole Southwest. Strenuous journeys to the head of Orion would have been made periodically in order to propitiate Masau'u in his fire god aspect. Even though the Spanish called the San Francisco Peaks *Sierra Sin Agua*, or "mountains without water," many springs among their piney environs offered an additional lure to those making pilgrimages to the high country. In fact, one of the chief springs of the four directions is found here.[21] Perhaps it is more than a coincidence, then, that one of the springs located in the San Francisco Peaks halfway between the highest point at Humphreys Peak and the "meeting place" at Elden Pueblo (in particular, five miles southeast of the former) bears upon the U.S. Forest Service map of Coconino National Forest the name *Orion*.

## *The Crown Chakra of Orion: Tuzigoot/Zeta Tauri and Other Verde Valley Ruins*

Once the grand chakra line is revitalized by *katsina* spirits inhabiting the Third Eye of Orion ensconced in the San Francisco Peaks, the psychospiritual energy moves southwest beyond the Mogollon Rim and is transformed by the unique terrain of the Verde Valley. Whereas the mountain home of the *katsinam* is represented by the sixth chakra, the Verde Valley corresponds to the upper-most, or seventh, chakra. On a microcosmic level this latter chakra located on the top of the cranium is called, according to Hindu and Tibetan tradition, the "Lotus of a Thousand Petals" or the "Wheel with a Thousand Spokes." Here duality is transcended and enlightenment, bliss, and immortality are attained. Although the true nature of this site is ineffable, the seventh chakra known as "the seat of the self-luminescent soul"[22] is the place of essential being where the individual self and the cosmic self are totally merged. "This psychoenergetic center is a luminous structure composed of a seemingly endless number of filaments that extend from the head upward into infinity. It corresponds to the level of ultimate Reality on the one hand and to the brain on the other."[23] Also identified as the "brahmic fissure," this chakra is the point at which consciousness leaves the body during the moment of liberation (*moksha*). On a macrocosmic level the sixth chakra's celestial energy which the San Francisco Peaks have drawn down from the star *katsinam* to the terrestrial plane achieves final union with the electromagnetic forces welling up from deep within the earth at the terrestrial seventh chakra. In other words, this site is a sort of New World Avalon, the quintessential paradise or a heaven on earth, a teleological Eden where ultimate divinity is realized.

Some believe the Verde Valley is the legendary Palatkwapi, the great red city of the south. It is easy to see how the blood-hued sandstone buttes and blazing orange cliffs found in the areas around Sedona and Sycamore Canyon might lead one to that conclusion, just as they did for one of the pioneers of archaeology in the Southwest, Jesse Walter Fewkes. "The region of the Red Rocks suggests the mythic land called Palatkwabi, or Red Land of the south, from which, according to their legends, came the Water House people, one of the most important components of the Hopi stock."[24] Collectively known by archaeologists as the Southern Sinagua (i.e., the ancient people living south of the Mogollon Rim), the Water (House) Clan and other Hopi clans such as the Sand, Rabbit, Sun, and Tobacco once thrived in this paradisiacal region.[25] The source of this natural cornucopia is the Verde River, which begins in Big Chino Valley and empties into the Salt River almost 150 miles to the south. Along with the valley's fertile soil and warm climate, the river and its tributaries (viz., Oak Creek, Beaver Creek, and Clear Creek) allowed for a burgeoning population in the twelfth and thirteenth centuries. In fact, here is another case where the Hisatsinom might have had it *too* easy, at least as seen in retrospect by the Hopi.26

According to the legend, the destruction of Palatkwapi by a deluge (which once very long ago reputedly wiped out the entire Third World as well) was causally linked to social, sexual, and religious discord. The Hopi believe that these social ills were inevitably brought on in part by irrigated (as opposed to dry) farming, as well as by the general indolence of an untrammeled existence. Bringing tremendous rain storms and flooding, the agent of devastation was the horned or plumed serpent called Palulukang (also discussed in the Wupatki section of Chapter 4), thought to inhabit, among other watery places, the so-called Montezuma Well in the Verde Valley.27 After the drowned Palatkwapi was abandoned, the people for the most part moved northward along the Palatkwapi Trail. (See the end of the Homol'ovi section in Chapter 4.)

One of the prime candidates for the actual village of Palatkwapi is Tuzigoot National Monument near the town of Clarkdale. (Fig. 30, p. 133) The name *tuzigoot* is an Apache word meaning "crooked water," a reference to the nearby Peck's Lake created eons ago by an oxbow in the meandering Verde River. Established initially in the early 11th century by a group of Sinagua migrating south from the Sunset Crater region, the pueblo saw its first major construction circa A.D. 1125, about the same time that the villages at Wupatki and Walnut Canyon as well as those on the Hopi Mesas were being built. One main expansion at Tuzigoot took place in A.D. 1200 and another in the late 1300s, with the peak population reaching about 225. Located on a narrow ridge 120 feet high running due north and south above the flood plain, the pueblo is constructed of uncoursed, white limestone and pink sandstone blocks along with river cobble and darker basalt boulders all held together with liberal amounts of mud mortar. Eighty-six out of an estimated 110 rooms have currently been excavated in this structure, which reached two or possibly even three stories high. The dimensions of the rooms are comparatively large, averaging twelve by eighteen feet. Similar in function to those at Walnut Canyon and Elden Pueblo, a large rectangular ceremonial room measuring seventeen by twenty-six feet with a raised bench at one end has also been found at Tuzigoot. On the northwest corner of the pueblo is an ample plaza area where ritual dances took place. Especially on the western side of the pueblo, one senses the pyramid-like architecture akin to the Maya of Mexico. In this case, however, the natural ridge provides most of the height. Here again, a geologic formation was merely augmented to provide an elevated temple whereupon worshippers could be even closer to the star beings.28

At the very top of the ridge was constructed a square two-story room whose roof undoubtedly served as an astronomical observatory. As we might expect, the corners of this platform are oriented to the intercardinal directions, which were of paramount importance to the Hisatsinom: at the northwest corner the summer solstice sunset point (300 degrees azimuth) faces the red rock country in Sycamore Canyon; at the southwest corner the winter solstice sunset point (240 degrees) sights a gap in the Black Hills above the present town of Jerome halfway up the mountainside (oddly named Cleopatra Hill); the winter solstice sunrise point (120 degrees) is far to the southeast down the Verde Valley where Tawa travels in the winter; and at the northeast corner the summer solstice sunrise point (60 degrees) is located on the rim of a large, river-eroded limestone bowl which surrounds the pueblo on all sides except the south and beyond which are the stunningly beautiful crimson canyons and buttes of Sedona.

*Fig. 30. Hilltop dwellings at Tuzigoot National Monument, Verde Valley*

Still renowned for its spectacular scenery, the contemporary town of Sedona and its environs located about twelve miles northeast of Tuzigoot is additionally blessed with numerous power vortices. Continuously fluctuating auras of electric or magnetic energy are undeniably palpable in specific spots on the landscape such as Bell Rock, Airport Vortex, Cathedral Rock, and Boynton Canyon. "The red rocks canyonlands of Sedona, Arizona host some of the most powerful vortex sites in the western United States. For reasons concerning cracks and fissures, faultlines, ley lines, grid intersections, underground rivers, high amounts of iron and magnesium in the soil, and a beauty of a negative ion count, Sedona has a personality all its own."[29] Although the causes are varied and the effects dependent upon the individual, the overall result is felt by almost everyone. Certainly Native Americans used the region as a tellurian altar to augment their prayers, and a few small ruins even show continuous habitation.[30] A full description of the specific properties of the Sedona vortices is beyond the scope of this book, but the influence of this region is a crucial component in the schema as we have been delineating it.

Returning to the ruin at Tuzigoot, we notice that its stellar correlative is Zeta Tauri, the lower "horn" of Taurus and an extension of Aldebaran in the Hyades cluster. (See Fig. 27, p. 121. A discussion on the terrestrial location of the Hyades is found in Chapter 8.) With a magnitude of 3.0 (about the same as Pi 3 Orionis, discussed below) and at a distance of about 940 light-years, Zeta Tauri is known by astronomers as a "shell star" because of its expanding ring of circumstellar gas caused by the star's rapid rotation.[31] On a terrestrial level this nimbus is associated with the expanded consciousness of the seventh chakra. If we recall from the previous chapter, Zeta Tauri was known to the Chinese as a stargate through which the A.D. 1054 supernova journeyed, and remains a focal point for that region of the sky. Indeed, this is about the time that the first Sinaguans of any appreciable number settled around the Tuzigoot site, even though Hohokam farmers migrating north from the Valley of the Sun had been living in the Verde Valley since about the seventh century A.D.[32] If this ruin truly does represent Zeta Tauri on the tellurian plane, then the crescent-shaped Peck's Lake a mile away might be emblematic of the crescent moon seen on the morning of July 5, 1054 as the "guest star" made its unannounced arrival within one degree of the star. It is possible that the Hisatsinom migrated to this specific spot about the time of the supernova's appearance as part of the covenant established with Masau'u. Perhaps Palatkwapi is just one more piece of the puzzle, one more synchronicity in the overall schema that gradually revealed itself to a people who constructed their villages in a pattern that obviously albeit mysteriously mirrors the stars.

Tuzigoot has yielded a plethora of artifacts, including an entire Mexican macaw buried beneath the pueblo floor, many large red or brown ceramic bowls, ollas measuring two feet in diameter used for storing corn, a wealth of carved shell jewelry, and one turquoise necklace twelve feet long consisting of 3,295 beads. (A prehistoric turquoise mine was once located near the contemporary town of Kingman, Arizona.) Similar to those found at Snaketown built by the Hohokam to the south, a rectangular paint palette now in the museum at Tuzigoot National Monument measures approximately three-and-a-half by five inches and has zigzag snake images carved along the borders with water spirals in the corners. (Again, the rectangle is symbolic of land and the body of Masau'u/Orion.) The

Sinagua also traded salt obtained from a mine located a few miles southwest of present-day Camp Verde 33, as well as cotton and minerals such as copper. (The United Verde Copper Company once owned the land upon which Tuzigoot sits, and tailings from its smelting operation still rest at the base of the ridge.)

One of the more intriguing artifacts from our standpoint is "a cache of 652 pieces of cut pipestone" found beneath a floor at Tuzigoot 34, along with a heavy block of the same hard, red mineral (also called catlinite) used in carving tiny fetishes found at Montezuma Castle (see Fig. 31, p. 138) about fifteen miles southeast of Tuzigoot.35 The only place in the world where catlinite is mined is at Pipestone National Monument in southwestern Minnesota. The Plains Indians who inhabit the surrounding region revere this substance, using it for the bowls of their sacred "peace" pipes. Some believe that the mineral found at Tuzigoot and Montezuma Castle is actually argillite instead of catlinite, the former originating locally— in particular, from a mine near the hamlet of Del Rio, a few miles north of Chino Valley.36 But if this mineral unearthed at Tuzigoot and Montezuma Castle is indeed catlinite, then an immense trade network must have existed not only south into Mexico but also north into the Great Plains region.

This theory is reinforced by an extension of the grand chakra system discussed above. A straight line starting from the Verde Valley (Palatkwapi) intersects both Walnut Canyon and the Hopi village of Shongopovi, proceeds northeast though the substantial Anasazi ruins at Mesa Verde in southwestern Colorado, crosses the Rocky Mountains not far from the headwaters of the Colorado River in the country of the Utes (a tribe linguistically related to the Hopi), traverses the traditional land of the Pawnee in central Nebraska 37, and terminates at the pipestone quarry in the Dakota (Sioux) territory of Minnesota. Extending well over a thousand miles long, this line was established on a northeast/southwest axis by the summer solstice sunrise and winter solstice sunset points. (This axis is specifically 51/231 degrees azimuth. See Chapter 2. Northeast is technically 45 degrees and the midsummer sunrise point is 60 degrees, while southwest is 225 degrees and the midwinter sunset point is 240 degrees.) If we include the southwest segment of this line which reaches all the way to the mouth of the Colorado River, we have a conduit of earth energy flowing over thirteen hundred miles long.

At the risk of straining the bounds of credulity, if we were to extend this same line a bit more than nineteen hundred miles northeast of Pipestone, Minnesota, it would pass just south Isle Royale in Lake Superior (the site of major copper mines conservatively estimated to have contained 500 million pounds of ore and radiocarbon dated at 2000 B.C.- 1000 B.C.38) to finally reach Newfoundland within fifty miles of a place called L'Anse Aux Meadows, the first Viking settlement in the New World, established circa A.D. 1000— about the same time that the initial Sinagua settlement at Tuzigoot was being built. Of course, this is the sort of coincidence, piled one upon another, meaningful or not, to which we have become accustomed.

The grand chakra system aligns a series of significant ceremonial and habitation sites in much the same manner as the ley lines, or the "old straight tracks," originally discovered in Britain by Alfred Watkins during the early 1920s. As the eminent astro-archaeologist John Michell remarks in regards to this world-wide system, "In several other parts of the world, lines linking holy centres are not only mythological paths down which the gods representing the various heavenly bodies pass at regular seasons, but have some further quality known only to native magicians. American Indians, especially the Hopi of the Southwest, appear to use them as cables of mental communication. In China they are known as *lung-mei*, the paths of the dragon, and run between astronomical mounts and high mountains."[39] In the Chinese context the dragon energy of *ch'i* corresponds on a microcosmic level to the kundalini energy, or "serpent power," denoted in the Hindu and Tibetan chakra system. Michell considers the "dragon currents" of Chinese geomancy to be identical in function to the ley lines found in Britain.

> "At certain seasons of the year the dragon passed overhead down a straight line of country, drawing in his wake the fertilizing powers of life. Astronomers observed its passage, and astrologers predicted the moment of its appearance, while geomancers marked its course with alignments of mounds and stones. Processions down the line from centre to centre for the annual invocation of the dragon current created straight tracks, sections of which survived until lately as traditional pilgrims' paths linking the holy places. It can still be found that the legendary haunts of the dragon stand in line with others, joined together by carefully set rows of stones and earthworks all over the country."[40]

In fact, Michell has discovered what he calls "St. Michael's line" running from Land's End in Cornwall in the southwestern corner of Britain through a series of at least ten interconnected hilltop churches and shrines, including the Glastonbury Tor and the stone rings at Avebury. The easternmost extension of the line touches the coast just north of Lowestoft, totaling a distance of 350 miles. Possibly related to Baron von Reichenbach's odic light or, more recently, Wilhelm Reich's orgone energy, this dragon current roughly follows an axis of 60/240 degrees (specifically, 63/243 degrees, according to Michell's calculations)[41]. In terms of our schema in the southwestern United States these azimuths correspond to the midsummer sunrise and midwinter sunset line found between Oraibi/Mintaka and Wupatki/Bellatrix. (The azimuthal locus for the midsummer sunrise in this area of Britain is 51 degrees, while the midwinter sunset is 231 degrees.)

St. Michael 42, one of the four archangels of Christianity who stand around the throne of god, was the legendary slayer of dragons who expelled "that old serpent" Satan from heaven, casting him "out into the earth." (Revelation 12:7-9) However, in pagan times the figure that came to be known as St. Michael was reputedly the *guardian* of the dragon ways across the country. Furthermore, he was associated with Hermes, the Greek god of roads and cairns who wields his wingéd, double-serpent (i.e., double helix) staff called the caduceus. In a first century account of his Gallic campaign Julius Caesar says that Mercury (the Roman equivalent of Hermes) was the god that the Gauls (who called themselves Celts) most reverence, although Caesar was too ethnocentric to give the native name for their deity.43 As we noted in Chapter 1, Hermes finds his New World correlative in the Hopi figure of Masau'u, god of land and death. In this web of associations, Christian iconography often shows St. Michael with a scale weighing souls of the dead 44, much like the traditional onus of afterlife judgment that both Masau'u and the Egyptian Osiris share. Hence, in Britain as well as in Arizona we see the same archetypal figure represented by St. Michael and Masau'u respectively in control of the dragon's pranic power as it courses across the land. If we recall that the flood described in Revelation 12:15 was caused by the dragon, we are mythologically propelled back to the New World and the destruction of Palatkwapi by Palulukang, the horned or plumed serpent.

It is possible that the entire middle Verde Valley was known as Palatkwapi, instead of just one village. The valley contains about fifty large pueblos of thirty-five to one hundred rooms each.45 The presence of eight ball courts in the region built between A.D. 900 and A.D. 1100 suggests cultural relations with the Hohokam to the south.46

Located five miles southwest of Montezuma Well (previously end-noted) near the town of Camp Verde, Montezuma Castle National Monument is a well preserved, five-story cliff dwelling recessed into a limestone alcove that overlooks Beaver Creek. Tucked away in a canyon of tall sycamores, the pueblo began construction in the early twelfth century about the same time as the first major construction at Tuzigoot. Perched a third of the way down from the rim of a cliff 150 feet high, the pueblo contains twenty rooms of mostly small stones hauled from below, a waist-high parapet on the upper floor, and a tower in the middle of a structure which stretches about ninety feet horizontally.47 The tower faces due south, while the rest of the rooms are constructed on either side along the gentle concave line of the alcove. Much like the cliff dwelling at Betatakin, Montezuma Castle afforded views of the southern sky across which Orion makes his winter journey. A window on the western side of the pueblo directly faces the winter solstice sunrise (120 degrees azimuth), while a larger window (or perhaps T-shaped doorway) on the eastern side looks toward the winter solstice sunset (240 degrees).

"On the wall of another room is an interesting pictograph incised in the mud plaster. This roughly rectangular figure measures about 6 by 8 inches, and is laid off into 4 sections by lines that intersect at the center. In the upper left and the lower right quarter are vertical wavy lines that suggest water." Again we are confronted with the rectangular motif representing Masau'u/Orion and his land.

About a hundred yards west of the cliff dwelling lies Castle A, a six-story pueblo containing approximately forty rooms at the base of the bluff. Archaeologists found charred roof timbers fallen in upon floors already drifted over with sand, indicating that a fire had occurred after the abandonment of the pueblo.

*Fig. 31. Montezuma Castle on Beaver Creek, Verde Valley*

As with all of the ruins in the Verde Valley, the people left here early in the 15th century.48 Why did the "Sinagua" leave this paradise of perpetually flowing streams and warm bountiful earth? Were they truly flooded off the land, or did Masau'u instruct them to fulfill his covenant and move on? These conundrums persist.

The other pueblos at Palatkwapi followed a similar pattern. Six miles south-southeast of Montezuma Castle are Clear Creek Ruins, which in Hopi are called Sakwavayu. Containing a total of about fifty rooms and what was probably at least one kiva, two pueblos were constructed on a precipice 400 feet high that overlooks the creek. Along the cliff side are a couple hundred small caves, some of which were hollowed out of the white limestone by hand with rooms built in front or walls across their mouths. Similar to the caves at Tsankawi Mesa in New Mexico, these are still stained with the soot of cooking fires. Functioning as excellent passive solar domiciles, the caves face due south toward the broad Wingfield Plateau. On tip of the mesa a triangular area lined with upright limestone rocks and a ridge of earth nearly two hundred feet on each side apparently functioned as an unroofed ceremonial dance plaza.[49]

From atop this mesa a spectacular panoramic view can be enjoyed. Nearly twenty-two miles to the northwest at the summer solstice sunset point (300 degrees azimuth) is Mingus Mountain (elevation 7,720 feet) in the Black Hills of Arizona. (This line extended farther northwest would pass near King's Ruin in Big Chino Valley, a bit over fifty miles away. See Chapter 2.) A little over nine miles to the southwest at the winter solstice sunset point (240 degrees azimuth) is Bald Mountain (elevation 6,089 feet).[50] Nine miles southeast of Clear Creek Ruin is Needle Rock, just south of the 120 degrees winter solstice sunrise point. (This line extended southeast would intersect Grasshopper Ruins and Kinishba Ruins, two major Mogollon sites at a distance of seventy miles and 110 miles respectively.) A near summer solstice sunrise line (57 degrees) extended from Clear Creek would intersect Chavez Pass Ruins and Homol'ovi Ruins (see Chapter 4), a distance of forty miles and seventy miles respectively. A little over fifty-five miles almost due north are the San Francisco Peaks.

Eight miles northeast of Montezuma Castle, three miles east of Montezuma Well, and less than a mile east of Beaver Creek, a forty room pueblo is perched on the top of a solitary limestone butte called Sacred Mountain. Perhaps functioning as a trade center, this pueblo with three room blocks outlining a plaza also hosted a ball court at its base. "This appears to be the latest court in the Verde Valley, dating to a time when they were no longer in use in their Hohokam heartland to the south."[51]

Not far from that pueblo is a petroglyph site known today as the V-Bar-V Ranch. This is a richly evocative site of great spirituality and complexity. Densely carved by indirect percussion with hammerstones and flint chisels on a vertical rock face of red sandstone darkened by patina, the petroglyphs include both male and female anthropomorphs (some with enlarged hands or multiple arms), zoomorphs (viz., deer, elk, cougars, antelopes, and either coyotes or dogs), blue herons, lizards, centipedes, clan markings such as Bear and Snake, both round and square spirals, concentric circles, grids, rectangles, abstract designs, sunbursts, equilateral crosses (i.e., stars), dots (one group forming what looks like a spiral galaxy!), and a possible star and crescent moon juxtaposition (the A.D. 1054 supernova again?). The glyphs have well defined edges and in general do not overlap. Many of the human and animal figures as well as the foot/paw prints have a small cupule signifying the heart of each glyph. One interesting grouping shows two frog people still with tadpole tails (or

**Fig. 32. Petroglyph at V-Bar-V Ranch**

possibly turtle people) emerging from a horizontal crack in the rock which represents the Underworld of the spirits. Above these images is carved a copulating couple together with a zigzag snake ending in a spiral (the latter not shown in Fig. 32). Thus, two traditional symbols of water are closely related here to a depiction of fertility.

We all know, however, that sometimes this life-giving element can also wreak havoc. The legend of the deluge at Palatkwapi concludes on a melancholy note:

> "The people picked up a few of the things they had saved from the destruction and began their journeys. The Rabbit Brush Clan, or Rabbit Clan as it came to be known, and the Tobacco Clan were the first to go. After them the Hawk and Eagle clans departed. Then the Sun Clan left, followed by others. The Water Clan and its subclans waited with the Sand Clan until the others had gone. The Water Clan chief, using a flint knife, inscribed on a large rock nearby the message that the Water People had come, lived for a while, then moved on, and he signed his message with the picture of a frog. When that was done, the Water Clan people and the Sand Clan people left this place, gathering a few ears of corn from the fields as they went, and began walking toward the north."[52]

## The Right Arm of Orion

As an extension of his shoulder located on the terrestrial plane at Homol'ovi, the upraised right arm of Orion reaches far to the south, more so than any of the sites yet discussed. His forearm follows Chevelon Creek upstream toward the Mogollon Rim, where rests his wrist (near the former cabin recently destroyed by fire of the popular Western novelist Zane Grey). From that point his fingers (sometimes conceptualized as holding a club) extend southwest toward Perry Mesa and what is now Horseshoe Reservoir on the Verde River. This upper extremity of Orion stretches into the middle of the Milky Way, which finds its tellurian correlative in the forested region of evergreens at the southern end of the Colorado Plateau.

Ranging just east of Interstate 17 from the town of Cordes Junction in the north to Black Canyon City in the south, Perry Mesa (recently declared Agua Fria National Monument by presidential decree) is a broad, grassy plateau dotted with occasional juniper trees. In addition to buckhorn cholla and huge prickly pear cacti scattered across the rocky landscape, the northern range of the saguaro is found at the southern end of the mesa. At one time this area about 113,000 acres in size also interfaced a number of ancient cultures: the western extent of the Mogollon people, the southern extent of the Sinagua, the northern extent of the Hohokam, and the northwestern extent of the Salado. Although more than four hundred prehistoric sites have been found, seven major village clusters provided a home for a population estimated to have been over 3,000. These pueblos of up to three hundred rooms each were located along the washes that drained off the edge of the mesa, while the main agricultural system of terraced fields and check dams were found toward its center. The culture flourished from A.D. 1250 to 1450, when it apparently dissolved or was absorbed into neighboring groups. (Fig. 33)

*Fig. 33. Rugged country at Perry Mesa Ruins, Agua Fria National Monument north of Phoenix. These multiple ruins of stacked masonry correspond to Chi 1 Orionis in the constellation's right hand.*

Because of the strategic locations of these pueblos containing a total of over 1,200 rooms, some archaeologists have created a scenario in which the prehistoric people on Perry Mesa form a culture of warring polities, supposedly making raids on the Hohokam or others and then retreating to their strongholds. These scientists cite as evidence supporting their hypothesis the presence of breast-high walls surrounding some of these pueblos.₅₃ However, as we noted regarding the walls near the so-called "forts" in Walnut Canyon, the imputation of military functions to a man-made structures which just as plausibly might have been ceremonial reflects more upon our own culture than that of the former inhabits of this region. It is currently fashionable in the academic world to iconoclastically contradict the erstwhile notion of the Anasazi and other ancient groups as "the Peaceful People" by pointing to evidence of extensive warfare or even cannibalism.₅₄ Indeed, the range of human experience is so broad and diversified that it is possible to find cultural examples fitting almost any hypothesis. Undoubtedly, archaeologists ages hence will discover evidence of the Holocaust, the dropping of atomic bombs on Hiroshima and Nagasaki, or other twentieth century atrocities and consequently label us "the Genocidal People," but we living in these times might question the veracity of this designation. If the ancient people of Perry Mesa could respond to such charges of warfare, what would they say?

Rock art is the only "language" through which the consciousness of these Ancient Ones can still be perceived. Perry Mesa is located in the mountainous, chaparral region between the Colorado Plateau and the upper Sonoran Desert. Hence the people who lived here did not grow crops to the degree that either the Anasazi to the north with their dry farming methods or the Hohokam to the south with their system of irrigation did. The people of this intermediate region lacked a true "agri-culture" (*agri-* etymologically meaning "field") but instead were primarily hunter-gathers who supplemented their diet by gardening. The petroglyphs and pictographs located mostly on the vertical cliff faces of the mesa reflect this cultural requisite. Accordingly, we find at Perry Mesa a preponderance of zoomorphs, especially depictions of elk, deer, antelope, and bighorn sheep. Sometimes shown with boat-shaped bodies and elaborately delineated antlers, examples of this rock art obviously served as an essential component in a system of sympathetic magic that shamans used to aid in the hunt. Few if any iconographic representations of warfare have been found. Thus, we can say that in all probability the people of Perry Mesa were relatively peaceful and tended to watch the star gods with the same sense of awe and veneration as the rest of the Ancient Ones of Arizona.

This region's sidereal correlative is Chi 1 Orionis, the tip of Orion's right hand. (See Fig. 27, p. 121.) Somewhat fainter than most of the other stars in the constellation, this celestial body has a magnitude of only 4.6. It is also anomalous vis-à-vis the rest of the stars that comprise Orion because of its relative nearness to Earth— only 29 light-years, in fact. Furthermore, it is a star much like our sun with a spectral type of G, indicating the same general temperature and age. The other star in Orion's right hand is Chi 2 Orionis, terrestrially corresponding to the ruins at Horseshoe Reservoir (not to be confused with Horseshoe Ranch on Perry Mesa or Horseshoe

Canyon in Utah.) This star has a magnitude of 4.7 and a light-year distance of 131. The farthest site south of all those yet discussed, Scorpion Point Village on the banks of the Verde River (before it was dammed) was a large pueblo occupied from A.D. 800-1000. Influenced by close connection to the Hohokam, it had two ball courts and grew an abundance of cotton, as evidenced by the plethora of seeds found in the excavated rooms. Road House Ruin, another site in the same area, possibly had ties to the Sinagua toward the north, since it, unlike the Hohokam, apparently used dry farming.[55]

We can conceive of the two stars Chi 1 and Chi 2 Orionis, representing Perry Mesa and Horseshoe Reservoir respectively, as forming a link between the Anasazi and the equally significant Hohokam culture. (See Chapter 12.) Orion's right arm, which reaches down from the high desert of the Colorado Plateau in the north to the low desert of the Sonoran Basin in the south, could have provided a symbolic bridge between these different environments. The data regarding these stars, specifically their relative closeness and similarity to our own Sun, will assume an almost monumental dimension when in the next section we discuss Orion's upper left limb.

*Fig. 34. Petroglyph of zoomorph inside sun shield, Perry Mesa*

*Fig. 35. Petroglyph of Orion's belt stars and sword, Perry Mesa*

## *The Left Arm of Orion*

"The view down the gulf of color and over the rim of its wonderful wall, more than any other view I know, leads us to think of our earth as a star with stars swimming in light, every radiant spire pointing the way to the heavens.... It seems a gigantic statement for even nature to make, all in one mighty stone word, apprehended at once like a burst of light, celestial in color its natural vesture, coming in glory to mind and heart as to a home prepared for it from the very beginning. Wildness so godful, cosmic, primeval, bestows a new sense of earth's beauty and size. Not even from high mountains does the world seem so wide, so like a star in glory of light on its way through the heavens."[56]

In his lush, exuberant prose John Muir expresses the majesty and divinity of Grand Canyon by invoking an image of celestial immensity, the awesome reaches of the night sky. Perhaps he knew more than he realized. A stellar correlative does indeed exist, but more specific than that of which the great naturalist had conceived.

The Hopi see Grand Canyon is the *quintessence* of their cosmology. The italicized term in its etymological sense is especially cogent to our discussion. The prefix "quint-" means five, a reference from medieval philosophy to the central fifth element ether, surrounded by the other traditional physical elements of earth, air, water, and fire. It is at the very heart of sacred space, represented in Anasazi/Hisatsinom rock art as a cross, a swastika, or a quadrilateral. Known as the great Sipapuni, Grand Canyon is located in the realm of the transcendental, a subterranean land of supreme spiritual significance for the Hopi. The central component of every kiva, or ceremonial lodge, is its *sipapu*, a small hole leading to the Underworld, both as an embodiment and an emblem of the greater passageway to this *sanctum sanctorum*. Marked by a large travertine dome, the actual point of entrance to this chthonic abyss is a mineral spring that lies along the Little Colorado River a few miles upstream from its confluence with the Colorado River. As a whole, Grand Canyon serves as the *omphalos*, or navel, of Grandmother Earth, to which all her children are inseparably linked. In his brilliant and passionate book *The Tragic, Sacred Ground*, Erling Duus describes a similar relationship in terms of the Lakota (Sioux) and the *axis mundi* of their holy Black Hills:

> "The Center of the Earth is not an appellation which can be derived simply from an outward manifestation, demonstrable and articulate to the rational consciousness. Rather, the source of this belief lies in the deep umbilical relationship whereby the body and soul of the people are attached in very identity to the mountains, to the underground of Wind Cave whence the people came, scaling upward to the granite peaks to look upon the new earth of creation. The Great Spirit, *Wakantanka*, and along with him the spirits of the ancestors are centered there more powerfully than at other places."[57]

Figuring in the mythology of most Native American tribes including the Hopi, a primordial journey of proto-human anthropoids was made from the nether plane upward to the present world. For the Hopi Grand Canyon is both the origin of their being and the source of all time. As mentioned in Chapter 1, the three previous "Worlds," or epochs, are located, one on top of the other, in the place beneath the bottom of the canyon. Throughout their lives Hopi males make obligatory pilgrimages to gather salt and perform oblations at the orifice of this interdimensional dynamo. When an individual dies, he or she journeys downward to join the ancestors there in an existence that to a great degree parallels the one lived here on the surface of the earth. Thus, the eschatological path into the spirit world is both spatially descendent and temporally retrograde. No wonder, then, that John Muir recognized this magnificent chasm which cuts through northern Arizona as a long-prepared-for *home*.

Virtually thousands of small, mostly unexcavated sites built by the Anasazi over the course of centuries lie eroding upon both rims and within the canyon itself. The largest of these is called Tusayan Ruin, located at the eastern end of the canyon's south rim near Lipan Point. In the 19th and early 20th centuries the term "Tusayan," which is a Spanish word meaning "people of the corn," was used to designate the province of Hopiland, especially the area of the three Mesas, but this usage has currently fallen into disfavor. Representing one of the westernmost pueblos of the Kayenta Anasazi, Tusayan Ruin contained approximately fifteen rooms, some two stories high. Constructed of limestone and mortar, it was built circa A.D. 1185 but abandoned by only the first or second decade of the following century. Home to about thirty people, seven or eight of these rooms were habitation units, while the rest were used for storage.[58] Tusayan was a U-shaped pueblo with the axis of each wing running northwest-southeast, not only to take advantage of the winter sunlight along the main living area and provide a plaza area but also to orient the structure toward the midwinter sunrise (120 degrees azimuth).[59]

Two partly subterranean, circular kivas with a diameter of nineteen to twenty feet each were also used ceremonially.[60] Four posts supported each of the roofs where a hatchway provided entry by ladder. It is thought that the kiva located on the corner where the southern wing joins the main row of living units had burned, only to be replaced by a second kiva located a few feet southeast of the northern wing in a refuse pile.[61] It appears from a diagram of the pueblo that the ventilator shaft of the former kiva was constructed to point northeast toward the midsummer sunrise (60 degrees azimuth), while the ventilator shaft of the latter kiva definitely points toward the midwinter sunrise. (Fig. 36, p. 146) This raises the possibility that the shafts not only functioned as air vents but also allowed the first few rays of sunrise to stream across the Coconino Plateau and penetrate the kivas on crucial solstice days. For this to occur, however, the vegetation was probably less dense, unlike today when the ruin itself rests in a pinyon and juniper forest.

Established at about the same latitude as Chaco Canyon far to the east, Tusayan had significant relations with a few other pueblo sites in the Four Corners region. As stated above, the ruin is oriented toward the southeast along an axis of 120 degrees azimuth. If we follow a line one degree south of this midwinter sunrise line for 135 miles, we end up about fifty miles east of Homol'ovi State Park at Puerco Ruin in Petrified Forest National Park.[62] On the other hand, if we follow a line from Tusayan along a 58 degrees azimuth reading (two degrees north of the summer solstice sunrise point) for a bit less than ninety miles, we arrive at Betatakin, fully discussed in Chapter 4. Continuing along this summer solstice sunrise line northeast another ninty-five miles, we arrive within a mile of Square Tower Ruin at Hovenweep National Monument. These three pueblos possibly could have functioned as reciprocal "sister" villages, relatively positioned along crucial solar pathways.

All the Hisatsinom ruins of Grand Canyon, including Tusayan, are represented sidereally by the left arm of Orion, sometimes depicted as holding a shield, the skin of a slain lion, or a perhaps a bow. This curving

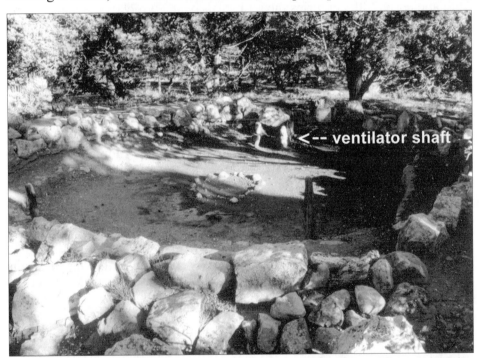

*Fig. 36. Round kiva with ventilator shaft aligned to winter solstice sunrise, Tusayan Ruin, south rim of Grand Canyon. Tusayan has a winter solstice sunrise relationship (southeast) with Puerco Ruin and a summer solstice sunset relationship (northwest) with Point Sublime. It also has a summer solstice sunrise relationship (northeast) with both Betatakin (Navajo National Monument) in northern Arizona and Hovenweep National Monument in southeastern Utah (Diagram 3, p. 32).*

line of six stars with Pi 1 at the top (south) and Pi 6 at the bottom (north) arcs across the eastern end of Grand Canyon, providing a link for chthonic energy via the constellation's arm to its torso and the correlative pueblos there. From this primordial Place of Emergence and destination for afterlife souls to the living villages of the Hopi found in the central part of the torso, the arm's east-west conduit serves as a fundamental spirit road between worlds. Moreover, it might even fulfill a more astonishing purpose: namely, that of an interstellar stepping-stone.

In this regard Pi 3 Orionis is of particular interest. This star is at the center of the shield or bow that Orion holds in his left hand, providing the initial point in the pathway along which the pyschospiritual energy of Grand Canyon is channeled— first to Wupatki/Bellatrix and then to the rest of the terrestrial constellation. Before we can talk about the significance of the terrestrial Orion, however, we must point out one aspect of the celestial one. In one sense Orion is itself astronomically unique. "Unlike most constellations such as Cassiopeia, which are meaningless line-of-sight coincidences, the constellation Orion is a group of stars associated in time and space."[63] In other words, many of the stars that comprise this apparent pattern forming an anthropoid hunter in the sky are in more or less the same stellar "neighborhood," which, by the way, is comparatively distant from Earth. For instance, Saiph, the farthest star in Orion, is 2,100 light-years away, while the closest, Betelgeuse, has a distance of about 520 light-years. The three stars of the belt are either 1,500 or 1,600 light-years from us. However, Pi 3 Orionis is anomalous in that it is one of two stars in the constellation which is, at least in cosmic terms, relatively close to us— only twenty-six light-years away. (The other is Chi 1 Orionis in the right arm, discussed in the previous section of this chapter.) The remaining Pi stars are consistent with the distance of the rest of Orion (with the exception of Pi 2, about ninety-three light-years away), but Pi 3 is conceivably reachable— that is, to a culture that has figured out SOL (speed-of-light) travel. (See Fig. 27, p. 121.)

In addition to a relatively close distance, the spectral type of Pi 3 somewhat resembles that of our own Sun. Technically called a G2 type, the Sun is a yellow dwarf star with a surface temperature of about 5,700 degrees K.[64] Pi 3 is a yellow-white dwarf star with a classification of F6, giving it a slightly hotter temperature of 6,000-7,500 degrees K.[65] Although not always the case, stars with similar temperatures are generally of the same size and age. Hotter stars are larger and younger while cooler stars are smaller and older. Only slighter larger and hotter than our Sun, Pi 3 has a magnitude of 3.19.[66] In addition, spectral analysis tries to detect the presence of ionized calcium, found in both G and F type stars. In essence, Pi 3 Orionis is quite a bit like the Sun, which is exactly what SETI (Search for Extra-Terrestrial Intelligence) researchers are looking for when they aim their giant radio telescopes toward the heavens to scan for signals of sentience.

Although life forms are probably ubiquitous throughout the universe, some scientists restrict their search to stellar objects closer to the Earth. According to Todd Henry of the Space Telescope Science Institute that oversees Project Phoenix, a "Best and Brightest Sample" includes only those stars within twenty parsecs (sixty-five light-years) as well as those which are similar to the Sun in color, size, age, and temperature.67 Pi 3 fits all those requirements. In fact, Pi 3 Orionis is star number 2185 in the SETI Star Catalogue. According to Dr. Peter R. Backus, manager of Phoenix Project, this star is too far north for its Australia radio telescope and a bit too far south for the one at Aricebo in Puerto Rico, given the limited amount of time allotted at the latter telescope. Thus, at this writing Pi 3 Orionis has not yet been surveyed.68

Orion's left arm (from Wupatki/Bellatrix to Grand Canyon/Pi 3) forms a summer solstice sunset line of 300 degrees azimuth. If we extend this line 200 miles into Nevada, we come within about twenty-five miles of Groom Lake, site of the infamous Area 51, otherwise known as Dreamland. (See Diagram 3, p. 32.) Like the Hopi Underworld of Grand Canyon, this region is replete with the chimeras of the subconscious, though it involves a more contemporary scenario of exobiology and extraterrestrial technology. If Orion's left (sinister) hand is conceptualized as holding a bow, then it is as if he were shooting his cold warrior-energy into the reputed repository of the alien Greys and their spacecraft. As stated in Chapter 1, the Hopi god Masau'u (whose celestial doppelgänger is Orion) bears a frightening resemblance to these creatures. (Fig. 2, p. 17)

With this in mind, perhaps it is more than a mere coincidence that another Orion line leads straight to the birth place of modern ufology. In Chapter 2 we said that the winter solstice sunrise line of 120 degrees azimuth connects Betatakin/Rigel and Canyon del Muerto/Saiph (Orion's feet) with Casamero Ruin south of Chaco Canyon, New Mexico. If we extend this line another 115 miles, we pass Mount Taylor (see p. 207) and directly intersect the Keresan-speaking Laguna Pueblo to arrive at Abó Ruins east of the Rio Grande at Salinas National Monument. This large pueblo built in the early 14th century with a Spanish mission added in the early 17th century may have been originally inhabited by ancestors of the Hopi and the Zuni.69 Following this solstice line roughly southeast another 125 miles brings us exactly to Roswell, New Mexico, close to the site of the putative July, 1947 flying saucer crash and retrieval of alien bodies.

A lesser-known saucer crash supposedly occurred nearly nine months later near Aztec, New Mexico. An undamaged disk about one hundred feet in diameter was said to contain the scorched, dead bodies of sixteen humanoids with an average height of three-and-a-half feet and an average weight of forty pounds. They had the typical huge heads and large, "slant" eyes of the Greys.70 This region is on a close summer solstice sunrise line of 65 degrees azimuth, connecting First Mesa/Alnitak and

Canyon de Chelly/Saiph with Aztec Ruins National Monument. (See p. 297, n. 8.) Are these still further cases of synchronicity (see pp. 40-41), echoing through time like ancestral voices in the caves of Grand Canyon?

As we have seen, Grand Canyon is of paramount spiritual and cosmological importance to the Hopi and was probably the same for their ancestors the Hisatsinom/Anasazi. For instance, below Point Sublime on the North Rim where one of the major Hopi shrines is located (see beginning of Chapter 2), enigmatic settlements located on top of nearly inaccessible pinnacles within the canyon have been spotted by helicopter with their original roofing apparently still intact.[71] Although these buildings resemble the placement of the island "forts" found in Walnut Canyon (see the section above on the head of Orion), the ultimate purpose of the structures remains a mystery.

We do know, however, that the presence of the Ancient Ones in Grand Canyon has been lengthy and pervasive. Effigies of bighorn sheep, deer, elk, or other animals dating from the Middle Archaic period more than 3,000 to 4,000 years ago have been found cached in some of its caves. Ranging from one to eight inches long and constructed from a single willow or cottonwood stem, these so-called split-twig figurines are thought to have played a part in a system of sympathetic hunting magic.[72] In addition, intriguing rock art found at the Shamans' Gallery (located in the western portion of Grand Canyon National Park) and at more than five other sites in the canyon has been dated from about this same period.[73] Executed in the Barrier Canyon (southeastern Utah) style, these life-size anthropomorphs stare back as ghostly presences of a distant and inscrutable past. "These are usually painted in dark red and are arranged in rows across the back walls of rock shelters and under overhangs. The figures are characteristically elongate and abstract in form, aesthetic factors that create an otherworldly aspect. Arms and legs may or may not be present... The figures are frequently decorated with white dots or linear patterns. Skeletal motifs also occur, and some figures have large staring eyes."[74]

What inspired the depiction of these imposing, eerie figures? Are they ecstatic inner visions of shamans or an attempt to render in paint upon Supai sandstone the tangible presence of the god Masau'u and his relatives? Although these pictographs indeed project an aura of the supernatural with their sometimes-horned heads and their frequently neckless, rectangular or trapezoidal bodies, are they truly "otherworldly," as the rock art expert suggests? If we consider the sidereal template of Orion reaching across the high desert to Grand Canyon, the mythical Place of Emergence, can we make that great stretch, both literally and figuratively, along his left arm to the firmament, in particular to Pi 3 Orionis? Is this sky portal the actual grand Sipapuni, the real origin of the Hisatsinom/Anasazi?

Considering the vast number of stars in the sky, we must admit that it is a very long shot. Nevertheless, the question remains: Could this be the code that the terrestrial/celestial schema of Orion is trying to convey? More specifically, are the Ancient Ones indeed the children of Masau'u who originated with their Father among the stars? The implications of an affirmative response to these questions, if they can be answered at all, would unequivocally alter the paradigms of our planetary evolution and prehistory. This leads to one final question: Are we prepared for the seismic shift in consciousness that such a far-reaching concept requires?

We might more readily answer 'yes' after exploring in the next chapter the unique spiritual phenomenon of the Hopi *katsinam*, especially those connected with the stars.

# Chapter 7
# A Rainbow Fading Into the Chasm
# Of Night—the Hopi Katsinam

"The shadows are now engulfing the village. The Kachinas who have been up all night, have nevertheless dominated the light of day from dawn to dusk with their insistent rhythm. Now amid the thunder of the drum they withdraw into the silent darkness of the sacred kiva like a rainbow fading into the chasm of night."[1]

Willoughby F. Senior

## *The Katsina Phenomenon: An Overview*

A scending at dawn from the subterranean shadows of the kiva, the *katsinam* (plural of *katsina*, also spelled *kachina*) stream into the sunlit plaza of the oldest village in North America. In a single file procession they step as one entity to the steady pulse of a single cottonwood drum. An oblong loop of spirit dancers soon forms inside the negative space created by clusters of low, masonry dwellings: a sacred circle within the square, one great *katsina* wheel turning in perfect synchronization to the rhythms of the seasons around the communal heart of Oraibi. Unlike the Plains Indians' sun dance songs that seem to aggressively pierce the firmament like rays of sunlight, these Hopi songs project a more moderate and reserved character. This is due in part to their voices being muffled by the extraordinary masks, which sometimes even resonate with a soft buzzing. More essentially, however, this sedentary native group's attention is primarily focused downward to the earth, urging the forces of fertility to rise. From daybreak to nightfall with only short intervals of rest, the singers' intoned prayers are pressed into the ground by a series of unremitting dance steps, thereby assisting the tellurian cycle of horticultural growth in an extremely harsh land. At last the sun slips beyond the western rim of the horizon and is gone, making its diurnal descent to the Underworld.

The annual departure to the Underworld of the *katsinam* coincides with the date when the setting sun is at a significant azimuthal point on the horizon. The sixteen-day-long Niman (Katsinam Going Home) Ceremony begins four days after the summer solstice.[2] Because the solstice occurs on June 21st, the last day of Niman is usually July 11. In some cases the ceremony extends past mid-July, but occasionally it has been known to occur as late as July 24.[3] On this latter date in A.D. 1300 (the approximate period that the *katsina* cult was instituted) the sun set at 292 degrees azimuth in relation to Oraibi, just over three degrees north of the great

Sipapuni (located on the Little Colorado River a few miles east of its confluence with the Colorado at the bottom of Grand Canyon— see Chapter 6). Even if the ceremony concluded on the more common date of July 11th, the sun set in the same year at about 295 degrees azimuth, only about six degrees north of the Sipapuni. Hence, at the end of Niman both the sun and the *katsinam* retire together to the point on the horizon where the Sipapuni that leads to the Underworld is located, thereby concluding the *katsina* season. Not surprisingly, the Powamu Society chief from the Katsina Clan assumes the duty of watching the western horizon after the sun god Tawa leaves his summer "house" on the solstice.4

The only other time that the sun set at 292 degrees azimuth in A.D. 1300 was in early May. At this same time Orion hovered over the western horizon, with Rigel just touching it at thirty-four degrees to the south. Of course, the sun's last rays would have obscured the constellation. Even though Orion was invisible, competent sky watchers nevertheless would have known that it was there by the relative positions of other constellations a few hours later. Perhaps it is no coincidence, then, that the Hopi conduct in May a spinach gathering ritual called Nevenwehe in which Masau'u (i.e., Orion), god of death and the Underworld, plays a major role.5

The long day of the *katsinam* —seemingly made even longer by the drum's ever present heartbeat and the drone of rain-bringing songs rising from parched throats— is at an end. As the sun god Tawa descends to his nightly nether abode, the dancers go down to repose once again in the darkness of the kiva— the quintessential model of the Underworld, an *imago inferno*, so to speak. After a brief evening thunderstorm undoubtedly induced by the psychospiritual energy of the ceremony, their effulgence fades in the mind's eye as gracefully as that prismatic emblem arching over Arizona's high desert plateau.6

Although the auditory dimension of the Katsina Phenomenon seems to issue from the earth itself, the visual aspect that the dancers display —i.e., their "rainbow"— is another matter altogether. Amid this desert landscape of pale sandstone and muted earth tones, the stately yet primordial presence of the *katsinam* strikes the eye with the startling brilliance of their vivid primary colors. Clan kilts and sashes, fox fur and turkey feathers, eagles plumes and bandoleers, blue spruce or pinyon ruffs, yucca whips and willow bows, moccasined feet and painted bodies, swastika gourd rattles and knee bells, turquoise pendants and tortoise shell leg tinklers— the variation is endless. A dizzying array of multi-hued costumes and accouterments clad and equip these sundry spirit messengers as they dance for rain or the general well being of the Hopi *sinom* ("people"). "The kachina is a *paho* [prayer messenger], so is the *tihü*, the figurine [i.e., the *katsina* doll]. Aside from the conventional significance of its details, the costume is also distinctly of a decorative intent because the deities are naturally attracted by beautiful objects. When the deities see elaborate and brilliantly decorated kachina personators, they say, 'Aha, what beautiful objects are those, they must be the admirable kachina of the Hopi!'"[7] With the exception of the Mudhead Katsina classified as a clown or trickster figure and associated with the subterranean Third World which preceded the present one, the *katsinam* project a general impression of otherworldly inscrutability that is awe-inspiring to humans but apparently endearing to the gods.

Perhaps the most preternatural feature of all is their masks. Originally made from buckskin but now from stitched rawhide or stretched cloth which extends completely around the head, they manifest multifarious forms: cylindrical, square, circular, ovoid, dome-shaped, etc. Some are adorned with horns, feathers, or dark hair; others, like the Niman (or Home Going) Katsina, have brightly painted tablitas rising from the tops of their heads like clouds stylized in stepped formation. Some appear three dimensionally bug-eyed, others merely have painted slits for eyes, while still others have no eyes at all. Several exhibit cylindrical or squash-shaped snouts, while some display sharp fangs or lolling tongues. A few have ears but many lack noses. Unless they are clearly representative of animal or bird spirits, some *katsinam* even project the uncanny appearance of wearing helmets of an undetermined alien origin rather than masks.

Regardless of style, however, the most important function of the mask is to impart temporary spirithood to its wearer. In other words, when a man [8] puts on a mask, he actually becomes the spirit that it represents. (Before we dismiss this as mere primitive belief, we should remember that the Eucharistic bread and wine are sacramentally transmuted to the actual body and blood of Christ.) The Hopi always refer to these masks by the term *íkwatci* (*kwaatsi*), "my friend or double," rather than the word *tuviku*, which literally means "mask."[9] Ritually fed and kept within the family and clan for generations, *katsina* masks are actual beings that supersede any notion of the purely representational. They are, in fact, the embodiment of the spirit world.

But who are these "friends?" Like most aspects of the exceedingly complex Hopi religion, this is not easy to determine. (Despite the fact that our book deals with the Anasazi/Hisatsinom rather than the modern Hopi, we shall try to answer in terms of the latter, since we can access evidence only from their oral tradition. However, the two are very closely aligned across the temporal continuum.) In the simplest sense the *katsinam* are intercessory spirits that can take on the form of any manifold physical object, phenomenon, or creature in this world. Being distinct from the Hopi pantheon, they are not worshipped per se, though certain deities, such as Masau'u, can alternately appear as *katsinam*. "Not only men and animals, but plants, stones, mountains, and storms, astral bodies, clouds, sky, and underground spirits which may be evil or beneficent toward human beings and which may be propitiated or defeated by certain prescribed acts. These spirits are personified as Katchinas [variant spelling of *katsina*], who come into our modern world trailing tatters of everything historical or legendary in the Hopi past."10 Most observers of Hopi culture, however, have more or less discounted the negative role of the *katsinam*, which, according to one prominent anthropologist, are perceived "...as a host of benevolent spirits who have the best interests of the Hopi ever at heart."11 In addition to restricting our discussion to this "past" (while at the same time acknowledging the many fine books written about contemporary *katsina* practices 12), we shall furthermore limit our inquiry in the following section of this chapter to the *katsinam* associated particularly with the celestial plane.

These animistic spirit helpers, whose legion is acknowledged to be more than two hundred and is constantly augmented by new types 13, inhabit the terrestrial realm during only half of the year. In particular the *katsina* season stretches from the winter solstice when they arrive from the spirit world until after the summer solstice when (viz., around mid-July) they return to their homes, which are either on the San Francisco Peaks and a few other primary mountains or in the Underworld and a few other primary springs. The former residence stresses their association with rain clouds that linger around the mountain tops while the latter residence emphasizes their subterranean connection to ancestral spirits. However, the Hopi conceptualize these two dimensions not as disparate but as complementary. This apparent dichotomy is merely another permutation of their dualistic cosmology. (The dual universe of the Hopi/Hisatsinom is discussed in Chapter 3.) "The clouds hide not only the faces of the Hopi's departed ancestors who, taking pity on their grandchildren, are bringing them rain, but an almost infinite variety of kachinas who have other functions beside bringing rain."14

During the non-*katsina* season other dances are held, but they do not involve these particular supernatural powers, which at that time are repeating the same ceremonies in the spirit world. After the kivas are ritually "opened" at the beginning of the *katsina* season, the sacred entities again stream forth through the *sipapu* of each kiva as well as through the great Sipapuni of Grand Canyon to perform their duties on Earth. The constellation of villages with their concomitant kivas hence forms a sort of supernatural transit plexus analogous to an urban subway system through which the *katsinam* may journey to emerge at various distant nodes upon the terrestrial body of Orion.

Etymologically the term *katsina* is perhaps derived from the word *kátci*, "spread out," "horizontal," or "surface of the earth" and *náa*, "father," thus giving to the term a literal meaning of "surface of the land father."15 In this sense the *katsinam* are possibly related to Masau'u, the god of the earth. One author believes that *kachi* refers to "life father" or "spirit father," but the horizontal sense of reclining can be interpreted as "...a 'sitter.' i.e., one who sits with the people (and among other things, listens to their petitions for rain and other spiritual and material blessings)."16 This description parallels that of the angelic entities discussed in the apocryphal Book of Enoch, who are deemed "the Watchers." In fact, one of the kivas on the First Mesa village of Walpi is called *Wikwa'lobi*, "Place of the Watchers." This kiva holds the esoteric rituals pertaining to the exoteric form of the Snake Dance Ceremony.17 In addition, Sótuknang, the Heart of the Sky god, is also known as "the Watcher."18 (See a further discussion of the Watchers in the final section of this chapter.)

The word *katsina* is also interesting in light of the fact that it is an apparent import. "There is no translation for katsina. It is certainly a borrowed word. (Emory Sekaquaptewa: personal communication.) Foremost, there is no initial syllable *ka-* in Hopi. Evidence to suggest it is a borrowed term from outside the Pueblo area, rather than being indigenous, lies in the similarity of its pronunciation in the Zuni language and in Keresan spoken in Acoma."19 From this evidence we can deduce that the *katsinam* and their correlates in other pueblo groups were derived from a single, monolithic source. Ultimately, we have a case in which these spirit beings of foreign origin wearing transmundane helmets and bizarre regalia once sat with the people and listened to their pleas for succor. These intermediaries of such primary deities as Masau'u (god of earth, fire, and death) or Sótuknang (god of the sky, lightning, and stars) once apparently walked amongst the Hisatsinom to provide physical aid and spiritual guidance. Still, whence did they come, and why?

Many Hopi legends suggest how the *katsinam* once presented themselves to the Ancient Ones in the flesh but now pay their annual visits merely in spirit form. In his marvelous autobiography, Don C. Talayesva states: "My fathers and uncles showed me the ancestral masks and explained that long ago the real Katcinas had come regularly to Oraibi and had danced in the plaza. They explained that since the people had become so wicked —since there were now so many Two-Hearts in the world— the Katcinas had stopped coming in person and sent their spirits to enter the masks on dance days. They showed me how to feed the masks by placing food on their mouths and taught me to respect them and pray to them."20 Among other things these comments reflect the ubiquitous native belief that former eras were spiritually pristine, while later times have unavoidably undergone a process of spiritual devolution and degradation. Some legends suggest that the *katsinam* first appeared during very ancient times, i.e., at the emergence into the Fourth World and the initial migrations. "The spirits of the masks that are kept in the maternal houses of certain lineages, the kachina chiefs, are thought of as clan ancestors, not progenitors, but as beings encountered in the early clan migrations just as plants and animals were encountered and 'taken into the clan'."21 If this is indeed the case, then the Hisatsinom were presented with these anomalous spiritual entities along with Masau'u in the process of establishing the villages that would eventually constitute the body of Orion we find manifested on the high desert.

Archaeological evidence as well suggests a foreign origin for the so-called "*katsina* cult." The capability of humans to merge with the various spirits inhabiting heaven and earth is *the* unique aspect of the Katsina Phenomenon that distinguishes it from all other North American masked dances.22 Considering this factor in conjunction with the uniform terminology for the *katsinam* among the pueblos of Arizona and New Mexico, we can conclude that this ritualistic system did not evolve gradually in an independent manner among the region's various indigenous groups. Instead we can imagine a scenario in which the Hisatsinom initially interacted with the physical creatures that came to be known as *katsinam* in a restricted geographic region and within a limited temporal span.23 Most archaeologists agree that the *katsinam* actually came from the south, viz. Mexico, and may have entered the Four Corners region via two separate routes: 1. the Rio Grande Valley from A.D. 1000-1200 and 2. the San Pedro Valley from A.D. 1250-1400.24 Of possible significance to our discussion of Chaco Canyon in the next chapter, petroglyphic and pictographic evidence from that first wave enigmatically shows many *katsina* figures with large, almond-shaped eyes and tiny, triangular noses.

Rock art expert Sally J. Cole believes that the *katsina* influence in Arizona, however, was the result of the second influx. At Homol'ovi (discussed in Chapter 4 of our book) she found eighty-nine examples of "mask-katsina representatives," some having the rectangular bodies and upraised arms akin to the Masau'u/Orion paradigm.26 "...it is surmised that katsina cult iconography is associated with more recent prehistoric occupations of the Little Colorado River region that include the period between A.D. 1250 and 1400 when aggregated pueblos of Homol'ovi were occupied."27 Thus, at least in Arizona the Katsina Phenomenon probably began about a century and a half after the first villages were established on the Hopi Mesas.

The presence of the *katsinam* has no doubt profoundly affected the Hisatsinom culture and altered the course of its development, both in ceremonial and architectural ways. This cult cuts across various clan affiliations; therefore, it functions integratively. An increased village size during this period of origination allowed for both greater centralization and greater concentration of the populace, which consequently maximized social continuity, thereby facilitating interclan cooperation. Furthermore, during this period the *katsina* cult became focused upon the sympathetic production of rainfall. This emphasis was perhaps the result of the adversities of the Great Drought, which occurred during the last quarter of the thirteenth century. By circa A.D. 1300 most of the Anasazi settlements to the north had been abandoned. In the new construction of pueblos during the late thirteenth and early fourteenth centuries, large enclosed plazas, each customarily equipped with its village *sipapu*, were incorporated as a ritualized space wherein *katsina* dances could be held. These plazas subsequently replaced the Great Kivas as centers of communal activity. In addition, smaller rectangular kivas mirroring the plaza structure (and, incidentally, the morphology of Orion) were built instead of the traditional round kivas.

At any rate, we can conclude that the *katsinam* were an extrinsic force that irrevocably altered the tenor of Pueblo culture. Initially they were perceived not as spirits but as benevolent physical entities who had come into the land of the Hisatsinom from some distant place. As the Hopi, Zuni, and Keresan language groups all attest, the very name of this cult is exogenous to the region. One myth in particular (a portion of which was mentioned in Chapter 5 in connection with the Sunset Crater volcanic eruption) reveals the eerily alien nature of the *katsinam*. After a series of ordeals on the San Francisco Peaks (paralleling the Greek myth of Psyche and Eros), a young bride accompanies her handsome Ka'nas Katsina husband back to her village of Mishongnovi.

> "This time on their way home, the two were going to travel by flying shield. Together they climbed onto the shield and the girl firmly shut her eyes. As the shield lifted off, the kachinas all gave out a boisterous yell. The spectacle was incredible; every sort of kachina conceivable was present. All of a sudden as the couple flew along, flashes of lightning were visible in the air and the rumble of thunder could be heard. When the shield rose higher, drizzle began to fall. The kachinas were now accompanying them. They actually followed the pair in the form of clouds.... Customarily, a bride is returned to her residence in the morning. Therefore the parents had headed to the edge of the mesa at this time to look out. Looking down from the rim of the mesa, they saw an incredible number of people coming across the plain. To their great amazement all were kachinas, singing and crying out their calls in a pandemonium."[28]

As it advanced toward Second Mesa from the sacred peaks, this entourage of diverse divine messengers bearing a huge quantity of corn and melons on their backs as gifts for the Hopi must have been a stunningly beautiful sight. In fact, the Hopi sometimes refer to the *katsinam* as "the beautiful creatures."[29] This designation emphasizes not only their aesthetically pleasing appearance, both to the gods and to the Hisatsinom/Hopi, but also their role as persons in a kinship system. As noted above, the *katsinam* were adopted into the clans along with various plants and animals during the migrations that followed the emergence from the Underworld. Hence, their presence had been clearly corporeal and tangible as opposed to supernatural and ethereal. In other words, their influence once was directly discerned on a material level. As time went on, however, the social and religious corruption —a recurring motif in Hisatsinom/Hopi thought— forced these strange but munificent "people" to abandon the Southwest. After that period which extends into the present, the *katsinam* may be accessed only via their spirit forms.

The "magical" flying vehicle, or *paatuwvota*, mentioned above is a recurrent *deus ex machina* in Hopi legends. The term *paa* refers to water; thus, *paatuwvota* can also mean the expanding concentric rings in water. This might be a metaphorical description for the way the peculiar aerial device appeared to function. A related word is *patuka*, or spindle, which might also describe the shield's spinning motion. The prefix *pa-*, on the other hand, denotes wonder or awe, which for a desert people is usually associated with water, but could also refer to this extraordinary means of transportation. The word *tuwvota* signifies a warrior shield. If we recall, the concept of war is frequently connected in Hopi ideology with the stars. Hence, the use of *tuwvota* rather than the term *ngœla*, "disk" or "circle," suggests a celestial origin for the *paatuwvota*.30

For pueblo peoples the shield has transcendent connotations in general. For instance, the Zuni, geographically and culturally the closest tribe to the Hopi though linguistically distinct, perceived this artifact on a number of various levels. "On a more esoteric level, beyond being an implement of war, the shield was viewed as a metaphor for transformation, or more specifically as a symbolic portal for the passage of the transformed spirit between two realms... The two realms equate conceptually with such universal dualities as 'nature' and 'supernature,' the material and spiritual, or (in the context of war) the living and the dead."31 Thus, even though the *katsinam* originally presented themselves in the physical realm together with their mystical paraphernalia, they represented a higher, more pristine state of existence symbolized by a passage to the spirit world.

### The Katsina "Friends" From the Stars: Mastop, Ahöla, Eototo, Sótuknang, and Sohu

Among the ever-burgeoning ranks of the *katsinam* are those whose aspects in some way reflect the sidereal realm. Briefly mentioned in Chapter 3 in connection with the winter solstice ceremony of Soyal, the Mastop Katsina is one of those. (Fig. 37, p. 159) This *katsina* found only on Third Mesa comes from the northwest— the direction of Grand Canyon's Sipapuni and hence associated with death. In fact, the translation of the name for this messenger is Death Fly.32 Always arriving in pairs, he and his twin appear on the second to the last day of the Soyal ceremony, a time of long nights and great darkness. Their bodies are painted black or dark brown and they both wear a woman's old, discarded kilt or in former times a bobcat skin. Usually one white handprint is painted on their chests, giving a rather arresting impression (at least to the contemporary eye), and other smaller handprints are painted on their legs and upper arms. They both carry a short black-and-white striped staff (à la Orion's club?) in their right hands with which to beat the dogs as they make their way through the village. Antically leaping about, each Mastop dashes up to a crowd of females, grabs one of them by the shoulders from behind, and makes a series of short hops which simulate copulation. After this somewhat humorous pantomime, they rush to the Chief Kiva in order to confer with the priests in disguised voices. Then they suddenly run back to the cluster of females, repeating this serious fertility ritual (despite the antics) until all of them have been approached in a similar manner.[33]

The celestial connection of Mastop is made apparent when viewing his black, cylindrical helmet with a rounded crown. On each side of the mask is painted a grouping of white dots representing stars. One author claims that the right side is the Pleiades and the left side is the Great Bear.[34] However, the V-shaped configuration just as easily could represent the Hyades of Taurus, or perhaps the belt of Orion in conjunction with Sigma Orionis, which trails off from Alnitak. This wedge-shaped grouping of stars on each side of the *katsina*'s head might even signify Orion's belt together with his sword, the latter containing Iota Orionis and the fertile star seeds of the Great Nebula, M-42 and M-43. (See final section of this chapter.) Given the virile aspect of Mastop, Orion's phallic sword is an appropriate mask decoration. However, Harold S. Colton, Director Emeritus of the Museum of Northern Arizona, claims that this *katsina* is

*Fig. 37. Mastop katsina doll, Museum of Northern Arizona*

*Fig. 38. Ahöla katsina doll, Museum of Northern Arizona*

also associated with Masau'u, thus stressing the dual aspects of fertility and death.35 As we have heretofore discussed in detail, Masau'u is the deity most closely related in Hopi cosmology to the constellation Orion.

Among the so-called chief (*mongwi*) *katsinam*, Ahöla, or Ahül, deserves our attention in particular. (Fig. 38, p. 159) As one of the *katsinam* who arrives at the winter solstice and who also formally opens the *katsina* season by visiting each kiva at the Powamu (bean sprouting) ceremony in February, this spirit messenger "...is a priest katsina of high order. He is commonly referred to as the Ahölwutaqa, meaning that he is an elderly, wise chief."36 The Hisatsinom passed down to the Hopi a legend of his determined leadership. "Led by Ahül they first started from the San Francisco Mountains, went far to the great river in the east [Rio Grande?] and then turned back west, and their houses are still at the waters where they stopped during this migration."37 The latter river mentioned is possibly the Little Colorado, where rest the ruins at Homol'ovi near Winslow, Arizona. (See Chapter 4.) In addition, this legend emphasizes the corporeal nature of Ahöla actually walking with his people, at least in the very early times, rather than providing merely an unseen spiritual presence.

Ahöla's most striking feature is a circular mask, fringed with a corona of eagle feathers and red horsehair. A black-and-white horizontal band divides the lower third of the mask, while a similar vertical band bisects the upper two-thirds of the mask. The lower third is customarily painted black, while dark equilateral crosses representing stars cover the upper two-thirds, the background of which is usually painted brown (though sometimes green) on his left side and yellow on his right side. Between the upper two-thirds and the lower third a black triangle points downward to a wooden beak. Ahöla wears a white shirt and white kilt, leggings of white mesh cloth, green moccasins, and sometimes a fox fur or spruce ruff around his neck. He is also seen occasionally with a red dance sash hanging on his right side. In his right hand he carries either a cornmeal bag or a ceremonial wand tied with eagle feathers, a crook, and an ear of corn. In his left hand he carries a netted gourd and *mongko* (see description in the next chapter), the chief *katsinam*'s badge of authority.38

Jesse Walter Fewkes, a preeminent ethnographer of the Hopi, believed that Ahöla was just one of many aliases of an ancient anthropomorphic Sky-god. Depending upon the specific village, this deity was variously called Wüwüyomo ("Ancient Being"), Wupamow ("Great-One-Above"), and Ahülani (from the Hopi word *ahülti*, or "return").39 He was even identified with the Star Priest of the winter solstice ceremony (see Chapter 2), and was also known as "Old Man Sun." Thus, he was responsible for the sun's return at midwinter dawn. At any rate, the importance of the celestial phenomena in Hopi religion should be acknowledged, despite those who contend that the Hisatsinom/Hopi were mainly concerned with the earth. "As every altar has one or more such designs [of the Sky-god] upon it, it is not too much to conclude that sky worship is one of the most important elements in the Hopi ritual."40

Another chief *katsina* of paramount importance is Eototo. (Fig. 39, p. 162) He is known as the father of the *katsinam*, partly because he knows all of the ceremonies by heart. As the spiritual counterpart of the village chief, his presence evokes great reverence among the people during his ritual duties at Powamu in February and Niman in July. His costume is very similar to that of Ahöla, and he too carries the netted gourd and *mongko*. Eototo's mask, however, is very different from Ahöli's. More like a helmet, this pure white, unadorned cylinder with a rounded crown lacks a nose and has mere black dots for eyes and mouth. Fewkes theorized that Eototo in his capacity as a germination spirit was in fact merely another manifestation of Masau'u. (In Chapter 3 we mentioned the close relationship between Masau'u and the germ god Muy'ingwa, alternately known in his *katsina* capacity as Alosaka, the Two Horn Priest.) Furthermore, Fewkes thought that Ahöla, the spirit of arrival, and Eototo, the spirit of departure, were complimentary aspects of the same Sky-god, each performing essential functions at the beginning and the end of every *katsina* season.

> "In the personnel of each there is a masked man [who is] their leader, known in the advent drama as the Sun-god; in the exit, the Germ-god. The shape of the mask of the former [viz., Ahöla], its radiating feathers and horsehair, represents the sun's disk; the head covering of the latter [viz., Eototo], a simple bag or gourd without ornament, a fitting symbol of the underworld. In their objective symbolism these two have little in common, and yet theoretically there is good evidence to regard them as variants of the same being, the magic power of the sky, the genitor of men, animals, and plants; one designated by the mask of the sun; the other, the ruler of the underworld, home of the ancients, the old Fire-god [i.e., Masau'u] or Germ-god [i.e., Muy'ingwa], male parent of all beings."41

Hence, we are confronted with a conflation of deities and *katsinam* that makes any strict nomenclature impossible. This inability to precisely categorize spirit beings does not bother the Hopi; therefore, it should not greatly trouble us either.

Another star being is found in the personage of Sótuknang, who is both a deity and a *katsina*. Some Hopi legends say that he was instructed by the sun god Tawa to create the world. The reader may recall from Chapter 1 that he is the same figure dressed in clothing covered with "icicles" that rescued a brother and sister from a great flood, taking them for a ride on his *paatuwvota*, or flying shield. His name literally means "heart of the sky" or "heart of the stars."₄₂ His name also "...connotes master or manager of the universe."₄₃ Hence, he is concerned with keeping the cosmos in balance. As heretofore mentioned, the star Aldebaran in the constellation Taurus is thought to be his fiery red eye. In addition to the implementation of his sidereal purview, thereby imparting a warrior nature in the mind of the Hopi, he also is the god of lightning and thunder, two violent forces that in the desert usually accompany life-giving rain. Unlike the deity Masau'u, however, Sótuknang remains dignified, silent, and aloof from the mundane activities of humans. Ergo, he became a strategic point of reference in the Christian missionaries' mostly unsuccessful attempt at evangelism.

In contradistinction to the germination god Muy'ingwa of the Two Horn Society, Sótuknang has either a single curved horn on the top of his head or a high peaked hat resembling a Phrygian cap. He wears moccasins

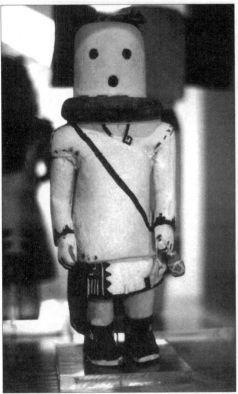

*Fig. 39. Eototo katsina doll, Museum of Northern Arizona. Note white, cylinder-shaped helmet. This katsina may be a variation of Masau'u/Orion, Hopi god of the Underworld.*

*Fig. 40. Sohu Katsina, embroidery applique (design by Clifford Bahnimptewa). Note three stars on its crest, representative of Orion's belt. For correlations to other cultures, see p. 182 and p. 241.*

and a plain white kilt, and his body is painted either blue-gray with the sediment from the bottom of a water hole 44 or white. His mask is adorned on both cheeks with either the opposing arrowhead emblem (the petroglyph which, as we saw in Chapter 2, denotes warfare) or terraced rain clouds. In his left hand he carries a framework of expandable crossed sticks representing lightning, and in his right he holds a bull roarer representing thunder.45

On a Flute altar in Oraibi Fewkes found a carved figure, reputed to be Sótuknang, of an anthropomorphic bird with zigzag lightning designs down long, slender legs. He thought this was a homologue of the Northern Plains mythical Thunder Bird 46, in Lakota (Sioux) known as *Wakinyan*. In addition to appearing in the mixed *katsina* dances, Sótuknang participates in the puppet ceremony usually held in March (described briefly in the Wupatki section of Chapter 4), which involves Palulukang, the horned (or plumed) serpent. In some cases Sótuknang is associated with Morning Star, so his Mesoamerican connection with the Mayan Kukulkán (the Aztec deity Quetzalcóatl), whose emblematic star is Venus, seems particularly apt. As omniscient chief of all creation, Sótuknang possesses the additional attribute of "Watcher" or "Protector."47 (See further discussion below.) This suitably complements one of the connotations of the actual word *katsina*, i.e., "one who listens."

Undoubtedly many other *katsinam* with sidereal aspects exist, but the final one we shall discuss is called Sohu, or Star Katsina. (Fig. 40, p. 162) His most prominent feature is the three vertical four-pointed stars arranged horizontally in a row across the top of his head.48 These, of course, bring to mind the most important constellation in Hopi cosmology, Orion, in particular his belt. These stars are interspersed between four vertical eagle feathers. This *katsina* has dark straight hair, goggle eyes, and diamond-shaped teeth. On his right cheek is painted an equilateral cross (star), on his left a crescent moon. He wears a fringed buckskin shirt and a kilt made of radiating turkey feathers, both of which are peculiar attire for a *katsina*. As Barton Wright succinctly notes, "He does not resemble the usual Hopi Kachina."49 Fewkes says that Sohu has stars painted on his forearms and legs. He holds yucca whips in both hands and a fox skin trails behind him.50

Fewkes remarks that the figure described above is the First Mesa (Walpi) version of Sohu, which he spells Coto. The Third Mesa (Oraibi) variation, he says, appears with a single large four-pointed star in the middle of a square mask. It also wears a trailing eagle feather headdress customary to the Plains Indians. The latter *katsina*, however, is commonly known as Na-ngasohu, the Chasing Star (or Planet) Katsina, and is thought to represent a comet.51 At any rate, these both have foreign elements which apparently derive from the east or northeast.

Perhaps they even originated in the territory of Skidi Pawnee, an extinct Nebraska tribe with many correspondences to the Hopi. For instance, the four-pointed star motif was also ubiquitously employed in the cultural accouterments of the Pawnee. A photograph of a Pawnee chief from the early 1900s shows a large four-pointed star on the front of his ceremonial hat.52 A leather star chart has also been recovered, showing the positions of various constellations using both four-pointed stars to represent the major sidereal points and equilateral crosses for the minor stars.

The four-pointed star is also a recurrent motif at Pottery Mound in New Mexico, located southeast of Acoma Pueblo on the west bank of the Rio Puerco, a tributary of the Rio Grande. A series of mural frescoes found in a number of excavated rectangular kivas depict four-pointed stars with human faces, which an Acoma informant has deemed "soul faces." Many of these star faces have feather ruffs, some of which are attached to rattlesnakes.53 Here too we find the feathered serpent archetype so rife in the mythology of Mexico. In fact, this large pueblo three to four stories high and occupied from A.D. 1300 to 1475 was built on a flat-topped, pyramid-shaped mound, which suggests a Mesoamerican influence.54

### The Watchers and the Summer Home of the Katsinam

In this chapter we have outlined the Katsina Phenomenon and have examined a few of the celestial *katsinam*. We have also noted that this colorful and diverse group of spiritual intercessors came to the American Southwest from somewhere afar. We have furthermore stated that the Hopi called them the Watchers or the Protectors (*Tuuwalaqa*).55 As mentioned above, this is precisely the term that the Apocrypha use to describe angelic entities. "The Apocryphal books tell us this: Originally the angels, or Sons of God, all surveyed the world and its beings from on high, and among them were those called the Grigori or Watchers. 'The Watchers' can be translated with several shades of meaning, and depending on the translator means 'observers' or 'sentinels, sleepless ones'; whether they are vigilant or simply curious, they watch."56 The Watchers are even mentioned in the canonized Bible, viz., in Daniel 4:13: "I saw in the visions of my head upon my bed, and, behold, a watcher and an holy one came down from the heaven;". Incidentally, this dreamer's name is Nebuchadnezzar (also Nebuchadrezzar), the legendary king of Babylon, who received prophecies regarding his fate. On the other hand, the Hebrew patriarch Enoch learned prodigious occult wisdom from these Watchers. In Chap. 92, verse 3 of his non-canonical book, he states: "Concerning these things will I speak, and these things will I explain to you, my children: I who am Enoch. In consequence of that which has been shown to me, from my heavenly vision and from the voice of the *holy angels* [italics added; a Qumran text reads instead "Watchers and Holy Ones"] have I acquired knowledge; and from the tablet of heaven have I acquired understanding."57 This is perhaps closely akin to knowledge found on the

Hopi stone tablets. (See Chapter 5.)

The term "the Watchers" also refers to the so-called fallen angels, who lusted after and mated with human females, thereby creating the Biblical race of giants (Genesis 6:1-4) called the Nephilim. (One of these gargantuan figures was Nimrod, who, as mentioned in Chapter 3, is equated mythologically with Orion.) In Arizona many similar legends exist in which *katsinam* take Hopi women as brides. For instance, a Póngo (Circle) Katsina marries an Oraibi maiden and fathers two children, who are also Circle Katsinam. After she commits adultery with a Hotóto Katsina, however, the husband kills her. Subsequently her "skeleton" (ghost?) continues to pursue him in order to avenge her death until both are finally turned into stars by Flute priests. "The two stars, Nangö'sohu [literally "chasing stars"] pursue each other because one constantly follows the other, sometimes overtaking it and then again remaining behind, are these two personages."58 Giants inhabit Hopiland as well, as demonstrated by the common presence of both the Chaveyo (Giant) and the Soyoko (Ogre) Katsinam.

Referring again to *The Book of Enoch*, we find that the chief Watcher is named Azazyel, who "...taught men to make swords, knives, shields, breastplates [i.e., artifacts of war, Orion's purview], the fabrication of mirrors, and the workmanship of bracelets and ornaments, the use of paint, the beautifying of the eyebrows, the use of stones of every valuable and select kind, and all sorts of dyes [i.e., articles of beautification], so that the world became altered."59 Finally the world's iniquity became so great with impiety and fornication (a common Hopi motif as well) that the loyal archangels (the "good" Watchers) swept down to annihilate the "evil" Watchers who reputedly had polluted human values. As a result, Azazyel was stoned to death, only to be cast into a lake of eternal fire on Judgment Day. (Chap. 10, verses 6-9) His grave is thought to be a heap of stones at the foot of the cliff of Haradan in the Sinai Desert, to which the scapegoat bearing Israel's collective sins was annually driven. Particularly relevant in this context is the comment made in Chapter 2 of our book that the chief Hopi deity Masau'u functions as the god of cairns. "Alternately, he [Azazyel] is sometimes said to have hurled himself into the sky and become the constellation Orion."60 At this point we should remember that Masau'u, whom we equated with Orion, is also frequently represented in *katsina* form, and thus is technically a Watcher as well.

In the pseudoepigraphal *Book of Jubilees* composed in the second century B.C. from earlier sources 61, we encounter a figure named Kainam, the grandson of Noah.

> "And the son grew, and his father [Arpachshad] taught him writing, and he went to seek for himself a place where he might seize for himself a city. And he found a writing which former (generations) had carved on the rock, and he read what was thereon, and he transcribed it and sinned

owing to it; for it contained the teaching of the Watchers in accordance with which they used to observe the omens of the sun and moon and stars in all the signs of heaven. And he wrote it down and said nothing regarding it; for he was afraid to speak to Noah about it lest he should be angry with him on account of it."[62]

Here we see that the teachings of the Watchers regarding astronomical lore are transmitted in much the same manner as the Hopi might have received information, viz., via petroglyphs. More importantly though, the name Kainam bears a striking resemblance to the plural form of the name for the Hopi spiritual benefactors, viz., the *katsinam*. Was the name of this antediluvian patriarch who held knowledge so secret that he was afraid to tell his grandfather somehow trans-oceanically transferred to the realm of the Hopi as a description of the Watchers?

We might also question how these *katsinam* fit into the geodetic Orion schema that we have described in this book. About twenty-five miles northeast of Shongopovi is the village of Piñon. "East of the trading post at Piñon there's an old ruins [sic] that belonged to the Kachina Clan. There were other clans living there, of course, but the Kachina Clan was the ruling group in that place. It's called Burnt Corn Ruins. The village was destroyed by fire, it seems."[63] (See Diagram 3, p. 32.) This ruin probably had about one hundred rooms and was established about the same time as the villages farther south on the Hopi Mesas, though archaeologists believe it was abandoned circa A.D. 1250.[64] This latter date is somewhat perplexing, in that it coincides with the probable establishment of the so-called *katsina* cult. In other words, the *katsina* ceremonies started approximately the same time that the Village of the Katsinam was physically deserted.

In the same general vicinity at the head of Oraibi Wash at an elevation of 7,200 feet is Kiisiwu, one of the four major springs of the Hopi.[65] This is the traditional summer home of the *katsinam* [66], to which pilgrimages are made in order to obtain ritually used water and Douglas fir (sometimes identified as spruce) branches. Thus, from the winter solstice until mid-July the *katsinam* inhabit Black Mesa, blessing it with their beneficent presence.

The sidereal correlation to this specific region is the Great Orion Nebula (M-42 and M-43) found in the sword that hangs down from his belt. Located at a distance of 1,300 light-years, this luminescent cloud of greenish gas and dust studded with stars emanating ultraviolet radiation is one of the largest emission nebulae in our galaxy [67] —about 20 light-years in diameter.[68] "...it creates, as does no other vista of the heavens, the single overpowering impression of primeval chaos, and transports the imaginative observer back to the days of creation. This irresistible impression is more than a poetic fancy, as modern astrophysics now confirms, for the Orion Nebula is undoubtedly one of the regions in space where star formation is presently underway."[69] Indeed, this veritable sidereal nursery contains many hot, young stars no more than 100,000 years old, especially in the region near Theta Orionis called the Trapezium.[70] Approximately one half of a degree south of the nebula at the tip of the sword is Iota Orionis, known by the Arabian name of Na'ir al Saif, or "Bright One of the Sword." It's magnitude is 2.76, a little dimmer than Saiph (Orion's right foot).[71]

The village where the *katsinam* dance appears in more than one Hopi myth. As stated above, these revered entities once existed in physical form but now interact with humans merely in the spirit. The former situation of two species mutually inhabiting a region somewhat resembles that of Paleolithic times, when Neanderthals coexisted with *Homo sapiens* in the same part of Europe. In the case of the Hopi/*katsinam* interface, however, the opposite result occurred, viz., the more spiritually advanced group disappeared, at least in the flesh, while the less sophisticated humans were left to continue the best way they could.

This locus on Black Mesa corresponds not only to the sword of Orion (or Azazyel, who taught men how to make swords) but also to his phallus. The star seed in his loins signifies primal creation, which the *katsinam* are mandated to assist. Their primary goal is basically one of fertility— both agrarian and human: to bring rain to the desert, falling upon the parched landscape as promiscuously as the trembling juices of an orgiastic ritual. The sidereal fire stoking Orion's manhood finds its terrestrial correlative in the combustible carbon found in great quantities on Black Mesa, hence its name. Where subterranean and "superterranean" waters meet, we find the Watchers, terrestrial angels in whose very existence the hermetic maxim of "As Above, so Below" is made manifest. These *katsinam* of an undetermined origin had come here in order to assist the humble Hisatsinom in their migrations toward an unique destiny. The spirits of these Watchers still help the Hopi to perform their annual cycle of amazingly elaborate ceremonies, the ramifications of which extend far beyond the dry mesas of Arizona. In fact, when the *katsinam* dance, they are doing so for all of humanity. They are, in essence, maintaining the precarious balance of the whole world.

*

In the next chapter we shall look beyond Orion configured in the red dust of Arizona to a few other constellations and their correlative ruin sites, discussing as well the celestial significance of a Hopi ritualistic artifact known as the *mongko*.

# Chapter 8
# If We Could See With Eyes
# Made Of Dust

"...hour of New Mexican stars, Anasazi stars, too, if we
could see with eyes made of dust. Unsmothered by town glow or smog,
the clear dark sizzles with their particulate fire. Lots of antique gods and
goddesses up there. What all didn't our ancestors see in the stars!"[1]
Reg Saner

### *The Hopi Mongko and Taurus (the Western Companion of Orion)*

The constellation Orion is not alone in our geoastronomical schema whereby both ritually vital natural loci and human-constructed habitation sites reflect certain sidereal points. If we could ascend to the heavens on a *paatuwvota*, or flying shield, in much the same manner as did the Mishongnovi bride and her Ka'nas Katsina husband mentioned in the previous chapter, we would see another constellation important to the ceremonial life of the Hopi. West of Orion is the brilliant constellation Taurus, its crimson eye Aldebaran burning through the night. The terrestrial counterpart is located about 150 miles due west of the Hopi Mesas in the western section of Grand Canyon National Park, where the Colorado River makes a great loop in the vicinity north of the village of Peach Springs on the Hualapai Reservation. The relationship between this specific landmark and the constellation on a star chart is completely proportional and reflects either a pervasive intelligence at work or, again, the factor of mere chance.

As we have seen above, Grand Canyon is considered by the Hopi to be the great Sipapuni, the Place of Emergence, the origin of a people who ascended from the subterranean plane called the Third World where they had previously lived, and currently the place to which the spirits of the dead return and the *katsinam* live. Although no specific ruin sites have yet been discovered for this western part of the canyon, habitation had been constant for thousands of years. "Of the Grand Canyon's two thousand or more aboriginal sites only three have been both excavated and stabilized. Of its 1.2 million acres, 500,000 have never been visited by archaeologist or historian."[2] This is in part due to the isolated and difficult terrain, especially on the north rim of the canyon. In an archaeological sense this area could be seen as *terra incognita*. However, various artifacts such as split-twig figurines as well as pictographs such as those found in the so-called Shamans' Gallery (both mentioned in the Chapter 6) indicate the cultural importance of this part of Grand Canyon.

The long history of native habitation here is reflected not only in artifacts but also in legends.

> "Around 1000 B.C. Uto-Aztecan groups were migrating around the Grand Canyon. Traditional Hopi stories say that a powerful *Hognyam* Bear Clan migrated from the Rio Grande to Colorado, then southwest to the Colorado River Valley. The Bow and Bear Clans [see below] were the first to arrive at Hopiland, and only they were allowed to be *Kikmongwi* or head spiritual leaders. Images of Hopi *Mongkohu*, the high spiritual leaders' crooked canes [specifically of the Flute Society], are painted on the Canyon walls. These are considered important power objects."[3]

In the Chapter 3 we mentioned the Hopi Two Horn Society, which directs the New Fire Ceremony during which Taurus achieves its midnight meridian passage (at least in A.D. 1100). One of the primary ritual articles of this society is the *mongko*. The importance of this sacred "badge" vis-à-vis Hopi cosmology should not be understated. "The supreme symbol of spiritual power and authority is the *mongko*. It gives evidence that each society [Two Horn, One Horn, and Flute] and the clans comprising it had completed their centuries-long migration. It is the Hopi 'law of laws.'"[4] A number of chief (*mongwi*) *katsinam* customarily carry the *mongko* in their left (i.e., sacred) hands: Ahöla (Ahül), Wuwuyomo (which greatly resembles Ahöla and may be a variation thereof), Eototo with his attendant Aholi, and Ahülani (Kuwan). (See a description of Ahöla and Eototo in the preceding chapter.)

In physical terms the *mongko* is a flat piece of wood forked or V-shaped at one end with the other end cut in the shape of terraced rain clouds. (Fig. 41, p. 170) In the middle a "perfect ear of corn" (*tsotsmingwu*) is sometimes tied lengthwise. At Oraibi this ear of corn is not connected to the *mongko*, because the former is believed to represent the maternal aspect. "The *mongko*, on the other hand, symbolizes the father. The owner of this emblem stick relies on it for assistance and draws courage from it as he carries it about when he practices his ritual."[5] (If we conceptualize both the *mongko* and the constellation Taurus not as a "V" but instead a "Y", we find an intriguing resonance on a microscopic level with the male Y chromosome.) From each end of the *mongko* are suspended either two turkey or two eagle feathers, and from the center hangs either a ball of earth in a cotton net or a reticulated water gourd— symbolic of both sky and earth. A few of the *mongkohus* are nearly six feet long, while some are more portable at about a foot long to one-and-a-half feet long. Still others are miniature (less than six inches) and reputedly made in the Underworld (symbolically, Grand Canyon), which indicates that they are the most sacred of all these artifacts.6 The *mongko* of the One Horn Society has a somewhat different form. The flat slat of an agave stalk is carved at one end to represent the horned or plumed snake Palulukang. The ethnographer Fewkes reminds us that the One Horn Society brought the Plumed Serpent cult (i.e., Quetzalcóatl) from Palatkwapi, the Red Land of the South.7 As we have seen, Palulukang is associated with both subterranean water and rainfall, thus reflecting its dual ophidian/aviary nature.

Although many cultures around the world have associated the zodiacal constellation Taurus with the bull or wild ox, it was also universally connected with the concept of water. In fact, the word Hyades (an open cluster representing the face of the bull) means "to rain" in Greek.

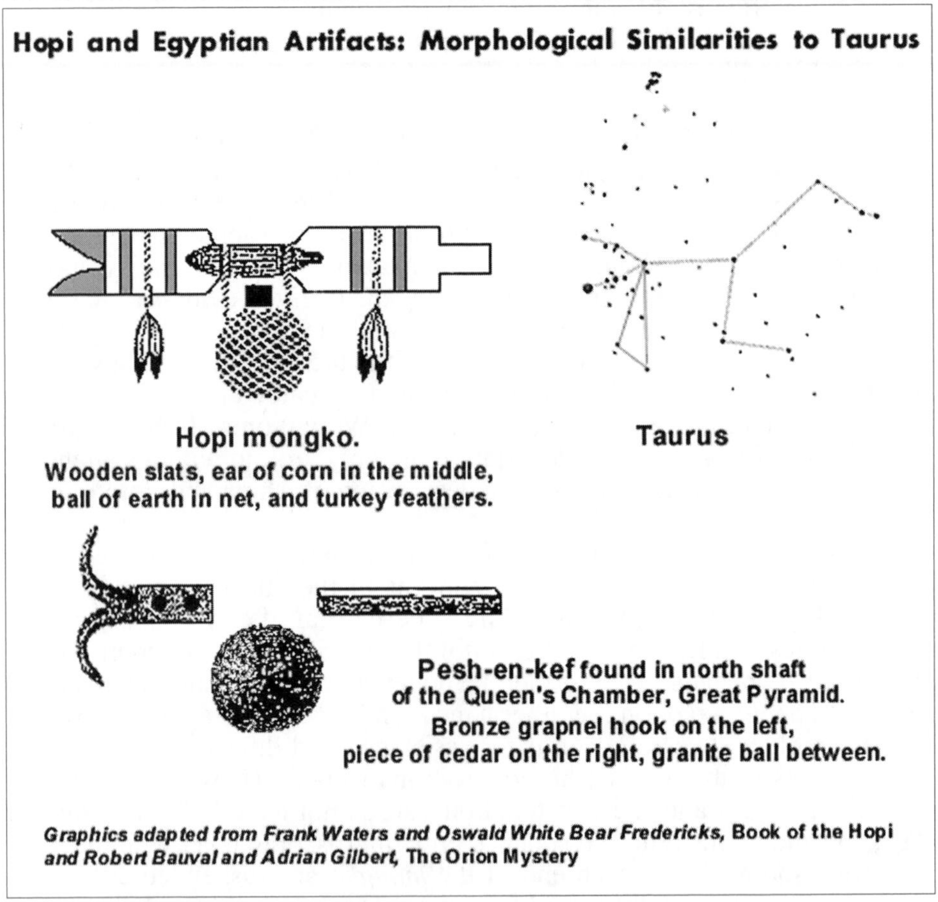

**Hopi and Egyptian Artifacts: Morphological Similarities to Taurus**

**Hopi mongko.**
Wooden slats, ear of corn in the middle,
ball of earth in net, and turkey feathers.

**Taurus**

Pesh-en-kef found in north shaft
of the Queen's Chamber, Great Pyramid.
Bronze grapnel hook on the left,
piece of cedar on the right, granite ball between.

*Graphics adapted from Frank Waters and Oswald White Bear Fredericks, Book of the Hopi and Robert Bauval and Adrian Gilbert, The Orion Mystery*

Fig. 41. The mongko (upper left), the Hopi "law of laws," is a ceremonial object still in use. In 1872 Waynman Dixon found the Pesh-en-kef (lower left) sealed in a shaft of the Khufu (Cheops) pyramid. It may have been used in the "opening of the mouth" ceremony. (For more on these artifacts from opposite sides of the globe, see pp. 246-7.)

Husbandmen and mariners in particular have found this group of stars to be a sign of coming storms and precipitation. Ovid calls them *Sidus Hyantis*, or "Rain-Bringing Stars." The Hyades —half-sisters of the Pleiades— apparently were stricken with grief after their terrestrial brother, Hyas, drowned in a well; thus, their copious tears of mourning became rain.[8] In the same tradition the poet Edmund Spencer calls the Hyades the "Moist Daughters," while Samuel Johnson's *Dictionary* deems them "a watery constellation." In his poem "Ulysses," Tennyson refers to "the rainy Hyades." [9] Consequently, the influence of Taurus is especially crucial in the desert where one's survival is totally dependent upon the presence of this inconstant element.

Aldebaran, the bloody bullseye of Taurus, has its specific Arizona correlation in the eponymous Grand Canyon Caverns. About twenty miles south of the canyon near the Hualapai Reservation, this dry limestone formation is completely devoid of life but rife with various types of crystals. It extends at least 210 feet underground (or as much as a twenty-one story building), though seismic testing has determined four lower levels ("kivas"), each larger than the one above with the lowest one still containing water and producing crystals. Findings have shown that the entire cavern system extends over 1,700 feet below the surface. The deeper portion has yet to be explored, but the two main rooms in the upper portion of the caverns, the Chapel of the Ages and the Halls of Gold, are 130 yards long and 210 yards long respectively. The latter room was so named because it was initially thought to contain rich deposits of gold ore, but the ruddy color (similar to that of Aldebaran) turned out to be merely iron oxide. "In early 1963, during the Cuban [Missile] Crisis, the United States government stored enough food in the caverns to support 2000 people for two weeks with food and water. It was never needed, but because of the cool-dry conditions of the caverns, 36 years later the food is still edible."[10] In 1958 a passage was found with a mysterious source of air. Test smoke artificially introduced into the passage eventually egressed almost fifty miles away near Huvasupai Falls in Grand Canyon. After that experiment,

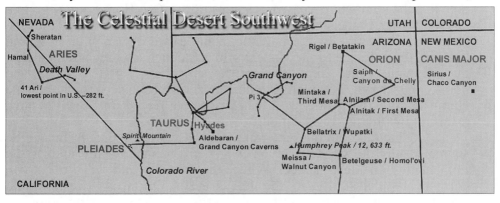

**Diagram 4 showing Aries, the Pleiades, Taurus, Orion, and Canis Major**

the original name was changed from Dinosaur Caverns to Grand Canyon Caverns.

The association between Taurus and caverns makes perfect sense if we remember the exquisite paintings of bulls found in the caves at Lascaux, France and Altamira, Spain. Near the entrance of the former complex is a naturalistic rendition of a bull, above which are suspended six dots. Some hypothesize that these represent the six visible stars of the Pleiades. If so, this would mean that Upper Paleolithic humans associated male bovines with the constellation Taurus about 16,500 years ago— at least 12,000 years before the zodiac is thought to have been conceived![11] In addition, the bull-obsessed Minoan culture of Crete kept its bull monster, the Minotaur, inside the dark recesses of the Labyrinth, which reflects the twisting, intestine-like passages of cave systems.

The Hopi word for Aldebaran is *Wuyok shóhü*, or "Broad Star."[12] Other meanings of the adjective *wuyok* include "large," "spreading," and "extending widely," as well as the sense of being "old."[13] All these could conceivably refer to both the dark grottoes of the unconscious and itself. The V-shaped symbol at the end of the *mongko* is a recurrent glyph which means "opening up," an obvious reference to both the *sipapu* of the kiva and the great Sipapuni of Grand Canyon.[14] Similar to the V-shape, the chevron found on some Hopi pottery is emblematic of the badger, specifically the inclined slopes of its burrow.[15] If we recall, one of the totemic symbols of the Underworld is the badger. During a healing ceremony A.M. Stephen himself was successfully treated for a throat condition by a member of the Badger Clan, who among other things prayed specifically to the star Aldebaran.[16] The early trader Thomas Keam noted the petroglyph design of the squash blossom as an altered horizontal rectangle whose top side is formed by an open V instead of a straight line, with an additional vertical straight line rising from the center of the V. This also represents the home of Alosaka (Muy'ingwa), the Hopi two-horned deity, on the eastern mountain of the San Francisco Peaks. This glyph furthermore signifies the coming of rain.[17] In this context it is interesting to note that the spirits of deceased members of the Two Horn Society go to a lake in the San Francisco Peaks known as Alosaka, while those of the One Horn Society retire to a small mountain called Kwanivi near Grand Canyon, the entrance to the Underworld.[18] Stephen also reports the belief that the eye of Sótuknang, the Hopi "heart of the sky god" with a single horn on his crown, is actually Aldebaran. As we have seen, both the One Horns and the Two Horns with their respective *mongkohus* seem to have an affinity with this constellation.

Related to both the subterranean spirit world beyond death and the source of all life, Grand Canyon in general metaphorically evokes the immensities of deep space. While the eastern end of the canyon corresponds celestially to the left arm of Orion, its western end encompasses the Hyades cluster of Taurus. The specific morphological correlation between the *mongko* and the constellation Taurus with its V-shaped end pouring out rain stresses again the ceremonial link between earth and sky. The *mongko* is thus invested with the sacred power of both canyon and constellation. Via the annual rituals of Wúwutcim and Soyal — the only two times when the *mongko* is displayed 19 — each assures the continuity between the mundane world and the spirit world.

## The Chaco Phenomenon and Canis Major (the Eastern Companion of Orion)

If we again zoom out high above Arizona in our fanciful flight through the looking glass where earth mirrors sky, another constellation beside Orion and Taurus comes into view. To the east we see the brightest star in the heavens, Sirius in the constellation Canis Major. A proportional distance on the earth —viz., 140 miles east of the Hopi Mesas (the same distance west from the Mesas that terrestrial Taurus is located)— brings us to Chaco Canyon (mentioned in Chapter 1, and again in Chapter 5 in relation to the supernova pictograph). This site is perhaps the greatest architectural achievement of the Anasazi, a sacred city with ceremonial roads extending both north and south for scores of miles.

A plethora of archaeological, architectural, archaeoastronomical, and cosmological data on Chaco Canyon exists. However, since our current book deals primarily with the Orion ruins and villages of Arizona, we shall take merely a cursory look at this grand site in northwestern New Mexico. Located along Chaco Wash, an intermittent stream in the arid and desolate San Juan Basin, this awe-inspiring group of a dozen large pueblos reflects a high degree of cultural synthesis. As Edgar Lee Hewett, one of the earlier archaeologists who researched Chaco Canyon, floridly remarks: "The mystery of the desert reaches its climax when, in the center of this area a hundred miles square without a flowing stream of any sort, we come upon a group of ruins such as Egypt and Mesopotamia and Asia Minor and Middle America have been supposed to monopolize."20

Begun in the early 900s, construction entered a boom phase sometime after A.D. 1030. More specifically, the respected co-authors William M. Ferguson and Arthur H. Rohn cite the date 1055 as the beginning of a twenty-eight year period called the Florescent Bonito Phase (named after the main pueblo).21 This, of course, was the year following the supernova explosion depicted in the Chaco rock art discussed in Chapter 5 of the present volume. Whether or not the construction surge and the celestial event are causally related is moot. At any rate, "...by A.D. 1050 the Chaco people had ascended to the peak of their golden age. Living conditions were in many ways better than those of the middle classes of Europe and at least equal to the best conditions in Mesoamerica."22

Some of the masonry structures erected during this period, such as the D-shaped Pueblo Bonito, once contained between 650 and 800 rooms, and rose four or five stories high. The walls were erected using a core of rubble and an ashlar veneer designed with great skill and aesthetic sensibility. Then, surprisingly, the walls were finished inside and out with a layer of plaster, hiding their exquisite beauty. Because religious ritual was omnipresent in the life of the Chacoans, many communal great kivas (e.g., those at Pueblo Bonito) or tower kivas (e.g., those at Chetro Ketl, Kin Kletso, and Tsin Kletsin in Chaco as well as in the outlying villages of Salmon Ruin to the north —see Chapter 2— and Kin Ya'a to the south) were also incorporated into the architecture. In terms of the smaller clan kivas, a ratio of one kiva to every twenty-nine domiciliary or storage rooms has been found [23], suggesting an exceedingly rich ceremonial life. An estimated 215,000 trees logged from forests located between twenty and fifty miles away were used in the construction of all the pueblos at Chaco.[24] In addition, an estimated fifty million pieces of sandstone were quarried and transported in order to build just one of the major village structures, Chetro Ketl.[25] Hence, a greatly efficient cooperative labor system must have been in place to accomplish such prodigious tasks.

The great kivas of Chaco Canyon are another example of superior engineering abilities employed in the service of sacred ceremonies. Measuring sixty-two feet in diameter, the great kiva at Chetro Ketl used

**Fig. 42. Pueblo Bonito, Chaco Canyon, New Mexico.**
**Round kiva in foreground.**

four vertical posts as roof supports, arranged in the shape of a square. One of these roof posts was found to be twenty-six-and-a-half inches in diameter. Four sandstone disks over three feet in diameter and weighing from one-half to three-quarters of a ton each were placed, one on top of the other, in each socket as footings for these upright pillars.26 Ten sealed niches in the circular wall of this kiva yielded numerous votive objects, including turquoise pendants and many strands of shells or turquoise beads. Some of these strands extended up to seventeen feet long and were crafted from over 17,000 turquoise beads.

*Fig. 43. Casa Rinconada, Chaco Canyon. Note T-shaped passageway.*

Another great kiva called Casa Rinconada, measuring nearly sixty-four feet in diameter, contained a subterranean stairway for the hidden entry of the priests. Unconnected to any pueblo village, this kiva also contained twenty-eight regularly distributed niches (suggesting perhaps a lunar significance) and six irregularly spaced niches (suggesting perhaps the Six Directions), one of which was precisely aligned to the summer solstice sunrise. One rare upper story corner window in Pueblo Bonito is also thought to have some solstitial significance. Another ancient astronomical device is known as the Sun Dagger, located at Fajada Butte in the mouth of the canyon. Using three upright slabs of sandstone about six feet high each to collimate the sun's rays onto two spiral petroglyphs, it registers summer and winter solstices, equinoxes, as well as major and minor lunar standstills.

D espite the barren and inhospitable environment, the people of Chaco attained a level of development which archaeologists call the Great or Classic Pueblo about fifty-to-a-hundred years before the rest of the Southwest. "In the years A.D. 1000 to 1100, the occupants of Chaco Canyon were one of the most sophisticated prehistoric societies north of Mexico. Some archaeologists believe they had the largest and most important religious, economic, cultural, and political center in what is now the United States."[27] Although not as extensive as the Hohokam irrigation system (described in Chapter 12), the Chacoans developed an impressive water control and distribution system that used dams to impound runoff and direct it via canals to headgates where it was subsequently diverted into the grid irrigation network of fields. This allowed the Chacoans not only to survive but also to thrive in an uncertain ecosystem. The climate a thousand years ago was much as it is today, and more favorable geographic locations that would more easily fulfill basic needs were not too far away. Surely, some non-pragmatic reason existed for the substantial Anasazi settlement in this barren canyon.

As mentioned above, the Chacoans also built an extensive network of over 400 miles of roads, frequently thirty feet wide— all for a culture that did not possess beasts of burden or the wheel. According to Ferguson and Rohn, "This road system is undoubtedly the greatest single achievement of prehistoric man in the Southwest."[28] Constructed on packed earth or bedrock and bordered by earthen or rubble berms, these highways proceeded in an arrow-straight line across various desert landforms, using stairways and ramps to negotiate canyons and buttes. This road network connected the various "outliers," i.e., a group of over seventy distant villages such as the northern Salmon Ruins and Aztec Ruins as well as the southern Kin Ya'a Ruin.[29] Along certain segments we find double or even quadruple parallel roadways, constructed most likely for ceremonial purposes. The people of Chaco also built a series of signal towers for communication via selenite mirrors, mica, or pyrite during the day and torches at night. In addition, horseshoe-shaped masonry shrines called *herraduras* (similar to the type of shrines that the Hopi currently erect) have been found along the route.

Starting in A.D. 1130 a minor fifty-year drought halted any further construction of pueblos, roads, or "lighthouses" and eventually caused a gradual depopulation of the region. By 1200 Chaco Canyon was more or less abandoned.

The above selected details regarding this high desert culture all exemplify the fact that the Chaco Phenomenon, as it is called, was somewhat an anomaly in terms of the Anasazi's understated "architecture of existence" that we discussed at the beginning of Chapter 6. Undoubtedly, the echoes here are of Mexico, both its magnificence and its grandiosity. It comes as no surprise, then, that physical evidence of a direct southern influence is readily apparent in the artifacts found at Chaco

Canyon: scarlet and green macaws, copper bells, shell trumpets, cloisonné-decorated sandstone, painted wooden birds, ceremonial canes, conical-shaped objects employed as stamps or seals, and other exotic artifacts.30 Adding to the architectural design at Chetro Ketl, both the colonnade formed by a number of square pillars (later filled in) and the circular tower (Fig. 51, p. 272.) point to a Mesoamerican influence. (Specifically, the latter is reminiscent of the astronomical tower called the Caracol at Chichén Itzá.) Behind Chetro Ketl the small ruin called Talus Unit Number 1 has a wide three-step stairway between two large rooms. Most likely unroofed, the upper room possibly contained an earthen platform akin to the temple mounds of Mexico. In addition, an expandable lightning lattice was found at Chetro Ketl.31 As we saw in Chapter 7 regarding the *katsinam*, this artifact that is still used in the contemporary Hopi spring ceremony Powamu relates to Sótuknang, who is a variation of the plumed serpent Quetzalcóatl.

Although the pueblos of Chaco Canyon might have superficially resembled the apartment complexes found in any major metropolitan area today, their religious and social function was probably quite different. "[Archaeologist W. James] Judge argues that Chaco Canyon in the 1000s became a ritual center (similar to the Maya cities during the 700 and 800s). By 1050 it was the center of a social, ritual, and economic system. Chaco Canyon, he suggests, was a ritual rather than a residential center; the pueblos were not year-round residences but accommodations for pilgrims."32 A few pertinent facts about the region indeed clearly suggest a sacred rather than a secular usage. For instance, the dearth of burials in the canyon implies that many people journeyed to Chaco on a periodic basis and then returned to their homes. In addition, much of the black-on-white pottery apparently originates from elsewhere, and a majority of the lithic material is of foreign origin.33 Furthermore, the number of storage rooms greatly exceeds the amount of corn that could have been grown locally. In fact, many more rooms existed at Chaco than the estimated population warrants. At one time archaeologists thought that the population must have been very great, a thronging city of perhaps as many as 20,000. Now, however, in light of the above evidence, most population estimates range between 6,000 and 2,000 or even lower, though without actual skeletal evidence this is mere academic conjecture.34

What, then, was the cosmological and cultural significance of these so-called "Great Houses" grouped together in a canyon naturally containing merely minimal material resources? As Douglas and Barbara Anderson succinctly query: "Was Chaco a Mecca, a Jerusalem, a Green River, a Rome, a Sears Roebuck warehouse?"35 We may never know exactly. However, a general consensus is emerging in regard to prehistoric life at Chaco Canyon. "Great Houses—the massively built, geometrically formal buildings associated with Chaco Canyon—were not, in any useful sense, pueblos. They were occupied, if at all, by only a few, clearly exceptional residents. They were not built to be apartments; they were built to be monuments."36

Very possibly Chaco Canyon served among other things as an *axis mundi*, a Center of the World —see Mircea Eliade's *The Sacred and the Profane*— to which pilgrimages were made according to a complex ritual cycle. "In this [Puebloan] worldview, peaks and pinnacles, springs and lakes, caves and other topographic features have cosmic significance, and the organization of pueblos, kivas, and roads is sometimes linked to topographic features and to solar and lunar orientations."37 According to this "divine cosmography," the sky and the Underworld were merely different dimensions of the same realm, and the landscape was a living entity whose being reflected both. Much like the three Mesas of the Hopi, Chaco Canyon of the Anasazi was the legendary Middle Place, midway between nadir and zenith. More specifically, the Great North Road that begins at the *S(h)ipapu*, the place of emergence from the womb of the Underworld (exoterically represented by Kutz Canyon near Salmon Ruins), and the Great South Road that terminates at Kin Ya'a Ruin, whose tower kiva is a symbolic link to the celestial realms, both find their pivotal point at Chaco Canyon.38 In fact, the distances from Chaco north to Kutz Canyon and from Chaco south to Kin Ya'a located near the geological prominent Hosta Butte are almost exactly the same. (The Great South Road is one-half a kilometer longer than the Great North Road.39) Hence, not only are the four cardinal directions included in this cosmological schema but also the two vertical directions so important to Anasazi eschatology. The spiritual nexus of Chaco would have drawn votaries along the network of sacred avenues from all over the region so that they could participate in the seasonal ceremonies made even more efficacious by this natural *sanctum sanctorum*. The system of long-distance communication would have facilitated the timing of these rituals to which the Anasazi obviously gave great credence.

Did the people in the surrounding areas bring commodities of corn, pottery, and other artifacts into Chaco to trade in exchange for ceremonial services? If so, this would have necessitated a theocratic hierarchy of priests— a sociopolitical situation we fail to find in the descendants of the Chacoans, viz., the modern-day Puebloans. Given the putative Mexican connection noted above, perhaps the people of Chaco were indeed influenced by the Toltecs, their contemporary neighbors to the south. This latter native group, for instance, possibly had built a great settlement due south of Chaco Canyon in the present Mexican state of Chihuahua. Constructed of puddled adobe instead of masonry, this impressive site called either Paquimé or Casas Grandes (not to be confused with the Hohokam site of Casa Grande south of Phoenix) might have been a link in a series of cities stretching southward into the tropical regions.

The archaeologist Stephen H. Lekson posits that Paquimé was one node on what he calls the Chaco Meridian. This line includes Aztec Ruins to the north, Chaco Canyon at the center, and Paquimé to the south.40 Lekson also allows for the possibility that the prehistoric and historic site of Culiacán (Viejo) west of the contemporary Sinaloan city of the same name is the southernmost node on this meridian, though further research is needed to confirm this. At any rate, he believes that an oligarchy comprised of high status elites centered in Chaco Canyon exerted control over a large area up and down the line. "The organization of labor, the organization of space, and prestige economies of exotica all point to Chacoan political influence or authority over this huge region."41 Whether actually coerced or merely organized, extensive labor was used to build those monumental architectural structures that were designed in part to impress or even awe visitors, some of whom had come from great distances. In addition, the importation of exotica —i.e., macaws, copper bells, and either olivella or abalone shells— established a "political-prestige economy"42 to offset the older local subsistence economy. Finally, the system of ceremonial roads also provided the means to channel widely scattered pilgrims toward the Center-place. As Lekson summarily puts it, "The North Road projected Chaco's power across distance..."43

For an agricultural society such as the Pueblo culture of this region, the concept of a straight north-south line must have been an abstraction with awesome spiritual implications: North, the direction of immutable circumpolar stars sweeping around their axis; and South, the way the sun journeys in the winter, the spirit road beyond this life. With their solstitial points the eastern and western horizons were both related to the mundane world of planning and planting, but the north-south road conceived of as a vertical axis would ultimately lead to the timeless realm of the spirits. Thus, according to Lekson's hypothesis, the combined effect of colossal architecture, exotic trade goods, and this mysterious meridian were the means by which a select group of Chacoans could concentrate and legitimate sociopolitical power during this period. As the influence of Chaco gradually waned in the 12th century, Lekson believes that this "Chaco hegemony" eventually shifted to other sites— first to Aztec and then to Paquimé.

The Chaco Meridian is located specifically at a west longitude of 107 degrees 57 minutes 25 seconds. Perhaps it is merely a coincidence that the Bighorn Medicine Wheel in Wyoming is located at 107 degrees 55 minutes 20 seconds. (If we consider all the other so-called coincidences involved in this subject, perhaps not.) The difference of two longitudinal minutes means that the latter site located nearly six hundred miles to the north is only about two-and-a-half miles east of the Chaco Meridian. Of course, very different cultures constructed their respective sites north and south; however, some similarities exist.

Located upon a promontory on the western slope of the Bighorn Mountains at an altitude of over 9,600 ft., the Bighorn Medicine Wheel is a stone circle about seventy-five feet in diameter with twenty-eight spokes (the same as the number of regularly spaced niches at Casa Rinconada) and a pattern of line-of-sight cairns. Possibly constructed as a prototype for the Plains Indian Sun Dance Lodge, this wheel contains a system of astronomical alignments with which we have become somewhat familiar: the summer solstice sunrise and sunset points as well as the heliacal risings of Aldebaran, Rigel, and Sirius— each separated by twenty-eight days.[44] To avoid becoming mired in details distant from the Southwest and the focus of our book, it is interesting at this point to merely note that these are some of the same types of archaeoastronomical alignments we find at Fajada Butte and Casa Rinconada in Chaco Canyon. Was the location of the Bighorn Medicine Wheel an intentional extension of the Chaco Meridian into the far north? Functioning in a capacity similar to the prime meridian of Egypt, this extremely long north-south line would have unified a macroregion and codified the theocratic influence of the Chacoans (or post-Chacoans) over an extensive territory. It is a far stretch, both geographically and conceptually, but nonetheless a tantalizing prospect for further research.

As we return to the Southwest, a central question once more arises to discomfit us: Was Chaco really one of the northern outposts in a cultural network extending far south into Mexico? Again, mere speculation without further evidence brings no firm answers. What we *do* know, however, is that the Chaco Phenomenon was one of the supreme architectural and cultural accomplishments in North America. It was, perhaps, merely an experiment in monumentalism, an ambitious detour in the ever spiraling development of an admirable people, one rather ostentatious step onward in the Great Migration of the Hisatsinom, a move which in the end proved to be spiritually ineffective, and thus was abandoned for a more subtle way to journey in balance through a world intimately connected to the realm of gods and *katsinam*— all as close as corn or rain.

The sidereal correlation to this voluminous Chacoan culture is, of course, the most luminous star in the firmament. Located in the constellation Canis Major, Sirius was widely known as the Dog Star. (See Diagram 4, p. 171.) In fact, many cultures throughout the world associate both the star and its constellation with canines. For the Greeks Sirius was the head of the Great Dog who was always waiting behind Orion, ready to fetch the game that his master hunts; hence, it was called the Dog of Orion. This asterism was also deemed Janitor Lethaeus, the Keeper of Hades; thus, it is Cerebus of the southern sky who watches over the lower heavens where demons reputedly live. (Here again we see the Underworld correlated to the celestial plane.) In Arabia, Sirius was known as Al Kalb al Jabbar, the Dog of the Giant. In one early Hindu myth it was Sarama, one of the Twin Watchdogs of the Milky Way. The *Rig Vedas* also referred to it as Sivanam, the dog who awakens the Ribhus (the gods of the mid-air) and summons rain. To the Nordic peoples Sirius was the she-wolf Greip, who bore the god Heimdall, the Shining One. The Assyrians recognized it as Kal-bu Samas, the Dog of the Sun, whereas the Phoenicians saw it as Hannabeah, the Barker. In Egypt this spiritually significant star was associated primarily with the goddess Isis, wife of Osiris (Orion), but was also linked to the jackal-headed god Anubis. The heliacal rising of Sirius (which in 3000 B.C. occurred during the summer solstice) coincided with the flooding of the Nile; hence, it was also called the Nile Star.45 In fact, this specific heliacal rising signaled the beginning of the Egyptian Sothic calendar. "The curious thing about Sirius is that out of an estimated 2000 stars in the heavens visible to the naked eye it is the only one to rise heliacally at this precise and nicely rounded interval of 365 and a quarter days..." —i.e., a solar year.46

In China this star was known as T'ien-lang, the Celestial Jackal or Wolf of the East, while what we conceive of as Canis Major's hindquarters was called Hou-Chi, the Bow and Arrow. In another Chinese legend from the Sung Dynasty (which, incidentally, is roughly contemporaneous with the span of Anasazi residence in Chaco Canyon), these same stars just mentioned represent Chang-hsien, the Patron of Child-Bearing Women who consequently offers up prayers to him for fecundity. If a woman conceives, it means that this white-faced, bearded figure customarily seen with a young boy by his side has shot the Heavenly Dog with his bow and arrow.47 Paralleling this latter connotation, the Babylonians referred to Sirius as Kakkab kasti, the Bow Star, while the Persians called it Tir, the Arrow.48 The Egyptian circular Zodiac of Denderah depicts the goddess Sati (or Satis) with a bow and arrow riding in the celestial barque of Sothis (Isis/Sirius). In one version of Sumerian mythology Sirius was called KAK.SI.DI., or the Arrow-Star.49 However, the sixth tablet of the Sumerian epic *Enûma elish* refers to a "Bow Star," which is called the lordly brother of the Anunnaki, a group of fifty celestial deities among whom he was placed by the great god of heaven Anu.50 Emphasizing the star's additional connotation as commander, one Sanskrit appellation denotes the Chieftain's Star, while Plutarch speaks of this sidereal presence as the Leader.

In another context Sirius was known as the Scorcher, referring to its prominence during the "dog days" of summer. This torrid season in particular was believed to bring fever, pestilence, and madness. The Assyrians furthermore saw the sidereal point as Su-ku-du, the Restless, Impetuous, or Blazing One. The Arabic Al-Shi'ra reflects the Sanskrit Surya, or Sun God, both literally meaning "The Shining One." Sirius was also known in many cultures as the Sparkling One, due to its brilliant scintillation. In former times, however, numerous references describe it as fiery red or ruddy, hence its name *rubra canicula*.51

Although it has only twice the mass and diameter of our own Sun, Sirius is forty times more luminous. As a white dwarf, its spectral type is A0 with a surface temperature of about 10,000 degrees K.52 It has a magnitude of minus 1.42 and is only 8.7 light-years from Earth. Sirius is a binary star; its companion Sirius B has a magnitude of 8.65 and is invisible to the naked eye. This extremely dense star revolves around Sirius A in a period of about fifty years.53

Robert K.G. Temple's mythologically rich book *The Sirius Mystery* discusses the work of anthropologists M. Griaule and G. Dieterlen with the Dogon of Mali. As heirs apparent of Egyptian hermetic knowledge, this tribe knew about the existence and periodicity of that invisible star as well as other celestial phenomena around which its members devised an entire ritual system. In fact, incredible as it may sound, the Dogon claim that their civilization was founded by a group of amphibious creatures with fish tails originating from the star system Sirius. These celestial emissaries were called the Nommos, which means "the Instructors" or "the Monitors," the latter designation harkening back to the role of the *katsinam* as watchers or listeners. Dogon drawings of the Nommos (Figures 32 and 34 in Temple's book) resemble both the Babylonian figure of Oannes and the Hopi figure of the Sohu Katsina discussed in Chapter 7.54 In terms of the latter, turkey feathers replace the fish scale pattern, and eagle feathers provide a substitute for the four upright protrusions radiating from the headdress. (The Hopi word *nömö* means "to be folded" or "pleated," a possible reference to the fish scale — or turkey feather— imbrication.55) However, the shape of the mask and its goggle eyes remain consistent in both Dogon and Hopi forms.

For the Lakota (Sioux), who practiced a system of ritual seasonal migration according to various constellations and their terrestrial reflections, Sirius represents the Tayamini Sinte, the tail of a great celestial buffalo whose backbone is Orion's belt and whose eyes are the Pleiades. The star's terrene equivalent is located in Hell Canyon of the southern Black Hills, where the Cheyenne River flows "in four directions," i.e., makes an oxbow loop.56 The extinct Skidi Pawnee saw Sirius as the Wolf Star, god of war and death.57 Its name was *ckiri ti'u:hac*, or Fools the Coyotes, a reference to the star rising before the Morning Star, thereby tricking coyotes or wolves into premature howling.58 We should remember that the name of the Skidi (or Skiri) band of the Pawnee literally means "wolf." As archaeoastronomer Von Del Chamberlain observes: "What could have been more appropriate than for the Wolf Band of the Pawnee, a people who took their way of life from the stars, to give their own name to the brightest star in the night?"59

Most germane to our discussion, the Hopi word Ponóchona [Ponotsona], meaning "The One That Sucks From the Belly,"60 is the name for Sirius. Although this term does not specifically associate the star with a canine, it clearly designates a mammal. For the Hopi and probably their ancestors, Sirius is apparently a guardian star involved with hunting magic and the burgeoning of the animal kingdom, about which we shall say more shortly. Suffice it now to sum up the archetypal connotations of this asterism. As we have seen, a cross-cultural, global connection with two well-defined motifs seems to exist: 1. the dog (or other mammals) and 2. the bow and arrow. At this point the reader may well be asking the question: How does this all relate to the people who resided in or made pilgrimages to Chaco Canyon?

In Chapter 4 we mentioned the Gran Chichimeca, a vast territory north of Mexico where putative nomadic barbarians lived. This generic term designates a group of people known as the Chichimecs, literally "Sons of the Dog." Instead of being a unified tribe, the Chichimecs were a loose aggregate of diverse bands whose character has been compared to that of the Germanic tribes who swept down from the north in the 5th century A.D. to attack Rome. The Chichimecs are frequently contrasted with the Toltecs, whose primary urban center was Tula (north of Mexico City in the State of Hidalgo) and who in that specific region and time period were considered the epitome of refined civilization. "'Chichimec,' on the other hand, means literally 'descendants of the dog,' and was used in one sense to refer to the hungry nomads who inhabited the wide-open spaces north of the cultivated fields, the hunters and gatherers who used the bow and arrow, dressed in deer skins, and ate raw meat."61 As the bellicose group from which the Aztecs are believed to have later descended, the Chichimec hordes (like the Germanic tribes on another continent six centuries before them) migrated down from the north, eventually reaching the Valley of Mexico sometime between the 11th and the beginning of the 14th century.62 According to archaeologist Charles Di Peso, at its greatest extent their territory reached from the 38th parallel near the headwaters of the Rio Grande in the San Juan Mountains of southwestern Colorado south to the Tropic of Cancer.63

Eventually the Chichimecs and the Toltecs forged an alliance whereby an exchange took place, the former providing military aid and the latter contributing the amenities of relative cultural refinement. According to legend, the figures of Mixcoatl and Xolotl were the first to use the *bow and arrow* in Mesoamerica rather than the less accurate atlatl.64 Mixcoatl, or "Cloud Serpent," was the apotheosized chieftain of the Toltecs. His son, who was named Ce Acatl Topiltzin (a.k.a. Quetzalcóatl), founded Tula (also called Tollan, or "Place of Reeds," a city whose life span exactly corresponds to that of Chaco Canyon, circa A.D. 900-1200). The son eventually buried his assassinated father at a site called the Hill of the Star, perhaps the snow-capped, extinct volcano named Orizaba. The presence of Topiltzin was frequently marked by an arrow that would pierce a tree, thereby creating a cross.65

Xolotl was the likewise apotheosized chieftain of the Chichimecs who invaded the Valley of Mexico in A.D. 1224 (shortly after Chaco was abandoned). In his deific manifestation he was the dog-headed god who accompanied the dead to the Underworld, as well as the controller of lightning (arrows?).66 Xolotl's son Nezahualcoyotl, which in the Nahuatl (Aztec) language means "Hungry Coyote," was the philosopher-poet-engineer-king who founded Texcoco (east of Mexico City).₆₇ The younger figure erected a ten-zone pyramid with an exterior black roof covered with stars. In a manner akin to the monotheistic reformations of the Egyptian pharaoh Akhenaton (who reigned during the Eighteenth Dynasty from 1353 to 1335 B.C.), this later Mexican structure was dedicated to an invisible god to whom no blood sacrifices were permitted.₆₈ At any rate, we see the motifs of both dog and bow ranging south of the U.S. border as well.

Further links between the American Southwest and Mesoamerica exist. About seventy-five miles south of the Tropic of Cancer, the ruins at La Quemada near the city of Zacatecas show an architecture and artifacts similar to those of Chaco Canyon, i.e., unhewn, unmortared stone and a dearth of sculptures or murals.₆₉ On the northwestern outskirts of Mexico City, the pyramid of Tenayuca, "...the only Chichimec monument in the Valley of Mexico we know thoroughly," is constructed in much the same manner as the walls of the Great Houses at Chaco. "Its numerous superstructures are each built in the same way: a stone and earth nucleus with smaller stones as veneer, covered in turn by a thick coat of stucco."₇₀ We have heretofore discussed the Mesoamerican influence of the round tower kivas at Chaco. We should add that the circular, tri-walled tower construction at Pueblo del Arroyo in Chaco is also thought to be an architectural concept imported from the south. It appears, then, that a great number of blueprints (or their prehistoric equivalent) were being shared longitudinally.

Given the above evidence, the Anasazi contact with the Chichimec-Toltec group is self-apparent. Obviously we can see that the two groups had some connection. However, the exact nature of this interface is unclear. A discussion of linguistics might provide the requisite light to traverse this shadowy terrain. The contemporary Hopi share the same language family with the ancient Chichimecs, viz., Uto-Aztecan.₇₁ In terms of the name of the latter group, however, the Hopi have no "ch" sound in their language; the closest phoneme is "ts-." The Hopi word *tsiitsi'rum* means "baring teeth." (*Tsiitsi* means "to divide" or "tear apart.") The word *mak* means "hunt." In an aural approximation of the word Chichimec, the combination of these two Hopi words has the sense of "to hunt with bared teeth," clearly connoting a canine trait. Incidentally, the Hopi term *tsiikwi* means "to straighten" (as in arrows).₇₂ Hence, these Sons of the Dog are associated in the Hopi language with a specifically dog-like characteristic, and possibly with the act of arrow-making. Here in yet another context we find a recurrence of the dual mythological motifs —dog and arrow— which, as we have seen, are widely linked to the star Sirius.

What do the Hopi call Chaco Canyon, that most massive of Anasazi/Hisatsinom ruins? There appears to be some reticence in this regard, both in the ethnographic data and among contemporary Hopi. (The explanation for this may become clear in our discussion below.) The word "Chaco" is apparently derived from the Spanish. For instance, the name *Chaka* was found inscribed on a Spanish map of the region dating from 1774.[73] Did the Spanish get this term from the Navajo, who in turn obtained it from the descendants of the Chacoans? At this point it is impossible to tell. The meaning for the Spanish word does have some interesting reverberations, however. *Chacal* means "jackal," and *chacoto* means "noisy mirth" or "racket"— the sound associated with the New World equivalent of the jackal, i.e., the coyote. In addition, *chacuaco* means "crude, boorish." *Chacra* (as in Chacra Mesa above Chaco Canyon) means "small farm," and *chagra* means "a person from the country, a peasant." All these connotations could readily apply to the Chichimecs.

We recall, of course, that Chaco Canyon lies about 140 miles northeast of the Hopi Mesas. Both the Hopi terms *hopoq* and *hopqöy* refer to the direction of northeast. *Hópoko* is known as the place of the summer solstice sunrise.[74] The word *hopoqki* is the "Northeastern Pueblo community or country where they bring back turquoise bracelets." Although this is a possible reference to the turquoise mine near the Rio Grande, it most likely refers to Chaco, especially since the Los Cerrillos mine is technically east-*south*east of the Hopi Mesas. After all, Chaco Canyon was the undisputed clearinghouse for the turquoise trade in the Southwest. Most importantly, the proper noun *Hopqöy* means "a mythical place in the northeast where marvelous building was accomplished by *powaqam*, 'sorcerers'. The suggestion has been made that this may have to do with the Chacoan ruins."[75] This term resonates with many of those found in the linguistic complex we have been describing. For instance, the Hopi word *pok* (or *poko*) means "dog," but it is also a homonym for "shoot arrows." *Hoohu* (pronounced "ho-o-hu") means "arrow" (and, metaphorically, "semen"). In addition, *hopaqa* refers to a small reed used in making arrows. The only term for any of the Chacoan ruins that appears to have a Puebloan origin —the rest are either Navajo or Spanish— is Hongo Pavi. As a possible corruption of the Second Mesa village name Shongopovi [Songòopavi], or "the place by the spring where the tall reeds grow," the word for this small ruin in Chaco Canyon is related to the Hopi word *hongap*, or "arrow material." (*Hongaptsikwànpi* is the grooved stone used for straightening arrows.) Although all these numerous cognates might create somewhat of a verbal blurring, they all enigmatically point to the Dog Star Sirius with its efficient weapon of choice, the bow.

Just as the Chichimecs should not be viewed as a discrete native tribe, what we know collectively as the Hopi is comprised of a number of sundry clan groupings, or phratries, and presumably the Hisatsinom society was structured in the same manner. In other words, the clan system has been an integral part of the Hopi polity since the first villages were constructed, and probably even before that time. Prior to the 1906 split at Oraibi, there existed twenty-four separate clans grouped into nine different phratries.76 One phratry in particular seems to have all the thematic variations of our present discussion. "The *Reed-Greasewood-Bow* grouping is evidently associated with the fall, with the waxing of Orion and the Pleiades in the night sky, with the onset of cold weather, with hunting (through the use of bow and arrow, and the link with dogs), and, secondarily, with war."77 (Of course, Taurus and Canis Major should be added to the configuration of prominent constellations.) The Reed-Greasewood-Bow phratry's *wuya*, or clan deity, is Pokonghoya, the Elder War Twin. Note the word *poko,* or "dog," in his name. Mentioned in Chapter 3, this phratry was responsible for the ceremonies from about late September to late January, basically the non-*katsina* season.

As chief of all warriors as well as chief of all dogs, the Reed Clan sponsors a prayer stick-making ceremony in December during Soyal (described in Chapter 2). On each of the four walls of its clan house, a totemic mural is painted. On the northeast wall —the direction of Chaco Canyon from the Hopi Mesas— a wolf is depicted.78 (This contradicts the normal totemic associations: usually the wildcat is placed in the northeast while the wolf is found in the southeast.) In the tradition of the Reed Clan the legendary home of the Dog People is a village in the east (northeast?) called Suchaptakwi. (Possibly formed from *sutsep*, "always" and *taqyuwsi*, "warrior-like.") Courlander states that this site is "probably" on the Rio Grande, but it is more likely a reference to Chaco Canyon.79

The Greasewood Clan refers to the wood traditionally used to make the phallic dibble. This prized item is ultimately placed upon a man's grave as a ladder whereby his spirit-breath may climb down to the Underworld.80 (Incidentally, the Hopi word for dibble is *sooya*. The related word *sootanta* means "to be having intercourse with a woman." Enigmatically, both words are cognates of *soohu,* or "star.")

The Bow Clan was the leader of the Hopi Third World, which was destroyed because of its wickedness by an immense flood.81 According to Thomas Banyacya of the Coyote Clan in Oraibi, the chief of the Bow Clan was also father to a pair of sons who were given charge of the *owatutuveni,* or stone tablets (see Chapter 5): "Now the Great Chieftain who led the faithful one[s] to this new life and land was a Bow clan and he had two sons who were of the same mother.... It was to these two brothers [that] a set of sacred stone tablets were given and both were instructed to carry them to a place the Great Spirit had instructed them."82 The connection of the Bow Clan with the custody of the sacrosanct stone tablets illustrates the importance of the former in Hopi history. Both the Bow Clan and the closely related Ko'kop-Coyote phratry are in charge of Wúwutcim, or the New Fire Ceremony, held in November. (See brief description in Chapter 3.) Originating from the northwest, this phratry includes such clans as the Gray Wolf, Fire, and Agave. Its *wuya* is Masau'u (Orion).

Some of the war-like members of Bow Clan eventually settled at Awatovi ("Bow Height") on Antelope Mesa south of Keams Canyon. (The

Hopi word for bow is *awta*.) Surprisingly, Courlander relates that when members of the Bear Clan first established their village at Masipa in circa A.D. 1100, they found the Bow Clan already living in their large village at Awatovi. This suggests a very early settlement in the area by the latter.[83] Archaeologists have found a series of kiva murals at Awatovi, some of which depict one of the Twin War Gods clutching a bow-and-arrow next to possibly Masau'u, who wears a bandoleer on his left shoulder instead of the customary right. Also depicted are number a *katsinam*, including Ahöla (described in Chapter 7) and Pooka, the Dog Katsina.[84]

In A.D. 1700 the only known incident of intra-tribal massacre took place at Awatovi, effectively destroying the village in the process. Suffice to say that the Warrior Societies (Motswimi) of all three Hopi Mesas raided the town and killed its male residents, not only because the latter let back in Spanish missionaries, who had been totally driven out of the territory twenty years earlier, but also because the village was a haven for sorcerers.[85] Even three hundred years later the Hopi are loathe to talk about this event that was seemingly so *qahopi*, so uncharacteristic of these "People of Peace."

Every society has its darker side (some more than others), and the Hopi tribe, despite its magnificent and complex religious rites, is no exception. This shadow nature is specifically manifested in the canine context that we have been discussing. "There is... an affinity of certain animals, notably wolf and coyote, with witchcraft. Both coyote and wolf are regarded as sources of *duhisa*, witch power."[86] The Yaya Ceremony was based on the shamanistic ability of shape shifting, or assuming the form of various animals. Those who performed this ritual obtained their power from the spirit people of the animal kingdom (who were decidedly distinct from the *katsinam*). Their abilities included fire walking and seeing over long distances in the dark. "About midnight a fog came in so thick the people could not see one another. 'This is a sign that your ceremony has been perfect,' said the leader of the animals. 'From now on your movements will be secret. Your protecting star will be Ponóchona [Sucks From the Belly], the star you must ask to increase the animal kingdom on earth."[87] (If the reader will recall, this refers to the star Sirius.) A.M. Stephen identifies the word *ya'yatü* as a Keresan word meaning "mother," thus emphasizing the nursing aspect of Sirius. He states that this was, on the other hand, a "phallic, wizard society" which performed many supernatural feats, such as falling from great heights without being harmed.[88] Eventually, however, the Yaya Ceremony was corrupted and a cult of sorcerers developed. Not unlike practitioners of witchcraft the world over, these Southwestern sorcerers would frequently cause foul weather, personal misfortune, disease, or even death. In order to assure their own survival, some of these people would be forced to take the lives of others, even those of their own relatives.

The main village at Panlangwu ("Red Rock Place"), now known as

Canyon de Chelly (See Chapter 4), was thought to be the headquarters of this cult.89 As evidence of this, a number of canine pictographs have been found in the side Canyon del Muerto at Antelope House Ruin and Twin Trail Ruin, including those with bared teeth. In addition, images of both dogs and arrows have been found in Pictograph Cave just east of White House Ruin in the main canyon.90 Among other locations, the sorcerers migrated to Chípiya (or Tsipiya), or Home of the Bighorn Sheep, now known as Aztec Ruins, and to Chaco Canyon where they spent a number of years.

Recently an even darker scenario than Lekson's hierarchical model of Chaco Canyon has emerged. Archaeologist Christy Turner has used extensive osteological and forensic evidence to suggest that a cult of cannibalism centered on Chaco Canyon developed during the time of its ascendancy.

> "By exclusion, correspondence, analogy, and distribution evidence, we propose that the majority of Chaco Anasazi cannibal episodes resulted from acts of violent terrorism, possibly combined with ritual, incited by a few zealous cultists from Mexico and their descendant followers who possessed the deadly ceremonial knowledge of certain Mexican socio-religious and warfare practices. If we are right, then it follows that the strong spatial and temporal concordance between Anasazi cannibalism and Chacoan great houses points also to a Mexican stimulus for rapid development of things Chacoan."91

He believes that these warrior-cultists also gained the social control needed to direct the construction of the massive buildings in Chaco by performing human sacrifice dedicated to the Mesoamerican gods Tezcalipoca and Xipe Tótec. The former was the jaguar (or sometimes eagle) god of the sun who wore a smoking mirror on his chest by which he observed and judged the deeds of men; the latter was the maize god of spring who wore a flayed human skin. In addition, Turner associates Xipe Tótec with the Hopi god Masau'u. Needless to say, this controversial hypothesis infuriates many contemporary Puebloan people. Other legends from the Native American Southwest, however, seem to corroborate these claims of cannibalism and witchcraft. The richly poetic novelist Leslie Marmon Silko from Laguna Pueblo (whose language is Keresan) talks about an ancient contest of sorcerers that closely resembles the Yaya Ceremony (in its corrupted form) mentioned above. "Way up in the lava rock hills / north of Cañoncito / they got together / to fool around in caves / with their animal skins. / Fox, badger, bobcat, and wolf / they circled the fire / and on the fourth time / they jumped into that animal's skin."92 Each witch assuming the form of his or her totem animal tries to outdo the other in paradigms of evil: corpses of infants simmering in blood, skulls cut away and brains sucked out, cinders from the burned hogans of the dead, bundles of flints and severed fingertips, penises, or clitorises— all the grisly minutiae of necromancy.93

Even though archaeological evidence suggests that the Diné (Navajo) did not enter the region until well after Chaco Canyon was abandoned, they nevertheless have legends regarding these ruins. One story involves an evil gambler named He Who Wins Men At Play, who came to Kin Teel (also spelled Kin Tiel), Navajo for "Wide House," which is actually either Pueblo Pintado found on Chacra Mesa ten miles east of Chaco Canyon 94 or Wide Ruin located exactly fifty miles due south of Canyon de Chelly. "He enslaved the people by gambling and winning from them their rights to freedom, after which he demanded that they build the huge pueblo for his house." Eventually a young Diné man together with divine assistance defeated the gambler, who was then "...shot into the sky as an arrow."95 Incidentally, the coveted object under a gambler's shell game cup in Hopi is called *soomoki*, which for some reason literally means "star bundle."

Ultimately, we can only speculate on the specifics of the complex interrelationships and mycelial migrations of native groups that occurred over a millennium ago around the Four Corners area. Are the two contemporary Hopi phratries mentioned above, i.e., Reed-Greasewood-Bow and Ko'kop-Coyote, either offshoots of or remnants of the Chichimecs, or were they merely influenced by contact with the latter? Did a small but imperious cult of Toltecs actually infiltrate the erstwhile egalitarian and relatively pacifistic Anasazi/Hisatsinom culture, thereby instituting a despotic regime that used a campaign of psychological terror and coerced labor to construct the massive pueblos at Chaco Canyon? As the author and editor David Roberts eloquently asks: "Had the Chaco Phenomenon been a spectacular aberration, a two hundred-year meteor of bloody and brilliant arrogance flashing and dying across the blank sky of centuries in which the Anasazi co-existed in harmony?"96 In this case a shift from the interrogative to the declarative mode is probably impossible. We can say with impunity though that the Dog People once lived at the geographic point whose uranographic correlative is the Dog Star Sirius. Whether or not the more violent hypothesis propounded by Turner et al. regarding Chaco Canyon and its environs is accepted, the constellation of recurrent cultural motifs heretofore discussed —viz., canine, bow and arrow, and fire— nonetheless reflects the archetypal resonances of the constellation Canis Major.

In the less than favorable environment of Chaco Canyon, the Dog People managed to construct during the 10th and 11th centuries over a dozen major pueblos, half of which are bow-shaped. For example, separated on a north-south line by about two-and-a-third miles, the axis of Pueblo Alto to the north is 1.1 degrees west of due north, while the axis of

Tsin Kletzin to the south is one degree west of due north. Both of these bow-shaped structures are metonymically shooting their arrows, i.e., their spiritual energy, to the south, toward the cosmological zenith. More perfectly though, the axis of the likewise bow-shaped (or D-shaped) Pueblo Bonito is only two-tenths of one degree east of due north, a geodetic exactitude approaching that of the Great Pyramid in Egypt. The cultural sine qua non of the bow icon is reinforced by a correlating petroglyph surmounted by a spiral found near the Sun Dagger on Fajada Butte.

> "The shape, unusual in rock art, corresponds with the floor plan of Pueblo Bonito, also D-shaped, and to the building's solar cycles. The lines of the petroglyph's diameter and perpendicular radius correspond with two principle walls at Pueblo Bonito that are accurately aligned to the north-south and east-west axes. A hole drilled into the petroglyph corresponds with the position of the primary kiva at Pueblo Bonito. The spiral over the D-shape may refer to the great house's cardinal and solar alignments. The D-shape is similar to the bow-and-arrow design used by historic Pueblos in depicting the sun. In Pueblo tradition, a bow and arrow offered to the sun will ensure hunting prowess. If the reading is accurate, the petroglyph may be the first recording of the relationship between Anasazi great houses and their beliefs."[97]

In contrast to the southward emphasis of Pueblo Alto and Tsin Kletzin, Pueblo Bonito is shooting its arrow north toward the nadir, paralleling the Great North Road that leads to the Sipapuni— in this case, Kutz Canyon.[98] Whereas many of the Anasazi architectural structures in the Southwest (such as Aztec Ruins) are solstitially aligned, those at Chaco that were just mentioned reflect via their north-south orientation the vertical tripartite axis of the Underworld, earth, and heaven. As the Center-place, Chaco Canyon most certainly must have functioned as the ceremonial fulcrum between provenance and predestination, ontogeny and teleology. As we have seen, however, nadir and zenith, the Underworld and the sky, are converse sides of the same coin. It comes as no surprise, then, that in one Hopi legend a kiva ladder descending to the Underworld is found at the very summit of the San Francisco Peaks.[99]

Just as the monumental Egyptian pyramids burst forth in a brief period of earlier construction (viz., the Third and Fourth Dynasties) rather than gradually emerging as a result of evolutionary growth over the many centuries of Pharaonic rule, what is arguably the greatest achievement of Anasazi architecture appeared during the so-called Developmental Pueblo Period (Pueblo II). Beginning in the 10th century, the rise of Chaco Canyon initially fixed the terrestrial/celestial template that we have described by centering upon the most brilliant star in the heavens, Sirius. Thereafter, the development proceeded westward with the establishment of Canyon de Chelly/Saiph in the mid-11th century and then southwestward with the settlement of the Hopi Mesas/Orion's belt at the beginning of the 12th century, continuing with the subsequent construction of Wupatki/Bellatrix in about the mid-12th century. The north-south axis would be added a century later with the appearance of pueblos at Tsegi Canyon/Rigel to the north and at Homol'ovi/Betelgeuse to the south.

Was the Chaco Phenomenon somehow connected with the Katsina Phenomenon that we discussed in the previous chapter? Although most of the archaeological evidence for the *katsinam* postdates the abandonment of Chaco Canyon, some of the legends of these spirit messengers suggest their participation in the earliest Anasazi/Hisatsinom migrations. Perhaps the initial wave (mentioned previously) of *katsina* influx from the south via the Rio Grande beginning circa A.D. 1000 did indeed influence the development of Chaco Canyon. For instance, one of the most common petroglyphic representations of the Jornada Style found along the Rio Grande in western Texas and southern New Mexico is the rain god Tlaloc, which is frequently shown with goggle or almond-shaped eyes, a triangular nose, and a trapezoidal head.

"A number of investigators have acknowledged parallels between the Tlaloc and kachina cults and have suggested that the kachina cult appears to be a variant of the Tlaloc cult. The kachinas as bringers of rain and clouds, with their homes on the tops of mountains or at water sources, bear obvious similarities.... Thus the Jornado style is important in providing positive evidence for a logical historical and cultural connection between the Tlaloc cult and the Pueblo kachina cult, the Jornada region being culturally affiliated with late developments at Casas Grandes [Paquimé], which were ultimately traceable to central Mexico."[100]

The mutual Chaco-Paquimé influence has been discussed earlier. A more significant question, however, is whether or not the two phenomena mentioned (viz., Chaco and Katsina) were in some way connected to the overall Orion Phenomenon, which, as we will see in the next few chapters, appears to have a world-wide influence. Before exploring in Part II of this book the global implications of the Orion Correlation, we will discuss one more constellation important to the ancient peoples of the American Southwest.

## *Death Valley and Aries (Plus a Few Other Companions of Orion)*

W e have heretofore mentioned that the terrestrial correlate of Taurus coincides with the large loop in the Colorado River formed by the Shivwits Plateau to its north. (Refer again to Diagram 4, p. 171.) We have also noted that the major star Aldebaran of that constellation corresponds to Grand Canyon Caverns. In addition, we find a Pleiades correlation located on the Colorado River just downstream from the point where it starts to flow southward in the final stretch toward its mouth. The constellation's terrestrial correlative is Grapevine Canyon, the largest petroglyph site in southern Nevada, located near what the Mohave call Avikwa'ame, or Spirit Mountain (Newberry Peak). The tribe also identifies this area as the House of Mastamho, the cosmogonic god who created both this mountain and the Colorado River.[101] (Note the linguistic similarity between this god and the Hopi god Masau'u.)

It is plausible that the constellation Monoceros, the Unicorn, is represented by the ruin sites in Petrified Forest National Park, together with Kinlichee and Kin Tiel (Wide Ruins) as well as those near the Zuni Indian Reservation, such as Hawikuh, Village of the Great Kivas, and Atsinna (El Morro National Monument). It is likewise plausible that Lepus, the Hare, is represented by a number of ruin sites in southwestern Colorado and southeastern Utah. The terrestrial/celestial coordinates for this constellation are as follows: Mesa Verde National Park/Delta Lepus; Hovenweep National Monument/Arneb; National Bridges National Monument/Mu Lepus; Canyonlands National Park/Epsilon Lepus; Lowry Ruin/Nihal; and Escalante Ruin/Gamma Lepus. (These site correlations are tentative and need more study.) The constellation Eridanus, the River, may well be represented by the now submerged ruins in Glen Canyon and those along both the upper Colorado River and lower Green River. We have also suggested that Gemini might be found to the southeast in a number of ruin sites below the Mogollon Rim, including Kinishba near Ft. Apache (corresponding to Alhena) and Besh Ba Gowah near the town of Globe (corresponding to Mu Gemini). The terrestrial correlations of Pollux and Castor are plausibly located in southern Arizona near the Chiricahua Mountains and the Dragoon Mountains respectively. The Hopi word for Castor and Pollux is *Naatupkom*, which literally means "siblings of the same sex." Is this merely a coincidence? Since these two stars do not necessarily resemble twins per se, it is highly improbable that the Hopi designation for these stars should coincide with that of the Western zodiac. The implied cross-cultural exchange of information is a tantalizing possibility, though perhaps ultimately unprovable.

Where, then, on our map of the Southwest is Aries located? If we move a proportional distance in a westerly direction from Orion, Taurus, and the Pleiades, we find that Aries rests snugly within the contours of Death Valley, with Sheratan and Hamal to the north near the Grapevine

Mountains (not to be confused with Grapevine Canyon previously mentioned) and 41 Aries to the south. Because we have entered the territory of nomadic rather than sedentary habitation, we do not expect to find any pueblo ruins, though petroglyph sites may prove to delineate the stars of this constellation in its mundane manifestation.

In fact, this region is rife with petroglyphic evidence of the Ram. According to David S. Whitley, one of the foremost experts on North American prehistoric art and a professor of archaeology at UCLA, the Coso Range just south of Death Valley National Monument is... "[o]ne of the most spectacular concentrations of rock art sites in North America—if not the world..."[102] This is a striking statement for an academic to make. Along this thirty mile stretch of canyon located within the boundaries of the China Lake Naval Weapons Center, over 14,000 pecked rock drawings are known to exist.[103] Dr. Whitley claims to have found over 350 engravings of bighorn sheep alone, which he estimates to be between 1,000 and 1,500 years old.[104] Whitley believes that this plethora of sheep petroglyphs formed part of a shamanistic ritual system to induce rainfall.

> "Since the shaman and his spirit helper, the bighorn sheep, were considered one and the same, and since the shaman's trance was a metaphoric form of ritual death, the shaman made rain by 'killing a bighorn' (or killing himself, a supernatural bighorn) and entering a trance. Thus, petroglyphs depicting a human shooting a sheep have nothing to do with hunting; they are metaphoric symbols indicating that a Bighorn Shaman came to this location and entered a trance to bring rain."[105]

These shamans sometimes traveled great distances on their vision quests. Whitley states that Numic speakers (i.e., Shoshone, as well as Northern and Southern Paiute) may have traveled even as far as Wyoming's Bighorn Basin (its name merely another coincidence?) to obtain power in warfare.[106] They might have also been attracted to both the world's largest mineral hot springs at the present town of Thermopolis and the Bighorn Medicine Wheel, which we mentioned earlier in this chapter in the context of the Chaco Meridian.

Constructed from piles of rocks, many so-called hunting blinds together with bighorn sheep bones have been found near springs in the Death Valley region as well, especially on its eastern side. Of course, in ancient cosmological thinking, springs represent not only essential life-giving oases in the desert but also portals leading to the spirit world. In addition, a number of serpentine rock alignments and circles have been discovered in this area, possibly corresponding to water and the Underworld.[107] The confirmed existence of at least one bighorn sheep petroglyph (but probably many more still to be found) in Titus Canyon of the Grapevine Mountains attests to the fact that the Bighorn Shaman's powers to control weather was needed throughout the entire Great Basin.108 Although hunting of mountain sheep undoubtedly occurred, more likely the emphasis was on their supernatural attributes connected with water.109

In this context we are reminded of the Hopi Al (Two Horn) Society, the members of which wear the involuted horns of the mountain sheep on their heads. This fraternity directs the November Wúwutcim, or New Fire Ceremony, which is thought to have developed from the annual Shoshonean pinyon pine-nut harvest festival and concurrent mourning ritual sometime after 1000 B.C.— a date squarely at the center of the Age of Aries, by the way. We might add here that the various clans migrating southeast from the Great Basin also brought the idea of fixing this festival's date according to the position of Orion and the Pleiades in the night sky.110 The early shamanistic tradition of associating mountain sheep with rainfall is carried on in the Pong (Pang), or bighorn sheep *katsina*, which in particular has the power to make rain as well as to cure spasms.111 The Hopi word for the sacred bighorn sheep is *pangwu*, or *pa'ngwu*. Breaking up this word, we find that *pa* (*paa*) denotes "water," but it also has the sense of "wonder, awe, surprise," etc. The suffix *ngwu* means "causing to occur." Thus, *pa'ngwu* literally means "causing water (or in the desert 'wonder') to occur," which points to the mountain sheep's shamanistic potentiality.

As a precursor of further evidence, the Egyptian word *ba* means "ram," and its palindrome *ab* means "horn" (of an animal).112 (As we will note in Chapter 11, the homophones of this palindrome mean "soul" and "heart" respectively.) Since no "b" sound exists in Hopi language, "p" is the closest phonetic approximation. Thus, the same root word is used in both Egyptian and Hopi to refer to the ram. Especially in Thebes, the people worshipped the great ram-headed deity Amon (Amun or Amen), also known as the "king of the gods" and thereby equated with the Greek Zeus.113

The Hopi constellation named *Soo'ala* literally means "star-horn," but the word *ala* (or *aala*) specifically designates the Two Horn Society. Thus, *Soo'ala* very possibly could refer to Aries, which traditionally represents the Ram. The word *soo'ala* also refers to a cat's cradle figure, whose angle of strings could be likened to the constellation's angled ram's horn. However, as with the case of the Gemini Twins, Aries does not resemble a ram or ram's head in particular, but only symbolically so. Is this yet another example of cross-cultural influence? (Incidentally, the Hopi word *ari* means shearing sheep, or cutting hair. Was there once some sort of hunting and ritual "shearing" of mountain sheep before the introduction of domestic sheep?) At least one African tribe from the Congo region (unfortunately not designated in this source) worshipped Ala, "...a Supreme Spirit of the Sky, a Jove, whose voice is thunder, who gives or withholds the rain, and whose hand hurls the lightning."114 (Of course, we need not be reminded of the name of supreme god of Islam.) These meteorological attributes are all in keeping with *pangwu*, from which the Hopi Ala (Two Horn) Society derives its power.

Legends of treasure buried and forgotten at various spots in the West abound, and sometimes the source of wealth is decidedly ancient. In conjunction with the terrestrial Aries of Death Valley, we find the following story. Author Bourke Lee relates that two prospectors named Fred Thomason and a Mr. White were working the bottom of an abandoned mine shaft at 4,500-5,000 feet above the Death Valley floor near Wingate Pass on the eastern flank of the Panamint Mountains opposite Furnace Creek Ranch, when the latter fell through into an underground cavern. Upon exploration of the hole, the two men were stunned when they realized that the tunnel extended twenty miles into the mountain and led to a vast subterranean city complex. The men claimed to have discovered gold spears and armbands, shields, many statues, including one of solid gold standing eighty-nine-and-a-half feet tall, and bins cut into the rock containing jewels and gold bars. In addition, they found huge, perfectly balanced stone doors (similar to those found at Coral Castle south of Miami, Florida) as well as a room, possibly used as a council chamber, containing a large polished round table inlaid with gold and precious gems. The complex appears to have been illuminated by some sort of natural gas system, and scientifically designed stone wheel barrows with a single balanced wheel in the middle had apparently been used to transport the valuable materials.

The city also served as a mausoleum, since the prospectors encountered over one hundred mummies wearing leather aprons (Masonic?) and gold ornaments or jewels. On the eastern side at the higher level of the complex was located a series of beautiful galleries with stone arches. "Those arches are like big windows in the side of the mountain and they look down on Death Valley. They are high above the valley now, but we believe that those entrances in the mountain side were used by ancient people that built the city. They used to land their boats there."[115] Hence, at one time these tunnels had been used as wharves for an inland sea that has since evaporated.

The two men claimed that they had tried to make a deal with the Smithsonian but finally refused because the institution would only offer them one-and-a-half million dollars instead of the five million for which they had asked. When they brought a team of experts from a prominent Southwest museum to view the fabulous city, a major storm had eroded the entrance and the site was reputedly lost forever. Such are the vague phantasmagoria that seize the brains of those peregrinating the desert in search of ancient treasures.[116]

Given this tale's incredible nature, one wonders whether or not it could contain any semblance of the truth? In tone and detail, it is much like the Egyptian City lost in Grand Canyon (described in the last chapter). But one fact emerges from the evidence found in both the Death Valley complex and the Egyptian City: the water level at one time must have been much higher. This stirs the imagination, and we are taken back to the end of what the Hopi call the Third World, which was destroyed by a deluge of enormous proportions. Despite the isolationists' dogma, could there really have been close contact between the American Southwest and the Old World or, we add with the utmost circumspection, even beyond? Part II of this book will attempt both to answer that question and to elucidate the ultimate implications of the ancient star cities we have called The Orion Zone.

# Part II

# Chapter 9
# To Calibrate the March Of Time

"As I pored over large-scale maps of the major ceremonial centers of Mesoamerica, I found that time after time they replicated the location principle which I first discovered at Izapa: Their solar orientation at one of the solstices invariably aligned with the highest mountain within view. (In other words, the location of the ceremonial center had been consciously chosen so as to align with the highest point at sunrise or sunset on either June 22 or December 22.) It was as though the sun-god himself had decreed the location of native American cities, for each of them employed a commanding topographic feature to calibrate the march of time."[1]

Vincent H. Malmström

## *The Hopi-Mesoamerican Connection*

In the section on Chaco Canyon in the previous chapter, sundry links to lands far to the south were discussed. This sphere of influence may have once extended even to the region of the Maya in southern Mexico, Guatemala, Honduras, and Belize. For instance, the roadways that radiate north and south of Chaco Canyon are structurally and perhaps ceremonially similar to those found in Maya-land. In the northeastern Mexican State of Quintana Roo one "white road," or *sacbe*, as it is called, stretches sixty-two miles from Cobá west to Yaxuná, the latter located a dozen miles southwest of Chichén Itzá.[2] Measuring thirty feet across, this road has the same width as the Chacoan road. In addition, the combined length of the North and South Roads (with Pueblo Bonito at the very center) measures sixty-three miles— nearly the same as the Mayan causeway. Incidentally, "White Road" is the term the Maya used to refer to the Milky Way, along with the phrase "Road of Awe."[3]

Another parallel between the Classic Maya and the Hisatsinom deals with the respective locations of their cities. Apparently neither people was very pragmatic in regard to the founding of their cities in close proximity to reliable water sources; hence, each group was forced to rely on human-made cisterns. John Lloyd Stephens, the first travel writer of Central America, states that about one hundred of these so-called "aguadas" were used to remedy the water situation of one city: "Within the whole circumference of Uxmal there is no well, stream, or fountain, and nothing which bears the appearance of having been used for supplying or obtaining water... The general opinion with regard to these aguadas is that they were 'hechas a mano,' artificial formations or excavations made by the ancient inhabitants as reservoirs for holding water."4 The ancient inhabitants of Third Mesa in Arizona used the exact same structure to allow them to exist in their arid landscape. "Cut into the sandstone of the mesa top around Old Oraibi are some forty to fifty cisterns, called *pa'tni* in Hopi, which formerly supplied the inhabitants of the pueblo with the greater part of their drinking water."5 It is estimated that these cisterns were six to eight feet deep with a carrying capacity of 1,500 gallons. In both cases the cistern is the solution whereby each group could live in locations chosen more by spiritual mandate than practical concerns, it appears.

A common architectural motif found all across the Anasazi Southwest, including at Chaco Canyon and Mesa Verde, is the T-shaped doorway or window. (Fig. 43, p. 175) We also find this far to the south at the Mayan city of Palenque in Chiapas. Specifically, a number of these T-shaped windows were incorporated into the building called the Palace. The Mayan daykeeper, artist, and historian Hunbatz Men explains the meaning of this motif:

> "A transcendental synthesis of human religious experience is inherent in the word *te*, Sacred Tree, which emerged from the words *teol* and *teotl* the names of God the Creator in Mayan and Nahuatl. These most revered and sacred words of the ancient people, symbolized by the Sacred Tree, were represented in the Mayan hieroglyphs as the symbol 'T.' Additionally, this symbol represented the air, the wind, the divine breath of God."6

In other words, the T-shaped doorway or window symbolizes the Sacred Tree at the Center of the World (*axis mundi*) upon which the spirit may shamanistically climb. In addition, it functions as the portal leading to the Great Spirit, through which the breath of life may pass. In Greek the letter T is called *tau*, which echoes the Hopi sun god Tawa. In his classic *Atlantis: the Antediluvian World*, Ignatius Donnelly states that *tau* was an important icon signifying "hidden wisdom" for not only the Mexicans but also the Peruvians, Egyptians, Phoenicians, and Chaldeans. In general, it was emblematic of rejuvenation, freedom from physical suffering, hope, immortality, and divine unity. Furthermore, in numerous cultures *tau* was connected to abundant water or rain-deities. For instance, in Egypt the *anhk*, or ansate cross, was the "key to the Nile" by which Osiris accomplished his annual riparian inundations.7 It is interesting to note that when Moses entered the Sinai desert, he found the Midianite tribe (also called the Kenites) wearing the T-shape on their foreheads. This icon, which represented their god of storms (bringing water) and war (thunder), later became known as the "Yahweh Mark."8 Much later Jesus was in fact crucified on a Tau or St. Anthony's cross instead of on the Latin cross we think of today.9 Thus, in many cultures the T-shape has associations of psychospiritual journeying and ultimate resurrection.

Another motif common both to ancestral Puebloan pottery and petroglyphs and to Mayan architecture and codices is the spiral or stepped fret. As discussed in Chapter 5 in terms of the Homol'ovi star map, this represents the portal between the worlds of the living and the dead. For the Maya this motif is represented by the letter G, or *ge*, and refers to the number zero. It also symbolizes the germ, the egg, the seed, or the essence. "All of the appearances of the 'G'... confirm for us the intimate relationship between the symbolic 'G' and the dead; between their union with cosmic laws and the understanding by the Maya that we are all products of the Great Spirit found in the essence of the Milky Way."[10] Quite incredibly, the Maya intuited the form of our spiral galaxy in this particular icon, which is commonly found not only all across Mesoamerica (e.g., on the facade of the House of the Governor at Uxmal) but also in Southwest pottery designs and rock art too numerous to mention, and even occasionally in the distinctive weave of sandals.[11]

Other correspondences emerge. Was the ceremonial game played in the huge ball court at Chichén Itzá akin to that played in the most northern albeit much smaller ball court located at the contemporaneous village of Wupatki (the left shoulder of Terra Orion)? This is a distance on foot of over two thousand miles! We can only speculate that the game had a common origin, though evidence from 1,350 miles away strengthens this argument. "A ball game marker, found at Teotihuacan, bears an incised symbol identical with the Hopi Indian friendship sign [viz., *nakwách*]. This could, conceivably, indicate a link between the ancient builders of Teotihuacan and the Hopi Indian Tribe of Arizona."[12]

Another factor that unites Hopiland and Mesoamerica is a common number system. The Maya and other southern tribes use a vigesimal system (based on 20) rather than a decimal system (based on 10). Hopi scholar Harold Colton has noted that Third Mesa likewise has always used a vigesimal system, but he believes that Second Mesa and First Mesa once used this system as well. All the other tribes surrounding Hopiland employ the decimal system, and the closest one with a vigesimal system is the Seri in the Mexican State of Sonora.[13] Hence, we can surmise that an enduring southern influence included numbers —a cultural mainstay— as well as architecture, customs, ideas, and legends.

Various ceremonial correlations also suggest a common origin of the Hopi and the Maya. In Chapter 3 we discussed the Hopi Wúwutcim, or the New Fire Ceremony, the culmination of which is timed to coincide with the appearance of both the Pleiades and Orion's belt through the kiva hatchway. "'It is only a short space of time before the three stars [in Orion's belt] are now in line [lengthwise] with the kiva opening, the center star directly above the fireplace [at midnight]. At this moment we begin our most important ritual according to the pattern first laid down on this planet Earth. Life began with fire. Thus we begin.'"[14] Waters states that in 1959 the beginning of this nine-day initiation ceremony was announced in the village of Shongopovi on November 11th.

Diego de Landa, the friar who both contributed a great deal of our knowledge about the historic Maya and, paradoxically, burned many of their codices, describes a similar ritual in his 1566 manuscript: "On arriving, and offering their prayers, they set the banner on top of the temple, and below in the court set each of their idols on leaves of trees brought for this purpose; then *making the new fire* [italics added] they began to burn their incense at many points, and to make offerings of viands cooked without salt or pepper, and drinks made from their beans and calabash seeds."15 This ceremony took place between 8th and the 13th of November. In his book *The Mayan Prophecies*, Adrian Gilbert has determined that in 1507, the year this ritual was last performed, the Pleiades crossed the meridian at midnight on November 11th, midway between the two dates.16

From the Second Mesa village of Shongopovi on November 11th, A.D. 1100 the Pleiades appeared to cross the meridian shortly before 11:30 p.m., and Alnilam (the middle star of Orion's belt) achieved culmination about two hours later. Thus, in both the Hopi and Maya cultures we find ceremonies with the same name and function, synchronized by the same sidereal complex.

In later Mesoamerican cultures, however, this ceremony assumed a particularly brutal aspect, where the original symbolic implications were interpreted literally:

> "Since by tradition fire was first acquired on this occasion, the ceremony itself involved putting out all the fires of the past eras and rekindling new ones. Thus, in the Nahua mind the fateful moment in which the Pleiades passed through the zenith—in relative proximity to Orion's Belt, which they visualized as a 'fire drill'—provided an appropriate opportunity for demonstrating humankind's gratitude to the gods for giving fire. To the Toltecs—and later the Aztecs—this meant cutting out the heart of the sacrificial victim and kindling the first new fire in his chest cavity."17

The resurrection of the sun on the winter solstice is a primary component of both the Maya and Aztec belief systems. As independent researcher John Major Jenkins states, "The rebirth of the sun on the December solstice is a widespread Maya belief. That the Maya believed the winter solstice to be New Year's Day is suggested by the fact that it is still the focus of a midnight ceremony among the Chamula Maya. Moreover, the Aztec sun god Huitzilopochtli, in some contexts appeared as the newborn sun on the December solstice."18 The above-mentioned ceremony corresponds to the Hopi Soyal ceremony described in Chapter 2, whereby Tawa, the sun god, is turned back from his southward course along the horizon, after which he gradually returns to the Hopiland with the vernal warming of the earth. Like the Wúwutcim, this nocturnal ritual is synchronized as well by the belt of Orion; hence, it is not a purely solar phenomenon. We should reiterate that the winter solstice is also the beginning of the *katsina* season, which lasts through July.

Scholar Richard Maitland Bradfield summarizes additional correlations between the Maya and the Hopi: "...what I believe happened was that a nexus of ideas, having to do with moisture, with the germination and growth of corn, and with the return of warm weather, was carried from northern Yucatan into the pueblo region at the formative point, i.e. around A.D. 700, in the development of the Pueblo culture."[19] He cites the Hopi Bean-germinating Ceremony of early February, the Water Serpent Ceremony of early March, and the Flute Ceremony of mid-August in every other year as examples of this nexus transferred to the north. In addition, he compares the Mayan Young Corn god with Muy'ingwa, the Chacs with the Hopi cloud deities, and Itzamna in his aspect as sun god with Tawa. It is significant that Bradfield keys in on the water aspect, since the Water Clan (which includes the Young Corn, the Cloud, the Tadpole, the Frog, the Snow, and the Rabbitbrush Clans), along with the Parrot Clan and the Katsina Clan, are thought to originally hail from lands to the south.[20]

One final Hopi ritual, the Snake-Antelope Ceremony (or Snake Dance, as it is sometimes called) appears to have a Mesoamerican correlation. Performed in mid-August in alternate years to the Flute Ceremony, the Snake-Antelope Ceremony is the most infamous in the popular consciousness, partly because its participants at one point place gophers snakes, bull snakes, or even rattlesnakes in their teeth. The primary purpose of the sixteen-day ceremony, however, is not to shock non-Indians but to assure sufficient rain for the final maturity of the crops. Prior to the concluding dance, before midnight on the eleventh day the marriage of the Snake Maiden and Antelope Youth occurs. Directly following this, the *pavásio*, or period of greatest concentration and singing of sacred songs, continues until Orion rises to hover upon the eastern horizon. (Waters mistakenly refers to the western horizon.)[21] On August 21, A.D. 1100 from the village of Shongopovi, Orion appeared to clear the eastern horizon about 2:00 a.m. Again we see a major Hopi ritual synchronized by this primary constellation.

Discussing the Maya serpentine motif, Adrian Gilbert points to the influence on Mesoamerican cultures of the rattlesnake in particular. "For according to [José] Diaz Bolio the Maya, and indeed all the other cultures of Central America worthy of the name civilization, were deeply involved in a rattlesnake cult."[22] The Maya associate the shaking tail of the rattlesnake with the Pleiades, which they call *tzab*, meaning "rattle."[23] As mentioned above, their culmination in the night sky synchronizes the Mayan New Fire Ceremony in the same way that Orion's crossing the meridian synchronizes the Hopi one. Many architectural examples of the serpent exist, especially in Uxmal and Chichén Itzá. The most well known instance is perhaps El Castillo, or the Pyramid of Kukulkán, at the latter site. At sunrise on the vernal equinox a serpentine shadow forms on the edge of the steps at the bottom of which is a sculpture of a snake's head. The Maya term for the plumed snake is Kukulkán; in Mayan *kukul* means "feather" and *can* means "snake."[24]

Evidence has even been recently found of a Mayan Snake Dance. One lintel at Yaxchilan depicts its ruler Bird-Jaguar and a subordinate lord dancing with snakes in their hands in the exact manner that we see on the Hopi Mesas. A similar scene is illustrated in House D at Palenque.[25] Historian of religion Karl W. Luckert also emphasizes the importance of the snake cult and its link to both cultures: "The religion of the Serpent seems to have reached the plateau of Anasazi-land, on which the realm of the Hopi Indians is located, in at least two distinct waves, probably more... The first wave is still pulsating in the Snake dances of the Snake Clan tradition; the second wave has survived in the Feathered-/or Horned-Serpent ceremonies of the Water and Maize [or Corn] Clans."[26] The latter ceremony known as Pa'lülükonti (theWater Serpent Dance occurring in March) is described more fully in the Wupatki section of Chapter 4, pp. 79-80. Both the celestial Feathered Serpent Palulukang (or Pa'lölökang— the prefix *pa-* indicating "water") and its terrestrial counterpart the rattlesnake, known as *tselölökang* (which is semantically similar to *tselölöta*, "dripping" or "beginning to rain"), still play a prominent role in Hopi ritual, much as they probably did for the tribes far to the south.

### The Mayan Orion As Celestial Hearthstones

For the Maya the direct associations to the constellation Orion are multiple and complex. On one level the constellation has a domestic connotation. During the destruction of their previous era (corresponding to the Hopi Third World, which was similarly destroyed by flood) the hearthstones began to fly about of their own accord. According to Dennis Tedlock, one translator of the Quiché "Council Book" called the *Popol Vuh*: "Andrés Xiloj remarked: 'It's like a cataract of stones from a volcano!' This incident may be the origin of the stars Alnitak, Saiph, and Rigel in Orion; today these three stars are said to be the three hearthstones of the typical Quiché kitchen fireplace, arranged to form a triangle, and the cloudy area they enclose (Great Nebula M-42) is said to be the smoke from the fire."[27] Indeed within the common Hopi fireplace at one corner of the room, usually three round stones (though sometimes more) served to hold up the cooking pot.[28]

However, once we turn to the sacred version of the more secular living quarters, i.e., the semi-subterranean kiva, we find that no chimneys were ever employed, and that a rectangular firepit called a *kwop'kota* was located in the center of the room. In this context it is interesting to note that the Hopi word *kwuhi* means "coals" or "embers," while the term *kwuhpu* refers to "lifted head." Hence, we have these terrestrial embers mirroring the celestial embers of the sky one can only see by looking upward.29 Another semantic "coincidence" is the pair of Hopi words *qööhi*, "fire" and *qötö'at*, "head."

The kivas in Hopiland are for the most part rectangular, perhaps reflecting the morphology of Orion that we noted in Chapter 3. We need not go further into the structural details of kivas here, except to mention one prominent feature of every kiva: a hole two inches or so in diameter located in the main floor and usually sealed by a wooden plug when not in use. "This feature is the sipapuh, the place of the gods, and the most sacred portion of the ceremonial chamber. Around this spot the fetishes are set during a festival; it typifies also the first world of Tusayan [Hopi] genesis and the opening through which the people emerged."30 Located at the western end of the kiva, this local *sipapu* corresponds to the main Sipapuni of Grand Canyon.

Whether we are speaking of the domestic hearth or the kiva fireplace at the center of the *imago mundi*, the ritualized fire symbolizes this cosmic triangle formed from the stars whose locations were established at the creation of the current "world." If we look at this Mayan sidereal triad in relation to the astro-terrestrial correlations of Arizona, we find Walpi (Alnitak) at one apex, Canyon de Chelly (Saiph) at another, and Betatakin (Rigel) at a third. At the heart of this grand equilateral triangle is Black Mesa, near the village of Piñon. Perhaps it is no accident, then, that this happens to be the region where ceremonial coal is obtained for the New Fire Ceremony. Hence, the Orion Nebula, a great celestial nursery constantly giving birth to new star systems, corresponds on Earth to the locus of the glistening black fuel whereby the new fire of the ancestral Puebloans is still perpetuated annually.

Another Mayan association to Orion is that of the Heart of the Sky. "In this area of Mesoamerica, the stars of Orion are seen in a true zenith position. This may be why they express the notion of centrality among the Quiché Maya, who associate Orion with a deity known as Heart of the Sky... Huracán is another way of referring to Hurricane, one of the three aspects of Heart of Sky, who appears with the plumed serpent in the creation epic."31 According to Tedlock, another epithet for this god is Thunderbolt.32 In Chapter 8 we identified this Heart of the Sky god as the Hopi deity Sótuknang, whose red eye is Aldebaran in the Hyades, which of course are adjacent to Orion. Not surprisingly, we find resonances of Sótuknang in gods to the south.

"When not masked, the personator of Sotuknangu wears a star-shaped hat from which feathers hang over his face. This deity is described as 'both Star and Lightning, the god who kills and renders fertile and who initiated the practice of scalping.' (cf. Elsie Clews Parsons, *Pueblo Indian Religion*) Thus we see in this Hopi god one version of Quetzalcóatl, with traces of Tlaloc (rain, fertility), and also Xipe Tótec, who was ritually honored by the taking of scalps."33

In this Hopi Heart of the Sky god we notice a conflation of Mayan/Aztec deities. However, in the Hopi god Masau'u we can also see shades of the goggle-eyed Tlaloc, whose rectangular body is found in petroglyphs throughout the Southwest, especially in the Jornada-style rock art of the Rio Grande Valley.34 Masau'u has also been compared to the fertility and death god of spring, Xipe Tótec, who was wont to wear a coat of flayed human skin, symbolizing rebirth in much the same way as a snake shedding its skin.

In Chapter 3 we conclusively identified Orion with Masau'u, Hopi god of earth and death. In the Mayan version of this complex, Heart of Sky is sometimes followed by Heart of Earth, the latter of which is never used by itself.35 Perhaps in the same manner the Hopi god Sótuknang is merely the celestial dimension of a totality that might be deemed Sótuknang-Masau'u, i.e., Heart of the Sky, Heart of the Earth. Instead of functioning as discrete entities, these two gods could possibly fulfill a dualistic role in the pantheon of Hopi deities. In Chapter 3 we established the essential dualism inherent in Hopi cosmology and ideology. If the Hopi were indeed influenced by the Maya, this trait may well be inherited.

> "To this day the Quiché Maya think of dualism in general as complementary rather than opposed, interpenetrating rather than mutually exclusive. Instead of being in logical opposition to one another, the realms of divine and human actions are joined by a mutual attraction. If we had an English word that fully expressed the Mayan sense of narrative time, it would have to embrace the duality of the divine and the human in the same way the Quiche term *cahuleu* or 'sky-earth' preserves the duality of what we call the 'world.'"36

In our case, we could substitute the duality of "celestial and terrestrial" for that of "divine and human."

### *The Maya and Hopi Solstice Alignments of Cities and Peaks*

The geographer Vincent H. Malmström has made the distinction between *site* and *situation*. The former signifies the immediate topography upon which a ceremonial center is located, while the latter refers to the relationship that a given site has to its surroundings.37 In this regard he has found over two dozen Mesoamerican and Central American prehistoric sites, each of which is solstitially situated —either summer or winter, sunrise or sunset— to a major visible mountain. For instance, the proto-Mayan city of Izapa (the site mentioned above in the epigraph to this chapter), founded circa 1300 B.C. on the current border of Mexico and Guatemala, is "situated" on a summer solstice sunrise line to the Volcán Tajumulco, highest mountain in Central America.38 In the Petén region the Mayan centers of Uaxactún, founded circa 100 A.D., and Tikal, founded a century later, are both oriented on a winter solstice sunrise line to Baldy Beacon and Victoria Peak respectively, the latter being the highest point in the Maya Mountains of Belize.39

Many of the early Olmec cities on Mexico's Gulf Coast are also positioned solstitially. For example, the Olmec capital of La Venta, founded circa 1000 B.C., is situated at summer solstice sunset to Volcán San Martín 40, while San Lorenzo, founded two centuries earlier, is situated at winter solstice sunset to Cerro Zempoaltepec.41

The Valley of Mexico has numerous solstitial alignments as well. The major ceremonial center of Teotihuacán 42, founded circa 200 B.C., is situated at winter solstice sunrise to Pico de Orizaba, about 115 miles to the southeast. This is the highest peak in Mesoamerica (18,855 ft.) and was known to the Aztecs as Citlaltépetl, or "Mountain of the Star." Directly south of the Aztecan city Tenochtitlan (now Mexico City) is Cuicuilco, a Pre-Classic site likewise oriented to the winter solstice sun rising over the volcano Popocatépetl. In addition, Tlatilco is aligned with Tlapacoya, and both are situated on the winter solstice sunrise line to the volcanic twin of Popo called Ixtaccíhuatl. This latter volcano also serves as both the winter solstice sunset focal point for Tizatlán and the summer sunset focal point for Cholula.43

Finally, as far north as the Tropic of Cancer we find Alta Vista (otherwise known as Chalchihuites), founded circa 400 A.D., which is situated on the summer solstice sunrise line to Cerro Picacho.44 In addition to these and more solstice orientations which he cites, Malström also has determined that a number of ceremonial cities were positioned to the sunset on August 13th, the day, according to the Maya, when the current world was created. (See the last section of this chapter.)

The purpose of presenting these solstitial alignments is not to mire the reader in tropical curiosities but instead to propose the legacy of interrelational loci that Mesoamerica plausibly bequeathed to the Four Corners region of the American Southwest. Our strongest case is the Oraibi-Wupatki-Humphreys Peak alignment. Both of these villages established in the twelfth century are exactly situated at the winter solstice sunset (240 degrees azimuth) to the highest and most ceremonially significant mountain in Nuvatukya'ovi, or the San Francisco Peaks. Of course, this is the home of the *katsinam* and the core of their activity for the annual cycle extending from the end of July to the winter solstice.

(Diagram 3, p. 32)

Another alignment exists between Betatakin, constructed in Tsegi Canyon after the mid-thirteenth century, and Antelope House also occupied during the thirteenth century in Canyon del Muerto (a northern offshoot of Canyon de Chelly). These two villages were situated at winter solstice sunrise (120 degrees azimuth) to Mount Taylor (11,301 ft.) in the San Mateo Mountains of New Mexico. Granted, no inter-visibility occurs between either of these two villages and the mountain, but the specific direction of this promontory so ritually prominent to both the ancestral pueblo people and the Navajo would have been well known.

An additional vector which is nearly on a summer solstice sunrise point (specifically, 62 degrees azimuth) runs northeast from Walpi on First Mesa, skirts the north rim of Canyon del Muerto, goes through Aztec Ruins (in Hopi, Hoo'ovi, or "Arrow-up") constructed on the Animas River in the early twelfth century (see Chapter 2), transits less than five miles south of the Chacoan outlier of Chimney Rock occupied until A.D. 1125 (also mentioned in Chapter 2), and terminates at Summit Peak (13,272 ft.) in the San Juan Mountains of south-central Colorado.

Finally, rounding out all the solstice points, a line from Mummy Cave Ruin in Canyon del Muerto, completed A..D. 1284, extends northwest on a more or less summer solstice sunset vector (303 degrees azimuth), skirts the northeastern face of Black Mesa, transits Dowozhiebito Canyon at a point a little over five miles north of Keet Seel, whose final construction phase was A.D. 1286, and arrives at Toko'navi (Navajo Mountain, 10,388 ft.) on the Arizona-Utah border, where a number of thirteenth century Hisatsinom villages were located and where the Hopi have erected a shrine to which periodic pilgrimages are still made.

These solstice points, or "sun's houses," on the horizon have become a quintessential part of Hopi cosmology. To each intercardinal direction has been associated a specific color as well as particular animal and plant species. (Fig. 44, p. 208)

From a ritualistic standpoint the most important "houses" are the summer solstice sunset in the northwest and the winter solstice sunrise in the southeast. If we look at the latter direction, we notice that its symbolic aviary totems are two non-native species: the parrot and the macaw. These birds come from Mesoamerica far to the southeast. Anyone who has witnessed a *katsina* Parrot Dance (as did this author at the Second Mesa village of Shongopovi in late May of 1995) is surely startled by the incongruity of parrot-spirits dancing on the high desert and is reminded of the long history of distant migrations the Hisatsinom had to endure.

The Hopi conceptualize these solstice points not as azimuthal abstractions but as doorways through which the sometimes harsh and awesome sun god Tawa daily goes to and from the Underworld. A description from the myth of the Warrior Twins' journey northwest to the

| Direction | Color | Prim. Animal | Sec. Animal | Plant | Bird |
|---|---|---|---|---|---|
| kwíniwi (NW) | yellow | mountain lion | deer | corn | oriole |
| tévyuna (SW) | blue/green | black bear | mountain sheep | beans | mt. bluebird |
| tátyuka (SE) | red | gray wolf | antelope | squash | parrot/macaw |
| hópoko (NE) | white | wildcat | elk | cotton | magpie |
| ómi (zenith) | black | golden eagle | jackrabbit | watermelon | cliff swallow |
| atkyami (nadir) | all colors | badger | cottontail rabbit | all plants | canyon wren |

*Fig. 44. Hopi directional table* 45

house of their father and mother, Tawa (Sun) and Huzruiwuhti (Hard Substances Woman), reinforces the perilous nature of these orifices. "The sky is solid at this point, and the walls constantly open and close like giant jaws ready to catch and crush any rash person attempting to pass the forbidden portals."46 The path of the rising and setting sun during the course of the year not only fixes the agricultural cycle (by telling the people, for instance, when to plant one type of corn or another) but also determines the boundaries of a sacred landscape in which Tawa long ago coördinated the schema of villages spiritually mandated by the earth god Masau'u to mirror the latter's celestial form: viz., the constellation Orion. In this universe similar to the one envisioned by Einstein, sacred space fuses with sacred time to both structure and energize the entire ceremonial cycle.

> "The location of those sacred places [solstice points on the horizon] connects sacred space to sacred time and is just as important to a Hopi's religious, cosmological, and intellectual framework as is the determination of the sacred times marking the ends of the year. When the sun pauses precisely at his house, this validates the intellectual construct of the four sacred directions which order sacred space and by which the Hopi order their understanding of the sun's habitual motion."47

Although the community in general was familiar with Tawa's houses, it was those members of the Patki Clan in particular who knew the solstice lore most intimately. (See more about the Patki Clan in Chapter 10.) "Prayer sticks, or *pahos*, offered to the sun are traditionally deposited at a shrine marking this direction at the time of the summer solstice by members of the Patki (Water) clan, from which the Sun Chief is chosen and which has primary responsibility for watching the sun near the solstices."48 As noted above, this clan is thought to have originated in Mesoamerica. Isn't it likely, then, that the tradition of positioning ceremonial cities to align with mountains on any of the four sunrise or sunset points had been an importation from the south?

## The Mayan Orion As the Celestial Turtle

In addition to their duties as sun watchers, the members of the Patki Clan are also ritually associated with turtles. "In the old days turtles were caught, in early summer, in a tributary of the Little Colorado river; before anyone might take a shell, it had to be smoked over and prayers offered by Pa'tki clan chief; the shell was then carefully cut off, and the flesh returned to the stream. Turtle shells were used as dance rattles, attached to the right leg, at dances held during the Pa'lülükoñ-ti ceremony in early March, and at the Nima'n festival [in middle to late July]."49 Turtles were known as "pets" of the clouds 50 and were regarded as sacrosanct by both the Hopi and the Zuni 51, probably because of their aquatic connotation. In addition to the knowledge of solstice orientations, did the Water Clan bring along another Mayan association to Orion?

The Maya conceived of Orion not only as hearthstones at the heart of the sky (discussed in a previous section of this chapter) but also as a turtle (mentioned in Chapter 3 in connection with the Bonampak murals). Referencing the Madrid Codex, epigrapher Linda Schele reinforces this parallel:

> "It shows a turtle with a triangle of stones on its back. The turtle in the codex is shown suspended from cords tying it to the skyband because Orion hangs below the ecliptic. Clearly Orion was the turtle from which the Maize God rose in the resurrection. The Milky Way rearing above the turtle had to be the Maize God appearing in his tree form as he does on the Tablet of the Foliated Cross at Palenque. The image of the first turtle really is in the sky."52

Here the motif of the triangle of stones is repeated, but significantly each of these round stones heaped on the turtle's back is marked with an equilateral cross— the Anasazi (and presumably the Mayan) glyph for star. "Although this turtle is often interpreted as a representation of the earth, Schele proposes that it represents stars in Orion and that the Maize God is the Milky Way represented in the form of the tree."53 (The reader will recall Hunbatz Men's quotation above from his discussion of *te*, the Sacred Tree.) The resurrection that Schele is speaking about pertains to One Hunapuh, or First Father, a figure from the *Popol Vuh*. Depicted on a number of Classic-period ceramics, this god is shown emerging from the cracked carapace of a turtle, flanked and assisted by his twin sons. (The irony of the sons helping give birth to the father was probably not lost on the Maya.) In this case the sky-earth itself is cracking, because we are witnessing the birth of the Fourth World. Both the earth and the stars are shifting away from their accustomed positions and assuming new alignments. Is this yet another myth of the ilk we see profusely illustrated in *Hamlet's Mill* (cf. Chapter 5 of our book), one that encodes in its symbology the precession of the equinoxes? Is this yet another example of the earth (in the form of the turtle) mirroring the sky (in the form of Orion's feet plus one of his belt stars)?₅₄ In this context Douglas Gillette eloquently elaborates on the dictum of "As Above, so Below":

> "When First Father later raised the World Tree he separated the images of the stones. One image stayed on the earth as the greatest of all 'power points,' around which all pyramid-temples and ballcourts would be built. The other image was lifted into the night sky as the triangular pattern of the three stars in the constellation Orion. The so-called Orion nebula, a cloud of gas and dust that can still be seen in the middle of this triangle, became the *ch'ulel*-bearing smoke [*ch'ulel*, "life-force"] of that first sacrificial fire that rose when the creator gods burned their own sacred blood, the very blood that they had used to paint images of the hearthstones."₅₅

In the mythology of many indigenous people, association of the turtle with the earth and its waters was archetypal. The Maya were known to use turtle shells ceremonially as musical instruments, beating them with antlers.₅₆ Even today the Hopi put dried antelope hooves inside turtle shells to make eerily sounding rattles which are affixed to their right knees during *katsina* dances. In fact, the Hopi go great distances to obtain these ceremonial objects, sometimes as far as the Verde Valley or even the Colorado River south of Needles, California.₅₇ But the association with the turtle may well have been cosmological as well as ceremonial. As the poet Gary Snyder relates: "Turtle Island— the old/new name for the continent, based on many creation myths of the people who have been living here for millennia, and reapplied by some of them to 'North America' in recent years. Also, an idea found world-wide, of the earth, or cosmos even, sustained by a great turtle or serpent-of-eternity."₅₈

Specifically, the cosmogony related in the Algonkin *Walam Olum* shows the Great Spirit Manito being supported on the back of an immense turtle. "Set in the traditional Midewiwin form of four plus four symbols or houses..., these stanzas concord with the ritual cosmogony of Mesoamerica."₅₉ Did the Mesoamericans, some of whom most certainly traveled north to the Four Corners region and beyond, believe that North America was indeed "Turtle Island," the place where the stars of Orion came down to earth in a strict pattern of pueblo villages? Is the hard shell of the cosmic turtle really the hardpan desert of Arizona? In our realm of archaeo-astropoesis, perhaps it is.

## The Cosmological Significance of July 26th and August 13th

D uring or shortly after the aforementioned Niman ceremony when the *katsinam* return to their home on the San Francisco Peaks, the monsoons arrive on the Colorado Plateau, bringing during a very brief period the greatest portion of the annual allotment of rainfall. It is also during this time that Orion achieves his heliacal rising, after having been invisible for over two months. (See the end of Chapter 3.) In other words, Orion, like those "pets" of Omau'u, the god of the clouds, brings with him the hope for sufficient moisture for agricultural success. Perhaps it is merely a coincidence that the first day of the Mayan year, July 26th, occurs approximately when the annual *katsina* ceremonial cycle is ending and the non-*katsina* part of the year is beginning. Or given all the other parallels, perhaps not. July 26 is also the second of two annual zenith passage dates of the sun at the Pre-Classic Yucatan site of Edzná, as well as at its contemporary site in the Valley of Mexico called Teotihuacán— both at 19.5 latitude.[60] Incidentally, anyone familiar with the work of Richard C. Hoagland and/or hyperdimensional physics will recognize the significance of this number.[61]

One could write an entire book on parallels between the mythology, architecture, and rituals of both the Maya and the Hopi, or more broadly, between the Mesoamericans and the Puebloans. In our case it is enough to show probable cause. We will leave the reader with yet one more "coincidence" that will bring us up to historic times.

In the Southwest of the mid-seventeenth century, tensions were high. It had been a century since the *entrada* of the Spanish, and their imperious occupation of the land and enslavement of the native peoples became an increasingly onerous yoke to bear. Finally one religious leader named Popé, a Tewa from San Juan Pueblo, had had enough. From his headquarters at Taos Pueblo, he began to orchestrate a full-scale rebellion against the Spanish. "A knotted cord was carried by runners to all the villages which had agreed to join the rebellion. This set the date for the general uprising to take place apparently on August 13, 1680."[62] Unfortunately Popé's plan was leaked, and he had to attack sooner than anticipated— early on the morning of the 10th. Nonetheless, Popé and his forces killed over five hundred Spaniards and destroyed many cathedrals. With the assault that came to be known as the Pueblo Revolt of 1680, the Spanish were effectively driven from the territory ranging from Taos to Zuni for over a dozen years.[63]

If we recall, the Maya are very particular about the date of the Creation of this world: August 13th, 3114 B.C. "The Classic Maya Creation days were August 13 and February 5."[64] The latter date is the "reciprocal opposite" of the former date. That is, the stars at dawn on February 5 are in about the same position as they are at sunset on August 13, and vice versa. (Between June 21st —the summer solstice— and

August 13, the number of days is fifty-two, the sacred number of Kukulkán.) Did Popé somehow know the significance of this particular August date? Did it have some ritual meaning shrouded by time and distance? With one chance in three hundred and sixty-five that his planned attack date was random, can we still really believe that no Mexican Connection exists?

One final point: If we were to stand at dusk in the village of Oraibi on August 13th (which, incidentally, is in the very middle of the sixteen-day Snake-Antelope Ceremony), the sun would appear to descend into Grand Canyon at Potavey'taqa (Point Sublime) —specifically azimuth 285 degrees— over ninety miles away. Here the Hopi have erected another major shrine to which they make periodic pilgrimages.

*

In this chapter we discussed the enduring legacy of Mesoamerica upon Hopi culture. The next chapter will extend the chakra line of the Arizona Orion as a vector channeling energy southwest toward the South Pacific, as we explore in the process the extraordinary Hopi link to Oceania.

# Chapter 10
# They Came From Across the Ocean
# —the Water Clan (Patki) and the
# Snake Clan (Tsu') Of the Hopi

"Those people who got here, the flood destroyed most of them but a few had survived. They were the remnant of something big. That's always the way, that some survive, except for the ones that were destroyed, no more to be remembered. But these Hopi people know that they came from across the ocean and migrated here. And they never forgot their religion."[1]

Homer Cooyama, Kykotsmovi, Arizona

## *Destruction by Deluge of the Red City*

Incredible as it may seem, the Hopi, those inveterate denizens of the desert, were once a seafaring people— or at least one of their clans was. In Chapter 1 we described the long journey across the ocean from the Third World destroyed by flood to the Fourth World where the people now live. In alternate versions of the myth a number of tall flowers or trees such as the sunflower, yellow pine, spruce and bamboo are planted, each in its turn, so that one might reach and pierce a hole (*sipapuni*) in the sky, allowing the people to use the vertical growth as a ladder to the world above. In all the versions, however, it is the bamboo either upon or inside which they finally ascend to their new life. "The use of the word 'bamboo,' coupled with the idea that it was a plant comparable to a tree, makes one feel that this origin myth has come a long way and represents a mingling of many habitats. Witness the literal translation of the words for the Bamboo Clan— Wukobacabi (meaning 'a large, or larger reed')."[2] We should reiterate that bamboo is not an indigenous species on the Colorado Plateau but is found in southwestern Arizona. "Along the formerly great Gila River (the now dry bed of which stretches across the Sonoran Desert of western Arizona) there were extensive marshes, swamps, and floodplains with cattail (*Typha domingensis*), bulrush (*Scirpus olneyi*), giant reed (*Arundo donax*), common reed (*Phragmites communis*), arrowweed (*Plucea sericea*), and man trees."[3] Either the giant reed or the common reed is possibly the plant referred to in the legend.

The man from the Coyote Clan whose words we used as an epigraph for this chapter makes the distinction between the two versions of the origin myth. "I'm familiar with that children's story. They want to block the real story [of origins] until the children are initiated into the kiva societies, that's why they tell this story [in the meantime]."[4] In other words, the true story told only to the initiates involves an ocean migration.

213

Another source reinforces this notion: "I'll tell you one thing, I don't hardly believe [that the people climbed up from the Third World in a bamboo]. I know that story a little bit, but I'm not interested in that."[5]

Perhaps in the children's version, bamboo (reed) is used only as a metaphor for the type of boat upon which the people sailed to their new home. The former plane, viz., the Third World, is designated as the Underworld and usually is associated with water or even with the sea. "The Kachinas are supernatural, anthropomorphic beings inhabiting the water-world that lies underlies the earth. While a certain spring called Kisíu-va [mentioned in Chapter 7] is regarded as their home, they are believed to be present also in all other bodies of living water, the Hopi conception being that all bodies of water are parts of *one great ocean* [italics added] underlying the earth, in other words, mere openings through the earth-crust into the water-world."[6] Instead of being merely a mythological construct of the archetypal inferno, perhaps this subterranean "water-world" is actually an ancient tribal memory of the real island or continent across the wide ocean where the Hisatsinom once lived before the great migration took place.

If the myth of the destruction of the Third World by a deluge is conflated with the similar devastation of Palatkwapi (mentioned in Chapter 6), then the Water Clan along with related clans such as Rain, Cloud, Snow, Wild Duck, Water Bird, Frog, Water Snake, and Corn, all of which are associated with this "Red City of the South," may be the key to unlocking the mystery of the seafaring Hopi. "The Bátki [Patki] clan and the Sand Clan come from Palátkwapi. When traveling, the Sand clan would spread sand on the ground and plant corn. The Bátki clan would cause it to thunder and rain (by singing), the crop would grow in a day and they would have something to eat."[7] While this quotation stresses the fertility aspect of the Patki Clan, the following one specifies the direction whence it originated and the ceremonies it brought. "The Patki clan came from Pala'tkwabi. No one knows just where that Red land is, but it is somewhere in the far southwest. Our people, the Water people, carried all these things you see at the altar on their backs. Men, women, and youths carried them. The Water people brought the Kwa'kwantü [One Horn ritual, part of the New Fire Ceremony], the La'lakontü [the Basket Dance, women's Corn Harvest Ceremony], and the Shoiya'luña [Soyal, the winter solstice ceremony] with them."[8] The ethnobotanist A. F. Whiting groups the Reed Clan with the phratry that includes the Water Clan.[9] This former clan again refers to the mode of transport used by these truly ancient mariners. (See discussion of the Reed-Greasewood-Bow phratry in the Chaco Canyon section in Chapter 8.)

The previously mentioned Sun Chief (*tawa-mongwi*), whose duty it is to calibrate the position of the sun at the solstices, is selected from the Patki Clan. Were the calendrical-cum-agricultural skills of this astronomer-priest adapted from erstwhile navigational ones? Did members of the Water Clan know the means not only to ritualistically manipulate meteorological conditions but also to read the stars and planets, thereby gauging their own position upon the ocean? If we are to take the Hopi legend of marine migration seriously, then these are reasonable assumptions. "On the [Sun Chief's] altar the nadir is represented in the south. Inferably Pala'tkwabi is the Underworld, i.e. the world before the Emergence."[10] From this we may assume that the Red City had an antediluvian existence. "Two elders are making Pa'lülükoñ [Water Serpent] prayer sticks, blue-green prayer sticks, some to be deposited at sun spring, others at the southwest for Pala'tkwabi."[11] Hence the Hopi even have a local shrine representing this distant land. Incidentally, blue-green is the symbolic color of the southwest. Despite its politically incorrect tone, a final piece of evidence adds to the conundrum: "One thing you hear from the Patki people is that in ancient times they were white, not Indian color. They say, 'My ancestors had white skins, but because of evil things that happened, we lost all that.' They also say, 'The Patki people are the ones who are supposed to teach the Hopis good moral values, how to lead good lives.'"[12]

Pala-tkwa-pi, "a mythical city in migrations legends, the Red-Walled City," literally "red-masonry-wall."[13] The Hopi word *paala* means "red," as in *paalàngpu*, or "a red thing." Yet the homophone of the former word means "moisture, liquid," as in *paahu*, or "water as occurring in nature." Thus, we have two key concepts, the color red and the element water, associated with Palatkwapi. Where exactly is this fabled city? Here we enter a more speculative realm.

The most conservative candidate is the red rock country of the Verde Valley, as posited in Chapter 6. This area, which ethnographer Jesse Walter Fewkes believed to be Palatkwapi, is certainly southwest of the Hopi Mesas. Furthermore, pueblos such as Palatki (Red House) provide the proper color, though this small ruin could not in any estimation be thought of as a "city." (Fig. 45, p. 216) One of the largest ruins in the region is Tuzigoot, whose Hopi name is Tsor'ovi, or Bluebird Way, perhaps referring to the Bluebird Clan. (See Chapter 6.) This ruin used red clay plaster, at least on its interior walls. In addition, the copper ore quarried and traded in prehistoric times also relates to the color red.[14] The other Palatkwapi requirement of water is amply fulfilled by the Verde River, one of the largest continuously flowing streams in northern Arizona.

The next candidate for Palatkwapi is the Hohokam region near the contemporary city of Phoenix, which is also southwest of Hopiland. (See Chapter 12.) According to the *Oxford English Dictionary*, the name of this metropolis (besides referring to the mythical bird that rose from its ashes) means in Greek "purple-red or crimson" and is associated with those legendary mariners the Phoenicians. Perhaps this refers to the large adobe (as opposed to masonry) pueblos such Snaketown and Pueblo Grande, which used red stucco for exterior walls. Extensive copper deposits both to the east near the town of Globe and to the southwest near Ajo reinforce the association of the color red. One geographic description of Palatkwapi perhaps points to this area specifically. "Far south, far beyond Prescott, a river flows from the northwest to the southeast. Another river flows from east to west. At their junction is a gap in the horizon. The river after its junction rushes down into a lower land and in this land is Pala'tkwabi."[15] The upper Verde River flows northwest to southeast before flowing due south and eventually merging with the Salt River, which flows east to west until it joins the Gila River a few miles to the west, the latter also flowing in the same direction. As mentioned above, the Gila was not as it is today —a dry riverbed— but instead a living riparian area with marshes and floodplains. In addition, the Hohokam were famous for constructing a network of irrigation canals that totalled perhaps five hundred miles in length.[16] (See Chapter 12.) This indeed satisfies the Palatkwapi requirement for water.

A third candidate for the mythic Red City is the adobe ruin of Casas Grandes (Paquimé, mentioned in Chapter 8 in connection with the Chaco Meridian) in northern Chihuahua, Mexico. However, this ruin is southeast of the Hopi Mesas rather than southwest. The archaeologist Charles Di Peso, former director of the privately funded Amerind Foundation, "...informs us that to the immediate west of Casas Grandes there is a valley in red-rock country very similar to Oak Creek Canyon in northern

*Fig. 45. Pictograph at Palatki Ruin. At right, star spirits walking Milky Way (charcoal). Middle, zoomorphs and water/snake symbol in circle. Sun shield (kaolin) at lower left and tall torso (hematite) at upper left.*

Arizona."₁₇ In addition, copper bells and ceremonial ax heads as well as copper rings, pendants, disk beads and sheet-copper armlets were produced at this site. Hence we have the relevant color association. "The Casas Grandes Valley itself is wide, fertile, and relatively well-watered, and the indigenous, Mogollon-like population experienced a general population growth."₁₈ The city had an irrigation system at least comparable to if not surpassing that of the Chaco Canyon complex. "Inside the city was a large reservoir filled by a ditch run from the river a few miles to the north. From this reservoir rock-walled underground ducts led throughout the city. They possibly served as both a water system and a sewage system."₁₉

This water system in particular may have lent itself to flooding. "...now the Bálölöokongs [water serpents] were shooting forth from the ground with streams of water in all parts of the village, from the fireplaces in the kivas, in the houses from the water vessels, and in fact everywhere. Water began to fill the houses in the village. Soon the houses began to fall, burying many of the inhabitants under falling walls."₂₀ Being made of mud instead of stone, these walls were susceptible to the violent water erosion of an inundation. The Hopi version of the flood is echoed almost word for word by the Maya *Popol Vuh*: "The desperate ones ran as quickly as they could; they wanted to climb to the tops of the houses, and the houses fell down and threw them to the ground..."₂₁

Although we tentatively had located Palatkwapi in the Verde Valley, and although it has variously been identified with either the Gila River region or Casas Grandes, the following description of Palatkwapi points to the Toltec-Maya area much farther south:

> "Many days [years?] ago the Hopitu lived in the south where the rocks and the earth are red and they lived happily there for many days, owning many sheep and horses and having many beautiful women. Also the art of making blankets, silver and gold ornaments, working the turquoise and many beautiful shells was far better understood than today. They manufactured many kinds of colored cloths from wool and cotton, using different kinds of dyes. Flowers were highly cultivated and used in many feasts and dances. It was while living in that country that the handsome cotton robe used by the high priest in the sacred duties of his office was made. It was highly figured by the weaving in of silver or copper threads; flowers, birds, vines of many kinds and the horned water serpent were to be found in the pattern."₂₂

The artifacts and rituals in this passage clearly indicate a Mesoamerican culture. We should add that the horned water serpent Palulukang, an analogue of the Mayan Kukulkán and the Aztecan Quetzalcóatl, was the agent of Palatkwapi's destruction due to the general iniquity if its citizens.

Even though the city of Palenque in Chiapas, Mexico is also southeast rather than southwest of the far Hopi Mesas, this great Mayan center could be viewed as the fourth candidate for Palatkwapi, partially due to the fact that the Hopi cosmologically conceive red as the symbolic color of the southeast. "Glowing red under a tropical sun 13 centuries ago, the thriving city-state of Palenque climbs a hillside at the edge of the Maya lowlands."[23] Archaeologists believe that Palenque's exquisite stucco walls were once painted a brilliant crimson. Even though the name of this Red City means "palisade" in Spanish, the Maya called it Lakam Ha, or "Big Water." As the late Linda Schele, epigrapher of the Maya, has written:

> "Crystalline waters laden with dissolved limestone tumble down the rocky creeks that divide the city into natural sections. Palenque's builders incorporated these streams into their city by channeling the water through aqueducts and containing walls, and by building bridges that crossed them. The most important of these streams, today called Otolum, flows out of a valley called *Toktan*, or "Cloud-center," to cut through the center of the ceremonial precinct. The biggest aqueduct takes the Otulum on the eastern side of the palace, which served as the administrative heart of the kingdom."[24]

With water so thoroughly integrated into the architecture of the city, the pragmatic aspect of the system must at one time or another been overshadowed by its deadly potential— thus, the sacred nature of water in its ever shifting duality, creative and destructive.

### The Arizona Chakra Line to the South Pacific

Although the vast subject of Atlantis —its former existence and location— is far beyond the intent and scope of this book, we would like to mention in passing that its name contains both criteria of Palatkwapi. In the Nahuatl language of Mesoamerica, the prefix *atl* means "water,"[25] while the suffix *antis* means "copper."[26] In addition, Poseiden, the primary city of Atlantis as well as the name of its first ruler, was known as the "red city."[27] The Hopi word for copper is *palasiva*, which simply means "red metal." Given these facts, we can reasonably surmise that Palatkwapi is the Hopi name for Atlantis.

The early archaeologist of the Maya Augustus Le Plongeon, along with his wife Alice, believed that the Maya were the root culture from which many other ancient cultures sprang. Unlike many initial archaeologists of the region, the Le Plongeons learned the contemporary Mayan language in order to communicate with the descendants of those who built the Mesoamerican pyramids and cities. In addition, Le Plongeon determined from hieroglyphic inscriptions at Chichén Itzá the exact spot upon which to dig for the famous Chac Mool statue, thereby successfully unearthing it. He posited that the Maya were capable of extensive ocean travel, allowing substantial intercultural influences between Mesoamerica and the Pacific islands. "He believed that Copán [in Honduras] and Palenque [possibly Palatkwapi] were completely alien to Maya culture. Sculptures at those sites showed deformed heads, and, according to Le Plongeon, the Mayas never followed such practices. Nor could the hideous faces carved there belong to the Maya race. In his opinion, the inhabitants of Copán and Palenque were more probably people from Tahiti or other Pacific islands that the Mayas had visited on their voyages to India."[28] Le Plongeon suggested that the Maya apparently had sailed the Pacific and either brought back island people or showed them the way to the Central American continent. In this regard, he concurs with Thor Heyerdahl, whose epic (albeit empirical) journey on the balsa raft Kon-Tiki caused him to theorize that the primary route of migration was from east to west.

Though a friend of the Le Plongeons, Colonel James Churchward held the belief that marine colonization of the Western Hemisphere proceeded in the opposite direction, viz., from west to east, originating from a continent in the Pacific Ocean called Mu or Mu'a, the "Motherland of Man." This reputed continent was once 5,000 miles in length from east to west and 3,000 miles in width from north to south. Its northern boundary was the Hawaiian Islands while its southern boundary was a line roughly between Easter Island and Fiji. With a population of sixty-four million, Mu had a highly civilized and enlightened society, and until about 12,000 years ago it functioned as the world's center for trade, commerce, and education. At that time cataclysmic earthquakes, volcanoes, and tsunamis destroyed this great continent, leaving only the remnants of those archipelagos we see today— or so goes the story. Whether or not one believes this unlikely scenario, the influence of the South Pacific islands upon North and South America is self-evident.

> "On some of the South Sea Islands, notably Easter, Mangaia, Tonga-tabu, Panape, and the Ladrone or Mariana Islands, there stands today vestiges of old stone temples and other lithic remains that take us back to the time of Mu. At Uxmal, in Yucatan, a ruined temple bears inscriptions commemorative of the 'Lands to the West, whence we came'; and the striking Mexican pyramid [viz., the Temple to Quetzalcóatl at Xochicalo, 50 miles...] southwest of Mexico City according to its inscriptions, was raised as a monument to the destruction of these same 'Lands of the West.'"[29]

In addition, Churchward opined that the so-called Cliff Dwellers, i.e., the Anasazi, were the last wave of colonizers to arrive from Mu. "That the Cliff Dwellers came from Mu is certain, for every one of their pictures that are used as guide-posts contains a reference to Mu. In fact, rock writings and pictures of the Cliff Dwellers, except those drawn for artistic effect, are permeated with references to Mu, both before and after her submersion. In addition to this, they invariably use the symbols that were in vogue in the Motherland."30

If Mu, or Mu'a, truly had a global influence, then one clue reinforcing this is the palindrome for "Mu'a," which is A-U-M, the divisible form of OM. This Sanskrit syllable represents the divine principle of Brahman, or God. In this regard the *Taittiriya Upanishad* states: "Thou art Brahman, one with the syllable OM, which is in all scriptures—the supreme syllable, the mother of all sound..."31 Hence, both the mother of all sound and the mother of all people are referred to by the same letters, albeit reversed.

The Hopi word *mu'a* means "hit or shot" as in "hit with an arrow." Referring back to the Arizona chakra system discussed in Chapter 6, the reader will recall that part of the line runs from the Hopi village of Shongopovi (terrestrial Alnilam) through Walnut Canyon (terrestrial Meissa) to the mouth of the Colorado River. If this line is extended southwest across the immense distances of the Pacific Ocean, it arrives at the Somoa-Fiji-Tonga island region south of the equator. We may visualize the kundalini, or serpent, energy of the chakra system shooting up the terrestrial spine of Arizona Orion like an arrow, then sailing from his crown in the Verde Valley to be directed southwest across the sea, finally arriving at the possible origin or interim home of the Hisatsinom.

If we disregard the notion that Atlantis should be located in the Atlantic Ocean (since the mythical continent has been placed by scholars in almost every corner of the globe, including Antarctica), it is nothing short of revelatory to discover that the Nahuatl root *atl* should mean not only "water" but also "war" and the "top of the head."32 The reader will recall that most Pueblo people believe the concept of war connotes the sidereal zone. In addition, we said that the crown chakra discussed in Chapter 6 was the terrestrial correlative of Palatkwapi, possibly located in Verde Valley. In metaphysical teachings the crown chakra is the highest spiritual level of "Serpent Power," extending its influence from the personal to the transpersonal and ultimately on into other worlds, i.e., more elevated spiritual realms. In a geographic sense Arizona Orion's crown chakra thus projects its serpentine force on a vector that intersects a former South Pacific homeland or at least a tropical resting place on the Patki Clan's prophesied journey through the Fourth World. In this context it is significant to note Churchward's statement that the immigrants from Mu were known as "Quetzals," whose name is related to the Aztec plumed serpent Quetzalcóatl.33

## *How the Snake Clan (Tsu') Came to Arizona*

The members of the Hopi Snake Clan recount a lengthy mythic narrative of their clan origin, which entails a trip across the sea. We shall provide merely a brief summary here. In the village of Toko'navi (near Navajo Mountain in southern Utah) lived a youth named Tiyo. This ever pensive, curious lad was accustomed to sit on the banks of Pisisbyu (the Colorado River) and ponder where its waters flowed. Why, he wondered, when the people's corn cobs grew to only the length of a man's finger 34, would this precious life force simply disappear in the direction of the south? He asked if anyone knew what was at the end of the river where all that water went? "His father said, 'No, we do not know. But in the end it must join somewhere with Patowahkacheh, the Great Water. *Some of our grandfathers were there in ancient times* [italics added], but no one now living is familiar with all the land through which the river passes.'"35 Finally the boy resolved to embark upon a journey to solve this mystery.

Inside a hollowed out cottonwood log sealed at both ends with piñon pitch to resemble a drum, Tiyo floated downstream until he came to the great ocean. Soon he drifted against the island of Koyanwuhti (Spider Grandmother), within whose kiva he solicited her aid.36 In the distance lay another kiva on an island belonging to the Snake People. After walking between islands upon a rainbow path that Koyanwuhti had created, Tiyo used a special medicine that she had given him to pacify, each in its turn, a mountain lion (symbolic of the northwest), a bear (the southwest), a wildcat (the northeast), a gray wolf (the southeast), and finally a gigantic rattlesnake (symbolic of the nether world). He then descended the ladder of the kiva whose walls were covered with ceremonial snake skin costumes and found a group of men with faces painted a metallic black (*yaláhaii*, specular iron 37). They were dressed in blue kilts, the color symbolic of the southwest, and wore many necklaces of shells and coral beads. Testing his stamina, the Snake People tried to make Tiyo dizzy by offering strong tobacco (marijuana?), but Koyanwuhti helped him by drawing off the smoke through, incredibly, his anus. "The young man described his journey. After that the kikmongwi [chief] said, 'Well, you have discovered what lies at the place where the river meets the Great Water. We are Snake People. We are different from other people you know. Now we will show you something."38 These alien people then donned their snake costumes and turned into all sorts of angry snakes— rattlesnakes, bull snakes, king snakes, etc. Among the men there had also been some maidens, who likewise turned into hissing, slithering serpents. Koyanwuhti urged Tiyo to keep up his courage, after which the Snake People reverted to their human form and accepted him as one of their own. They subsequently taught him the Snake Ceremony, which to this day is danced biennially in August on the Hopi Mesas. In addition, he took the prettiest of the snake maidens as his wife.

In other versions of the myth, Tiyo also visits the island kiva of Hurúingwuhti (Hard Beings Woman).39 During the day while Tawa (the sun) is aloft, she appears as a withered crone but at night when he returns to this western house, she transforms into a beautiful woman. Alternate versions describe Tiyo spending the night with the lovely Hurúingwuhti in order to win her favor, thereby receiving many coveted turquoise beads, red coral, and seashells. In the morning, however, she (as in the previous variant) reverts to a repulsive hag.

Tiyo eventually returned with his snake *mana* (maiden) to Toko'navi. "At that time only the Divided or Separated Spring (Bátki) [Patki] clan and the Póna (a certain cactus) lived at that place, but with the arrival of this young couple a new clan, the Snake clan, had come to the village."40 After the couple's return, Tiyo's wife gave birth to a brood of snakes, which began to bite so many Hopi children that he was forced to return to the Snake People in order to offer them his herpetological offspring. Thenceforth the woman bore only human children.41 Later the Snake Clan migrated— initially to Kawestima (see Chapter 4 re. Betatakin and Keet Seel) and subsequently to Walpi.

Hence, we have perceived an essential Hopi myth in this legendary oceanic voyage that led to the origin of the Snake Clan; the fact that its first two members joined the Patki Clan at Toko'navi (along with the Póna Clan, which is part of the phratry that includes the Snake Clan 42) merely emphasizes their common maritime tradition. It is interesting to note that the so-called "serpent effigies" of the god Palulukang, the Horned or Feathered Serpent (analogue to Quetzalcóatl), are kept by these two clans. At Walpi the Snake Clan was responsible (along with the Reed Clan); at Sichomovi the Water Clan was responsible.43 As the above narrative indicates, some of the ancestors of the latter once lived far away in the Great Water. But is it truly possible that the ancestral Hopi used the equatorial counter current of the Pacific to make their way to the Western hemisphere and ultimately to Arizona?

### Hopi Grandfathers in Tongatapu

Just before we began our recitation of Tiyo's epic journey, we mentioned that if the "chakra line" formed by the terrestrial Orion's orientation upon the landscape were extended southwest, it would eventually reach the vicinity of the island of Tongatapu. At one time this was not merely the minor tourist destination it is today. As David Hatcher Childress says,

"Actually, the evidence suggests that Ancient Polynesia, with Tongatapu its capital, was an extremely sophisticated nation which sailed the vast Pacific in huge ships, built gigantic pyramids, roads and monuments, and had great universities where navigation, astronomy, climatology and theological history were taught. This maritime empire existed for thousands of years and traded with powerful countries all around the Pacific rim, including North and South America. The people lived an idyllic existence for many hundreds of years until Polynesia fell into decline and a dark age swept through the Pacific."[44]

Or, according to Hopi myth, a flood swept through, inundating many large islands or even the reputed continent of Mu. Prior to this devastation, however, the city of Mu'a (see p. 220) at Tongatapu along with the neighboring site of Lapaha —both of which were located at the east-central part of the island on a lagoon large enough to accommodate ocean-going vessels— had been constructed of perfectly fitted, massive stone blocks rivaling those found at Baalbeck in Lebanon or Tiahuanaco in Bolivia.[45]

In addition, the only major megalithic structure in the Pacific, which is known as the Ha'amonga of Maui, is located at Heketa on the northeastern coast of the island. Its name literally meaning the "Burden of Maui" is not a reference to the Hawaiian island but to a Polynesian god. In Hopi *haani* or *haawi* means "come down" or "descend," while *mong* refers to "chiefs"— thus Ha'amonga might be interpreted as "the chiefs who came down (from the sky?)." The epigrapher Barry Fell opined that the legends of Maui were based on an actual maritime explorer of Oceania, who sailed east from the Indian Ocean across the Pacific in 232 B.C. "The word *mawi* in Egyptian means a guide or navigator, but it also sounds very like the Polynesian name Maui. In Polynesian legend Maui was a great sailor who, in the figurative speech of Polynesian tradition, was said to have 'fished up new lands' from the sea...—a poetic way of recording his discovery of lands hidden beneath the horizon."[46] The Hopi word *maawi* means "to pick beans or fruit," which suggests pulling up food from the soil in the same manner that Maui pulled up islands from the bottom of the sea.

Going beyond linguistics, we see that the Ha'amonga of Maui is a massive trilithon constructed of two upright, rectangular pillars rising fifteen feet and weighing fifty tons each, together with a rectangular lintel eighteen feet long and weighing approximately nine tons. Built perhaps as early as 1500 B.C., this structure probably served a purpose similar to that of Stonehenge, viz., as a solar, lunar, and stellar observatory. In fact, notches in the stones of the trilithon mark the summer and winter solstices [47], which are also the key calendric positions for the Patki Clan of the Hopi. Childress even suggests that this megalith was used to calibrate the constellations, including Orion, which in Tongan was known as Toloa.[48]

In a book called *Tongan Astronomy*, T.H. Fale, a native of that island, states: "Toloa was the most important constellation my people used.

Because Toloa can tell them all directions in the sky at night, also where the sun will rise and set at daytime. This knowledge and use of Toloa makes it very important in understanding the great knowledge possessed by Tongan navigators."[49] The constellation Toloa literally means "wild duck" and is apparently comprised of Orion's belt, his left shoulder (Bellatrix), and his left arm. The curve of Orion's shield (Pi 1 Ori - Pi 6 Ori) delineates the bird's wings, with its left pointing east and its right pointing west. Fale says that this represents the equator in the same manner as do the two incised "V"s on the Ha'amonga. The head of the celestial duck points south toward the two Magellanic Clouds (the large one in Tucana and the small one in Dorado). Its tail points north, and by sailing in that direction into the Northern Hemisphere one can find the North Star. Three major constellations (called the Houmatoloa, or the three Toloas) fall in line toward the south and basically help to orient navigators in the South Pacific: Toloa (parts of Orion), Toloa lahi (False Cross, probably Cygnus, or the Northern Cross), and Toloatonga (Crux, the Southern Cross), the latter pointing toward the South Pole.

The name Toloa also refers to a specific terrestrial site on the island. "Tonga oral tradition implies that the first capital of Tonga was at Toloa, an area somewhere near the current Fua'amotu International Airport. Its precise location is not known but small mounds are known to exist in this area. Toloa seems to have vanished."[50] It may be just one more coincidence among many, but the azimuth of the heretofore mentioned chakra line that runs southwest from Shongopovi to Walnut Canyon, then continuing through the rest of Arizona and out into the Pacific, is 231 degrees, whereas the line running southwest from Heketa where the trilithon is located to Toloa where the earliest inhabitants of Tonga lived is 228 degrees.[51] The three degree discrepancy may have to do with either the inaccuracy of the scale on the Tonga map or the vast distance between Arizona and Tongatapu. Nevertheless, the similarity between azimuths gives one pause.

Is the Orion star-village (i.e., sky-ground) correlation in Arizona a legacy of a much older navigational tradition originating in Oceania? Furthermore, can we say with impunity that the members of the Hopi Patki Clan, who are the current sky watchers of the desert, once assumed the sacred office of bearing this maritime lore across tide and time, current and crosswind? A clue to answering these questions might lie in the concept of zenith stars. Many island cultures were once (and to some degree still are) cognizant of the astronomical fact that if a particular star passes directly overhead at its culmination, the observer's terrestrial latitude will be equivalent to the star's declination, or celestial latitude. On Tonga this type of asterism is known as a *fanakenga*, "the star that points down to an island, its overhead star."[52] In Tahiti this star-island connection is called a "pillar of heaven"; in Maori it is known as a "prop of heaven."[53] One hymn found written on an Easter Island *rongorongo* board invokes not only the first-born son of the earth but also the "prop of heaven."[54] Sky pillars greatly assist navigators in determining how far north or south in a relative sense is their location at any given time. For example, both Tahiti and Vanua Levu (Fiji) are on the same latitude, viz., 17 degrees South, whereas the declination for Sirius in Canis Major is almost —17 degrees. Thus, the sky pillar for both islands is the brightest star in the heavens, even though Tahiti is over 2,000 miles east of Vanua Levu. Regardless of where one happened to be sailing, if this brilliant beacon were blazing directly overhead, then the latitude would be same as that of both Tahiti and Fiji.

At present the declination of Rigel, Orion's left foot, is a little over —8 degrees, whereas the latitude of the Tokelau Islands north of Samoa is exactly 9 degrees South; hence, at that location the constellation's brightest star would probably be considered a zenith star. Currently the declination for Alnilam, the middle star of Orion's belt, is approximately —1 degree, whereas the latitude of the 'para Micronesian' island of Ninigo is also 1 degree South.[55] Therefore, it is likely that the belt itself is or was considered a sky pillar on that island. Acknowledging these facts and remembering that through the ages the stars shift their positions in the sky, we might ask at what time period the declination of Orion's belt was equivalent to the latitude of Toloa, Tonga's earliest city whose very name refers to the constellation.

Toloa is located approximately 21 degrees 10 minutes South. At that latitude Alnilam was a zenith star in circa 3800 B.C. In other words, if one stood on the island of Tonga during that time period, the belt of Orion would pass directly overhead. Is this the era when this highly developed culture flourished? This may be the case if we admit to the possibility that sky pillars have the ability to spiritually energize the earth and facilitate the rise of civilization at a given spot.

In this context we should mention one more point related to the orientation the Arizona Orion Correlation. As with the Giza Correlation (see next chapter), the head of Orion points downward or south, the reverse of the way it is seen in the Northern Hemisphere sky with his feet pointed toward the southern horizon. On the other hand, the Southern Hemisphere sky presents Orion with his head pointing downward toward the northern horizon. Did ancient Hopi mariners retain the memory of Orion arcing across that sky with down-turned head and transport this image to the desert of Arizona? Granted, this notion may strain the reader's credulity, if the concept of the Hisatsinom originating in the South Pacific has not already done so. Let's look at some more evidence of this connection.

Before the deluge occurred a thriving Pacific civilization dominated trade networks and linked diverse cultures on a global scale. Not only were goods exchanged but also ideas and language. Why else would we find so many phonetic and semantic similarities? For instance, one linguistic parallel involves the Patki Clan itself. If we recall, the name literally means "water house" or "houseboat." Is it merely a coincidence, then, that the term for the primary ocean-going vessel in the Tahitian and

Tuamotuan archipelagos is *Pahi*?56 In most Polynesian dialects the word *Tonga* means "south,"57 while in Hopi the term *tatkya* refers to the same direction. In addition, the Hopi *tongo* means "made contact with" or "touched it," while in the same language *tapu'ami* equates to "bridge." Tongatapu is perhaps one of the islands with which the members of the Patki Clan made contact, using it as a bridge in their journey eastward.

On one of the most easterly of these "bridges" known as Easter Island, or Rapa Nui, the natives refer to a legendary homeland called Hiva. In this regard Graham Hancock writes: "We learn that it was once a proud island of enormous size, but it too suffered in the 'great cataclysm' and was 'submerged in the sea.' Afterwards, a group of 300 survivors set out in two very large ocean-going canoes to sail to Te-Pito-O-Te-Henua ["the Navel of the World"— Easter Island], having magically obtained foreknowledge of the existence of the island and of how to steer a course using the stars."58 The reader will recall that the Hopi term *kiva* is a sunken or subterranean ceremonial lodge. When descending into this structure via the ladder that extends through its roof, one is symbolically entering the previous era known as the Third World, which is conceptualized as antediluvian.

Hancock goes on to describe the ancient astronomers of Easter Island: "Traditions state...that ages ago there existed on the island a brotherhood of 'learned men who studied the sky.' These Tangata Rani were instantly recognized because they were 'tattooed on their faces with coloured spots'— somewhat like the astronomer priests of Heliopolis in ancient Egypt, who wore distinctive leopard-skin cloaks with coloured spots."59 We should note here that the Hopi god Masau'u is also conceptualized as having multicolored spots or splotches on his head, especially in his *katsina* form.

Incidentally, Easter Island at W109 degrees, 22 minutes happens to lie on the exact longitude of Hopiland, specifically Canyon de Chelly — the first site of the terrestrial Orion schema to be established— at W109 degrees, 30 minutes.

## The Nagas: Origin of the Hopi Snake Clan?

The Snake Dance (mentioned on p. 202) has both attracted and repulsed non-Indian spectators since the late nineteenth century. During this infamous ritual performed every other August on the Hopi Mesas of Arizona, participants handle a mass of venomous and non-venomous snakes. Some even put necks and bodies into their mouths. Unlike ophiolatry (serpent worship), the Snake Dance is instead a plea for agricultural fertility and rain in a beautiful but harsh desert landscape. However, many spectators would be surprised to learn that this bizarre rite came from India, the traditional land of snake charmers.

As we saw, an ancient Hopi myth describes a migration from the flooded Third World (or Era) to the Fourth World. The ancestral Hopi escaped on reed rafts and made their way to the mouth of the Colorado River, up which they traveled to seek their final destination upon the Colorado Plateau. Another stepping-stone on this monumental journey may have been the remote South Pacific islands of Fiji. Northwest of Tongatapu, this island is the location where once was held the highly secretive Baki, a youth initiation and fertility ritual.60 Because the Hopi language does not recognize the sound of the letter 'b', the word *paki* serves as a near homonym. Coincidentally, this Hopi word means "entered" or "started being initiated." In addition, *Yabaki* in the language of Fiji means "year," while the Hopi word with the same meaning is *yahsangw*, sharing the identical prefix.

One of a number of walled sites where Fijian boys would enter manhood was called a "naga" or "nanaga." In this regard, Childress states that "...one of the ancient races of Southeast Asia is the Nagas, a seafaring race of people who traded in their 'Serpent Boats' similar to the Dragon ships of the Vikings."61 Here we can see a resemblance to the Aztecan "Quetzals," i.e., Quetzalcóatls, and the Hopian Tsu'ngyam, or Snake Clan. The Nagas originated in India and established religious centers and even cities throughout the country, including the Kingdom of Kashi on the Ganges, Kashmir to the north, and Nagpur in central India. In addition, the Nagas inhabited the great metropolitan centers of Mohenjo-Daro and Harrappa in the Indus River Valley. "In the nearby city-state of Lothal the Nagas founded a port city on the Arabian Sea which carried on frequent trade with Dragon Empires around the world while using a universal currency of cowries."62 As masters of arcane wisdom and sorcery, the Nagas bequeathed to Mesoamerica among other things the concept of the *nagual*, which is too complex to deal with here but is thoroughly delineated in the popular series of books by Carlos Castaneda that detail his tutelage with the Yaqui sorcerer Don Juan Matus.

It is very possible that the Nagas were the Snake People whom Tiyo met on his epic journey across the ocean. The Hopi word *nga'at* means "medicine root," referring to the healing or magical properties of a plant's water source. In this context it is significant to note that the vegetal root is both chthonic and morphologically snake-like. The related term *nakwa* refers to "...feather(s) or some other object on a string worn as a headdress or to signify the wearer has a particular role for the duration of a religious function."63 The ritual aspect of this plumage suggests the feathered aspect of the serpent. Another related term, Na-ngasohu, is the name of the Chasing Star (or Planet) Katsina described in Chapter 7. (*Nanga* means "to pursue" and *sohu* means "star.") This *katsina* wears a Plains-style eagle feather headdress. The Hopi word *Naka* is a proper name referring to a late 19th century chief of the Katsina Clan, whose traditional duty was to direct the Bean Dance at the February Powamu, or purification ceremony.64 His name is related to *naqvu'at*, which means "ear." Finally, the Hopi noun *naaqa* refers to "ear pendant," frequently made of abalone.

It is plausible that this type of jewelry was originally worn for the purpose of respectful mimicry rather than mere adornment. In this regard Childress describes the so-called Long Ears: "As tall, bearded navigators of the world, they were probably a combination of Egyptian, Libyan, Phoenician, Ethiopian, Greek and Celtic sailors in combination with Indo-Europeans from the Indian subcontinent. According to Polynesian legend, these sailors also has the famous 'long ears' that are well known on both Rapa Nui and Rarotonga."₆₅ The renowned mariner, archaeologist, and scholar Thor Heyerdahl states that the ruling families of the Incas in Peru artificially lengthened their earlobes in order to distinguish themselves vis-à-vis their subjects.₆₆ (An earmark indeed! Perhaps the frequent depiction in drawings and sculptures of Buddha having very long earlobes is also no coincidence.) James Bailey, who believed this ruling class was comprised of Aryan and Semitic peoples originating from the Indus River Valley, comments upon Heyerdahl's extensive work on Easter Island: "He showed that there lived on Easter Island the survivors of two distinct populations; the long-ears, a fair or red-headed European people who used to stretch their ear-lobes with wooden plugs so that they reached down to their shoulders and a Polynesian group of conventional Polynesian type, with natural ears. The first people had been known on the island as 'long ears', the second people as 'short-ears.'"₆₇ The former group supposedly attained an average height of six-and-a-half feet, and had white skin and red hair.

This resonates with the curious claim cited on p. 215 that the Patki Clan was originally Caucasian. It is also curious that the war-like Fire Clan, who lived with the Snake Clan at Betatakin (see Chapter 4), were known by the sobriquet "redheads." The tall, long-eared statues of Easter Island called the Moai, some with red topknots, were carved apparently to represent these characteristics. Due to the Long Ears' imperious control of the Short Ears, however, the latter finally revolted and exterminated all but one of their oppressors. This single survivor was allowed marry a Short Ear, and as a result the couple's descendants inhabit the island even today.₆₈ Noting the ear-plugs worn by certain tribes of Tanzania, Bailey comments on the ubiquity of this Long Ear artifact: "The ear-plug is itself symptomatic of contact with sea-people and I believe has a common origin all over the world, wherever it is found."₆₉ Although rare in the American Southwest, at least one example of a ring-type ear-plug carved from schist has been found in some Hohokam ruins near present-day Phoenix.₇₀

Not only do we find artifacts common to both desert and maritime people, but we also can identify related themes in myths from disparate cultures. For instance, the distinguished scholar Cyrus H. Gordon relates the incredible narrative (written in the first part of the second millennium B.C.) of an Egyptian sailor ship-wrecked upon the "island of Ka" (see Chapter 11 for the relationship between the Hopi *katsina* and the Egyptian Ka) located somewhere in the Red Sea or Indian Ocean in the region of Punt (Somaliland). Abounding in beautiful birds as well as delicious fruits, vegetables, and fish, this paradise was ruled by a giant serpent forty-five feet ("thirty cubits") long with gold plated skin, lapis lazuli eyebrows, and a beard extending three feet ("two cubits") in length. After this Serpent King had threatened to incinerate the sailor if he remained silent, the latter told how a fierce storm had driven him and his crew to that distant island. In turn, subsequent to describing his brethren and children, which numbered a total of seventy-three including himself, the sovereign serpent stated: "Then a star fell and these (serpents) went forth in the flame it produced. It chanced I was not with them when they were burned. I was not among them (but) I just about died for them, when I found them as one corpse." Before he allowed the sailor to depart in his boat loaded with myrrh and other fine spices, giraffe tails, elephant tusks, and monkeys, the Serpent King made the following curious remark: "It will happen that when you depart from this place, this island will never be seen again, for it will become water."₇₁

Whether or not this serpent had long ears, the tale does not say, but we are perhaps witnessing another instance of the legendary Nagas. Added to the serpentine motif, one theme particularly redolent of Atlantis or Mu is contained in this fabulous story: an Edenic island suddenly disappears beneath the waves due to some celestial cataclysm that destroys many lives. Do the Hopi myth of Tiyo's journey to the Island of Snakes and the Egyptian myth of the anonymous sailor's journey to the Island of Ka have a common source? We probably will never know for certain. Likewise, we can only speculate on the significance of the seventy-three serpents described in the latter myth. Encoded therein may possibly be what is called a precessional number, about which astronomically astute navigators were probably aware. Because of the phenomenon known as the precession of the equinoxes (mentioned in Chapter 5), the stars of the zodiac rising on the eastern horizon on the first days of spring and fall shift backwards (from Pisces to Aquarius, for instance) one degree every seventy-two years due to the precession, or wobble, of the Earth's axis. In the Egyptian tale the Serpent King's relatives —seventy-two of them— were all destroyed by some sort of falling asterism. Hence, the "skyscape," or sidereal configuration, that the people had known for roughly a lifetime or more was destroyed as well, only to be replaced by a slightly altered one.

To believe that so-called "primitives" would not have had the sophisticated knowledge or observational skills to recognize the one-degree difference is in effect to take the isolationist's stance that early civilizations were technologically incapable of navigating across great stretches of ocean. All of the myths of those civilizations, however, clearly point to the opposite, i.e., to the diffusionist's stance. We are *not* by any means suggesting that an elite corps of Old World Whites came to "save" the scattered bands of "savage" Native Americans, thereby allowing the latter to flourish (before, paradoxically, accomplishing almost total cultural genocide in the 16th through the 19th centuries). This scenario denigrates both cultures, assigning spurious attributes to each: an inherently monolithic imperialism to the former and an evolutionary inferiority to the latter. In short, this is racism at its worst. What we *are* saying is that the collective ingenuity of the peoples of North and South America together with the peoples of Oceania allowed them to sail to distant lands very early on, while the peoples of Europe and Asia used the same sort of collective ingenuity in order to make landfall on equally distant lands. The astronomical and navigational skills possessed by seafarers from all parts of the globe must have been the common currency of the day.

### From the Crown Chakra to the Galactic Heart

If the reader will recall, the grand chakra line is positioned upon the terrestrial plane at about 230 degrees azimuth in relation to Shongopovi/Alnilam. Following this line to the southwestern horizon —the direction of southwest is technically 225 degrees— we find the setting point for the constellation Sagittarius at the end of the Milky Way. Much like Gemini and Orion making their nightly winter passage across the southern quadrant of the sky on the eastern and western edges of the Milky Way respectively, at the opposite end of this spirit road Sagittarius on its eastern side and Scorpius on its western side make a summer passage across the same region. More specifically, the area that Sagittarius encompasses is known as the galactic center. Dense with nebulae and star clusters, this active galactic nucleus is a "strong radio emitter,"[72] suggesting that a black hole dominates it. In addition to the energy from the visible spectrum as well as that from infrared, gamma rays and x-rays that the heart of our galaxy emits, a particular type of non-thermal energy known as "synchrotron radiation" is also generated. This is a sort of electromagnetic radiation produced when electrically charged particles approaching the speed of light pass through a magnetic field.[73] At any rate, the alignment of Hisatsinom sites on the terrestrial plane forms the grand chakra line which points directly to this energy-intensive galactic center as it sets on the southwestern horizon.

The heart of our spiral galaxy was intuited by the Maya and represented on the facades of their temples. The beginning of the Mayan New Year on July 26th roughly coincides with the conclusion of the Hopi Niman ceremony which signals the end of the annual *katsina* cycle. On this date in 200 B.C. the galactic center (Right Ascension 17:45.6, Declination —28:56)[74] was at 230 degrees azimuth shortly before midnight, with Antares in Scorpius just hovering above the southwestern horizon. This year is significant because it is the approximate date for the establishment of the proto-Maya culture at Izapa (near the present border of Guatemala and the Mexican State of Chiapas). The ingenious inhabitants of this city most likely formulated the Mayan Long Count calendar system.[75]

The Maya call the galactic core the Hunab Ku, or literally the "One Giver of Movement and Measure," while the Milky Way is referred to as Kuxan Suum, or "the Road to the Sky Leading to the Umbilical Cord of the Universe."[76] As scholar of the Maya and New Age writer José Argüelles states:

"If the Kuxan Suum, like a resonant, galactic walkie-talkie, could be the transmitting agent of the information necessary to transport the Maya as high-frequency synchronization scouts from a system outside of ours to our planet, Earth, it also bears resemblance to the Hopi *sipapu*. Described as the tunnel or passage leading to and from the different worlds, the sipapu is the thread or lifeline not only linking galactic core, star systems, and different planets, but linking different eras as well. Thus, when one world era closes and another is about to begin, the sipapu is the passage showing the way."[77]

Hence, the Sipapuni of Grand Canyon is not the only interdimensional gateway. The portal at each end of the Milky Way could also function in the manner of the Hopi *sipapu*, with the southern stargate leading straight to the Great Mystery of our local black hole. (As with most things astrophysical, "local" is a relative term. The galactic center is about 28,000 light-years away.)

As stated in Chapter 6, the vital energy of individual consciousness is projected from the Crown Chakra into the universal dimensions of the Absolute. In terrestrial terms, the Crown Chakra correlates to Tuzigoot and other Sinagua ruins in the Verde Valley of Arizona. The resonant energy collected within the Orion configuration of ancient star cities is channeled southwest across the Sonoran Desert to the mouth of the Colorado River, after which it continues in the same vector across vast stretches of Pacific Ocean, traversing the equator and ultimately arriving in the region of Tongatapu, which may have served as a "stepping stone" in the migration of the Hopi Patki Clan to their home in the Four Corners area of the U.S. This island and others in the region could even be the remnants of the primordial mother continent of Mu and the origin of the Hisatsinom and other tribes.

In celestial terms, conversely, by heading southwest toward the setting of Sagittarius we are traveling to our galactic heart. The Hopi word for the Milky Way is *songwuka*, literally "the big reed." The cognate *so'ngwamiq* means "towards the end" or "towards the source." The related term *songowu* refers to the reeds used to make the traditional storage case for a woman's wedding robe woven of white cotton that will be buried with her after her death. We recall the mythological significance of the hollow reed in the Hopi migration from the previous Third World to the present

Fourth World, and the fact that reed boats were used to navigate to the west coast of North America. If we break down the word *songwuka*, we find that *soo-* is the prefix of the word "star" and *ngwuvi* is a root that means "climb." From all of this we can deduce that *songwuka* is the galactic tunnel through which the ancient star people journeyed in order to descend to their terrestrial home. The first village settled on the Hopi Mesa was called Songohpavi (Shongopovi— see Chapter 4), literally "place of the reed." Perhaps this name not only describes the moist area of settlement where an abundance of reeds once grew but more importantly it commemorates the Ancient Ones' crossing over to Earth through the metonymic reed we know as the Milky Way.

Mesoamerica also has a number of locations designated by this specific appellation. The ancestral home of the Aztecs was known not only as "place of the heron" but also the "place of the reeds." (See Chapter 12.) Initially assumed to be the feathered serpent Quetzalcóatl making his prophesied return, Hernando Cortés and his *conquistadores* arrived on the Atlantic coast on Easter 1519, which was the Aztec year Ce Acatl, or One Reed. This year marked the end of a fifty-two year cycle when the world would either be destroyed or renewed. Sadly for the Aztec leader Moctezuma of Tenochtitlán, the former occurred.[78] Linda Schele speculates that the original "place of the reeds" was the Gulf Coast swamp of the Olmec heartland, where civilization, writing, the arts, and organized warfare for this whole region began. Later the name was applied to the major Toltec center of Teotihuacán.[79] Maya cities with this same identification include Uxmal, Copan, Tikal, and Utatlán.[80] (As we will see in the next chapter, both Teotihuacán and Utatlán had been oriented to reflect various aspects of the constellation Orion.) Whereas the ancient Egyptian afterlife similar to the Greek Elysian Fields was called the Field of Reeds, the more mundance usage of the reed was as an instrument of writing— hence its cultural significance.[81] Given the variety of geographical loci for the "place of the reeds," we may conclude that it is not so much a reference to flora as it is a designation of a place of high culture and ancient wisdom— the sort of location where astronomer-priests would normally scan the heavens for doorways through which the soul could make its passage to the Otherworld.

At the end of Chapter 5 we discussed the concept of stargates, or sky portals leading to and from interdimensional realms. The northern stargate is located between Taurus and Gemini above Orion's right hand, whereas the southern stargate is located between Scorpius and Sagittarius. In a tome written by 33rd degree Mason and Grand Commander Albert Pike and ponderously titled *Morals and Dogma of the Ancient and Accepted Scottish Rite of Freemasonry* (its secret knowledge "not being intended for the world at large..."—from the Preface), we find further evidence of these passageways of the spirits. "The equinoxes were the gates through which souls passed to and fro, between the hemisphere of light and that of darkness. The milky way was also represented, passing near each of these gates: and it was, in the old theology, termed the pathway of souls. It is, according to Pythagoras, vast troops of souls that form that luminous belt."[82] As we previously stated, souls are incarnated by descending through the northern gate and are ex-carnated by ascending through the southern gate. Just as one can not view both Orion and his nemesis Scorpius at the same time in the night sky, the northern and southern stargates can not both be open at once.

\*

In the following chapter we will discuss various Orion Correlations around the globe, focusing on the pyramids at Giza. We shall furthermore explore the Hopi-Egyptian connection and examine an Anasazi artifact depicting phoenix-like birds perched upon three pyramids.

# Chapter 11
# Ancient and Mysterious Monuments
# —an Extraterrestrial Archetype

"Is it possible that the incorporation of a 'celestial plan' in ancient and mysterious monuments from many different parts of the world, and a particular focus on the three stars of Orion's Belt... could be parts of a global scientific legacy passed on by a lost civilization of very remote times?"[1]
Graham Hancock

"The world that surrounds us, then, the world in which the presence and the work of man are felt—the mountains that he climbs, populated and cultivated regions, navigable rivers, cities, sanctuaries—all these have an extraterrestrial archetype, be it conceived as a plan, as a form, or purely and simply as a 'double' existing on a higher cosmic level."[2]
Mircea Eliade

## *The Global Orion Legacy: South America, Mesoamerica, North America, Europe, and a Few Other Locations*

Whether one interprets the word "extraterrestrial" as Eliade undoubtedly did, i.e., as a psychospiritually dictated bond between the transcendental and the mundane planes, or one favors the more contemporary theory of so-called "alien" intervention of technology imported from the stars, virtually no one can deny the world-wide evidence of an uncanny mirroring of sky and earth. For instance, the above quotation from Graham Hancock's globally encompassing book entitled *Fingerprints of the Gods* is actually excerpted from a caption of a photograph depicting a huge spider geoglyph 150 feet long found on the Nazca Plain in southern Peru. The German mathematician and astronomer Maria Reiche, who studied this and other Nazca figures and lines for over forty years, believes that the spider's legs were shaped to represent the outstretched limbs of Orion with its waist forming his belt. She furthermore posits that a particular line intersecting this anatomically correct arachnid from the Amazon jungles was oriented toward the heliacal setting of this constellation, perhaps for the purpose of coördinating solar and lunar calendars.[3] Made in the desert like the other figures by removing the darker colored pebbles in order to leave exposed the lighter ones, this spider is located close to what is known as the Great Rectangle, a geometric form of which, as noted in Chapter 3, has associations with Orion. Located nearby, an anthropoid figure deemed "the Owlman" also bears an eerie resemblance to the Hopi god Masau'u.

Farther north in Guatemala, the archaeologist José Fernandez has determined that all of the primary temples at the Post-Classic Quiché

Maya site of Utatlán ₄ (established about the time the Hopi Mesas were first being settled) were oriented like the Nazca spider to the heliacal setting points of the stars in Orion.₅ "Capital city of the Quiche nation, Utatlán was the most powerful city in the Maya highlands before it was razed by the Spanish in 1524."₆

Just over thirty miles north of Mexico City the massive site of Teotihuacán also apparently reflects the stars of Orion. In particular, the configuration formed by the Pyramid of the Moon, the Pyramid of the Sun, and the Pyramid of Quetzalcóatl spatially correlates to Mintaka, Alnilam, and Alnitak respectively, i.e., the belt.₇ Although other astroarchaeological data continue to be amassed at this site, the clear link to this constellation reinforces its primacy in the indigenous cosmology of the region.

Author Page Bryant has suggested that two sites erected by the Mound Builders of North America are potentially Orion Correlations as well. Both O'Byam's Fort in Hickman County, western Kentucky and the Hill Works in Ross County, Ohio (about thirty miles northeast of the Serpent Mound) consist of three major mounds corresponding to the belt stars, with one of the three slightly offset in each case.₈

Knights Templar researcher Jeff Nisbet has discovered an Orion Correlation in Scotland. To very briefly sum up the template: the islands of Fidra, Lamb, and Craigleith located off the southern coast of the Firth of Forth represent the belt stars of Alnitak, Alnilam, and Mintaka respectively. Northeast of the belt, the Isle of May correlates to Bellatrix. Northwest of May on the Fife Peninsula a few miles south of Eden River once lay a stone circle called the Dunino Circle, now lost. If again found, this may correspond to Betelgeuse. A line drawn northwest between May and the hamlet of Dunino comes to rest at Dunsinane Castle of Shakespeare's *MacBeth*. A line drawn southwest from May through Fidra leads to the famous Rosslyn Chapel. Due south of Craigleth is the Castle of Yester, which corresponds to Rigel. A line drawn from this isle through Yester intersects the Cisterian Abbey of Melrose to eventually reach the Glastonbury Tor in England.₉

Orion Correlations indeed seem to be popping up all over the world. According to the Czech magazine *WM*, the belt stars are perfectly mirrored by three pyramids of stone in Montevecchia, a town in northern Italy about forty kilometers from Milan. The highest of these pyramids is 150 meters tall. Identified by satellite and aerial imagery, these structures so overgrown with vegetation that they were originally mistaken for natural hills are thought to be over 3,000 years old.₁₀

About one hundred miles west of Aswan in the Sahara Desert lies an archaeological site called Nabta Playa. Only ten to eleven feet in diameter, this megalithic calendar circle has a north/south line-of-sight as well as a summer solstice sunrise alignment. According to former NASA physicist Thomas G. Brophy, Ph.D., three stones inside the circle mirror the pattern of Orion's belt at the meridian for this season during the period

6,400 to 4900 B.C. Three other interior stones represent the shoulders and head of the constellation for the astoundingly early date of 16,500 B.C. Another set of megaliths south of the circle aligns to the vernal equinox heliacal rising in 6300 B.C. of six key stars in Orion (Alnitak, Alnilam, Mintaka, Betelgeuse, Bellatrix, and Meissa). This vernal equinox heliacal rising happens only once per precessional cycle (nearly 26,000 years).

Even more astonishing is the fact that some of these megaliths are arranged proportionally to correspond to the physical distance from Earth of each of the aforementioned stars except Meissa. In addition, other megaliths in this group are arranged proportionally to correspond to the same stars' radial velocity, or the speeds at which these stars are moving away from us. "The companion megaliths in each distance alignment match corresponding megaliths in each velocity alignment in such a way as to fit the physics of orbital motion, and thus probably represent actual companion objects to the six primary stars. Meaning: The designers of the megaliths had a basic understanding of physics, and knowledge of astronomy that rivaled or surpassed ours today."[11] Compounding the complexity of this astrophysical map, a sculpture carved into the bedrock has been found buried beneath the surface sediment. This sculpture accurately depicts the Milky Way Galaxy, showing the relationship between our sun and the vernal equinox heliacal rising of the galactic center circa 17,400 B.C. Given the astronomical encoding of this site, Nabta Playa's homage to Orion reveals an understanding of the cosmos that shatters our traditional notions of the ancient world.

Other promising candidates for sites corresponding to the Orion constellation need further research. For instance, southwest of X'ian in China's Shensi Province is a pattern of large ancient pyramids constructed of clay that appear to mirror the belt stars. Also, recent study of the eponymous Great Zimbabwe located in the country formerly known as Rhodesia shows that on the winter solstice three bright stars in the constellation rise over three stone monoliths on the eastern arc of the Great Enclosure. In addition, a current Internet buzz on the Graham Hancock Message Board brings up the possibility that three henges at the Thornborough Neolithic Monument Complex in North Yorkshire, England correlate to the belt stars. If so, the template is arranged similar to the Arizona Orion, with his head pointed southwest. Finally, the Jordanian author Rami Sajdi posits that the belt stars of Mitaka, Alnilam, and Alnitak correspond to the Middle Eastern sites of Jerusalem, the Essene community of Masada on the Dead Sea, and Petra respectively.[12] The diverse cultural sites in Peru, Mesoamerica, North America, Scotland, and perhaps other locations on the globe focus on this particular constellation with an archetypal intensity. If it hasn't already done so, an unavoidable question arises: Are we witnessing a worldwide Orion legacy propagated by a single cohesive force or intelligence? Let's take a look at the most famous Orion Correlation, viz., the Giza pyramids.

## *The Egyptian Orion*

The primary "Orion Correlation Theory" was developed in Robert Bauval's and Adrian Gilbert's international bestseller *The Orion Mystery*,13 which, incidentally, provided in part the impetus for writing this book. The co-authors have discovered an ancient "unified ground plan" in which the pyramids at Giza form the pattern of the belt of Orion. According to their theory stated briefly here, the Great Pyramid (Khufu) represents Alnitak, the middle pyramid (Khafre) represents Alnilam, and the slightly offset smaller pyramid (Menkaure) represents Mintaka. In addition, two ruined pyramids —one at Abu Ruwash to the north and another at Zawyat al Aryan to the south— correlate to Saiph and Bellatrix respectively, while three pyramids at Abusir farther south correspond to the head of Orion. Bauval and Gilbert also believe that the pyramids at Dashour, viz., the Red Pyramid and the Bent Pyramid, represent the Hyades stars of Aldebaran and Epsilon Taurus respectively. Furthermore, this schema correlates Letopolis, located due west across the Nile from Heliopolis, with the brightest star Sirius. As co-author Gilbert states in a later book:

> "It was Bauval's contention that the part of the Milky Way which interested the Egyptians most was the region that runs from the star Sirius along the constellation of Orion on up towards Taurus. This region of the sky seemed to correspond, in the Egyptian mind at least, to the area of the Memphite necropolis, that is to say the span of Old Kingdom burial grounds stretching along the west bank of the Nile from Dashur to Giza and down to Abu Ruwash. At the centre of this area was Giza; this, he determined, was the earthly equivalent of Rostau (Mead's Rusta), the gateway to the Duat or underworld."14

The region in Hopi cosmology corresponding to the Duat is called Tuuwanasavi (literally, "center of the earth"), located at the three Hopi Mesas. Similar to the ground-sky dualism of the three primary structures located at the Giza necropolis, these natural "pyramids" closely reflect the pattern of Orion's belt. (See Diagram 1, p. 24.) In addition, the entry to the nether realms is known in Hopi as the Sipapuni, located in Grand Canyon. Culturally significant to a sacrosanct degree, this area mirrors the left hand of Orion. (See Diagram 2, p. 28.) Whereas the Egyptian Rostau is coextensive with the *axis mundi* of the belt stars formed by the triad of pyramids, the Hopi gateway to the Underworld in Grand Canyon is adjacent to the Center-place but still close enough to be archetypally resonant in that regard. (More on the Rostau in the next section of this chapter.)

Regarding the theory that Orion is projected upon the deserts of both Egypt and Arizona, we find both discrepancies and parallels. In terms of distinction, the Egyptian plan is on a much smaller scale than the one incorporating the Arizona stellar cities, using tens of kilometers rather than hundreds of miles. Furthermore, the bright stars of Betelgeuse and Rigel are perplexingly unaccounted for in the Egyptian schema. (Recently two independent Egyptologists, Larry Dean Hunter and Michael Arbuthnot, claimed to have found all the stars of Orion represented by constructions on the Egyptian landscape. However, their terrestrial correlations are somewhat different than those originally put forth by Bauval and Gilbert.[15]) In addition, the Giza terrestrial Orion from head to foot is oriented southeast to northwest, while the Arizona Orion is oriented southwest to northeast. Of course, the pyramids are located west of the Nile River, while the Hopi Mesas are located east of the "Nile of Arizona,"[16] i.e., the Colorado River. We should also point out that Abusir is not in the correct location to fit the constellatory template of Orion's head. Bauval and Gilbert state that Abusir is "...a kilometre or so south-east of Zawyat al Aryan..."[17] (i.e., Bellatrix, or Orion's left shoulder), but it is in fact about six kilometers southeast. In other words, Abusir is nearly four miles south-southeast of where it should be according to the star correlation theory. Unlike Bauval, Gilbert, and Hancock, the present author has not yet journeyed to Egypt, but the consultation of any scale map will verify this statement.[18]

Despite these few differences, the basic orientation of the Egyptian Orion is similar to that of the Arizona Orion, i.e., south, the reverse of the celestial Orion. According to E.C. Krupp, Ph.D., Director of the Griffith Observatory, this is one of the factors that invalidates the Orion Correlation Theory.[19] This critique, however, is the result of a specific cultural bias in which an observer is looking down upon a map with north at the top and south at the bottom. Imagine instead that the observer is standing on top of the Great Pyramid (or for that matter, at the southern tip of First Mesa) and gazing southward just after midnight on the winter solstice. The other two pyramids (or Mesas) would be stretching off to the southwest in a pattern that reflects the belt of Orion now achieving culmination in the southern sky. We can further imagine that if the upper portion of the terrestrial Orion were simply lifted perpendicular to the apparent plane of the earth while its feet were still planted in the same position (Abu Ruwash and an undetermined site in the case of Egypt; Canyon de Chelly and Betatakin in the case of Arizona), then this positioning would perfectly mirror Orion as we see it in the sky.

Another similarity between Egyptian Orion and Arizonan Orion is the respective periods of construction, viz., just under two hundred years each. From the beginning of Khufu's reign (Fourth Dynasty, circa 2585 B.C. when construction of the Great Pyramid was probably started) to the end of Niuserre-Izi's reign (Fifth, Dynasty, circa 2392 B.C. when the last of the Abusir pyramids was constructed) is 193 years.[20] On the other hand (or continent), tree-ring dates from White House Ruin in Canyon de Chelly indicate that construction began in A.D. 1060.[21] In Tsegi Canyon the earliest tree-ring date from Keet Seel is A.D. 1250, indicating commencement of construction at this time.[22] The former site establishes terrestrial Saiph (Orion's right foot) while the latter establishes terrestrial Rigel (Orion's left foot). All the rest of the sites of terrestrial Orion in Arizona were constructed between these two dates. The chronological difference between the respective sites in Canyon de Chelly and Tsegi Canyon is 190 years. Hence, the time it took to establish the Orion template in both Egypt and Arizona is approximately the same: almost two centuries.

### The Egyptian, African, and Middle Eastern Connection

In their later book *The Message of the Sphinx*, co-authors Robert Bauval and Graham Hancock describe, among many other things, the cosmic journey of the Horus-King, or the son of the Sun, to the Underworld: "He is now at the Gateway to Rostau and about to enter the Fifth Division [Hour] of the *Duat* — the holy of holies of the Osirian afterworld Kingdom. Moreover, he is presented with a choice of 'two ways' or 'roads' to reach Rostau: one which is on 'land' and the other in 'water'."[23] We have been blessed with a wealth of hieroglyphic texts, both on stone and on papyrus, with which we can reconstruct the Egyptian cosmology. On the other hand, unless we consider petroglyphs more as a form of linguistic communication than as rock "art," the Hopi and their ancestors had no written language; hence we must rely on the oral tradition.

In this regard the Oraibi *tawa-mongwi* ("sun watcher") Don C. Talayesva describes an intriguing parallel to Rostau. As a young man attending the Sherman School for Indians in Riverside, California during the early years of the twentieth century, he became deathly ill and, in true shamanistic fashion, made an inner journey to the spirit world. After a long ordeal with many bizarre, hallucinatory visions, he reached the top of a high mesa and paused to look. (Is it simply another coincidence that the Hopi word *tu'at*, also spelled *tuu'awta*, meaning "hallucination" or "mystical vision," sounds so close to the Egyptian *Duat*— indeed spelled by E.A. Wallis Budge, former director of antiquities at the British Museum, as *Tuat*, that seemingly illusory realm of the afterlife?)

> "Before me were two trails passing westward through the gap of the mountains. On the right was the rough narrow path, with the cactus and the coiled snakes, and filled with miserable Two-Hearts making very slow and painful progress. On the left was the fine, smooth highway with no

person in sight, since everyone had sped along so swiftly. I
took it, passed many ruins and deserted houses, reached the
mountain, entered a narrow valley, and crossed through the
gap to the other side. Soon I came to a great canyon where
my journey seemed to end; and I stood there on the rim
wondering what to do. Peering deep into the canyon, I saw
something shiny winding its way like a silver thread on the
bottom; and I thought that it must be the Little Colorado
River. On the walls across the canyon were the houses of
our ancestors with smoke rising from the chimneys and
people sitting out on the roofs."[24]

In this narrative the narrow, dry road filled with cacti and
rattlesnakes, where progress is measured by just one step per year, is
contrasted with the broad, easy road quickly leading to the canyon of the
Little Colorado River. A few miles east of the confluence of this river and
the Colorado River is the actual location of the Hopi "Place of Emergence"
from the past Third World to the present Fourth World. Physically, it is a
large travertine dome in Grand Canyon to which annual pilgrimages are
made in order to gather ritualistic salt. In correlative terms the Milky Way
is conceptualized as the "watery road" of the Colorado River at the bottom
of Grand Canyon— that sacred source to which spirits of the dead return
in order to exist in a universe parallel to the pueblo world they once knew.
Alternately this stellar highway is seen as traversing the evergreen forests
of the San Francisco Peaks, upon whose summit is a mythical kiva leading
to the Underworld.

Talayesva's account describes many traditional otherworldly
motifs, including "the Judgment Seat" on Mount Beautiful, which supports
a great red stairway, at least in his vision. (This peak is actually located
about eight miles west of Oraibi.) We also hear of a confrontation with the
Lord of Death, in this case a threatening version of Masau'u (the Hopi
equivalent of Osiris), who chases after him. Thus, like the Egyptian
journey to the Duat, the Hopi journey to Maski (literally, "House of
Death") has two roads— one on land and one on water. In this context we
must decide whether or not the latter is really a code word for the sky. In
the "double-speak" of the astral-terrestrial correlation theory, are these
spirits in actuality ascending to the celestial river of the Milky Way? Is this,
then, the purpose of the grand Orion schema? —to draw a map on earth
which points the way to the stars?

Another startling piece of evidence from the Hopi oral tradition
comes from one Jasper Poola of First Mesa. "Some Hopis have told me, for
instance, that the original *sipapuni* (earth navel) was in Egypt, India, or
Jerusalem—that is, somewhere in the Old World."[25] This suggests a
considerably wider range of Hopi migration than hitherto acknowledged.
Parallels between the Old World and the New can even be found in the

field of comparative linguistics. For instance, the Hopi word *sohu* (or *soohu*) simply means "star," but in their belief system stars are conceptualized as supernatural entities, with those of Orion being ceremonially paramount.[26] As we saw in Chapter 7, the Hopi even have a Sohu Katsina, an intermediary spirit who dances wearing a mask with three stars in a row on its crest.[27] (Fig. 40, p. 162) In some of the world's oldest funerary literature known as the Egyptian Pyramid Texts, the word *Sahu* refers to "the star gods in the constellation Orion."[28] In addition, we find an important verification for the sky-ground dualism of the Orion Correlation Theory in both the homophone *sahu,* which means "property," and its cognate *sah-t,* which refers to "landed property," "estate," "site of a temple," "homestead," or "environs." Because the term *sahu* simultaneously refers to both stars and ground, this conceptual mirroring aligns the two realms, i.e., "...on earth as it is in heaven." These and other language correlations corroborate if not a Hopi migration from the Old World, then at least a pre-Columbian contact with Middle Eastern or North African mariners, perhaps Phoenician or Libyan.[29]

An additional parallel between the Hopi language and those of the Middle East can be found in the name of Orion itself. In Chapter 3 we mentioned that the Hopi word *Hotòmqam* (referring either to the belt stars or to Betelgeuse, Alnilam, and Rigel) literally means "to string up" or "strung together," as beads on a string. The middle belt star Alnilam is an Arabic word literally meaning "string of pearls." The Hopi word for bead or necklace is *tuukwavi,* but the related word *tuukwi* means "butte" or "mesa." From this linguistic nexus we may assume that the Hopi meant to string up not only the stars of Orion but also the three Mesas upon which their culture was founded. Another example of their emphasis on sky-ground dualism can be found in the phrase *tukwi omaw,* or cumulous cloud, literally "heaped or stepped cloud." Its petroglyphic representation resembles a stepped pyramid, the Egyptian hieroglyph of which means "stairway, stepped throne, ascend."[30] As we noted in the previous paragraph, the Egyptian *Sahu* refers to the stars of Orion, and *sah-t* refers to land, whereas the cognate *sa-t* means "beads." The near homophone *saa-t* means "wisdom, knowledge," while *saa hat* is "knowing of heart, i.e., wise."[31] The Hopi word *saha'at* means "calf of the leg" (used to walk the land) while the Egyptian word *sat* refers simply to "leg."[32]

A further interesting Hopi/Egyptian linguistic parallel presents itself in *Ka.* In our Chapter 7 discussion of those supernatural intercessors the *katsinam,* we noted that this syllable was a foreign import and was pronounced the same in Hopi, Zuni, and Keresan (the latter spoken in some of the pueblos of New Mexico). In other words, for the Pueblo people of the Southwest the initial syllable *ka-* is not native to their lexicons. In the Egyptian ontology *Ka* refers to the etheric double.[33] A statuette resembling the deceased was frequently constructed for the *Ka* to inhabit. In addition, food offerings were often made to the *Ka,* a custom which still exists in

Hopiland during the November Wúwutcim ceremony when spirits of the dead return to the villages.34 The hieroglyph for *Ka* is two uplifted arms whose elbows form right angles. The palms are open and the shoulders are fused together, thus forming a U shape.35 Among the petroglyphs of the Anasazi this characteristic "prayer stance" is found in great numbers all over the Southwest. (See Fig. 3, p. 50.) "The most frequently encountered anthropomorphic stance is the 'prayer/blessing' position with both arms raised to the heavens and both feet on the ground."36 In this stance the knees frequently form right angles like the elbows. Incredible as it may seem, the non-indigenous *ka-* of the *katsinam* may have been influenced somehow by the Egyptian conception of *Ka*.

One more Hopi/Egyptian linguistic parallel involves the root word of the premier god Masau'u. This deity, of course, connotes death and the Underworld. The Hopi word *mas* refers to "gray" or "ghostly," while *maasi* means "human skeleton." The Egyptian word *maas* means "to slay, to kill."37 On the other hand, Masau'u in some accounts is said to have a handsome appearance beneath his horrific mask. In more recent cases he even is spoken of as the Great Spirit or the Creator, giving him an almost monotheistic aura.38 He is furthermore referred to in prophetic terms as the Redeemer who will return on the last day of the Fourth World during the third great war and execute what is called the Purification.39 It is this latter Masau'u that the pioneering occult researcher George Hunt Williamson evokes when he associates the Hopi god with the Messiah.

> "The great master-teacher of the Hopi people is *Massau*. Notice the astonishing similarity between this word and the Aramic [Aramaic?] *meshiha*, the Hebrew *mahsiah*, and the Greek *messias*. These words mean: *anointed*. To the Hebrews, the *Messiah* is the expected king and deliverer. To the Christians, the *Messiah* is Jesus, the Christ, son of Mary. And to the Hopis, *Massau* (Massua, Masao) is the deliverer who came before and who will return from the *east* as the 'true white brother.'"40

In the ancient Egyptian language *m'tha* is one of the words that means "to anoint," while on another level it refers to "phallus and testicles." In fact, Budge relates that the appellation *M'tha au* means "Long Phallus, a title of Osiris."41 Here we see conclusive evidence that the Hopi Masau'u, Lord of the Sipapuni, is etymologically linked with Osiris, Lord of the Duat.

This correspondence also underscores the fertility aspect of the former god, with his phallic dibble and enlarged head shaped like a squash. During an agricultural ritual outside the strict ceremonial cycle, Masau'u is impersonated for the purpose of engendering the growth of crops. "The impersonator is smeared [anointed?] with rabbit's blood, and in some accounts he carries a small cylinder filled with seeds with which he clubs people until the sack bursts and the seeds spill out. On the Second Mesa the sack is filled with cotton, while at Old Oraibi it is a short club covered with an inverted rabbit skin."[42] Later in the ceremony Masau'u is forced to inhale the smoke from a juniper bark torch, after which he falls to the ground as if dead. Soon, however, he rises again as a potent deity of both human and agricultural fertility, thereby assuming a resurrectional aspect as well. In Chapter 7 we discussed the Mastop (Death Fly) Katsina, whose name may derive from a combination of Masau'u and *totop*, or "fly" (insect).[43] (Fig. 37, p. 159) On the last day of the Soyal ceremony the Mastop rushes among crowds of young Hopi women to pantomime copulation. Here again we see Masau'u via this related *katsina* symbolically connected to human procreation.

In this regard we may recall the extraordinary potency of Osiris as well. Even after his death and dismemberment at the hands of his brother Set, Osiris along with his sister/wife Isis managed to conceive a son, the falcon-headed Horus.

> "The goddess reconstituted the body of Osiris, cunningly
> joining the fragments together. She then performed, for the
> first time in history, the rites of embalmment which restored
> the murdered god to eternal life. In this she was assisted by
> her sister Nephthys, her nephew Anubis, Osiris' grand
> vizier Thoth and by Horus, the posthumous son whom she
> had conceived by union with her husband's corpse,
> miraculously re-animated by her charms."[44]

In the mythological renderings of both Masau'u and M'tha'au (Osiris) we see the archetypal motifs of fecundity and eternity repeated with an uncanny similitude.

Adding another intriguing linguistic parallel, premier Atlantis scholar Ignatius Donnelly cites the existence of a black tribe dwelling on the Niger River in Sudan ruled by a light-skinned royal family named Masas. "*Masas* is perhaps the same as *Mashash*, which occurs in the Egyptian documents applied to the Tamahus."[45] This latter group, he suggests, refers to the present-day Tuaregs. An Egyptian monument from 1500 B.C. depicts this bearded figure wearing a robe on which are circles or spots, reminding us of the characteristic splotches on the skin of Masau'u.

The Hopi oral tradition provides further corroboration of that tribe's putative Middle Eastern origin. The prominent Hopi scholar Harold Courlander received the following information from Louis Numkena, Sr. of Moencopi in 1968: "My uncle has been telling that story about where we come from ever since I was a kid. Most of that story I can't tell you. My uncle said, 'Keep it to yourself.' But I can tell you a little part. In the beginning, he told me, we started from Jerusalem. He was an old man, but he still knew about that Jerusalem. I don't know where that is. Well, that's the place where we're from."46 Both Don C. Talayesva (quoted above) of Oraibi and Ned Zeena of Walpi verify an origin for the Hopi somewhere in the Middle East. Christian missionaries trying to proselytize the Hopi have made fewer inroads with this tribe than with any other Pueblo people, so it is doubtful that these informants were thus influenced.

On the other hand, the renowned nineteenth century photographer Edward S. Curtis brings us a case of the interaction between elder members of Motswimi, or the Warrior fraternity, and a younger Hopi man, who had indeed been exposed to biblical training: "In the evening the members sat smoking and telling stories. A young man educated at school entertained the audience with tales from the bible and instruction in the methods of the Unites States Government. The biblical stories held the men deeply interested because of the similarities noted in the customs of the Hopi and those of the ancient Hebrews."47

One can readily imagine the parallels that the elders drew. For instance, both the Hopis and the Israelites received their life plan on sacred stone tablets. In the case of the former, Masau'u, god of fire and death, appeared near the opening of the Sipapuni, whence the people had just ascended from the Third World. In the case of the latter Yahweh descended to Mount Sinai in clouds of smoke and fire in order to deliver His saturnine commandments.

Both groups were spiritually directed to make an extended exodus in the desert before reaching their "Promised Land." The Hopi were guided by a moving star or other celestial body in the east or southeast (see Chapter 1) that eventually led them to the Tuuwanasavi, whereas the Hebrews used a "pillar of fire" as a beacon to direct them to Jerusalem. In terms of religious ritual, the Hebrew "altars of earth" (rather than of gold or silver, Exodus 20: 23-24) which the Lord commanded them to erect likewise remind us of the humble yet efficacious altars made by Hopi religious leaders in their kivas.48

The Hopi are not a monolithic tribe originating from a single location but instead are a number of clans arriving from different directions to eventually aggregate in northern Arizona. The Hebrews were organized in a similar manner. "...all the evidence shows that the Jews are not a race or even a historical nation as they have come to believe; they are an amalgam of Semite groups who found a commonality in their statelessness and adopted a theological history based on a Sumerian sub-group."49

Finally, both groups have a vital tradition of prophecy that has profoundly shaped their world view. Other correlations undoubtedly could be made, but the Hopi-Hebrew connection remains a fascinating enigma.

Many major writers and scholars are also wont to see correspondences between the New World and northern Africa or the Middle East. For instance, Jon Manchip White, who has authored books on both the American Southwest and Egypt, perceives a parallel between the "Painted Kiva" at the Kuaua Ruins of Coronado National Monument in New Mexico and the tomb murals of Egypt. "Once again, without wanting to exaggerate, I must say that going down into this kiva reminds me of entering one of the smaller tombs of the nobles in the Valley of the Kings. Its birds, animals, and agricultural scenes have much of the immediacy and innocence of their Egyptian counterparts; they both reflect an easygoing agricultural society, living in partnership with nature."50

In his groundbreaking book *America B.C.* the epigrapher Barry Fell posits that Libyan seafarers circa 500 B.C. interacted with the Zuni (Shiwi), imparting a mixture of North African dialects such as Coptic, Middle Egyptian, and Nubian. (Although culturally associated with the Hopi, the Zuni have a language unrelated to any other in the Amerindian language family.) Fell also believes that the unique style of pre-historic Mimbres pottery found in western New Mexico and eastern Arizona incorporated the Libyan alphabet which describes the painted scenes of the people and animals depicted.51 In his next book Fell draws a correlation between the architecture of northern Africa and that of the American Southwest.

> "Herodotus reported that Troglodytes (people who live in holes in the ground) inhabited Libya. They still do! Communities may combine to excavate a circular depression in the desert rock, some 60 feet in diameter, and 20 feet deep. Then out of the circular wall thus produced, individual rock-cut apartments are excavated, all opening into the central depressed area, the 'hub' or *qaba*. This technique provides a cooler dwelling, sheltered from the sun's heat. Ventilation shafts connect the apartments with the surface of the desert overhead. This arrangement, seen in the mountainous desert to the west of Tripoli, and extending into Tunisia, may be the origin of the circular *kivas* of the so-called *pueblo* towns of the southwest United States. Similarly, the square adobe buildings of the Berber villages appear to match the pueblos of North America..."52

D r. Fell goes on to say that the Habbé of Mali fashioned baskets very similar to the ancient American variety and constructed cliff dwellings akin to those at Mesa Verde. "Indeed, were these people known only from their artifacts, they would be classified in America as late Basket Maker II or III, and their ruined cliff dwellings would be called Pueblo."53 David Roberts, who has written about both Egypt and the southwestern U.S. for *National Geographic* magazine, confirms Fell's remarks: "As a mountaineer, I had spent years exploring the harsh country of the American Southwest, where the Anasazi Indians had lived among sandstone cliffs strikingly similar to those of the Tellem [a predecessor of the Habbé] and Dogon half a world away."54

On p. 182 of Chapter 8 we discussed the morphological similarities between the the Sohu Katsina of the Hopi (Fig. 40, p. 162) and the amphibious creatures called the Nommos as seen in Dogon drawings reproduced in Robert K.G. Temple's book *The Sirius Mystery*. The Dogon tradition of the Nommos may have originated in Babylonia or Sumeria with a semi-daemon called Oannes (also known as Enki or Ea), the bringer of civilization to the region. In some depictions he looks like the traditional merman; in others he appears to wear a crown and cape fashioned from the head and body of a fish. In his left hand he carries a "sacred basket," which, as Temple claims, represents the geodetic net of longitude and latitude similar to that found on the *omphalos* stone of Delphi.55 If we recall the description of the Hopi *mongko*, one part of this emblem of power and authority is either an earthen ball or a water gourd encased in a cotton *net*. (Fig. 41, p. 170) The *mongko* is carried in the left hand by all the chief *katsinam*, who are considered to be intercessory spirits, not gods— the exact status of both Oannes of the Babylonians and the Nommos of the Dogon. Hence we find two similar artifacts apparently serving the same spiritual purpose in what is now Iraq, Mali, and Arizona.

Surprisingly, the Hopi *mongko* may be related to other artifacts from two distinct cultures on the opposite side of the globe. The independent researcher Crichton E M Miller has rediscovered an instrument shaped like a Celtic cross and plumb line that allowed for transoceanic journeys as well as the construction of ancient structures. "The device was able to determine time, find latitude and longitude, measure the angles of the stars, predict the solstices and equinoxes, and measure the precession of the equinoxes. The instrument could also determine the ecliptic pole, as well as the north and south poles. The information it provided generated maps and charts, designed pyramids and henges. Used in combination with these structures, observers were able to record and predict the cycles of nature and time."56 Miller also claims that the Dixon relics found at Giza were actually pieces of an Egyptian version of this instrument. (again, Fig. 41, p. 170) This so-called *Pesh-en-kef* allowed for alignment of the pyramids to the cardinal directions with utmost precision.57 It could also measure time by sightings across Orion's belt at its meridian (i.e., due south).58 Miller believes that the Hopi *mongko*, the Egyptian *Pesh-en-kef*, and the Celtic cross may all be affiliated. "There is no doubt in my mind that the Hopi *mongko* is related to Egyptian artifacts in concept, particularly the Bay or Merkhet. The *mongko* is obviously a stellar sighting instrument, although the Hopi have forgotten its use as have the Christians in the case of the cross."59

The Great Pyramid of Khufu (Cheops) was most likely built before 2500 B.C. during the last portion of the Age of Taurus. Hence, the bronze fork at the top of the *Pesh-en-kef* plausibly represents the Hyades of Taurus. As we have previously noted, the *mongko* also reflects the morphology of that constellation, which in our particular sky-ground schema correlates to the western part of Grand Canyon, the primeval Place of Emergence from the Underworld. The Hopi Two Horn Society uses the *mongko* during the New Fire Ceremony in November during the Taurid meteor shower. We have also said that between Taurus and Gemini is located the stargate on the northern end of the Milky Way. (More on this in Chapter 12.)

## *The Anasazi Bennu Bird*

The Hopi word *hik'si*, or "breath-body," appears to be related both in sound and in concept to a certain Egyptian word. "The phoenix also had another important function: it was the bringer of the life-giving essence, the *hikê*, a concept akin to our idea of magic, which the great cosmic bird carried to Egypt from a distant and magical land beyond the earthly world."[60] According to Herodotus, the Heliopolitans claimed that this phoenix had the size and form of an eagle with red wings tipped in gold. Arriving from Arabia (i.e., the east) once every five hundred years, it carries either the corpse or the ashes of its father encased in myrrh to the shrine of the sun.[61] The appearance of this legendary bird was thought to herald a new age or calendrical cycle.

The phoenix was also called the Bennu bird, sometimes depicted as a gray heron perched atop a pyramid or obelisk. The Bennu (Benu) was reputedly the *ba* (soul) of Ra and the *ab* (heart) of Osiris, each term being a palindrome of the other.[62] In essence this sacred fowl periodically regenerated from its ashes is a primary symbol of eternal life. "The Bennu not only typified new birth of the sun each morning, but in the earliest period of dynastic history it became the symbol of the resurrection of mankind, for a man's spiritual body was believed to spring from the dead physical body, just as the living sun of to-day had its origin in the dead sun of yesterday."[63] The Bennu was even an instrumental element of the cosmogony. For instance, the Shu Texts describes "...that breath of life which emerged from the throat of the *Benu* Bird, the son of Rê in whom Atum appeared in the primeval nought, infinity, darkness and nowhere."[64] Rising from the primordial abyss, the *hikê* ("life-breath") is carried in the beak of the sacred bird of rebirth. It is highly improbable that the Hopi word *hik'si* would both phonetically and conceptually echo the Egyptian word *hikê*, but that seems to be the case. Incidentally, the related word *Heka* signifies the Egyptian serpent-god of divine incantation but also refers to Meissa, the Third Eye of Orion and apex of a sidereal pyramid.

The powerful icon of a bird perched on the apex of a pyramid is not the sort of image we would expect in the context of the Anasazi, but a striking example of this has indeed been found. (Fig. 46, p. 249) At the beginning of the twentieth century the prominent archaeologist Jesse Walter Fewkes unearthed a stone slab covering a grave at Chevelon Ruin

(Sakwavayupki, occupied between A.D. 1280 and the 1380s) not far from Homol'ovi near the present town of Winslow, Arizona. This slab was painted on two sides; the obverse side exposed to the elements was mostly obliterated, though an image of a dragonfly is apparent. On the reverse side, which was turned downward, the image is clearer. Here we see a rectangle formed by a white border with black on the outside enclosing three isosceles triangles or pyramids of nearly equal size. These pyramids are painted black with a white square inside each one located near the base. The negative space (i.e., the background) of these pyramids is colored yellow. Most significantly, a red bird, perhaps a macaw or parrot, is perched atop all three of these pyramids. Each of the stylized birds has a triangular body with the base forming its dorsal side and the apex (where its feet would be) touching the apex of the pyramid. Facing to the right, they all have curving beaks and bifurcated tails. The bird at the center is the only one that has eyes. It should be noted that the four colors used on this slab are the traditional Hopi directional colors: yellow (northwest), black or dark blue (southwest), red (southeast), and white (northeast). Unfortunately Fewkes does not provide the dimensions of this slab, but it must have been large enough to cover the grave.65

What is the meaning of these figures? Fewkes suggests that the triangles are rain clouds, though this symbol is usually depicted by a stepped pyramid. The white square at the heart of each pyramid signifies in this case inner space, perhaps an Underworld of sorts. The three pyramids could possibly represent the three Hopi Mesas, or perhaps the three major promontories in the San Francisco Peaks: Humphreys, Agassiz, and Fremont. As heretofore mentioned, these three mountains curiously resemble the three primary pyramids at Giza, especially if approached from the west. (Fig. 47, p. 249) Frequently depicted on ceramics and petroglyphs, the exotic parrot or scarlet macaw represents the warmth and moisture of the tropical jungles far to the southeast, the direction symbolically implied by their redness. Used in prayer stick making and other ceremonies, their multi-hued feathers may also symbolize the nadir, the Underworld direction of "many colors."66 The whole bodies of both parrots and macaws have also been found in burial sites at Wupatki, Tuzigoot, Chaco Canyon, and other places. Furthermore, Fewkes found other grave slabs at Chevelon and Homol'ovi with circular holes worn into them, ranging in size from a broomstick to an arm's width. Somewhat condescending vis-à-vis the modern Hopi, he remarks on their purpose: "Explanations more or less fanciful have been suggested for these perforated stones, one of which was that the rock had been placed above the body and the hole in it was for the escape of the soul or breath-body."67 Given the above evidence, it would not be unreasonable, then, to assign to these three birds atop their pyramids in Arizona the same function that the journeying soul of the Bennu in Egypt performs— the omnipresent quest for immortality.

This Bennu iconography is also associated with the Benben, a black conical stone, possibly meteoric 68 used as a pyramidion, or apex of a pyramid. The Egyptian word *ben* denotes both the nominative "seed" or "semen" and the infinitive "to copulate" or "to impregnate"— all particularly apropos of the phallic obelisk.69 In addition, the cognate *ben-t* means "cincture, belt, girdle,"70 and might refer obliquely to Orion's belt. Alnitak, the most eastern star of the belt (corresponding to the Great Pyramid, or Khufu), literally means "the Girdle," while Mintaka, the most western star (corresponding to Menkaure), is called "the Belt."71 As with every example of truly divine omnipotence, the positive aspects are counter-balanced with the negative. Hence the word *ben* also means "evil, wickedness," and the words *ben-t* or *benut* can also refer to pustule, boil, abscess, or pus 72— all of which are attributes of the Hopi god Masau'u.

Conceptualized as an *omphalos*, or navel of the world, the Benben played a key role in the cosmogony. "The sun cult of Heliopolis taught that out of the waters of Chaos, arose the primeval mound in the shape of the pyramidal stone, the *ben-ben*, or High Sand, in the sanctuary of Heliopolis. It was on the *ben-ben* that the Creator first manifested himself, either in the form of a heron-like phoenix (the bird of light which dispelled the darkness over the waters) or as Atum, the demiurge in human form."73 In this context it is interesting to note that the Hopi Center of the World called Tuuwanasavi, literally "sand-middle," is described as "a *sandy* plain four miles southwest of Oraibi."74 On one topographic map this spot is marked with the words "SAND DUNES." In addition, the original name of

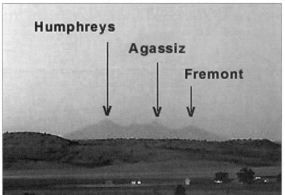

*Fig. 46. Painted grave slab, Chevelon Ruin (Bureau of American Ethnology)*

*Fig. 47. Arizona "pyramids" as seen from about 60 miles to the southwest*

Oraibi was Ojaivi, which means "Round Rock,"[75] possibly a version of the *omphalos* stone.

In this chapter we have seen a number of architectural and cultural parallels between the American Southwest and Egypt or Africa and the Middle East in general. The reader must decide for him/herself whether or not these are all mere coincidences, which seem to abound in discussions of this ilk. Are these correspondences between the continents just co-extant yet physically unrelated cultural developments, or are they definitive evidence of previous contact between the two regions? Again the reader must weigh the evidence to see whether or not these diffusionist claims are valid.

In the next chapter we will return to the phoenix in the context of the modern metropolis of the same name, and we will further delve into the subject of stellar thresholds by discussing the Phoenix stargate.

# Chapter 12
# Beyond That Fiery Day

"When we know that Arizona's Phoenix, now the metropolitan abode of a million souls, rose from the desert on the site of the vanished Hohokam, we realize the aptness of the name. If we embrace the Egyptologist Sir Flinders Petrie's cyclic view of history, then do we wonder how many centuries time has allotted this fair city before its funeral pyre is ready. And beyond that fiery day, what even more miraculous bird will arise from its ashes."[1]

Lawrence Clark Powell

## *Phoenix: the Stargate of the Orion Zone*

Of all the questions posed in this book, perhaps the most significant is the following pair: What is the function of the terrestrial Orion schema in Arizona, and how does the celestial Orion relate to it? In other words, why did Masau'u, the Hopi god of transformation, direct the Hisatsinom throughout their migration period to settle at given locations and build villages, or "star cities," that would eventually form the gestalt of the constellation Orion in a very precise way upon the high desert?

We have noted that Orion is the most important stellar configuration in many Hopi sacred rituals, such as the New Fire Ceremony (Wúwutcim) and the winter solstice ceremony (Soyal). Orion at his meridian synchronizes key segments of these rituals during which he sends down his numinous energy through the hatchway of the kiva, thereby binding sky with earth and providing celestial guidance in the terrestrial cycle of Hopi ceremonies.

Robert Bauval suggests that this sort of influence may even be talismanic. In discussing an eleventh century manuscript written by an Arab scholar from Andalusia (whose name has apparently been confused with the title of the work), Bauval observes: "The Picatrix deals essentially with a form of hermetic magic known to scholars as 'Celestial Magic' or 'Astrological Magic.' As we have seen, this sort of magic attempts to 'draw down' to earth the power and influence of stars and planets. The idea is to select a special object or monument, which is called a talisman, and through rituals, ceremonies and magical incantations induce the astral energies of 'spirits and angels' to dwell in it."[2] In the Arizona case each Anasazi village, or at least its village shrine or its main kiva, is the focus of the stellar force, both of Orion's unique energy as a whole and of the influence that each individual star has on a given village. In terms of the former, one esoteric source sums up the dual nature of incarnation symbolized by Orion:

> "The seeming strength and desirability of the animal forces in man (*beautiful, blooming, strong, a mighty hunter*) and the apparent bondage of the individual to those forces (Canst thou. . . loose the bands of Orion?" [Job: 38:31]). Man has a very dim comprehension that back of even his apparently animal forces and propensities that seem to bind him so tightly to the flesh there is something that is divine, there is some wonderful truth. Yet, like the stars that represent truths apparently far beyond man's present conception, his inner forces and powers, with their origin and possibilities, are just beginning to be faintly understood by him."₃

It is interesting to note that Job 38:33 echoes the basic Hermetic maxim "As Above, so Below," and, we might add, the primary theme of this book: "Knowst thou the ordinances of heaven? canst thou set the dominion thereof in the earth?"

In terms of the influence of individual stars upon their correlative ancient villages, fixed star astrology provides some evidence. For instance, Rigel, which corresponds in our terrestrial schemata to Betatakin, involves the active promulgation of knowledge and education, both in teaching and in learning about the vicissitudes of civilizations and overall world views.₄ Both the Snake Clan and the Hopi culture hero Tiyo, who journeyed to a Pacific island to gain ophidian knowledge and magic, originated from this region. Conversely, Bellatrix, which corresponds to Wupatki, signifies not only courage and a martial spirit but also personal growth and self-awareness.₅ Those who chose to live at the base of the volcanically active Sunset Crater were obviously brave souls and seekers of cosmic truth. On the other hand (or literally and more specifically, the right shoulder of Orion), Betelgeuse, which is associated on the terrestrial plane in Arizona with Homol'ovi, symbolizes natural talents, charisma, success, fame, or even immortality.₆ Living by the waters of the Little Colorado, the only perennially flowing stream in the region, the inhabitants of these successful villages famous for their cotton production must have viewed the bounty of their existence as a sacred gift naturally endowed by the Creator. The influence of Cingula Orionis, or Orion's belt, seems particularly apt vis-à-vis the Hopi. "The joint influence is to give strength, energy, industry, organizing abilities, notoriety, good fortune, lasting happiness, a sharp mind and a good memory... Good fortune as regards the growing of grain crops."₇ If applied to the Hopi culture, all of these characteristics could be considered germane.

The reader will recall from Chapter 2 that the word "zona" refers to the belt of Orion and that the disparity between the establishment of a terrestrial correlation of the stellar trinity upon the high desert beginning in the twelfth century and the naming of the Arizona Territory in the nineteenth was possibly the result of one type of synchronicity. A less psychological explanation exists, however. The first usage of "Arizona" appears to have been written by one Padre Ortega sometime before 1754, when he referred to the "Real of Arizona."[8] The Spanish word *real* means "military encampment," but the adjective form meaning "royal" is also implied. In addition, the Spanish term *arisco* can mean "churlish, surly" or even "vicious," while *ariete* means "battering ram" (reminding one of the constellation Aries near Orion) and *arimez* means "projection"— all traditionally active, masculine, and violent attributes in keeping with the archetypal Orion. Furthermore, the Spanish word *zona* refers to "belt" or "girdle" as well as to "zone." Alternate spellings for Orion include "Arion," "Oarion," "Aorion,"[9] so the prefixes *Ari-* and *Ori-* might have been interchangeable. The Greek *aristos*, as in "aristocracy," means "best" or "noblest," while the related Sanskrit word *arya*, as in "Aryan," means "of high rank" or "noble." The Italian word *aria* also means "air" (as in "arid") or "melody." In light of all these etymologies, perhaps the padre was merely recording what was already established in the region we now know as Arizona. If we lend credence to diffusionism rather than to the more academically accepted isolationism, it is plausible that Indo-European speaking Aryans such as the Nagas did at one time travel to Arizona (i.e., Ary-zona), where they shared linguistic concepts phonetically with the Hopi.

For instance, the Hopi suffix *-sona* refers to "one who relishes" while *tsoona* means "he's forward, not shy, or having fun exuberantly," all of which suggest characteristics of Orion. In addition, the term *orai* (homophone of the first two syllables in "Orion") means "Rock on High"[10] or "Round Rock,"[11] after which Oraibi was named, one of the initial Hopi Mesa villages. Furthermore, the Hopi word *soona* means "germ, kernel, edible part of any seed, or heart of a tree." Like the center of the constellation Orion, this could be a reference to the heart of Hopiland, whence sprouts the sustenance of the sacred corn or other agricultural mainstays.

In the third chapter of this book we stated that the name Orion is derived from the Akkadian *Uru-anna*, which means "Light of Heaven." Moira Timms comments further on the term: "Over time, the language corrupted to 'Aryan,' which is what the ancient Persians called themselves, and which became the modern idiom, 'Iran.' Arab astronomer Al Babadur said the constellation was originally called the 'Strong One,' but another, Scaliger, affirmed the name was a corruption of the Arab 'Al Shuja' (the Snake)."[12] As we saw in Chapter 10, the Hopi Snake Clan may have been influenced by South Pacific islanders or even East Indians.

The upper limbs of the mighty giant Orion also transmit their puissance to correlative sites on the ground. As discussed in Chapter 6, the left arm of the terrestrial Orion's reaches northwest from Wupatki to Grand

Canyon, known by the Hopi as the grand Sipapuni, or Place of Emergence. Out of this stunningly beautiful geologic rift the Ancient Ones ascended from their previous plane of existence (viz., the Third World) in order to inhabit the present one. In particular, the middle of Orion's bow or shield is the very sun-like star Pi 3 Orionis, only twenty-six light-years distant, which is relatively close in galactic terms. Orion's left (or sacred) hand points to the place of origin. (See Diagram 3, p. 32.)

Is this, then, one of the purposes of the Orion Correlation in Arizona? To point to the particular star system whence the Ancient Ones traveled? It would be far easier for a Hopi elder to point to that star and say, "That's where we came from." However, memories fade and people die. By constructing a configuration of stone villages during centuries of migration upon the high desert in order to reflect the Orion home world, an everlasting monument was created. Perhaps the people of our current era, the precarious end of the Fourth World, are specifically the ones for which this mirrored message of sky and earth was written.

Orion's other arm has equal significance in terms of the terrestrial template. (See Fig. 27, p. 121.) Also noted in Chapter 6, the right arm points to the interdimensional northern stargate (between Gemini and Taurus) at 33 degress declination (celestial latitude). On the earth this corresponds to the metropolis of Phoenix, located at 33 degrees 30 minutes (terrestrial) latitude.

XXXIII, of course, is a sacred number according to ritual Freemasonry; in most cases there is no higher degree or level to which a Mason may aspire. In a Biblical context, we see that King David ruled in Jerusalem thirty-three years, Jacob had thirty-three sons and daughters, and Jesus Christ was crucified at age thirty-three. This number even permeates the biological realm studied by science: thirty-three is the number of turns in a complete sequence of DNA.[13]

According to one numerological reckoning, thirty-three is 3 + 3, which equals 6. "Symbolic of ambivalence and equilibrium, six comprises the union of the two triangles (of fire and water) and hence signifies the human soul. The Greeks regarded it as a symbol of the hermaphrodite. It corresponds to the six Directions of Space (two for each dimension), and to the cessation of movement (since the Creation took six days)."[14] A pair of interlocking triangles forms the Star of David on the Great Seal of the United States. Six is the number of the four horizontal cardinal directions plus the vertical zenith and nadir, the latter corresponding to the *axis mundi* of the World Tree (or Jacob's ladder) upon which shamanic journeys are undertaken. "Six, the number of the material world and therefore of time and space, is the number chosen by the Egyptians to symbolize temporal and spatial phenomena."[15]

Thus, 33 (or 3 + 3 = 6) is the perfect number to represent the stargate of incarnation at the Phoenix locus where the soul becomes accustomed to the limitations of the body in the physical universe of space/time.

In addition, the major Hohokam site of Snaketown is located only about five miles north of the 33rd parallel and the astronomical observatory of Casa Grande about five miles south of the line.

## The Hohokam: Early Denizens of the Northern Stargate

We stated at the end of Chapter 10 that in 200 B.C. the galactic center was on the Orion chakra line of 230 degrees azimuth at about midnight. This is also within a century of the inception of the Hohokam culture in the Valley of the Sun. As we all know from the Einsteinian concept of relativity, space by its nature also includes time. The light that we see today from Saiph (Orion's right leg, corresponding to the Canyon de Chelly ruins, the first of the Orion Correlation "star cities" to be constructed) left that star 2,100 years ago, approximately the same period that the Hohokam were originally establishing themselves in the area one day to be known as Phoenix. In fact, they inhabited the Valley of the Sun perhaps as early as 300 B.C. (about the time of Alexander the Great and the Ptolemaic Dynasties in Egypt) and built one of the world's most extensive irrigation systems.

The name Hohokam is a Pima/Tohono O'odham word meaning "those who have vanished," or more literally, "all used up."[16] The Hohokam created an estimated total of 500 miles of canals to irrigate over 25,000 acres in the Valley of the Sun— all constructed with mere digging sticks, stone implements, and woven carrying baskets. Surprisingly, no wheelbarrows or draft animals were used. The main canals leading from the Salt and Gila rivers measured up to seventy-five feet across at the top and fifty feet wide at the bottom.[17] South canal no. 3 at Park of the Four Waters appears to have been about twelve feet deep [18], though most of the distribution canals were between two and four feet deep. From the Salt River near Pueblo Grande (a major Hohokam site within the Phoenix city limits), North and South canals extended almost eight miles long each, sending water to villages nearly ten miles away from the river.[19] Some of these waterways were lined with a concrete-like substance known as caliche, so that even today they could be incorporated into the modern water system for the Phoenix metro area.[20] These main canals branched into smaller lateral canals with headgates to divert the water into the network of fields. Overall, the construction of the canal system was a colossal undertaking.

As the early Southwest archaeologist H.M. Wormington observes, "The scope of the canal project suggests comparisons with the erection of the huge pyramids of Egypt or the great temples of the Maya."[21] At the risk of appearing politically incorrect, we must question whether or not the Hohokam had "outside" assistance in the construction of this monumental irrigation project. "The organization and coordination for the planning, construction, maintenance and operation of the system must have required social and civic efforts far beyond what might be expected of a primitive people one step removed from a hunting and gathering existence."22

Even if we disregard the "who" and focus on the what," we must admit that this technology allowed a florescence of culture thitherto unprecedented in North America. "The Phoenix Basin achieved a total population of between 30,000 and 60,000, one of the highest densities of people —living along the largest system of irrigation canals— anywhere in prehistoric North America."23 (The larger number is about the size of present-day Prescott, Arizona combined with a few of its surrounding towns.)

Unlike the Anasazi stone structures to the north, most of the Hohokam adobe dwellings have melted into the desert. The low desert people once lived in semi-subterranean pit house structures with jacal walls. Typically two to four houses were clustered around a central plaza with their doorways facing inward. This architectural arrangement known as the *rancheria* suggests a kinship system, with related households forming a clan that contained sixteen to twenty individuals.24 Each compound had its own communal cooking area, trash mound, and cremation cemetery.

In contrast to the inhumation custom of the Anasazi, the Hohokam had elaborate cremation rituals with ceramics and lithics burned along with the deceased. Associated with the mortuary ceremony were buried caches of deliberately destroyed stone effigies and clay figurines of both humans and animals.25 Two classes of humanoid figurines have been found at Hohokam sites: torsos and heads. "The torsos are strongly suggestive of similar human figurines found in the Basket Maker culture of the [Colorado] plateau, and this latter group may well have taken the idea of modeling them from the Hohokam. The heads find no close parallel in the Southwest, but are strongly suggestive of those typical of the Archaic horizon in the Valley of Mexico."26 Also found among the cremated remains were rectangular schist palettes (the morphology of Orion, as we saw in Chapter 3) with raised borders frequently incised or sculpted with snakes, lizards, birds, or other animals. Additional offerings to the dead included fine pottery vessels, copper bells, quartz crystals, and shells from the Pacific or the Sea of Cortez etched with the acidic juice of the saguaro cactus to form designs. Vanity was also a part of life for the Hohokam, who admired themselves in a sort of mirror. "The pyrite 'mirrors' are actually mosaic plaques on which pieces of reflective iron pyrite were glued to a round stone base, very similar to ones in Mayan ruins."27 At any rate, one might conclude that the emphasis on cremation is symbolic of the phoenix himself rising from his ashes. (See the next two sections of this chapter.)

During the Colonial Period (A.D. 550-900) ball courts began to be extensively used. Nearly two hundred of the former structures have been found in Arizona, from Wupatki in the north (see Chapter 4) to below Tucson in the south. However, over forty percent of them are located in the Phoenix Basin.28 The court itself was probably an *imago mundi* whereon players used a ball made from *guayule*, a rubber-like material from a plant native to Chihuahua, in order to decide their cosmic fate. The oldest and largest court was found at a site the Pima call "place of the rattlesnakes," or Snaketown (perhaps a Naga stronghold— see Chapter 10), about nineteen miles due south of Pueblo Grande. This oval playing area was 197 feet in length and sixteen feet in height, with its embankments allowing for over 500 spectators.29 In addition to the sacred connotation of the game, David R. Wilcox, chief archaeologist for the Museum of Northern Arizona, believes that it served the economic function of linking dispersed settlements in an exchange system, thereby fostering trade between different native groups— Hohokam, Sinagua, Salado, and Mogollon.30

The primary architectural development of the Sedentary Period (A.D. 900-1100) was the use of the platform mound, over forty of which were located in the Phoenix Basin.31 Whereas the ball court represented a communitarian or egalitarian phase of Hohokam development, the platform mound signaled a shift toward a more hierarchical social structure.32 The earliest mounds began as circular accumulations of earth, rubble, and trash capped with caliche, though sometimes they were accompanied by retaining walls. "In appearance like a truncated pyramid with a flat top, platform mounds apparently served as a stage-like area for performing ceremonies. That this custom was borrowed from Mexican peoples seems certain."33 Later platform mounds were constructed in a rectangular shape with rounded corners, oriented to a north-south axis. In addition, wooden palisades or adobe compound walls signify a restricted visual and spatial access to ceremonial activities. The further segregation of an elitist class of priesthood from the "commoners" is demonstrated by the construction of domicile and storage rooms on top of the platform mounds of the later period. "There were also massive adobe-walled enclosures which were filled in and formed raised platforms on top of which structures were built. It has been pointed out that similar pyramidal bases were found in Mexico."34 Unlike the ball court phenomenon which spread across both low desert and upland regions, this type of North American "flat-topped pyramid"35 was restricted to the major tributaries of Arizona.

At Pueblo Grande we find one of the largest platform mounds, which was once 300 feet long, 150 feet wide, and twenty-five to thirty feet high (including the height of the buildings). Over 720,000 cubic yards of fill of granite, sandstone, river cobbles, and dirt were used to construct this truncated pyramid. On the southeast corner of the platform mound was a room with an unusual corner door to let in the rays of the summer solstice sunrise, which fell against another door in the south wall. The former door also lines up with one more solstice observatory called Hole-in-the-Rock on Papago Buttes about two-and-a-half miles to the northeast. The last rays of the winter solstice sunset would have also entered the southern doorway, so the room was undoubtedly used to calibrate the Hohokam agricultural calendar. On the southwest corner of the mound was found a number of debris-filled cells, which included a

**Fig. 48. Pueblo Grande Ruin
near Phoenix Sky Harbor airport**

human burial and the skeleton of a large bird. (Some inhumation was practiced in the later stages of Hohokam development.) In this area were also discovered four giant adobe columns four feet in diameter and six feet in height, evenly spaced in the center of the room. This odd type of architectural feature has only been located on platform mounds and probably served some ceremonial purpose. Surrounding the platform mound was an adobe wall three feet thick and up to eight feet high. The rooms, compound walls, and courtyards later built atop this artificial mesa were apparently designed in a labyrinthine fashion to emphasize their hierarchical function. In addition, Hopi pottery, obsidian nodules, shells, stone beads, and piles of stone axes were unearthed in an area to the north. Because of Pueblo Grande's commanding view of the surrounding landscape, a few 19th century settlers were known to have sat atop this monumental example of Hohokam architecture to enjoy their picnics.

During the latest stage of Hohokam development, viz., the Classic Period, A.D. 1100-1450, at least three and probably more adobe and caliche "great houses" three to four stories high were built, the most famous of which is the astronomical observatory and administrative center at Casa Grande Ruins National Monument (mentioned in Chapter 2) located about forty miles southeast of Pueblo Grande. In the construction 1,440 cubic yards of dirt and 600 roof beams were used. The ponderosa pine and white fir beams, each thirteen feet in length, had to be hauled and/or floated down the Gila River from sixty miles away.[36] The entrenched walls measured four feet thick at ground level and two feet thick at the top.[37] (Fig. 49, p. 259)

These "great house" structures were also frequently surrounded by adobe compound walls. "In the last century [viz., the 19th], when the rich agricultural potential of the Phoenix Basin was rediscovered by European-American settlers, the Pueblo Grande site was put under cultivation to produce cotton. Even the three-story big house was demolished and its fill was used to help level fields."[38] This major archaeological ruin once rested where Van Buren St. is today— about one-quarter mile to the north of the platform mound.

Before discussing Hohokam representations of the heron, which is symbolically linked to both the phoenix and the eagle, we shall look at the historic founding of Phoenix in Aztlan, or the "place of the heron."

*Fig. 49. Casa Grande with modern protective roof near Coolidge, Arizona*

## Phoenix: the Masonic Heart of Aztlan

In the autumn of 1867 Bryan Philip Darrell Duppa and other founding fathers of the fledgling city of Phoenix were picnicking at Pueblo Grande Ruins near what is now the intersection of East Washington St. and 44th St. near Phoenix Sky Harbor airport. The question arose as to what this future municipality should be called. One Southerner wanted to deem it Stonewall, after the Confederate general. Another offered the name Salina, which means "salt marsh," but that too was voted down. Then Duppa spoke: "This canal was constructed in an age now forgotten. Prehistoric cities lie in ruins all around you. A great ancient civilization once thrived in this valley. Let the new city arise from its ashes. Let it be called Phoenix."[39]

Born into the English landed gentry, "Lord" Duppa was one of the best-educated men in the Amercan West. Classically trained in Paris and Madrid, he knew French, Spanish, Italian, Latin, and Greek. The library that he carried with him into the wilderness included Ovid, Juvenal, and Homer in the original. An eccentric and a loner, he occasionally was given to fits of eloquence and could quote Shakespeare by the hour, especially if facilitated by a shot or two of red-eye.

Months earlier Duppa had been seen in Prescott, the new prospecting town a hundred miles to the north. His ostensible business was to check up on some gold mining shares owned by his prosperous uncle, whose New Zealand sheep ranch he had helped to establish. Before arriving in Arizona, Duppa had traveled extensively throughout Australia and was the sole survivor of a shipwreck off the coast of Chile. Although water rather than fire was the threatening element, this event may give a clue to his personal choice for the name.

Duppa was alluding to the description of the mythical phoenix by the Greek historian Herodotus. At the end of each temporal cycle this brilliantly plumed male bird flies to Heliopolis in Egypt and builds a nest of cassia twigs in a myrrh tree as his pyre upon which he will be resurrected. Thus a new cycle is initiated. All this scholarship must have impressed the settlers, because the name began to be used officially. Or so the official story goes.

At the end of the previous chapter we discussed the association of the phoenix with both the sun cult's Bennu bird perched atop an obelisk (thought to symbolize the *axis mundi*) and the Benben stone of meteoric iron. Is it more than just a coincidence that this Egyptian bird whose center of worship was the Pre-Dynastic City of the Sun should lend its name to the largest city in the 19th century Valley of the Sun? Is the name something more than the whim of some erudite inebriate misplaced in the hinterlands of America?

Perhaps it is no accident that most if not all of the first citizens of Phoenix were Freemasons. John T. Alsap, for instance, was an attorney, judge, first territorial treasurer and first mayor of Phoenix. He also served as the first worshipful master of Arizona Lodge No. 2, F. & A.M. as well as the first grand master of the Masonic Grand Lodge of Arizona.[40] Even earlier, he had beem first master of Arizona's first Masonic Lodge called Aztlan, located in Prescott, the first territorial capital. (A lot of "firsts" here.)

*Aztlan* is a Nahuatl word meaning either "place of the heron" or "place of the reeds," as we saw in Chapter 10. The Aztecs inhabited this mythical land after emerging from Chicomostoc, the Seven Caves located in the bowels of the earth.[41] (In Hopi, *kiiqö* means "village ruin" and *kiiqölö* means "cave.") The *chichimeca azteca*, or the Chichimecs (see the section on Chaco Canyon in Chapter 8.) "...are the people we know as Aztec, which is derived from Axatlan [or Aztlan]: the legendary place from which the Chichimeca migrations are said to have begun in the lands of Mictla, the Country of the Dead."[42] This land was reputed to be located in the far north, so perhaps this land of the dead is a reference to the Hopi territory of Masau'u, deity of death.

Chicano folklore identifies Aztlan as that portion of Mexico taken over by the U.S. after the Mexican-American War of 1846 (in part, the Arizona Territory). Proof that the Nahuatl speaking peoples originated from this region comes from the present existence there of a number of tribes from the Uto-Aztecan-Tanoan linguistic group, including the Hopi.

The nomadic proto-Aztecans were thought to have lived in Aztlan for 1014 years ("twice four hundred years and ten times twenty years and fourteen years"[43]), after which they migrated south to Tollan, Tula, and ultimately Tenochtitlán (Mexico City). Aztlan is also conceptualized as an island, and some speculate that the name even refers to the legendary continent of Atlantis. According to comparative linguistics scholar Gene D. Matlock:

> "American Chicano political activists and poorly-informed historians like to mention a place called Aztlán as the primordial founding city of the Toltecs and Aztatecas. But there never was an Aztlán in Nahuatl mythology. It was called Aztatlán. On Mexico's West coast, there is an Aztatlán, Nayarit. The Sanskrit word Asta means 'Place of the Setting Sun' or 'Westernmost Extreme or Boundary.' Could Aztatlán be the westernmost boundary of what was once Atlantis? Additionally, the 'Aztecs' were never Aztecas, but Aztatecas. Again, Asta means 'Westernmost Extreme or Boundary.' Aztateca = 'Westerner.'"[44]

Why, then, did Brother Alsap name his lodge Aztlan? The heron is thought to be the naturalistic model for the Egyptian Bennu bird, or phoenix. More specifically, the hieroglyph for *bennu* means both "purple heron" (*Ardea purpurea*) and "palm tree."[45] In Chapter 10 we mentioned that one of the denotations for the word "phoenix" is "purple-red" and that Phoenicians were known as "red men." We further stated that the Hohokam territory is one of the candidates for Palatkwapi, the legendary Hopi "Red City of the South."

Psychologist C.G. Jung suggests that alchemy was the bearer of archetypal lore in a dark time that was hostile to mythological thinking; ergo, we expect to find pertinent lore in the alchemical literature. "In alchemy, [the phoenix] corresponds to the colour red, to the regeneration of universal life and to the successful completion of a process."[46] Even Pike's Masonic *Morals and Dogma* comments in this regard: "...the entire work [i.e., the Great Work of alchemy] has for its symbols the Pelican and the Phoenix."[47]

The heron is furthermore an Egyptian symbol of morning and the generation of life, and, together with the ibis and the stork, carries a favorable connotation.[48] Likewise, the Bennu embodies the morning star Venus, appearing on the Persea (laurel) Tree in Anu (Heliopolis)[49] to receive, Homerically speaking, "dawn's rosy fingers." This ornithological curiosity is also the incarnation of the heart of Osiris (counterpart to the Hopi god Masau'u) and the soul of Ra (counterpart to the Hopi god Tawa). In addition, the heron and the Bennu were among a number of animals, including the hawk and the serpent, in which a discarnate soul could inhabit for as long as it wished.[50]

Did Lord Duppa and Judge Alsap consciously try to merge Mesoamerican and Egyptian mythologies in the wilds of Arizona? Alsap's Bachelor of Law and Doctor of Medicine degrees both prove that he was no dummy himself. Was the establishment of Aztlan (Masonic Lodge No.1) and Phoenix (Masonic Lodge No. 2) an attempt to symbolically merge Prescott (the heron) and Phoenix (the Bennu) in the same way they would soon actually be linked by stagecoach? (Duppa later settled for a while at Agua Fria, twelve miles due east of Prescott along that stage line, where he lived in a crude dwelling made of scrub oak and cottonwood slats stitched together with rawhide.) Was it a clandestine Masonic intent that a new Atlantis (Aztlan) should rise in Arizona and a new Heliopolis (Phoenix) should be its heart?

Other questions about the first territorial capital arise (no pun intended). Why was Prescott named to honor the prominent 19th century historian William Hickling Prescott, who never set foot in the town? Were the run-of-the-mill settlers really all that interested in *History of the Conquest of Mexico* and *History of the Conquest of Peru*, the titles of two of his major books? From the former work we discover the origin of the native groups that Cortés confronted in the Valley of Mexico: "The inhabitants, members of different tribes, and speaking dialects somewhat different, belonged to the same great family of nations who had come from the real or imaginary region of Aztlan, in the far north-west."[51] In other words, the Arizona Territory. Is this why two major thoroughfares in the town of Prescott are named Cortez Street and Montezuma Street, to the east and west respectively?

Still more questions come up: Why did the territorial capital suddenly shift in 1889 from Prescott to Phoenix? The mercantile owner, postmaster, and territorial representative John Y.T. Smith greatly influenced this movement. He too was another "pioneer Mason" of Phoenix. After governmental authority finally rested with the southern city, spiritual symbolism superseded natural potency. Did secret powers dictate that instead of the heron the phoenix should arise?

Whatever the reason, Columbus H. Gray, who served as a territorial senator and member of Maricopa County's Board of Supervisors, began to construct during Phoenix's early years a Masonic hall at the corner of Jefferson St. and First St. Before it was completed though, he sold it to Mike Goldwater, grandfather of Senator Barry Goldwater, himself a 33rd degree Mason. By 1890 one John A. Black could list a number of the fraternal organizations operating in the city: "The secret societies are well represented; there are lodges of Masons, Odd Fellows, Knights of Pythias, Ancient Order of United Workmen, Grand Army of the Republic, Chosen Friends and Good Templars."[52]

Duppa spent his last days in the Valley of the Sun and crossed the bar in 1892. He was initially buried in the Odd Fellows Cemetery but later re-interred in Greenwood Memorial Cemetery by the Maricopa Chapter of the D.A.R. Most likely he was a Mason too. "Membership in both the Masons and Odd Fellows has been common as evidenced by numerous pins showing the square and compass conjoined with the three link chain."53 The three links symbolize the principal tenants of Friendship, Love, and Truth. However, in this context the Masonic square could represent the rectilinear body of Orion while the compass in the same emblem could suggest the circular horizon. The addition of the Odd Fellows triad of links could be emblematic of the Orion's belt.

Further evidence of Duppa's Masonic association comes from one source that connects him to Jacob Waltz, the famous Lost Dutchman, by identifying both men as Masons. This German prospector supposedly discovered a fabulous gold mine in the Superstition Mountains east of Phoenix. As with many lost treasures of the Wild West, its location remains a mystery. According to Charles Frederick Higham and Barney Barnard from their book *True Story of Jacob Walzer And his Famous Hidden Mine (The Lost Dutchman)*, "Jacob von Walzer [sic], the man known as the Lost Dutchman was a Mason as was Darrell Duppa, the Englishman, who named the city of Phoenix."54

Masonic influence in Phoenix continued well into the twentieth century. Arizona's first governor, George Wiley Paul Hunt, served seven terms between 1912 (the year of statehood) and 1932. He was also a prominent and longstanding Freemason.55 As a populist and supporter of trade unions, he spoke and wrote in a simple and sometimes grammatically incorrect style. Nonetheless, like Duppa, he loved classical literature, which gained him the moniker "Old Roman." A man of contradictions, Hunt also had been known to address Theosophical Society meetings. His final resting place in Phoenix's Papago Park is within sight of the archaeo-astronomical observatory called Hole-in-the-Rock mentioned in the previous section. Oddly enough, Hunt's family mausoleum was constructed in the style of a large white-tiled Egyptian pyramid.

Many historians (especially non-academic, local history buffs) portray early pioneers as hardy, pragmatic individualists who were more concerned with prospecting, gambling, and imbibing whisky than with studying arcane lore. In most cases, this is probably true. In the same sense, most Masons are ordinary businessmen who merely want to further their careers while both offering charity to

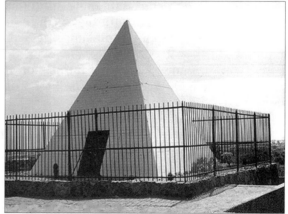

*Fig. 50. First Arizona governor's tomb*

the community at large and enjoying the camaraderie of the order. However, inside both each citizenry and each lodge exists a cabal of operatives who long to achieve power and further their own ultimate goals or those of their ancient organization. Darrell Duppa, John Alsap, George Hunt, and others of Aztlan may have been such men.56

### Birds of a Feather

Examining the pottery of the Hohokam, we see that Aztlan, or the Place of the Heron, certainly lives up to its name. More realistically portrayed than in the Anasazi geometric style, numerous examples of water birds have been found. For instance, from his comprehensive excavation of Snaketown in 1964-1965, Emil Haury unearthed 157 depictions on pottery shards of herons or cranes painted in the positive, and a few in the negative.57 Clearly the heron was a major totem for the Hohokam. "The Great Blue Heron is the most conspicuous large water bird in Arizona. It formerly nested in colonies in the Salt River Valley and still does locally."58 At Snaketown a single specimen of *Ardea herodias* was found partially burned, perhaps ritually. (Did the Hohokam know about the myth of the phoenix?) In addition, from a Casa Grande burial site a chevron-shaped pink shell bordered by inlaid turquoise exquisitely shows the extended wings and tail of a bird in flight— perhaps the mighty heron.59 Even as far north as Petrified Forest National Park a petroglyph of a large heron whose beak is stabbing a humanoid figure can be found. Quite significantly, in the rock below and slightly to the left of this heron is carved a triangle, making it appear that the bird is perched upon a pyramidion.

The heron/phoenix, then, was an abiding spiritual presence not only in the Valley of the Sun but in all of Arizona (Aztlan) from the Colorado Plateau extending south into the Valley of Mexico. In some cases the mythic bird was conflated with another natural species, the eagle. The flag of Mexico, which depicts an eagle sitting atop a prickly pear cactus and clutching in his claws a rattlesnake (thus suggesting the plumed serpent Quetzalcóatl— in Hopi, Palulukang), was patterned after a similar Aztec sculpture. In the latter example, however, the snake holds in its beak the hieroglyph meaning "water that burns," or *atl-tlachinolli*. The red fruit of cactus represents human hearts, the blood of which must be sacrificed to the flames.

> "But is it really necessary, after what the myths have taught us, to prove still once again that the divine spark is freed only when matter is burned up? Quetzalcoatl's message is just this. We have seen how the individual soul of the King of Tollan was freed from his cremated body, and also how the cosmic soul emerged from the old man covered with

sores. [viz., Nanahuatzin, the pustuled figure who immolated himself, a counterpart to the Hopi god Masau'u. See Chapter 2.] These two narratives show very clearly that the liberating fire is the fire of sacrifice and of penitence; and it is known that the institution of the priesthood had but one purpose: to teach the practices leading to the detachment from our earthly condition."[60]

In this context it is interesting to note that the phoenix originally depicted on the Great Seal of the United States issued in 1782 was changed to the less occult eagle in 1902.[61] It should be remembered that the Great Seal is Masonic in design and that a sizable number of the country's founding fathers were Freemasons, including George Washington, Benjamin Franklin, and Grand Master John Hancock. In fact, fifty out of the fifty-six signatories of the Declaration of Independence were Freemasons.[62] Above the eagle are thirteen stars arranged in the shape of Solomon's Seal. In addition to the copious numerological speculations (thirteen colonies, twelve apostles + Jesus, twelve signs of the zodiac + Orion, etc.), the interlocking triangles represent two cosmic modes. "For several millenniums, the ***Mogen David*** (six-pointed star) has been the official symbol of Judaism. The upward-pointing triangle symbolizes the ***Ayeen*** (The Eternal Void). The downward-pointing triangle signifies the ***Yesh*** (The Material Universe). These two triangles are eternally fastened together. Each one is the image of the other."[63] In other words, the Star of David is a symbol composed of interlaced *tetrakyses*. (See reference to 33 or 3 + 3 = 6 at the end of the first section in this chapter.)

A Pythagorean *tetrakys* (also spelled *tetratys*) is an equilateral triangle composed of nine points along its perimeter, with a tenth point at its center. "The tetratys represents metaphysical reality, Plato's 'ideal world', complete within the framework of a four-term system."[64] In short, the upturned apex signifies the southern stargate of ex-carnation (celestially located between Sagittarius and Scorpius, terrestrially located in the South Pacific—see the last section of Chapter 10). Conversely, the down-turned apex of the *tetrakys* represents the northern stargate of incarnation (celestially located above Orion's right hand between Gemini and Taurus, terrestrially located at Phoenix, Arizona). In this regard the mythologist Joseph Campbell states: "The eagle is the downcoming of the god into the field of time. The bird is the incarnation principle of the deity. This is the bald eagle, the American eagle [on the obverse of the Great Seal]." Campbell goes on to note that the eagle has nine tail feathers. "Nine is the number of the descent of the divine power into the world."[65] (Refer again to David's "The Dual Stargates of Egyptian Cosmology," mentioned in the last section of Chapter 5. www.theorionzone.com/egyptian_stargates.htm) On the reverse of the Great Seal is the pyramid with the all-seeing eye of divine Reason at its apex. This might also represent the cosmic "Third Eye" of Hindu philosophy or the mystical *chante ishta*, "eye of the heart," of the Lakota (Sioux). It is here that God has favored our undertakings or our accomplishments (*Annuit coeptis*) in the New World Order (*Novus Ordo Seclorum*). This glorious orb is also known as an *udjat*, or the "sound eye" of the Egyptian god Horus, the son of Osiris, frequently depicted as a falcon. In his provocative book *The Golden Thread of Time*, Crichton E M Miller discusses the significance of this symbol:

> "So where is the connection with the Eye of Horus on the dollar bill? The faces of the pyramid were cased in polished marble and were reflective and designed to show an image of the sun when it was due south on the prime meridian. No one may look upon the face of '*God the Creator*', as they will be blinded, but to look upon the sun in a reflection is safer. Because the sun is lower in the winter than the summer, at noon, it could be seen as a reflection low upon the southern face of the great pyramid. '*The Mighty Eye of Horus*' would be seen as a fiery image for all to see. As the year went by, the sun would rise daily up the face of this great instrument until it could be seen at the apex of the pyramid, on the Ben Ben stone at noon on the Summer Solstice as '*The all seeing Eye of God*'."[66]

Hence, we find the falcon associated with the southern face of the pyramid in particular and by extension the southern stargate. On the reverse of the dollar bill one can see both sides of the Seal simultaneously, the eagle on the right and the pyramid on the left. If the right end of the bill (eagle) is positioned to the north near Orion (the northern stargate) and the left end (pyramid) to the south near Sagittarius-Scorpius (the southern stargate), then the ONE in the middle (where In God We Trust) faces east, along with the pyramidal eye, to catch the first rays of dawn, while the eagle gazes toward the south, locus of ex-carnation, or as Mesoamerican scholar Laurette Séjourné (quoted above) put it, "...detachment from our earthly condition." As the Rose Croix doctrine states, "The ROSE was anciently sacred to Aurora and the Sun. It is a symbol of *Dawn*, of the resurrection of the Light and the renewal of life, and therefore of the dawn of the first day, and more particularly of the resurrection: and the Cross and Rose together are therefore hieroglyphically to be read, *the Dawn of Eternal Life* which all Nations have hoped for by the advent of the Redeemer."[67] Indeed, the circular sun-rose resting upon the Tau cross formed by the horizon and the first ray reaching the observer comprises the sacred Egyptian *ankh*.

As we have suggested, the phoenix-eagle connection appears to have a long historical precedent.

"Both Herodotus and Pliny noted the general resemblance in shape between the phoenix and the eagle; it is reasonably certain that the modern Masonic eagle was originally a Phoenix. The body of the Phoenix is described as having been covered with glossy purple feathers, while its long tail feathers were alternately blue and red. Its head was light in color and about its neck was a circlet of golden plumage. At the back of the head the phoenix had a peculiar tuft of feathers, a fact quite evident, although it has been overlooked by most writers and symbolists."[68]

This tuft of feathers at the rear of the bird's head is evident in both the naturalistic heron and the mystical phoenix as shown in Pike's *Morals and Dogma*. In particular, the phoenix is illustrated as the chapter heading for the Masonic Knight Rose Croix (XVIIIth) Degree mentioned above.[69] "The Degree of Rose [Cross, iconographically displayed in the text as a Maltese cross—see Chapter 13] teaches three things;—the unity, immutability and goodness of God; the immortality of the Soul; and the ultimate defeat and extinction of evil and wrong and sorrow, by a Redeemer or Messiah, yet to come, if he has not already appeared."[70] The word INRI on His crucifix, thus, not only means *Iesus Nazarenus Rex Iuaeorum* but also *Igne Natura renovatur integra* ("Entire nature is renovated by fire.")[71] The pyrological connotation of the earlier phoenix is retained in the solar significance of both the later eagle and the Son (Sun) of God/Man.

In this chapter we mentioned the talismanic aspect of the stars, focusing on the upraised right arm of Orion, which in terrestrial terms of our schema correlates to the Phoenix Basin, located at 33 degrees latitude, a significant number in Freemasonry. We also described the ancient Hohokam inhabitants of this region as well as the Masonic origins of the city of Phoenix located at the heart of Aztlan. Both the phoenix/heron/eagle complex (northern stargate) and the falcon/pyramid complex (southern stargate) were discussed in terms of the Masonically inspired Great Seal of the United States.

In the final chapter we shall reveal the influence in both the American Southwest and elsewhere of the precursors of the Masons, viz., the Knights Templar. In addition, the Western Star and the Maltese cross will be analyzed, the latter globally dispersed icon being a crucial part of the Hopi prophecy of the End Times. Finally, we shall take an intuitive leap (though not a blind one) into the realm of the Ant People. Here we will describe the role they played in Hisatsinom culture and explore their possible origin in the stars that created The Orion Zone.

# Chapter 13
# Rapidly Into the Far Future

"Many of the stars in Orion are hot and young, evolving rapidly and ending their lives in colossal cosmic explosions called supernovae. They are born and die in periods of tens of millions of years. If, on our computer, we were to run Orion rapidly into the far future, we would see a startling effect, the births and spectacular deaths of many of its stars, flashing on and winking off like fireflies in the night."[1]

Carl Sagan

### *A Four Corners Plague and the Knights of the Round Temple*

Two key periods in Hisatsinom history have had significant impact in the development of its culture. The first was subsequent to A.D. 1100 with the conclusion of the diaspora that began after the destruction by flood of the Third World and the people's entrance into the current Fourth World. This phase is architecturally marked by a shift from isolated pit houses to pueblos, with an increased communal aspect entering into religious observance. The other key period occurred two hundred years later, some time around A.D. 1300 when many villages on the Colorado Plateau that had been inhabited for a century or more were suddenly and "mysteriously" abandoned.

At least isolationist archaeologists find the depopulation of Anasazi villages in the first part of the fourteenth century mysterious. However, if one takes a more diffusionist viewpoint, the concurrent Black Death might provide a causal explanation.[2] According to co-authors Christopher Knight and Robert Lomas, the bubonic plague, which killed as much as one-third of the populations of China, the Muslim world, and Europe during the 1300s, spread westward from Norway to Iceland and Greenland, and thence on Viking ships to the New World.[3] (The reader will recall that an extension of the Arizona chakra line to the northeast ultimately arrives on the coast of Newfoundland near one of the primary Viking settlements, L'Anse Aux Meadows. See Chapter 6.)

The dry climate and large rodent populations of the southwestern United States make this region particularly susceptible to the spread of disease. Those living in larger pueblo villages, which were increasingly more common after the beginning of the twelfth century, must have been especially hard hit. The survival strategy would have been to seek conditions of decreased population density; thus, the Ancient Ones moved to smaller, more widely dispersed villages. John G. Bourke, aid to General Crook in both the Sioux and Apache campaigns, made the following observation: "The Navajoes say that the cliff-dwellers [i.e., the Anasazi] were carried off by a bad wind. He [an old Diné man named Nalihe] repeated this statement without explaining his meaning. Was this bad wind a pestilence or an epidemic? Such a supposition is not altogether unreasonable."4 If indeed a factor, this grim precursor of other infectious diseases such as smallpox and measles that would later decimate many Native American tribes is another piece of evidence in favor of pre-Columbian contact.

In addition to bubonic plague, typhus may have played a role in the emptying of the Colorado Plateau. Lice have been found on the scalps of naturally mummified bodies both in the American Southwest and Peru. The Tarascans of Michoacán called typhus *cocolixtle meco*, or "spotted fever." Designated by a related term, the Chichimecs (discussed in Chapter 8) had a custom of painting their bodies with red stripes and spots. This tribe was the forerunner of the Aztecs, who called typhus *matlazahuatl—matlatl* meaning "net" and *zahuatl* "eruption." An Aztec hieroglyph depicts a man with a net of erupting spots holding his head with his nose bleeding.5 The Aztec god Xipe Tótec was sometimes shown with boils and scabs covering his body, although he was also wont to wear flayed human skin.6 (He is also related to the bubonic god Nanahuatzin, whom we mentioned in Chapter 2.) At least one source (noted in Chapter 8) associates Xipe Tótec with the Hopi god Masau'u. Given the latter's ability to cause oozing sores as well as his depiction as a *katsina* doll painted with splotches, this seems reasonable. The reader will recall from Chapter 10 and Chapter 11 respectively the references to the Tangata Rani of Easter Island and the Masas clan of Sudan, both of which had spots on their clothing or skin. In anticipation of the serpentine theme dealt with below, we may add to the list the distinctive clay figurines from the Mesopotamian Ubaid culture of 4500 B.C. These statuettes exhibit small convex circles scattered on their shoulders and chest. Curiously enough, they also have reptilian heads.

Did the same sort of infectious diseases that manifested as boils in Egypt (Exodus 9:10-11) or that afflicted the Philistines of Ashdod, purportedly because they purloined the Ark of the Covenant (I Samuel 5:6; 6:4-5), somehow hitch a ride on vessels traveling to the New World in the late thirteenth century A.D. or before?

During the early fourteenth century the Rio Grande pueblos were established and additional settlements along the Little Colorado River were constructed. During this period the Katsina Cult also began to develop in Arizona. (See Chapter 7.) The years preceeding this cultural shift (between 1100 and 1300) were the approximate time span when the Orion template was impressed upon the high desert in the form of "star cities." It is interesting that the word "template" is homophonically similar to both "temporal" and "temple," the latter term forming the *raison d'être* for the

Knights Templar, whose existence coincides with the exact temporal span about which we are talking. This group may have played a role in the American Southwest that few people realize.

A detailed description of this fraternal order is beyond the scope of our book. To summarize a complicated and often contradictory story, we, therefore, shall be as brief as possible. In A.D. 1118 the leader Hugues de Payens established the Knights Templar from a core group of eight other Crusaders whose ostensible purpose was to guard travelers to the Holy Land. This date is nineteen years after the Holy City was captured from the Saracens in the First Crusade. Although members of the order had to take an oath of poverty and chastity, most of them came from affluent French families and/or royalty. Officially known as the Order of the Poor Knights of Christ and of the Temple of Solomon, the Knights Templar was garrisoned at the Temple of Jerusalem; hence their name. In truth, this proto-Masonic secret society was at its onset probably more of an archaeological team than an army. No one really knows what the Templars unearthed during the nine years of their excavations, but speculations include the legendary Ark of the Covenant, the Tables of Testimony (i.e., the stone tablets upon which God wrote the Decalogue to give to Moses after he shattered his first set), the Holy Grail, and arcane Essenic or Gnostic documents as well as manuscripts dealing with the life of Christ that predate the Synoptic Gospels. In addition, the Copper Scroll found in 1947 at Qumran on shore of the Dead Sea mentions an immense treasure in gold bullion and sacred artifacts hidden within the Temple of Solomon's extensive hypogeum once used as a stable for an estimated two thousand horses.

Whatever these "warrior monks" found, it made them incredibly rich in an incredibly brief period of time. As is usually the case, political power and prestige accompanied their wealth.[7] In their international bestseller *Holy Blood, Holy Grail*, co-authors Baigent, Leigh and Lincoln aver in regard to the Templars: "At their zenith they were the most powerful and influential organization in the whole of Christendom, with the single possible exception of the papacy."[8] In fact, they single-handedly invented the institution of modern banking and the international finance system, loaning huge sums of money to nearly every monarchy in Europe.[9]

Although most of these events are peripheral to our book, the navigational expertise of the Knights Templar is particularly pertinent. During the twelfth century the organization had grown to a point where it was becoming a formidable naval power, utilizing both military and commercial vessels. Templar sailors were among the first to use a magnetic compass.[10] By the beginning of the fourteenth century the order possessed a fleet of at least eighteen galleys docked at its main seaport of La Rochelle on France's Atlantic coast.[11] According to Crichton Miller, the writer and yachtsman whom we previously quoted, the Knights Templar may have discovered in their excavations of Solomon's Temple a navigational instrument shaped like a Celtic cross and plumbline which allowed them to make extensive maritime journeys.12 (See description of his theory on p. 246.) "It may be much older than the structures at Giza, since it also appears responsible for the construction of Neolithic henges in Europe, some of which predate the pyramids by thousands of years. The secrets of the astrolabe cross were rediscovered by the Knight Templars and other secret societies throughout the Middle Ages."13 If this instrument were as powerful as it seems, would it not also have been possible to use it in order to construct a template of Orion on the Arizona desert? If the answer to this question is 'yes', then we have indeed entered a bizarre realm far beyond usual academic conceptions of history.

Various nontraditional authors claim that the Templars even had contact as early as 1269 with the New World, where they increased their wealth by seizing Mexican silver.14 If correct, this year is significant because it antedates the approximate time of the abandonment (discussed above) of many pueblos on the Colorado Plateau. This would allow for a causal link between the arrival of the Templars in the New World and the spread of the bubonic plague in the American Southwest. Fearful of the increased status of the Knights Templar yet covetous of their increased prosperity, King Philippe IV of France conspiring with Pope Clement V had then Grand Master Jacque de Molay and some of his followers arrested on that unlucky day of Friday the 13th in October, 1307. Charged with heresy, blasphemy, witchcraft, necromancy, abortion, and homosexuality, Molay and his ardent supporters were eventually tortured and burned at the stake. However, the Templars apparently had been warned beforehand of the impending arrest because the entire fleet escaped unscathed from the harbor with the bulk of its wealth and presumably all of its esoteric scrolls in the ships' holds. Co-authors Knight and Lomas assert that they were bound for two distinct destinations: Scotland and America. Free in Scotland from the papal bull banning their organization, the Knights Templar established themselves and eventually built Rosslyn Chapel, which we briefly mentioned in Chapter 11. Because the construction was completed by 1486, we are perplexed in trying to find an explanation for the sculptured maize cobs and aloe cactus on an inner wall of the chapel—six years before... "Columbus sailed the ocean blue."15 Knight and Lomas also believe that the latter group of Knights Templar reached Cape Cod or Rhode Island early in 1308, where they began to establish settlements. These New World explorers left evidence of their presence, most notably a round tower of typically Romanesque design constructed at Newport, Rhode Island.16

Architecturally akin to circular structures of Ireland and Sardinia, many examples of round towers also exist in the American Southwest. In Chapter 8 we mentioned the Chetro Ketl round "tower kiva" three stories high in Chaco Canyon along with those of Kin Kletso and Tsin Kletsin in the same area. (Fig. 51, p. 272) In addition, the Chacoan outliers of Salmon Ruin to the north and Kin Ya'a to the south have similar structures. At

**Fig. 51. Round tower kiva of Chetro Ketl at Chaco Canyon, New Mexico**

Mesa Verde in southwestern Colorado, many round towers also can be found, including those at Cliff Palace, Sun Temple, Cedar Tree Tower, and Far View Community. The Hovenweep complex in southeastern Utah shows examples of this type of ceremonial structure as well. One building at the south end of Mummy Cave Ruin in Canyon de Chelly (terrestrial Saiph, home to the Snake Clan and others) may possibly have been circular, though because of structural deterioration and erosion it is difficult to determine. In fact, many of the earlier round kivas may have served as foundations for higher towers above them, but a nearly a millennium of weathering has taken its toll.

Although most of these towers antedate the 1308 arrival of the Knights Templar, the Anasazi were perhaps influenced by an earlier visitation by them or even by Phoenician explorers. The round towers found in Ireland are thought to have been built by Phoenicians, so perhaps they spread this particular architectural feature globally. "Like the Pagan temples, the round churches were microcosms of the world. In the late Middle Ages, they became the prerogative of an enigmatic and heretical sect, the Knights Templar... The round form of church became especially connected with the order, and in the centre of the rotundae of their churches stood not an altar but a perfect cube of hewn stone which was one of the mysteries of Templarism."[17] This cube within a circle represented the earth (or more exactly, the "four corners of the earth,"

272

referring to either the cardinal directions or the sunrise and sunset solstice points) within the celestial sphere of the heavens. As opposed to the Latinate cross representing the body of Christ, this circular structure symbolized in Christian terms the worldly or even the satanic domain. In addition, the round structure signified an *omphalos* where tellurian serpent forces accumulated.

At one time Wukoki Ruin at Wupatki National Monument (terrestrial Bellatrix—see Chapter 4) possibly had a round or D-shaped tower on its south end. All that remains is a curved wall about a foot high, the center of which faces southwest toward the winter solstice sunset directly over the San Francisco Peaks. Two gaps in the wall are oriented toward the south and the west. In the three-story square building on the north end of the ruin, one window is oriented toward the summer solstice sunset and one toward the winter solstice sunrise, so astronomical orientations were obviously as important to the people who once lived there as to the Yucatan Maya who built the round Caracol observatory at Chichén Itzá three hundred years earlier. As previously mentioned, Wukoki is a former house of the Snake Clan.

In fact, the Hopi referred to round towers as "snake houses." In Chapter 10 we described the origin of the Snake Clan, the narrative mentioning that the wife of the culture hero Tiyo gave birth to a brood of venomous snakes, which kept getting loose. In one version of the myth Masau'u explains to the snake-mother why her children no longer can have a house to live in. "And Masau said, 'No, the snakes have no houses, because they have bitten and killed Hopitu they should never again have a house, but should live under rocks and in holes in the ground.' But he also said the snakes houses (the round towers) which were built for them should never again be destroyed and that all coming generations of people should know the snake's doom, never again to have a house."[18] In these mythological terms we are obviously not talking about rattlesnake pens but instead are referring to either the domiciles or the temples of a dangerous, snake-like race.

In a Christian context these creatures unequivocally suggest the Devil and his minions. "And the great dragon was cast out, that old serpent, called the Devil, and Satan, which deceiveth the whole world : he was cast out into the earth, and his angels were cast out with him." (Revelation 12:9) In one sense the Hopi were forced to cast out their "snakes" too. Andrew Collins makes reference to an apocalyptic fragment from the Dead Sea Scrolls called the Testament of Amran. In his dream-vision Amran, the father of Moses, sees the Watcher called Belial. (See end of Chapter 7 for a discussion of the Watchers.) He is "terrifying in appearance, like a serpent..." and "his visage [is] like a viper..."[19] The figure of Belial referenced in II Corinthians 6:15 means "lawlessness," "worthless," or "reckless" and is an appellation of Satan.[20] The word "serpent," Mr. Collins adds, is synonymous with both the Enochian Watchers and the Nephilim, the latter denoting the biblical "giants in the earth" referred to in Genesis 6:4. Most significantly, the Hopi myth referred to above concludes with an offering to the recovered snakes.

> "When the snakes were all collected and they were gathered together at night they took the first snake they had found and washed its head and gave it the name Chüa (he of the earth) and decorated it with beads and ear rings. Then the Youth [viz., Tiyo] opened a bag and gave the people cotton and beads and said as the snakes had brought rain the people should now be happy and content, and on every celebration of the Snake festival good things would be given to them. Then the snake mother died."[21]

In his book on angels Collins goes on to say that the Nephilim are also known as the sons of the Anakim. "The word Anak is generally taken by Jewish scholars to mean 'long-necked', or 'the men with the necklaces'..."[22] In this context it is curious that the Hopi term *naaqa* means "turquoise necklace" or "ear pendant " and that *anaaq* means "ouch!", an interjection used to express extreme pain, such as that caused by a snakebite. Is this, then, a reference to the Indo-European Nagas, those snake-worshipping seafarers we encountered in Chapter 10? Are these the so-called Long Ears, who stretched their lobes with ear-plugs, an example of which archaeologists found in a Hohokam ruin near Phoenix? And one further coincidence: Chüa, the Hopi name for the worshipped snake that initiated their biennial ceremony is homophonically similar to "Chna," an English transliteration of the Greek word referring to the Phoenician land of Canaan [23]. The biblical Anakim were known to have hailed from southern Canaan, in particular from the city of Hebron.[24]

Are the Phoenicians, then, the round tower builders who came to the American Southwest in order to oversee the creation of the Orion Zone on the high desert of the Hisatsinom? Were the Knights Templar the recipients of this Naga/Phoenician legacy, carrying forth the ancient traditions bequeathed from Egypt? Do these structures form a global network centered on ophidian fertility symbols? Furthermore, were the Irish round towers also "snake houses," or phallic temples used by a race of serpent people whom St. Patrick in the 5th century A.D. ultimately had to chase into the sea?

In more recent times were the pioneer Freemasons (described in the preceding chapter) bearing the Templar torch passed on to them through the ages in order to bring it to the 33rd parallel in the very heart of the old Hohokam territory, now deemed the "New Land of the Phoenix"?[25] And finally, is the terrestrial Orion's right hand really holding that torch instead of a warrior's mace, a gnostic flambeau enlivened with the fire of purification that points the way to the stargate of Phoenix, a symbolic city awaiting the consummation of this cycle, the Hopi Fourth World, in order to rise again and be reborn?

Perhaps we are uncovering more questions than answers. Nonetheless, round towers survive as a testament to the awesome spiritual power of the Knights of the Round Temple. Their serpentine eyes gaze across the centuries, now and then sending a shiver up the spine.

### The Star of la Merika and the Blood Cross

In addition to round towers, the Knights Templar left other legacies in the New World. In Westford, Massachusetts, for example, the image of a knight in full battle regalia made by punched holes in a slab of rock was found in 1956. On his shield is a five-pointed star above the crosstree of a mast. The splayed rigging and the stylized hull of the ship resemble the Masonic compass and square. Barry Fell speculates that this image was made during the 1398 voyage of Prince Henry Sinclair, Earl of Orkney. He bases this notion on a similarity between the shield and a coat of arms belonging to a sept of the Sinclairs.[26] It is commonly known that his family was the primary force behind the construction of Rosslyn Chapel. Knight and Lomas believe that the medieval knight in stone was actually the tombstone of Sir James Gunn, who reputedly died on the late fourteenth century voyage to the New World.[27]

More importantly, the star on the shield is thought to represent the American continent, the utopian land to the west. "...it became our firm conviction that the continent of America took its name, not from the 'also-ran' explorer Amerigo Vespucci, but from the star of the west called Merika, which the Nasoreans believed was the marker of a perfect land across the ocean of the setting sun."[28] (The original followers of Jesus were known as the Nasoreans, also called the Essenes, who formed the original Jerusalem Church.[29]) Robert Bauval provides an interesting take on this matter.

"The name 'Merica' or 'Merika' sounds very Egyptian to me. It could be the composite of 'Meri-Ka', which would translate in ancient Egypt as something like 'Spiritual Land of the Pyramids (i.e. Egypt)'. This name would fit exactly the idea that under the star Sirius in the west, as seen from Bethlehem, was, in actual fact, the Great Pyramid. A pun, too, can be seen in the name 'Meri-Ka' and that of 'Mary Ka', i.e. 'The spirit of Mary', which certainly would not have escaped the Christian mythmakers of Egypt and Judea."[30]

The preeminent Egyptologist I.E.S. Edwards notes that the term *Mer* referred to a pyramid, literally, a "Place of Ascension."[31] The French word *mer* is, of course, "sea," while *mère* means "woman." Across the sea to the west hovers the brightest star in the heavens, Sirius, the archetypal woman in the form of Isis, whom the Christian Church knew as the Virgin Mary. In this context it is astounding that the Hopi word for "bride" or "woman married to a clansman" is *mö'wi'at*. As we noted in Chapter 7 in our discussion of *katsinam*, the *ka* sound is foreign to the Hopi language; thus, the substitution of *-at* in this near homophone of Merika. In addition, the Hopi term *moro* means "immersed." Perhaps, then, neither co-authors Knight and Lomas nor Robert Bauval are incorrect. The western Land of the Pyramids crowned by the star could indeed refer to America, where Maya and Aztec pyramids as well as Mound Builder and Hohokam platform mounds abound— all places of spiritual ascension.

The State flag of Arizona also displays the Star of la Merika. On a background of seven red rays and six yellow rays, an Egyptian-style, five-pointed star represents the heliacal setting of Sirius. Curiously, the horizon of the Earth is represented at the bottom half of the flag by a dark blue, usually the color reserved for the sky. ("As Above, so Below.") The star's copper color is exoterically explained by the existence of the State's many copper mines. Esoterically, however, Sirius/Isis was traditionally associated with copper. A Babylonian cuneiform text calls Sirius *Kak-si-di*, which means "shining like copper," and Homer's epic *The Iliad* compares Achilles' copper shield to the star.[32] The reader should also be reminded that small copper handles were found on a door at the end of the narrow "air shaft" leading from the Queen's Chamber in the Great Pyramid and aligning with the altitude of Sirius in 2750 B.C., approximately when the pyramids were built.[33]

The Knights Templar and possibly the earlier Phoenicians and Nagas also brought the blood cross, a.k.a. cross pattée, a.k.a. cross formée, a.k.a. Maltese cross, the latter a reference to the Island of Malta where one of the world's oldest temples dedicated to the goddess cult is located. One geoglyph found near the lower Colorado River contains a Maltese cross nearly ten feet in diameter next to what is perhaps one or possibly two Templar figures, since the second appears to be holding a shield.[34] (As mentioned in Chapter 2, the geoglyphs of Arizona and California are desert figures constructed in a manner similar to the Nazca lines of Peru.) Archaeologist Emil Haury compares shell pendants discovered at Snaketown as well as Hohokam pottery designs found there and elsewhere in the Valley of the Sun with the Mexican "Cross of Quetzalcóatl,"[35] i.e., the Maltese cross. The reader will recall the Templars' very early connection with Mexico.

Located on the western base of the Sacramento Mountains in New Mexico, the Three Rivers Petroglyphs site is one of the largest rock art sites in the Southwest. Incidentally, this site is located at the same latitude as both Phoenix and the geoglyphs: 33 degrees. The park contains over 20,000 petroglyphs carved atop a ridge by the Mogollon culture between 900 and 1400 A.D.[36] One of the geometric designs located there is a

Maltese cross within a circle surrounded by a ring of seventeen dots.37

The Hopi are also familiar with this cross, which is represented by two hair discs laid perpendicular to each other. Also known as *nögla* or "butterfly whorls," these items are traditionally worn by maidens because the butterfly is a symbol of fecundity. "The Maltese cross is the emblem of a virgin; still so recognized by the Moki [Hopi]. It is a conventional development of a more common emblem of maidenhood, the form in which the maidens wear their hair arranged as a disk of 3 or 4 inches in diameter upon each side of the head. This discoidal arrangement of their hair is typical of the emblem of fructification worn by the virgin in the Muingwa festival [Powamu, the Bean Germination Ceremony] ..."38 (See petroglyph of a Hopi *mana* in the Preface. Muingwa, also spelled Muy'ingwa, is the Hopi god of germination related to Masau'u. See end of Chapter 3.) Furthermore, in 1881 Bourke (cited above) discovered a Maltese cross carved into a ritual pipe used in the Snake Dance Ceremony.39

Many instances of Maltese crosses painted on Hisatsinom pottery can also be found, indicating the same symbology. In fact, some of these ceramic examples closely resemble pottery from the fourth millennium found at Susa, the capital of Elam (the biblical Shushan in present-day western Iran).40 Among ruins of Sikyatki at the base of the Hopi First Mesa an unusual rectangular "medicine box" had been discovered. On one side was painted a white Maltese cross, inside of which is a star formed by four triangles whose apexes point outward from a small circle at its center.41 Thus, in this case the Maltese cross is combined with the Star of la Merika.

Commenting on this ancestral Hopi pottery, Jesse Walter Fewkes writes: "There are several specimens of figures of the Maltese cross, and one closely approximating the Saint Andrew's cross. It is scarcely necessary to say that the presence of the various kinds of crosses do not necessarily indicate the influence of Semitic or Aryan races, for I have already shown that even cross-shape prayer-sticks were in use among the Pueblos when Coronado first visited them."42 This prominent archaeologist of late 19th century who in this instance illustrates his isolationist bias would find it very difficult to accept the Knights Templar visitation of the New World at least a century and a half before Francisco Vasquez de Coronado but perhaps as much as 400 years prior to this first Spanish foray through the Southwest.

Speaking of St. Andrew's cross, we find an interesting "coincidence" by visualizing an Egyptian style pyramid from a vantage directly above its apex: the four sloping sides of the three dimensional pyramid become an X-shaped St. Andrew's cross in two dimensions. This type of cross is also frequently found in the New World. Graham Hancock found the top of the Mayan Magician's Pyramid at Uxmal covered with them, and he recalls finding them as well at the Andean site of Tiahuanaco and at the Olmec center of La Venta.43 The scholar Karl W. Luckert, who has studied in depth both the Olmecs and the Hopis, finds a similar commonality: "The so-called St. Andrew's Cross, which can be seen on numerous Olmec statues, appears again in the Hopi sand altar [in the Antelope kiva during the Snake Ceremony]. Apparently it has been derived from the diamond pattern on the backs of rattlesnakes."[44] Fewkes also comments on the celestial significance of St. Andrew's cross: "These crosses, like that with four arms representing the Sky god in modern Hopi symbolism, probably represent the Heart of the Sky. A similar cross is figured on paraphernalia used in modern Hopi rites or on altar slabs; when it is represented by a wooden frame, it is called *tokpela* [literally, "sky"], and hangs before the altar. The same object is sometimes attached horizontally to the top of the helmet of the personification of the Sky god."[45] Hence, we see this type of cross associated with both the serpent and ascension.

If we shift the St. Andrew's cross slightly on it base, we have the Greek cross, a simple equilateral figure akin to that used by the Red Cross, the international philanthropic organization to which people frequently donate their blood. In this context it is interesting to note that the African tribe the Dogon, according to Robert Temple, also use this symbol. "The star of women is represented by a cross, a dynamic sign which calls to mind the movement of the whole Sirius system."[46] Again we are back to the feminine Star of la Merika. In addition, the Anasazi petroglyphic icon that represents "star" is the same as the Greek cross.

Finally, one medieval text known as the Osnabrück Register of Santa Maria combines in a few poetic lines all the elements with which we have been dealing.

> Hail, clear-shining star of the sea, Mary, divinely born for
>     the enlightenment of nations. . .
> Virgin, ornament of the world, queen of heaven, elect
>     above all like the sun, lovely as the light of the
>     moon. . .
> Let us drink in steadfast faith of the sweet stream that
>     flowed from the rock in the desert, and, girding
>     our loins that the sea has bathed, gaze on the cru-
>     cified brazen serpent.[47]

Hence, we find compressed in this matrix of images the star (probably Sirius setting) above the ocean, the Virgin Mary (or the Egyptian Isis or the Hopi Spider Grandmother), the enlightenment of countries (especially the Orion Zone of America), a royal figure encompassing both the terrestrial and the celestial plane ("As Above, so Below."), one of the elect on high who is as holy as the sun (i.e., both the Son and the Hopi god Tawa) and beautiful as the moon (perhaps a crescent, symbol of the Shriners, an organization of 33rd degree Masons), water flowing in the desert (of Palestine or Arizona, for instance), a journey across the sea (from the Hopi Third World to the Fourth World), the cross (in all its four-armed permutations), and the serpent (perhaps plumed or horned) of sacrifice and redemption. (The latter is a reference to the Knight of the Brazen Serpent, the XXVth degree of Freemasonry.)

Instead of bathing in the celestial brine of the Milky Way, Orion girds up his loins, takes his staff in his hand, and goes his way, awaiting the apocalyptic ascension of the Phoenix.

## Hopi Prophecy of the End Times

In general the Hopi culture is particularly prone to prophetic proclamations that merge with the ancient myths of their ancestors. The Hopi had foreseen moving houses of iron (trains), horseless wagons traveling on black ribbons (automobiles), people speaking through cobwebs (telegraph and telephone lines), a falling "gourd of ashes" (the atomic bomb), women wearing men's clothing (the women's liberation movement), humans journeying along a road in the sky to live in the heavens (Skylab, MIR or the International Space Station), and the door of the House of Mica (the United Nations) closing four times on Hopi pleas for peace.48

Just after the emergence from the subterranean Third World at the beginning of the present Fourth World, a figure known as Pahana, or Elder White Brother, took with him a corner of the Fire Clan's four inches square stone tablet and proceeded eastward toward the rising sun.49 At the same time the Younger (red) Brother stayed back, traveling the spiral road of migrations, constructing pueblos throughout the American Southwest, and eventually settling in the villages much as we see them today. (See Chapter 1.) Similar to the Mesoamerican myth of Kukulkán or Quetzalcóatl, it was assumed that Pahana would return at the end of the cycle to save the righteous people from foreign forces destroying the land. "'Many will turn away from the life plan of Maasau'u,' the younger brother warned his elder brother, 'but a few of us who are true to his teachings will remain in our dwellings. The ancient character of our heads, the shape of our houses, the *layout of our villages* [italics added], and the type of land upon which our village stands, and our way of life. All will be in order, by which you will find us.'"50 The "layout of our villages" could, of course, refer to the Orion Correlation in Arizona.

These prophecies are verified by contemporary omens and portends, the ilk of which has been especially rife during the millennial shift.

> "Blood will flow. Our hair and our clothing will be scattered upon the earth. Nature will speak to us with its mighty breath of wind. There will be earthquakes, floods, and strange fires in different places causing great disasters, changes in seasons, and in the weather, disappearance of

wildlife, and famine in different forms. There will be gradual corruption and confusion among the leaders and the people all over the world, and wars will come about like powerful winds. All of this has been planned from the beginning of creation."51

Whereas the Hopi accept these symptoms with a certain degree of fatalism —after all, they have gone through this three times before—the dominant Western culture perceives the age in which we live as plagued by random chaos, despair, hopelessness, and uncertainty. In the eyes of many, the End Times are indeed upon us.

Given our discussion of the blood or Maltese cross vis-à-vis the Knights Templar and the Freemasons, it should come as no surprise that this icon also plays a key role in Hopi prophecy. At a time preordained by the Creator, Pahana will return wearing a red cap or a red cape. Some modern Knights Templar orders wear a red pillbox hat, and the traditional Shriners' red fez also comes to mind. The red cross on the white mantle might possibly fit the "red cape" description as well. Pahana will verify his authenticity by bearing the stone piece that will match up to the rest of the tablet. He will be accompanied by two helpers, one of which carries a masculine swastika representing purity as well as the four directions. The first helper also brings a Maltese cross with lines between the arms representing menstrual blood, while the second helper conveys merely a sun symbol.52 The combined forces of these three icons will "shake the world" and bring about global purification.53

Pahana is probably not a single figure but an anthropomorphized composite of a group, since it is said that his population will be great. In this context it is significant to note the following: "The Greek word PHOENIX, derived from the Egyptian word PA-HANOK, actually means, 'The House of Enoch'."54 Thus, Pahana is homophonically connected both to the Phoenix and an Enochian group, perhaps the Watchers. In addition, the related name "Panch" is the Sanskrit term for Pani, referring to a Phoenician, thus corroborating the etymology.55 We find the Tibetan usage of this term especially relevant. For instance, the Panchen Lama (or Tashi), second in spiritual importance to the Dalai Lama, is derived from the Chinese word *banchán*, transliteration of the Sanskrit *pandita*, or pundit, literally "learnéd man." At any rate, the Hopi Pahana supposedly has no religion but his own. This sounds very much like the type of charge that fundamentalist opponents of the Freemasons lay against them, and it was partially the reason that leaders of the Knights Templar were tortured and executed. Ultimately, if Pahana and his two helpers fail to bring about an abatement of human inequities, an unnamed one from the west will come "like a big storm." He will unmercifully purge the evil doers, though he too is said to be a large number of people.56

"The Purifier, commanded by the Red symbol [Maltese cross], with the help of the Sun and the Meha [swastika], will weed out the wicked who have disturbed the way of life of the Hopi, the true way of life on Earth. The wicked will be beheaded and will speak no more. This will be the purification for all the righteous people, the Earth, and all living things on the Earth. The ills of the Earth will be cured. Mother Earth will bloom again and all the people will unite into peace and harmony for a long time to come."[57]

However, if the Hopi nation totally disappears, the motion of the planet will become eccentric, a great flood will again engulf the land as it did at the end of the Third World, and eventually the ants (see the next section of this chapter) will inherit the Earth. Some commentators have noted that these hoary emblems of Hopi prophecy represent the Central Powers of World War I (the Iron Cross) and the Axis Powers of World War II (the Swastika and the Rising Sun), whereas the final purification of the planet will present itself as World War III.

As mentioned in Chapter 1, Pahana's role of Purifier is sometimes conflated with that of Masau'u. "At the time the Hopi were about to embark on their migration, Maasaw [Masau'u] stated that he would journey toward the rising sun. After making this statement, he removed himself from their sight, but not before promising that he would return someday in the future. When the elders talk about this promise by Maasaw, they claim that his return would mark the last day of the world. Of course, no one knows for certain when that day will be."[58] This last statement echoes the Biblical passage of Revelation 3:3 (a harmonic of a Masonic number?): "Remember therefore how thou hast received and heard, and hold fast, and repent. If therefore thou shalt not watch, I will come on thee as a thief, and thou shalt not know what hour I will come upon thee." As demonstrated in Chapter 3, Masau'u is the terrestrial dimension of the constellation Orion.

In this State "Enriched by God" (*Ditat Deus*— the Arizona motto) we have seen how Masau'u/Orion, primary Hopi god and most conspicuous constellation in the sky, has been brought down to Earth as a configuration of Anasazi star cities constructed between the mid-eleventh and the late thirteenth centuries A.D. As a recent newspaper headline regarding Troy stated, it is not so much the 'where' but rather the 'wherefore' that is important. Orion Correlations are found all over the globe, yet the question remains: What is their ultimate purpose?

One plausible explanation is durability of design. Unlike artifacts depicting an earth/sky map such as the Hopi stone tablet with Orion's belt mentioned in Chapter 5, the grander scale of an actual constellation of villages constructed upon the landscape can never be lost or destroyed.

Although many of the original villages have fallen into ruin, the stone foundations of these sites that collectively correlate to Orion remain. We have also suggested that this geodetic template is talismanic, channeling both the general archetypal warrior energy of Orion to Hopiland and the specific energies of each star to the corresponding village. Because the constellation continues to play such a significant role in Hopi rituals, the acknowledgment of his numinous power would be an essential requirement in an animistic world where stars are indeed souls.

Perhaps the most monumental explanation for a tellurian presence of Orion in Arizona relates to each of his arms. While the belt stars are 1,500 to 1,600 light-years away, two stars —one in each of his hands— are relatively close. His left arm reaches toward Grand Canyon, origin of the ancestral Hopi people. In the middle of this hand is Pi 3 at a distance of only twenty-six light-years. His right arm reaches toward the galactic plane's northern stargate, whose terrestrial representation formerly was the Hohokam culture and presently is the Masonic city of Phoenix. The tip of Orion's right-hand fingers is Chi 1 at a distance of only twenty-nine light-years, corresponding to the puebloan ruins on Perry Mesa. Both stars are similar in temperature and size to our Sun, thus harboring the possibility of planets revolving in orderly solar systems much like our own. It is as if Orion reaches across the cold stellar night toward our Earth and beckons. Did Masau'u, the Hopi god of the Underworld (or in this context the "Overworld") who orchestrated the Arizona Orion template, originate from either of these stars?

## The Anthills of Orion

After such a lengthy analysis of The Orion Zone of the American Southwest, we should certainly discuss the name *Orion* itself in relation to Hisatsinom/Hopi mythology. A number of words cluster like glistening stars around Orion in the lexicon. *Origin* points to the basic, primal nature of the constellation which serves perhaps as an interstellar source of terrestrial life, while *orient* refers to the east whence Orion comes. *Orifice* literally means "mouth" and suggests the stargate to which Orion's right arm points (see previous chapter). *Orison* denotes a prayer, and *oracle* refers to a divine utterance. *Oriole* is, of course, a golden bird, while *orichalcum*, which literally means "mountain copper," is the highly prized copper-gold alloy that reputedly covered the walls of Atlantis. If we need a plant, perhaps *origanum*, or the aromatic mint wild marjoram, will do. Of course, the animal association is fulfilled by Orion's role as hunter.

These folk etymologies are all very interesting, but Orion's actual Indo-European root is, in a word, astounding. The name *Orion* is formed by dropping the initial 'm' in the stem *morui*, which supposedly means "ant."[59] Perhaps the constellation's narrow waist suggests this insect. According to the *Oxford English Dictionary*, *moru(zh)iue* is a variation of *moryeve* and literally means "morning gift," that is, the gift given by the husband to the wife on the morning after the consummation of their marriage. This connotation stresses the fertility aspect of Orion. After his absence for a couple months, Orion's heliacal rising arrives as a gift in early summer when the corn is beginning to sprout.

As noted in Chapter 3, the Hopi term for Orion is *Hotòmqam*, which literally means either "to string up" (as beads on a string) or "trey." This could refer to the three stars of Orion's belt but also to the tripartite form of the ant: head, thorax, and abdomen. These shiny, bead-like sections of the ant's body may indeed have their celestial counterpart in what the Hopi consider the most important constellation in the heavens. The appearance of Orion through the overhead hatchways of Hopi kivas still synchronizes many annual sacred ceremonies.

The ant has in fact played a crucial role in the survival of the Anasazi. During both the destruction of the First World by fire and the Second World by ice, the Ant People had provided refuge in their subterranean kiva to the ancestral Hopi. Only the virtuous members of the tribe following a certain cloud by day and a certain star by night were able to find the sky god Sótuknang, who elected to save these "chosen people" by leading them to the Ant People for protection. In this legend the ants are portrayed as generous and industrious, teaching the Hopi the merits of food storage and giving them aliment when supplies ran short. In fact, the reason why the ants have such thin waists today is because they once deprived themselves of provisions.[60]

In another account of the earliest eras, the Hopi themselves are described as ants. "When they were way underneath, they were ants."[61] The word "underneath" refers alternately to the Ant Kiva and the First and Second Worlds, the latter of which are conceptualized as being subterranean, i.e., beneath both the previous Third World and the present Fourth World. According to another rather brutal myth entitled "Why the Ants Are So Thin," a great number of Ants were living east of Toko'navi, or Navajo Mountain, the prehistoric home of the Snake Clan and the Sand Clan. Incidentally, the Hopi word *Toko'anu* literally means "flesh ant," the large dark red ant with a painful sting. During an initiation into the Katsina Society two of these Ants dressed up as fierce, giant-like Hu Katsinam and flogged the Ant children so hard that they were almost cut through in the middle of their bodies, hence their slenderness.[62] Here the insects are described not in the allegorical manner of an Aesop fable but in an almost anthropomorphic way.

The two Hopi clans called *anu* (ants of various kinds) and *pala anu* (red ants) help to form the Horn-Millet phratry, along with a number of other clans such as the deer, elk, antelope, and mountain sheep. This phratry combined with the war-like Reed-Greasewood-Bow and the Ko'kop-Coyote phratries (both mentioned in Chapter 3 in connection with the November Wúwutcim and the December Soyal ceremonies) ritualistically control the winter months when Orion is the paramount constellation and Masau'u the preeminent god. In addition, the black ant (*sisiw'anu*, literally "piss ant") is believed to be the source of witch power.63 Red ants and other stinging insects are frequently associated among Pueblo peoples with warfare, also the purview of Masau'u. For instance, at the Village of the Great Kivas in New Mexico a Zuni war chief was known to have carved a petroglyph of a red ant along with other venomous insects, thus enhancing his power to sting his enemies in battles.64 In the Zuni culture red ants are associated not only with the Warrior Society (Priests of the Bow) but also with the Snake Society and the eponymous Red Ant Society— the latter two involved as well with healing powers. "Furthermore, in addition to the Bow priesthood at Zuni (the Zuni Warrior association),... [Ruth] Bunzel lists the Ant Society, Wood Society, the Great Fire Society with its Arrow Order, the Hunt, and Cactus Societies as all being primarily war societies, and all are devoted to the Beast Gods [of the four intercardinal directions plus the zenith and nadir]."65 Thus, the ant is associated with warfare and/or hunting, both traits related to Orion in particular and stars in general.

The ant was further known for its wisdom brought forth from the Underworld (in Hopi, Maski). For instance, the Ant fraternity at Santo Domingo Pueblo was known to sing a song "in an unknown foreign language" to the snakes, though it contained the word *"Sípapûni,"* the traditional portal to the nether world.66 An example from Zuni Pueblo also stresses the wisdom of both ants and snakes. "In the context of ritual activity, Zunis offered prayers not only to the Beast Gods of the six directions but also to the snakes (sometimes described as rattlesnakes) and ants of the six directions. According to Matilda Stevenson, some of the medicine men who came to this world from the fourth Underworld were transformed into the six Beast Gods, and 'the others were converted into rattlesnakes and ants to preside with wisdom over the earth.'"67 Much like Masau'u, ants together with snakes possess knowledge of both the surface of the earth and the chthonic regions.

Even non-Puebloan tribes such as the Diné (Navajo) stress the cultural importance of ants.

> "Navajos associate their traditional house structure, or hogan, with ant mounds. Ants are the only insect for which an entire chantway is named: Red Antway. This ceremony is performed to counteract the deleterious consequences of consuming or disturbing ants. Ants are the most anthropomorphized of all the insect characters; many depictions show no insect features, so without being fully aware of the story line an observer would not realize the importance of ants."68

Again, we see that ants are conceptualized as virtually a different race of humans rather than as hymenoptera. To the north of the Diné territory a "very sacred" medicine bundle called an "Ant bundle" was once used to enhance hunting magic by one southern band of the Skidi Pawnee, who in many ways resembled the Hopi.69 Far to the south among the Maya, legends exist of ant-like men who built stone cities and roads during the First Creation (World). These peculiar creatures possessed magical powers and could summon stones into proper architectural positions by just whistling. "*Zayamuincob* can be translated as 'the twisted men' or 'the disjointed men,' suggesting a connection with 'hunchback.' The word may also be connected with *zay*, 'ant,' for there is also a Yucatec tradition of an ancient race called *chac zay uincob*, 'red ant men.' They were industrious like the ants which take out the red earth and make straight roads through the forest."70 The reference to "hunchback" is, of course, reminiscent of Koko Pilau (Kokopelli), the humpback flute player, who is the ubiquitous insect-like figure of Southwest petroglyphs.

The Hohokam (discussed in the previous chapter) were renowned for their red-on-buff pottery. They produced many examples of fine aesthetic quality and design using the paddle-and-anvil method rather than the coil-and-scrape technique of the Anasazi. On the other hand, the pottery was also functional, with a few jars having the capacity to hold almost thirty gallons of water.71 However, one ceramic vessel in particular is relevant to our discussion. Found at Snaketown from the A.D. 950-1150 period, it is a flat-bottomed, cylindrical bowl upon which a series of dancers is painted in maroon-red. The dancers heads are all turned to their left and they appear to be linking hands. Each of their bodies is curiously comprised of two diamond shapes with tips touching (see Chapter 2), looking much like the narrow waists of the Ant People and the constellation Orion. If the reader will recall, this also resembles the petroglyph for war: a pair of arrowheads with contiguous apexes. What is striking about the figures is that every other one has what appears to be a pair of antennae pointed forward rather than just one vertical plume (?) curving toward the back of the head. Each antennaed figure also has a number of closely spaced horizontal lines across his/her face, possibly suggesting a mask or perhaps representing a numinous force or an aureole akin to those found on depictions of medieval saints.72

Are these, then, the Ant People— Hohokam style? The Pima creation story called "Chuhwuht," or Song of the World, may shed some light on this. The Creator wandered in the primordial chaos of darkness and water, searching for his purpose. He then drew from his heart a large greasewood stick, upon which he rested during his journey. Next he brought forth tiny ants from his body and put them on the stick. From the gum of its wood the ants formed a round shape, and the Creator took the ball and rolled it under his foot while singing: "I make the world, and lo! / The world is finished." While he was rolling the ball underfoot, it gradually grew larger and larger until it become the world.73 This myth is interesting, for one reason, because it correctly identifies the world as a sphere. More important, however, is the fact that ants together with the Creator were crucial in forming the world. This mythic narrative is one way of relating the idea that the Ant People initially shaped the world, both literally and figuratively, as the indigenous people knew it.

The Pima also have an explanation for the end of the Hohokam culture. "They say that the *Sivanyi* (Hohokam) offended their hero, Elder Brother, and even tried to kill him. In retaliation, the Pima and Tohono O'odham (Papago) made war upon them and destroyed the Sivanyi villages, including Casa Grande and Pueblo Grande."[74] Contrasted with the current archaeological view that the Pima and Tohono O'odham descended from the Hohokam, this account suggests that there existed two distinct cultural groups at war with each other. As previously stated, the Hopi word *siva* means "metal," perhaps in particular, "copper." The suffix *-ni* is a nominalizer, so the word *Sivanyi* could mean something like the "Metal Ones." Hohokam artifacts include copper tinklers supposedly imported from Mexico, to which the epithet perhaps refers. But considering the spectrographic analysis of the metallic content in these artifacts in comparison with both Lake Superior and Mexican copper, Harold Gladwin, the renowned archaeologist of Snaketown, conversely states that the artifacts were probably local and had been manufactured onsite.[75] Each tinkler has a pear-shaped resonator slit at the bottom to insert the copper bead clapper. Twenty eight of these small bells were found in one room of Snaketown, fallen where the house had burned.[76] The narrow spatial focus for these artifacts suggests that an elite group of priests had used them for ritual purposes. Even more speculatively, we might ask whether the Metal Ones actually did wear some sort of metallic clothing. Or perhaps the Ant Peoples' gray skin and mechanical movements were construed as somehow being metallic.

At this point let us summarize the characteristics of the Ant People to which the Hopi legends refer: 1. They are the salvation of the ancestral Hopi, allowing them to survive inside a subterranean vault during the devastation of two different worlds. 2. They teach the virtues of generosity, assiduity, and thrift. 3. They are not merely allegorical figures but an unique species whose ectomorphology, mannerisms, and idiosyncrasies resemble those of ants. 4. They are associated with warfare and the hunt. 5. They possess both the positive magic of healing and the darker forces of sorcery. 6. They have intimate knowledge of both the Underworld and the powers of the earth plane. 7. They work in league with the Hopi sky god Sótuknang. These specific traits provoke us to ask the simple question: Just who were these formic creatures, anyway?

All of these characteristics enumerated could reasonably apply to Masau'u, who, as we determined in Chapter 3, is the terrestrial analogue of Orion, whose name means "ant." When this constellation dominates the winter skies, the ants are deep in their "kivas," or mounds.[77] Although this ostensibly seems contradictory, the zenith and the nadir are actually one shamanistic axis comprising the Underworld of spirits over which Masau'u reigns. In other words, two cosmological realms exist in the Hopi *Weltanschauung*: on the one hand, they conceptualize the surface of the earth and the site of human activity; on the other, they imagine a combined sky/underground region and the home of the spirits, in particular the *katsinam*. Were the Ant People, then, actually multiple versions of the Underworld god Masau'u, who is also a *katsina*?

Furthermore, we might ask about the Ant's People's traditional domicile. In the construction of their kivas, did the Hopi try to imitate the conical structure of ant mounds? The earliest kivas of the Anasazi were circular, but during the Pueblo period their form changed to rectangular in order to mirror the shape of the plaza where the *katsina* dances were held. The even earlier pit houses, whose morphology gave rise to the kiva, were round as well, perhaps as an homage to the initial sanctuary provided by the Ant People. Usually incorporated in the structure of the kiva were large cists into which globular pottery jars filled with food were put.78 This perhaps honored the ants' propensity to lay food away for future use deep within the earth. The subterranean realm connotes both the individual afterlife and the collective prior "Worlds," the latter destroyed due to human iniquities. Both the ant mound with its dark tunnels and the kiva with its *sipapu* embody the nether plane, which paradoxically arches up across the skies to serve as home to the star spirits. What then are we to make of these buried chambers within which a small group of uncorrupted Hopis were saved— not once but twice? Were they actually part of a cavern complex, of which the kiva is merely a mnemonic replica?

## *The Caves of Orion*

Both ants and snakes resonate deep in our psyches as archetypal denizens of dual worlds: the earth plane and the Underworld. The Colorado Plateau provides a number of sites where access to the latter can be gained. In Chapter 4 we mentioned the extensive cavern system near Sunset Crater and Wupatki Ruin, the latter of which even has a blow hole. About eighteen miles northwest of Flagstaff is Lava River Cave (a.k.a. Slate Lakes Lava Cave), an ice cave about three quarters of a mile long where the temperature hovers around freezing.79 A little over twelve miles east of Peach Springs, Arizona are Grand Canyon Caverns, the extensive cave system described in Chapter 8. In addition, the ceremonial catacombs and winding stone stairways at Casa Malpais near Springerville, Arizona were briefly end-noted in Chapter 2. All of these cavernous domains could have reinforced legends regarding ants. One subterranean site, however, is particularly intriguing vis-à-vis the Ant people.

Tentative evidence of a Lost Ancient City in Grand Canyon continues to emerge from Arizona researchers such as Jack Andrews and

Barry McEwen.[80] Popularized by the President of the World Explorers Club, David Hatcher Childress [81], the original story tells of an explorer named G.E. Kinkaid, who while working for the Smithsonian Institution in 1909 may have achieved the most monumental archaeological discovery in North America. At 2,000 feet above the Colorado River and nearly 1,500 feet down a sheer wall of Grand Canyon, he found the entrance of an immense system of passageways and chambers artificially carved into the rock. Fronted by thirty yards of stone steps (which, Kinkaid speculated, once led to the former level of the river), the main passage was twelve feet wide and extended "several hundred feet." In a subsequent expedition Kinkaid and Smithsonian Professor S.A. Jordan  explored "several hundred rooms," some of which radiated "like spokes in a wheel" from the huge chamber at the end of the main passage. Therein they found numerous artifacts, including a life-size Buddha-like sculpture sitting in the lotus posture with a lotus held in each hand.[82] In addition, various vases, urns, cups of copper and gold, smelting tools, enameled and glazed pottery, and stone tablets with some sort of hieroglyphic writing were discovered. In one large room Kinkaid and Jordan saw an aggregation of male mummies wrapped in bark fabric or clay and standing upright on hewn shelves. This along with the discovery of broken swords implies that the whole complex once served as a "warriors' barracks," accommodating perhaps 50,000 men. A number of granaries containing seeds and even a main dining hall forty feet wide and seven hundred feet long were also found, complete with cooking utensils.

Although this ancient "Lost City" reminiscent of Derinkuyu in central Turkey [83] (discussed below) was supposedly located forty-two miles upriver from El Tovar Crystal Canyon, contemporary explorers have not been able to relocate it. The only remaining hard evidence is a front page article in the April 5, 1909 issue of the *Phoenix Gazette*. If the story once had any veracity, its implications, which surely would have shattered all conventional archaeological paradigms, eventually forced the Smithsonian to cover it up. Is this, then, the site where the Hopi were given refuge by the Ant People? Until the Lost City is again found, it remains a conundrum.

In preceding chapters we discussed the possibility of an Old World origin of at least some of the clans forming the Hisatsinom. Author Thomas O. Mills, who was a close friend of the late Oswald White Bear Fredericks (Frank Waters' main informant), suggests that the "ant mounds" within which the Hopi were taken in order to survive were actually one of the monumental Seven Wonders of the Ancient World. "What would have looked like a huge anthill to a Hopi? Where could this have been? What structure that resembles an anthill is big enough to hold a large number of people...? If the structure could withstand the destruction of the earth, it should still be standing today. It would have to be one of the first structures on earth and have a place where the Hopi could be taught to be industrious."[84] The structure is, of course, the Great Pyramid along with adjacent smaller pyramids. As is well known, the Giza Plateau is replete with subterranean passageways, some of which are still being discovered and explored today. Mills goes on to identify the Great Pyramid (Khufu) with Taiowa, the Creator (or Tawa, the Hopi sun god); the slightly smaller, middle pyramid (Khafre) with the sky god Sótuknang; and the smallest pyramid (Menkaure) with the present Fourth World, while the three adjacent satellite pyramids represent the previous three Hopi Worlds.[85]

Another Old World candidate for the Ant People's hypogeum is Cappadocia in Anatolia. In this Turkish region thirty-six underground cities complete with ventilation shafts and interconnecting tunnels have been discovered. It is estimated that 200,000 people could have comfortably inhabited these complexes. "The largest one, Derinkuyu, covers 2 ½ square miles; only eight levels have been thoroughly explored out of twenty known to exist; and just this one complex could have adequately housed around 20,000 people."[86] Although these caverns carved out of volcanic rock were used by Christians escaping Arab persecution during the 7th century A.D., Ömer Demir, the premier historian and archaeologist of Derinkuyu, suggests that the oldest parts of the citadel may have been constructed as early as 9500-9000 B.C.— that is, during the end of the last Ice Age! Another interesting characteristic of the site is that the ceilings of oldest rooms are around seven feet high, whereas those of the more recent rooms are much lower.[87] We should remember that the Watchers and the Nephilim (as well as Masau'u) were traditionally taller in height, while Hopi people are typically shorter in stature. If the implications of this notion seem too outlandish, we remind readers of the statements made by Hopi informants (cited in Chapter 11) of a Hopi origin in the Middle East.

From Persia comes the mythic figure of Yima, who is particularly pertinent to our discussion. Similar to the death god Yama of India, Yima (or Jemshid or Jam) lived in a subterranean stronghold called a *Var*. In some ways Yima parallels the biblical Noah, filling his underground fortress with sundry species of plants and animals. The threat, however, is not from flood but from "vehement frost"[88], which is precisely what destroyed the Hopi Second World. Incidentally, the Hopi term *yama* means "crossed over," while its cognate *yawma* refers to "carrying objects." The good spirit Ahura Mazda, who ordered Yima to build his subsurface citadel, also commanded the following: "But put no deformed creature, nor impotent, nor mad; neither wicked, nor deceitful, nor rancorous, nor jealous..."[89] These are just the ilk of humanity who were also banned from the Ant People's refuge for the Hopi. As ruler of the Golden Age, Yima has been compared to Kronos or Saturnus [90], whose Hopi counterpart (as we determined in Chapter 3) is none other than Masau'u, also god of death. Finally, *var*, the Iranian word from Zoroastrian tradition, is related to the Hopi word *waranta*, which means "laid it away for future use" or "saved," something which ants do extraordinarily well. *Var*, literally meaning "subterranean fortress or city,"[91] might also have been the source of the Hopi word *ki-va*, the subterranean ceremonial chamber. The Hopi prefix or

*Fig. 52. Round kiva, San Ildefonso Pueblo, New Mexico. Ancient Hopi kivas were circular like this but later became rectangular.*

suffix *ki* refers to "house," while the Sumerian word *ki* means "earth."₉₂ In Sanskrit, *var* or *vara* means "protector, defender, encirclement, cover, or fortune," all of which could refer to an underground fastness and storage facility. The Sanskrit *var* can also mean "ocean" or a "receptacle of water,"₉₃ which is confusing until we recall that the Underworld as well as the sky were frequently conceptualized as a vast ocean.

Each February the Hopi perform the Powamu, or Bean Sprouting Ceremony, inside the kivas. "The central part of the Powamu is the germination of beans. To keep the symbolism straight some corn is planted, but beans have two advantages: they grow faster at this time of year and the results are edible. The kivas make excellent hot houses in which all sorts of containers full of dirt and bean seeds are placed, while the fires are kept up day and night."₉₄ Does this ritual commemorate a time when the Hopi sprouted beans inside caverns in order to survive? We might note in passing that the Hu Katsinam mentioned in the myth "Why the Ants Are So Thin" (p. 283) are an integral part of Powamu ceremony that initiates children into the Katsina Society.₉₅

## The Giants of Orion

All across the American Southwest one can find pictographs (rock paintings) and petroglyphs (rock carvings) depicting eerie creatures with spindly bodies, large eyes, and bulbous heads that sometimes project antennae. (For instance, Fig. 53, p. 292. Also see the description of the Shamans' Gallery rock art of Grand Canyon at the conclusion of Chapter 6.) The figures are frequently shown in what is called the "prayer stance," i.e., the elbows and knees positioned at right angles, similar to the bent legs of the ant. Are these rock drawings the representations of the Ant People? Are they an actual record of the meeting between indigenous humans and the alien Ant People? Were they truly "alien," as we've come to use the term after 1947 and the UFO crash near Roswell, New Mexico?

One etymological clue offered by Knight and Lomas might provide at least a partial answer. "The word 'Nephilim' is of uncertain origin, but it has been observed by specialist scholars that the root Aramaic word *nephîliâ* is the name of the constellation Orion, and therefore, Nephilim would seem to mean 'those that are of Orion.'"[96] The Nephilim mentioned in the New English Bible (alternately spelled "Nefilim") are, of course, familiar to readers of Zecharia Sitchin, who translates the Sumerian root NFL (*not* the football league!) as "*...those who were cast down upon the Earth!*"[97] These creatures are the same as the "giants in the earth" found in Genesis 6:4 of the King James version. Just before the great Flood "the sons of the gods," interpreted as either fallen angels or the Watchers, mated with "the daughters of men," or human women, to produce these giants. (See last section of Chapter 7 for a discussion of the Watchers.) At any rate, it is interesting to note that the Hebrew word meaning "ant" is *nemâlâh*, a near homophone of Nephilim.[98] If the Nephilim are indeed "of Orion," this could mean that the sires of these Ant People were cast down from the skies, perhaps from as far away as the constellation Orion itself. In this context we find of interest the Watchers' chief angel Shemyaza, who was ultimately banished to Orion because of their corruption of humankind.

> "Although the Watchers' leader, Shemyaza, is cast into the abyss alongside his brothers, in other versions of the story he undergoes a more dramatic punishment. Since he was tempted by a beautiful mortal maiden named Ishtahar [Ishtar] to reveal the Explicit Name of God in exchange for the offer of carnal pleasure, he is tied and bound before being made to hang for all of eternity between heaven and earth, head down, in the constellation Orion."[99]

The image of an angel hanging upside down in the constellation of Orion symbolically suggests the orientation of the Orion Correlations in both Arizona and Egypt, viz., south— opposite of the axis of the celestial Orion. Some conjecture that Shemyaza and Azazyel (the latter mentioned at the end of Chapter 7) are two names for the same entity because of their proxity and similar context in Chap. 9, verses 5 and 6 of *The Book of Enoch*. Incidentally, in their book *Uriel's Machine*, Knight and Lomas have identified the sculpture of an inverted angel hanging on the eastern wall of Rosslyn Chapel in Scotland. "Without doubt this is a representation of Shemhazai [Shemyaza] who was instrumental in causing the Flood."[100] More than a Christian church, Rosslyn is a late medieval monument to the perduring symbology of Freemasonry.

The notion that the Hopi actually were ants in the earliest eras is conceivably the result of what only could be called the miscegenation of the celestial Watchers and terrestrial women. If the Hopi had intercourse (both sexual and social) with the Ant People, their offspring naturally would have some of the latter's physical and social characteristics. In this case, we see not only a physical merging of the two races but a symbolic one as well, i.e., "As Above, so Below." While the Nephilim / *nemâlâh*

*Fig. 53. Petroglyph from Cottonwood Creek Ruin near Winslow, Arizona. The ET-like figure on left is possibly Masau'u, holding hands with a human. The figure on right may be Soyoko (Ogre) Katsina, who has a snout with sharp teeth and a baton or bow in his left hand.*

(Hebrew for "ant") parallel is interesting, the Hopi term for "ant" is downright intriguing: *anu*. This is the exact name of the Assyro-Babylonian sky god Anu, whose Hopi counterpart is Sótuknang, a god closely associated with Masau'u. In Hopi the word *naki* means friend, prayer feathers, food offerings, or sand—a nexus of concepts pertaining to this insect that sometimes flies. A combination of the two words (*anu-naki*, or "ant friend") may be related to Sitchin's Anunnaki. One Sumerian cylinder seal from around 2250 B.C. shows the pantheon of primary deities wearing peaked hats; the sky god Sótuknang also wears a pointed headdress. Like their Middle Eastern counterparts, the Hopi divinities were present at the creation of the universe and continued to be instrumental in the culture's development.

Anu was also the name of the Egyptian city of Heliopolis, where the famed *benben* stone of meteoric iron was kept. In addition, *anu* in the Egyptian tongue meant not only "products," "revenues," and "something brought in" but also "gift, tribute, offerings."[101] This refers to both the ants' capacity for storage of provisions and the reverence afforded the Ant People. Furthermore, Anu (or Danu) was also the appellation of the Celtic mother goddess and patroness of the dead.

A couple of biblical references further solidify the notion of ants *as people* (or at least a separate race of bizarre people, extraterrestrial or not) rather than insects. For instance, Proverbs 6:6 describes the ant as being wise, completely in keeping with the Hopi account of the Ant People. In addition, Proverbs 30:25 states: "The ants *are* a people not strong, yet they prepare their meat in the summer..." Even if we discount this direct identification of ants as people, how on earth would insects be able to "prepare their meat"? And "in summer," no less! As far as we know, neither fire ants nor legionary ants, both of which are sometimes carnivorous, utilizes the process of curing or drying meat. Even if one

**Fig. 54. This petroglyph at Homol'ovi State Park may represent a triangualar craft, in Hopi called a paatuwvota, or "flying shield."**

concedes to the possibility that "meat" might simply be a poetic metonym for food in general, the same cannot be done with "people." Unlike the American Indians, the Hebrews were not accustomed to describing various animal species as "people." They were never so egalitarian.

Were the Ant People (*nemâlâh*) the descendants (called Nephilim) of women who mated with rebel angels? Did Orion, whose name means "ant," come down to Earth in Arizona in order to become Masau'u, the ant-like god of the spirit world? Were the Ant People willing to save the virtuous people from two different natural cataclyms that ravaged the Earth because the former saw in humans the genetic reflections of themselves? Were the kiva-like caves in which the Hopi found refuge really the anthills of ancient star beings? Perhaps these questions are, in the end, unanswerable. Perhaps it is enough just to raise them.

The Zuni have a poem about ants that is chanted:

> They are so wise,
> > they always remember where their home is.
> They travel great distances,
> > but always find their way back.
> We make offerings to ants for their wisdom,
> > so that we will have the ability
> > > to keep the prayers in our memory.102

Are the "great distances" the Ant People have to travel in truth interstellar ones? Do these descendants of the Watchers still watch over us, or have they found their way back home to the arms of Orion? Do we have the ability to keep them in our memory? Perhaps somewhere in the far future it will all become clear.

# REFERENCES AND NOTES

## Preface

1. Michell, *Secrets of the Stones*, p. 112.
2. Campbell, *Hero With a Thousand Faces*, p. 3.
3. Ernst Cassirer, *Language and Myth*, p. 11.
4. Whiteley, *Rethinking Hopi Ethnography*, p. 12.
5. Patterson, *Hopi Pottery Symbols*, p. 38.
6. Snake Priest and eldest of the elders, Chief Dan of Hotevilla entered the Sipapuni and began his journey to the spirit world on January 15th, 1999 at the age of 108.
7. Roberts, *In Search of the Old Ones*, pp. 86-87.
8. The Cline Library Image Database, Cline Library, Special Collections and Archives Department, Northern Arizona University [Web site online]; available from the World Wide Web, <http://http://www2.nau.edu/~libei-p/scadb/search/da_advanced.cfm>; accessed 30 September 2006.
9. Mitton, *The Penguin Dictionary of Astronomy*, p. 283.
10. "The Book of Job," *The Holy Bible* (King James Version), Chapter 38, Verses 31 and 33.

## Chapter 1: Leaving Many Footprints

1. Schaaf, *Ancient Ancestors of the Southwest*, p. 13.
2. Dan Katchongva quoted by Mails and Dan Evehema, *Hotevilla*, p. 48.
3. Pike, Donald G., *Anasazi*, p. 12.
4. Titiev, *Old Oraibi*, p. 162.
5. Oppelt, *Guide to Prehistoric Ruins of the Southwest*, pp. 7-8.
6. White, Jon Manchip, *A World Elsewhere*, p. 11.
7. Wormington, *Prehistoric Indians of the Southwest*, p. 41-42.
8. Ferguson and Rohn, *Anasazi Ruins of the Southwest In Color*, p. 4.
9. Reid and Whittlesey, *The Archaeology of Ancient Arizona*, p. 187.
10. Folsom and Folsom, *Ancient Treasures of the Southwest*, p. 10.
11. Barnes, F.A., and Pendleton, *Canyon Country Prehistoric Indians*, p. 63.
12. Wormington, *Prehistoric Indians*, p. 86.
13. Schaaf, *Ancient Ancestors of the Southwest,* p. 35.
14. Widdison, ed., *The Anasazi*, p. 10.
15. Pike, Donald G., *Anasazi,* p. 148.
16. Mails and Evehema, *Hotevilla*, p. 17.
17. Secakuku, *Following the Sun and Moon*, p. 2.
18. Ferguson, *Anasazi Ruins*, pp. 47-50.
19. Cunkle, *Talking Pots.*
20. Benedict, *Patterns of Culture*, p. 73.
21. Ibid., pp. 79-80, p. 119.
22. Scully, *Pueblo*, p. 4.
23. Fewkes, *Tusayan Katcinas and Hopi Altars*, p. 252.
24. a. Courlander, *The Fourth World of the Hopis*. b. Nequatewa, *Truth of a Hopi*. c. Mullett, *Spider Woman Stories*. d. Schaaf, *Ancient Ancestors*. e.Waters and Oswald White Bear Fredericks, *Book of the Hopi*.
25. Ibid., p. 12.
26. Velikovsky, *Worlds In Collision*, p. 40-43.
27. Thomas Banyacya. "The Hopi Message To the United Nations" [online]. The Hopi

Information Network, 1996; available from World Wide Web: <http://www.InfoMagic.COM/~abyte/hopi/messages/nations/html>, p. 2; accesed 25 June 1998.
28. Nequatewa, *Truth of a Hopi*, p. 97.
29. Waters, *Mexico Mystique*, p. 273.
30. Schaaf, *Ancient Ancestors*, p. 14.
31. Nequatewa, *Truth of a Hopi*, p. 24.
32. Dan Katchongva, Danaqyumtewa, trans., Thomas Francis, ed. "From the Beginning of Life to the Day of Purification: Teachings, History & Prophecies of the Hopi People" [online]. The Hopi Information Network, 1996; available from World Wide Web: <http://www.InfoMagic.COM/~abyte/hopi/messages/katch1.html>; accessed 26 June 1998; originally published by the Committee for Traditional Indian Land and Life, Los Angeles, 1972, p. 2.
33. Courlander, *The Fourth World of the Hopis*, p. 204.
34. Waters and Fredericks, *The Book of the Hopi*, p. 19.
35. Ibid., p. 20.
36. Calvin, *The River That Flows Uphill*, pp. 94-95.
37. Courlander, *The Fourth World of the Hopis*, pp. 17-25.
38. Waters and Fredericks, *The Book of the Hopi*, p. 17.
39. Malotki and Lomatuway'ma, *Maasaw*, p. 3.
40. Courlander, *The Fourth World of the Hopis*, p. 22.
41. "The Public Statement of the Keeper of the Hopi Fire Clan Tablets, during his Prophetic Mission to the New Mexico State Capital at Santa Fe, December 1990" [online]. The Hopi Information Network, 1996; available from World Wide Web: <http://www.InfoMagic.COM/~abyte/hopi/messages/santafe.html>. p. 1; accessed 26 June 1998.
42. Nequtewa, *Truth of a Hopi*, p. 25.
43. Mullett, *Spider Woman Stories*, p. 41.
44. Malotki and Lomatuway'ma, *Maasaw*, p. 4.
45. Mails and Evehema, *Hotevilla*, p. 42.
46. "The Public Statement..." [online], p. 1.
47. Barbara Hand Clow, Introduction to Boissière, *The Return of Pahana*, p. xix.
48. Banyacya, "The Hopi Message..." [online], p. 1.
49. Martin Gashweseoma, "Cry of the Earth Conference, General Assembly, United Nations, November, 22, 1993" [online]. The Hopi Network, 1996; available from World Wide Web: <http://www.InfoMagic.COM/~abyte/hopi/mesaages.cry.html>, p. 1; accessed 25 June 1998.
50. Malotki and Lomatuway'ma, *Maasaw*, p. 74.
51. Waters and Fredericks, *The Book of the Hopi*, pp. 31-33.
52. Titiev, *Old Oraibi*, p. 60-61.
53. Katchongva, "From the Beginning of Life..." [online], pp. 5-6.
54. Seaman, *Hopi Dictionary*, p. 51.
55. Eliade, *The Sacred and the Profane*, p. 64-65.
56. Waters and Fredericks, *The Book of the Hopi*, p. 21.
57. Malotki and Lomatuway'ma, *Maasaw*, p. 63-64.
58. Courlander, *The Fourth World of the Hopis*, p. 33.
59. Whiteley, *Bacavi*, p. 11.
60. Nequatewa, *Truth of a Hopi*, p. 35.
61. Mindeleff, *A Study of Pueblo Architecture in Tusayan and Cibola*, pp. 17-18.
62. Anthony F. Aveni, "The Star of Bethlehem," *Archaeology*, Vol. 51, No. 6, November/December, 1998, p. 37.
63. Katchongava, "From the Beginning of Life..." [online], p. 6.
64. Ibid., p. 7.
65. Waters and Fredericks, *The Book of the Hopi*, p. 35-36.

66. Silko, *Yellow Woman and a Beauty of the Spirit*, p. 40.

## Chapter 2: The Sky Over the Hopi Villages

1. Bradfield, *An Interpretation of Hopi Culture*, pp. 287-288.
2. Tyler, *Pueblo Gods and Myths*, p. 26.
3. Mails, *The Pueblo Children of the Earth Mother*, Vol. II, p. 47.
4. Page and Page, *Hopi*, pp. 217-223.
5. Grigsby cited in Hancock and Faiia, *Heaven's Mirror*, p. 127.
6. Malville and Putnam, *Prehistoric Astronomy in the Southwest*, p. 23.
7. Inhabited from A.D. 1026 (or possibly earlier because of the underlying pit house) through 1300, King's Ruin has a thirteen-room foundation, twelve of which could have been two stories high. The five hundred pieces of unworked shells found at the site indicate substantial trade with the Pacific. Necklaces of turquoise, black shale and argillite were also found. One of the former materials consists of 2,031 beads that stretched sixty-six inches long. Fifty-five graves were also discovered, containing sixty-six individuals, most of which were buried in the extended posture with heads oriented toward the east, awaiting Pahana's return. Johnson, *A View of Prehistory in the Prescott Region*, pp. 8-9.
8. Occupied for a few generations after A.D. 1088, abandoned and then reoccupied between 1225 and the late 1200s, Salmon Ruins near the San Juan River contained from between 600 and 750 rooms. It also had a tower kiva built on a platform twenty feet high, which was made of rock imported from thirty miles away. Ten miles north of Salmon is Aztec Ruins National Monument (an obvious misnomer) located on the Animas River. At its peak development it contained about 500 rooms. Like the former, this latter site was originally inhabited in the early twelfth century by people of Chaco Canyon and then re-inhabited from 1225 to 1300 by people of Mesa Verde. In addition, it has a restored Great Kiva.
9. Inhabited from A.D. 1226-1276, Wide Ruin, or Kin Tiel, about fifty miles due south of Canyon de Chelly, is an oval shaped pueblo of 150 to 200 rooms with a number of kivas. Atsinna pueblo, located atop a high mesa at El Morro National Monument, was a mid-thirteenth century rectangular structure, part of which was three stories in height. It had 500-1000 rooms and two kivas, one circular and the other square.
a. Noble, *Ancient Ruins of the Southwest*: b. Oppelt, *Guide to Prehistoric Ruins of the Southwest*.
10. Constructed in the mid-eleventh century, Casamero Ruin was a small thirty-room pueblo. However, its Great Kiva, one of the largest in the Southwest, was seventy feet in diameter—even slightly more spacious than the better known Casa Rinconada at Chaco Canyon about forty-five miles to the north. Noble, *Ancient Ruins*; and Oppelt, *Guide To Prehistoric Ruins*.
11. Lister and Lister, *Those Who Came Before*, p. 224.
12. Located in the Mogollon Mountains of west-central New Mexico, Gila Cliff Dwellings National Monument is a ruin comprised of forty rooms in five separate caves located 150 feet above the canyon floor. The timbers of these structures have been tree-ring dated in the 1280s. The late Mogollon, or Mimbres, people are known for their exquisite black on white pottery, using realistic though stylized designs. The site was abandoned by 1400. Noble, *Ancient Ruins*, pp. 7-8.
13. Casa Malpais is a thirteenth century Mogollon site of a hundred rooms with a square Great Kiva (one of the largest in the Southwest), catacombs, ceremonial rooms, three winding stone stairways, and an astronomical observatory. Because of the nature of the artifacts found, such as crystals, ceremonial pipes, and soapstone fetish stands, it is thought to have been primarily a religious center. Smith, "House of the Badlands," *Arizona Highways*, pp. 39-44.
14. Located nearly ninety miles southeast of Homol'ovi and about twelve miles north of Casa Malpais, the Raven Site (privately owned by the White Mountain Archeological

Center) was occupied as early as A.D. 800 through A.D.1450 and had more than eight hundred rooms and two kivas. Cunkle, *Raven Site Ruin.*

15. Reid and Whittlesey, *The Archaeology of Ancient Arizona*, p. 220.

16. Occupied from A.D. 1085-1207, Ridge Ruin, a thirty-room pueblo with three kivas and a Maya-style ball court, was the site of the so-called Magician's Burial. Thought by Hopi elders to be of the Motswimi, or Warrior Society, this apparently important man was interred with twenty-five whole pottery vessels and over six hundred other artifacts, including shell and stone jewelry, turquoise mosaics, woven baskets, wooden wands, arrow points, and a bead cap.
a. Houk, *Sinagua*, p. 7. b. Oppelt, *Guide to Prehistoric Ruins*, pp. 99-100.
c. Reid and Whittlesey, *Archaeology of Ancient Arizona*, pp. 219-220.

17. The eponymous Winona Village, which was occupied at the end of the 11th century, contained about twenty pit houses and five surface storage rooms. Oppelt, *Guide To Prehistoric Ruins*, p. 99.

18. The Emilienne Ruin had a foundation of twelve rooms, most of which could have been two stories high, plus eleven outlying one-room units.

19. The Fitzmaurice Ruin, occupied from A.D. 1140-1300, had twenty-seven rooms in which were found beads, pendants, bracelets, and eighty one amulets, including crystals, animal fetishes, obsidian nodules (so-called "Apache Tears") and a curious six-faceted, truncated pyramid carved from jadeite and measuring 1.5 centimeters wide.
a. Barnett, *Excavation of Main Pueblo At Fitzmaurice Ruin*, p. 95. b. Johnson, *Prehistory in the Prescott Region*, p. 16.

20. Similar to the Nazca lines of Peru, these intaglios of human, animal, and star figures, some over a hundred of feet long, were made by removal of the darker, "desert varnished" pebbles, exposing the lighter soil beneath. Reid and Whittlesey, *Archaeology of Ancient Arizona*, pp. 127-129. According to the Mohave and Quechan tribes of the lower Colorado River region, the human figures represent the deity Mastamho, the Creator of the Earth and all life. Notice the similarity between the name of this god and that of the Hopi earth god Masau'u. These figures are thought to be between 450 and 2000 years old.

21. Also at 1:15 a.m. on this date Bellatrix is at 240 degrees azimuth and Meissa is at 242 degrees azimuth. Forty minutes later Alnilam is at 240 degrees, the azimuthal degree at which the sun will set at 5:15 p.m. on this same day. Incidentally, at this winter solstice sunset time Orion is just rising on the opposite horizon, thus emphasizing the pivotal relationship of Orion/Masau'u and the Sun/Tawa.

22. Edmund Nequatewa cited in Loftin, *Religion and Hopi Life In the Twentieth Century*, p. 33.

23. Waters and Fredericks, *Book of the Hopi*, pp. 158-161.

24. Bradfield, *An Interpretation of Hopi Culture*, pp. 134-135.

25. Alexander Stephen cited in Williamson, *Living the Sky*, pp. 79-82.

26. Waters and Fredericks, *Book of the Hopi*, pp. 161-162.

27. Sofaer, "The Primary Architecture of the Chacoan Culture: A Cosmological Expression," *Anasazi Architecture and American Design*, p. 98.

28. Williamson, *Living the Sky*, p. 40.

29. "Calculating the declination and azimuth" [online] Victor Reijs and His BBS Geniet, 1996; available from the World Wide Web: <http://geniet.mypage.org/aarde.htm>; accessed 26 September 2000.

30. Sofaer, *Anasazi Architecture*, pp. 96-120.

31. Sofaer and Sinclair, *Astronomy and Ceremony in the Prehistoric Southwest.*

32. Malville and Putnam, *Prehistoric Astronomy in the Southwest*, p. 51.

33. Sofaer, *Anasazi Architecture*, p. 98.

34. Malville and Putnam, *Prehistoric Astronomy in the Southwest*, p. 25.

35. Whitman, *An American Primer*, p. 31.

36. Barnes, *Arizona Place Names*, p. 27.

37. Allen, *Star Names*, p. 315.

38. Smith, *Smith's Bible Dictionary*, p. 49.
39. Malotki and Lomatuway'ma, *Maasaw*, p. 177.
40. Hancock and Faiia, *Heaven's Mirror*, pp. 16-17.
41. Jung, *The Portable Jung*, p. 512.
42. Kaiser, *The Voice of the Great Spirit*, pp. 34-35.
43. Widdison, *The Anasazi*, pp. 55-56.
44. West, *Serpent In the Sky*, p. 37.
45. Cunkle *Talking Pots*, pp. 115-120.
46. Nequatewa, *Truth of a Hopi*, p. 22.

## Chapter 3: Orion Rising In the Dark Crystal

1. Grossinger, *The Night Sky*, p. 313.
2. We are using the sidereal coordinates for A.D. 1100. At that time Orion rose concurrently with the sun on June 21st, the summer solstice, and achieved heliacal rising in early July (about the 7th). At present, Orion rises concurrently with the sun at the beginning of July and achieves heliacal rising about July 21. Mark A. Haney, *Skyglobe 2.04 for Windows* [floppy disk] (Ann Arbor, Michigan: KlassM Software, 1997). This and all subsequent astronomical calculations were made by this excellent program.
3. Allen, *Star Names*, p. 304.
4. *New Larousse Encyclopedia of Mythology*, p. 144.
5. Smith, *Smith's Bible Dictionary*, p. 474.
6. Allen, *Star Names*, pp. 306-310.
7. E.C. Krupp, *Beyond the Blue Horizon*, pp. 215-216.
8. Aveni, *Skywatchers of Ancient Mexico*), pp. 34-36.
9. Goodman, *Lakota Star Knowledge*, p. 44.
10. Griffin-Pierce, *Earth Is My Mother, Sky Is My Father*, p. 163-166.
11. Miller, *Stars of the First People*, pp. 176-178.
12. Malotki, *Hopi Dictionary*.
13. Stephen, *Hopi Journal*, p. 233.
14. Waters and Fredericks, *Book of the Hopi*, pp. 137-153.
15. Stephen, *Hopi Journal*, p. 150.
16. Stephen, *Hopi Journal*, p. 84 and p.87, n. 1.
17. Titiev, *Old Oraibi*, p. 135.
18. Malotki and Lomatuway'ma, *Maasaw*, p. 81.
19. Ibid., p. 20.
20. Bradfield, *An Interpretation of Hopi Culture*, p. 323.
21. Ibid., p. 288.
22. Powell, *The Hopi Villages*, p. 26.
23. Stephen, *Hopi Journal*, p. 1225.
24. Cunkle, *Talking Pots*, p. 106.
25. Patterson, *A Field Guide To Rock Art Symbols of the Greater Southwest*, p. 178.
26. Cunkle, *Talking Pots*, p.110.
27. Huxley, *The Way of the Sacred*, p. 212.
28. Hancock, *Fingerprints of the Gods*, p. 262.
29. Frazier, *The New Golden Bough*, p. 653.
30. Malotki, *Maasaw*, pp. 244-245.
31. Bradfield, *An Interpretation of Hopi Culture*, pp. 280-284.
32. Jones, *Astrology*, p. 244.
33. Jung, *Aion*, pp. 74-75.
34. Arroyo, *Astrology, Karma & Transformation*, pp. 71-72.
35. Van Toen, "Alice Bailey Revisited," *Spiritual, Metaphysical & New Trends In Modern Astrology*, p. 160.
36. It should be remembered that astrologically the *planet* Saturn assumed attributes of the

Roman god Saturnus, who was mythologically related to the *constellation* Orion. In this plexus of associations we can also see a kinship between Saturnus and the Hopi god Masau'u.

37. Stephen, *Hopi Journal*, Map 4.
38. Hancock, *The Mars Mystery*, pp. 259-284.
39. Ibid., pp. 175-177.
40. Mallery, *Picture Writing of the American Indian*, Vol. I, p. 320.
41. Titiev, *Old Oraibi*, p. 176.
42. Fewkes, *Tusayan Katcinas and Hopi Altars*.
43. Whorf, *Language, Thought, and Reality*.
44. Secakuku, *Following the Sun and the Moon*, p. 64, p. 70.
45. McCluskey, "Historical Archaeoastronomy: The Hopi Example," *Archaeoastronomy In the New World*, p. 37.
46. Ellis, "Pueblo Sun-Moon-Star Calendar," *Archaeoastronomy In Pre-Columbian America*.
47. Loftin, *Religion and Hopi Life In the Twentieth Century*, p. 127.
48. Tyler, *Pueblo Gods and Myths*, p. 33.
49. Malotki, *Maasaw*, p. 120.

# Chapter 4: The Cosmo-magical Cities of the Anasazi

1. Malville and Putnam, *Prehistoric Astronomy in the Southwest*, p. 60.
2. Scully, *Pueblo*, pp. 379-380.
3. Folsom and Folsom, *Ancient Treasures of the Southwest*, p. 22.
4. Bryant, *Starwalking*, p. 217-218.
5. Eliade, *The Sacred and the Profane*, p. 41.
6. Lawrence, *Mornings In Mexico*, p. 141.
7. Nequatewa, *Truth of a Hopi*, p. 35.
8. Despite its defensive conservatism, the contemporary Hopi reservation is not immune to power lines or satellite dishes. Even an occasional solar panel can be seen perched atop an old masonry home, bring the dubious world of electric lights and television to some of the oldest structures on the continent.
9. Burnham, *Burnham's Celestial Handbook*, Vol. 2, p. 1302.
10. The Hopi culture is both matrilineal and matrilocal. The women are the "owners" of the houses, whereas the men have authority over the various religious societies in the kivas. Of course, the former area is not exclusively restricted in terms of gender, but, though less recognized, neither is the latter an exclusively male domain. Some archaeologists have suggested that Anasazi/Hisatsinom women participated in the actual construction of the pueblos and may have even been their primarily builders.
11. Mails and Evehema, *Hotevilla*, pp. 94-95.
12. Scully, *Pueblo*, pp. 314-315.
13. James, *Pages From Hopi History*, p. 12.
14. Morgan, *Ancient Architecture of the Southwest*, p. 195.
15. Scully, *Pueblo*, p. 309.
16. Burnham, *Burnham's Celestial Handbook*, p. 1302.
17. James, *Pages From Hopi History*, pp. 136-138.
18. Mails and Evehema, *Hotevilla*, p. 295.
19. Claiborne, *The Summer Stargazer*, p. 79.
20. Burnham, *Burnham's Celestial Handbook*, p. 1305.
21. Courlander, *The Fourth World of the Hopis*, p. 234, p. 236, p. 238.
22. Allen, *Star Names*, p. 314.
23. Powell, *The Exploration of the Colorado River and its Canyons*, p. 345.
24. Cordell, *Prehistory of the Southwest*, p. 355.
25. Scully, *Pueblo*, p. 319.

26. Burnham, *Burnham's Celestial Handbook*, p. 1308.
27. Scully, *Pueblo*, p. 289.
28. Waters and Fredericks, *The Book of the Hopi*, pp. 43-44.
29. Thybony, *Canyon de Chelly National Monumen*, pp. 9-10.
30. Ferguson and Rohn, *Anasazi Ruins of the Southwest*, pp. 176-178.
31. Schaaf, *Ancient Ancestors of the Southwest*, p. 43.
32. Morgan, *Ancient Architecture of the Southwest*, pp. 136-137.
33. Ferguson and Rohn, *Anasazi Ruins of the Southwest*, pp. 184-185.
34. Mays, *Ancient Cities of the Southwest*, pp. 45-46.
35. Noble, *Ancient Ruins of the Southwest*, p. 101.
36. Anderson, "Wupatki National Monument: Exploring into Prehistory," *Wupatki and Walnut Canyon*, p. 13.
37. Houk, *Sinagua*, p. 8.
38. Lister and Lister, *Those Who Came Before*, pp. 217-219.
39. Folsom and Folsom, *Ancient Treasures of the Southwest*, pp. 42-43.
40. "A Game With the Gods: Ancient Ballcourts of the Southwest" (video), Echo Productions, Flagstaff, Arizona, 1997.
41. Downum, *The Sinagua*, p. 22.
42. Barnes, *Arizona Place Names*, p. 496.
43. Seaman, *Hopi Dictionary*, p. 54.
44. Bradfield, *An Interpretation of Hopi Culture*, p. 244.
45. Morgan, *Ancient Architecture of the Southwest*, p. 137.
46. Oppelt, *Guide to Prehistoric Ruins of the Southwest*, p. 102 and p. 104.
47. Morgan, *Ancient Architecture of the Southwest*, pp. 137-138.
48. Ferguson and Rohn, *Anasazi Ruins of the Southwest*, pp. 242-246.
49. Reid and Whittlesey, *The Archaeology of Ancient Arizona*, p. 220.
50. Courlander, *The Fourth World of the Hopis*, p. 77.
51. Schaaf, *Ancient Ancestors of the Southwest*, p. 45.
52. Thybony, *A Guide to Sunset Crater and Wupatki*, p. 32.
53. Ibid., p. 26 and p. 29.
54. Ferguson and Rohn, *Anasazi Ruins of the Southwest*, p. 246.
55. Houk, *Sinagua*, p. 2.
56. Morgan, *Ancient Architecture of the Southwest*, p. 138.
57. Sartor, "Meteorological Investigation of the Wupatki Blowhole System," *Plateau*, p. 26.
58. Nequatewa, *Truth of a Hopi*, pp. 103-104.
59. Ferguson and Rohn, *Anasazi Ruins of the Southwest*, p. 246.
60. Thybony, *A Guide to Sunset Crater and Wupatki*, p. 41.
61. Oppelt, *Guide to Prehistoric Ruins of the Southwest*, p. 101.
62. Allen, *Star Names*, p. 313.
63. Burnham, *Burnham's Celestial Handbook*, p. 1301-1302.
64. Scully, *Pueblo*, p. 302.
65. Titiev, *Old Oraib*, p. 123.
66. Fewkes, *Hopi Katcinas*, p. 53.
67. Wright, *Hopi Kachinas*, p. 56.
68. Secakuku, *Following the Sun and Moon*, p. 22.
69. Reid and Whittlesey, *The Archaeology of Ancient Arizona*, p. 200.
70. This first pueblo at Homol'ovi was begun about the same time as the construction at Betatakin, located nearly due north. In fact, Oraibi is the same exact distance on this north-south line from both Betatakin and Homol'ovi.
71. Walker, *Homol'ovi*, pp. 15-30.
72. It is a common misconception that the Spanish introduced adobe construction to the New World.
73. Allen, *Star Names*, pp. 310-311.

74. Burnham, *Burnham's Celestial Handbook*, p. 1281, pp. 1289-1292.
75. Courlander, *The Fourth World of the Hopis*, p. 72.
76. Byrkit, *The Palatkwapi Trail*, pp. 4-8.
77. Mays, *Ancient Cities of the Southwest*, p. 51.
78. Morgan, *Ancient Architecture of the Southwest*, p. 133.
79. Ferguson and Rohn, *Anasazi Ruins of the Southwest*, pp. 171-172.
80. Schaaf, *Ancient Ancestors of the Southwest*, p. 46.
81. Reid and Whittlesey, *The Archaeology of Ancient Arizona*, p. 196.
82. Calvin, *How the Shaman Stole the Moon*, p. 105.
83. Ibid., pp. 118-119.
84. Burnham, *Burnham's Celestial Handbook*, pp. 1299-1300.
85. Scully, *Pueblo*, p. 24, p. 26, and p. 30.
86. James, *Pages From Hopi History*, p. 27.
87. Stephen cited in Patterson, *A Field Guide to Rock Art Symbols of the Greater Southwest*, p. 108.
88. Waters and Fredericks, *Book of the Hopi*, p. 44.
89. Schaafsma, *Indian Rock Art of the Southwest*, p. 148.

## Chapter 5: Windows Onto the Cosmos

1. McCoy, *Archaeoastronomy*, p. 3.
2. Mitton, *The Penguin Dictionary of Astronomy*, p. 99.
3. Zeta Tauri, an extension of Aldebaran serving as one of the horns of the constellation, could certainly be perceived as the symmetrical focus of this region of the sky. Not only does the line from Aldebaran connect to it, but also the "chakra line," the right hand of Orion, and the left foot of Castor in Gemini all appear to center upon the place where the supernova exploded.
4. Allen, *Star Names*, p. 391.
5. Brandt, *Archaeoastronomy in Pre-Columbian America*, p. 46.
6. Williamson, *Living the Sky*, pp. 182-184.
7. Richard C. Hoagland contends that because the supernova event did not fit into the perfect symmetry of medieval cosmology, observers simply refused to countenance what their senses were telling them. Hoagland, *The Monuments of Mars*, p. 91.
8. Barnes, *Canyon Country Prehistoric Rock Art*, p. 298.
9. Patterson, *A Field Guide to Rock Art Symbols of the Greater Southwest*, p. 108.
10. Malotki, editor, *Hopi Dictionary.*
11. Williamson, *Living the Sky*, p. 86.
12. Patterson, *A Field Guide to Rock Art Symbols*, p. 66.
13. Miller, "Two Possible Astronomical Pictographs Found In Northern Arizona," *Plateau*, pp. 11-12.
14. Krupp, "Engraved in Stone," *Sky & Telescope*, April 1995, p. 61.
15. Brandt and Williamson, *Native American Astronomy*, pp. 171-177.
16. Brandt, *Archaeoastronomy in Pre-Columbian America*, pp. 50-53.
17. Cunkle and Jacquemain, *Stone Magic of the Ancients*, p. 99.
18. Brandt, "Pictographs and Petroglyphs of the Southwest Indians," *Astronomy of the Ancients*, p. 31.
19. Page and Page, *Hopi*, pp. 156-157.
20. Waters and Fredericks, *The Book of the Hopi*, p. 39.
21. Courlander, *The Fourth World of the Hopis*, p. 56.
22. Ibid., p. 39.
23. Ibid., p. 72.
24. Mails, *The Hopi Survival Kit*, p. 153.
25. Ley, *Watchers of the Skies*, pp. 149-150.
26. Patterson, *A Field Guide to Rock Art Symbols,* p. 65.

27. Schaaf, *Ancient Ancestors of the Southwest*, p. 57.
28. Thybony, *A Guide to Sunset Crater and Wupatki*, p. 16.
29. Malotki, *Earth Fire*, pp. 1-13.
30. Courlander, *The Fourth World of the Hopis*, pp.133-138.
31. Malotki, *Earth Fire*, pp. 65-84.
32. Essay by Peter Piles in Malotki, *Earth Fire*, pp. 112-113.
33. Reid and Whittlesey, *The Archaeology of Ancient Arizona*, pp. 217-218.
34. Dan Katchongva, Danaqyumtewa, trans., Thomas Francis, ed. "From the Beginning of Life to the Day of Purification: Teachings, History & Prophecies of the Hopi People" [online]. The Hopi Information Network, 1996; available from World Wide Web: <http://www.InfoMagic.COM/~abyte/hopi/messages/katch1.html>; accessed 26 June 1998; originally published by the Committee for Traditional Indian Land and Life, Los Angeles, 1972, p. 5.
35. Mails and Evehema, *Hotevilla*, p. 24-25.
36. Waters and Fredericks, *Book of the Hopi*, pp. 30-33.
37. Kaiser, *The Voice of the Great Spirit*, p 55.
38. Titiev, *Old Oraibi*, pp. 60-61.
39. Stephen, *Hopi Journal*, p. 390.
40. Ibid., pp. 1032-1033.
41. Patterson, *A Field Guide to Rock Art Symbols*, p. 205.
42. McCluskey, "Historical Archaeoastronomy: The Hopi Example," *Archaeoastronomy in the New World*. In Chapter 2 we noted that the northwest was symbolized by a mountain lion instead of a deer and the southwest by a bear instead of a mountain sheep. This variance is the result of more than one animal representing a particular direction.
43. Waters and Fredericks, *Book of the Hopi*, p. 32.d
44. Williamson, *Living the Sky*, p. 92.
45. Cunkle and Jacquemain, *Stone Magic of the Ancients*, p. 164.
46. Schaafsma, "Rock Art at Wupatki—Pots, Textile, Glyphs," *Wupatki and Walnut Canyon*, p. 22.
47. Waters and Fredericks, *Book of the Hopi*, p. 104.
48. Nancy Olsen cited in Cole, *Katsina Iconography in Homol'ovi Rock Art, Central Little Colorado River Valley, Arizona*, p. 105.
49. Stephen cited in Patterson, *Hopi Pottery Symbols*, p. 28.
50. Waters and Fredericks, *Book of the Hopi,* p. 113.
51. McCreery and Malotki, *Tapamveni*, p. 16.
52. Cunkle and Jacquemain, *Stone Magic of the Ancients*, p. 151.
53. Patterson, *Rock Art Symbols*, p. 158.
54. Haney, *Skyglobe 2.04 for Windows*.
55. Bradfield, *An Interpretation of Hopi Culture*, p. 275.
56. Malotki, *Hopi Dictionary*.
57. Waters and Fredericks, *Book of the Hopi*, p. 150.
58. McCluskey, "Historical Archaeoastronomy: The Hopi Example,"*Archaeoastronomy In the New World*.
59. Malotki, *Hopi Dictionary*.
60. Ibid.
61. Waters and Fredericks, *Book of the Hopi*, p. 149-150.
62. Mitton, *The Penguin Dictionary of Astronomy*, p. 61.
63. Santillana and Deschend, *Hamlet's Mill*, p. 2.
64. Ibid., p. 148.
65. Ibid., p. 239.
66. Ibid., p. 140.
67. Ibid., p. 213.
68. Sturluson, *The Prose Edda*, p. 32, p. 43.
69. Santillana and Dechend, *Hamlet's Mill*, p. 210.

70. Ibid., p. 306.

71. Bradfield, *An Interpretation of Hopi Culture*, p. 391.

72. For example, Crichton E M Miller in his recent book *The Golden Thread of Time: A Quest for the Truth and Hidden Knowledge of the Ancients* (Rugby, Warwickshire, United Kingdom: Pendulum Publishing, 2001); <http://www.crichtonmiller.com>. Also in the same volume, see Gary A. David's original overview essay "The Orion Zone: Ancient Star Cities of the American Southwest."

73. Santillana and Dechend, *Hamlet's Mill*, p. 242.

74. Prabhavananda and Manchester, *The Upanishads*, p. 36.

75. Gilbert, *Signs in the Sky*, pp. 202-205.

76. Ibid., p. 209.

77. Plog, *Ancient Peoples of the American Southwest*, p. 117.

# Chapter 6: The Architecture of Existence

1. Hall, *West of the Thirties*, p. 71.

2. Derived from Hindu and Tibetan mysticism, a *chakra* (which literally means "wheel") is one of seven psychic energy centers within the body. Arranged vertically along the spinal column, each chakra activates a specific psychophysical domain.

3. Bruyere, *Wheels of Light: A Study of Chakras*, Vol. I, p. 44.

4. Loftin, *Religion and Hopi Life In the Twentieth Century*, pp. xv-xvi.

5. a. Noble, *Ancient Ruins of the Southwest*, p. 153. b. Oppelt, *Guide to Prehistoric Ruins of the Southwest*, p. 96. c. Lister and Lister, *Those Who Came Before*, p. 214.

6. Bremer, *Walnut Canyon*, p. 69.

7. Ibid., p. 105.

8. Baldwin and Bremer, *Walnut Canyon National Monument*, p. 157.

9. Ibid., p. 113.

10. Thybony, *Walnut Canyon National Monument*, p. 11.

11. Baldwin and Bremer, *Walnut Canyon National Monument*, p. 158.

12. Pilles, "The Sinagua: Ancient People of the Flagstaff Region," *Wupatki and Walnut Canyon*.

13. Baldwin and Bremer, *Walnut Canyon National Monument*, p. 157.

14. Burnham, *Burnham's Celestial Handbook*, Vol. 2, p. 1308.

15. Allen, *Star Names*, p. 318.

16. Located three miles east of Elden Pueblo and built at about the same time and in the same style, the related Turkey Hill Pueblo contained over thirty rooms and one rectangular underground kiva.

a. Oppelt, *Guide to Prehistoric Ruins*, p. 100.

b. MacGregor, *Southwestern Archaeology*, p. 329.

17. a. Noble, *Ancient Ruins of the Southwest*, p. 147. b. Oppelt, *Guide to Prehistoric Ruins*, p. 100. c. Morgan, *Ancient Architecture of the Southwest*, p. 129.

18. Malotki and Lomatuway'ma, *Stories of Maasaw, A Hopi God*, p. 289.

19. Waters and Fredericks, *The Book of the Hopi*, p. 202.

20. Allen, *Star Names*, p. 318.

21. The spring of the southwest is located in the San Francisco Peaks; the spring of the northwest is at Betatakin; the spring of the southeast is near the town of Springerville; the spring of the northeast is located near the village of Piñon on Black Mesa. Geertz and Lomatuway'ma, *Children of the Cottonwood*, p. 78. However, the spring of the northeast known as Kiisiwu is thought to be a shrine symbolic of a spring found farther northeast at Spruce Tree House in the major Anasazi settlement of Mesa Verde in southwestern Colorado. Waters and Fredericks, *Book of the Hopi*, p. 49.

22. Johari, *Chakras*, p. 89.

23. Feuerstein, *Tantra*, pp. 150-151.

24. Fewkes, "Two Ruins Recently Discovered In the Red Rock Country, Arizona," *The*

*American Anthropologist*, p. 266.

25. Courlander, *The Fourth World of the Hopis*, p. 210.

26. One of the dangers of the seventh chakra: When a person reaches *samadhi*, or ecstatic release, the physical body begins to atrophy on this "plane of laziness." Johari, *Chakras*, p. 89.

27. Designated by another Anglo misnomer, Montezuma Well is a limestone sinkhole 470 feet across and fifty-five feet deep. It fills with warm spring water at the rate of one-and-a-half million gallons per day. The outlet beneath the well which empties into Beaver Creek allows the healing waters heated to a temperature of seventy-five degrees to flow at a rate of 1,000 gallons per minute past a single, huge Arizona sycamore hundreds of years old. Leading from the well is a mile-long irrigation canal dug to an average depth of three feet. A few masonry rooms are nestled along the inner wall of the blue-green well, while two small pueblos of eleven and seventeen rooms each are located near the rim. One large community room of about two hundred square feet provided space for ceremonial activities for the estimated 150-200 people who lived at or near the well. a. Hodge, *Ruins Along the River*, p. 21-26. b. Lamb, *Montezuma Castle National Monument*, p. 10.

28. a. Houk, *Sinagua,* p. 12-13; Lister and Lister, *Those Who Came Before*, p. 174. b. Buddy Mays, *Ancient Cities of the Southwest*, p. 43. c. Morgan, *Ancient Architecture of the Southwest*, pp. 130-131. d. Noble, *Ancient Ruins of the Southwest*, pp. 155-157. e. Reid and Whittlesey, *The Archaeology of Ancient Arizona*, p. 225.

29. Barlow, *Sacred Sites of the West*, p. 22.

30. Located in Loy Canyon of Prescott National Forest, Palatki and Honanki must have been incredibly gorgeous places to live. Inhabited circa A.D. 1150 to 1300, Palatki, or "Red House," was a two-story pueblo 120 feet long with at least seven ground floor rooms in a single row with a bow-shaped front wall built at the base of towering red cliffs. Not far from the ruin is located probably the largest group of pictographs in the Verde Valley. Spanning three thousand years of human habitation from the Archaic Period to historic times, this rock art arranged in a number of alcoves was executed in a variety of colors, including white (kaolin), red (hematite), black (charcoal) and occasionally yellow (limonite). The subjects include sun shields, a star chart showing the Milky Way, and a few tall, ghostly figures similar to those found in Utah's Barrier Canyon. Located about four miles from Palatki is Honanki, or "Bear House." Constructed as well on a talus slope, this somewhat larger ruin rose two or perhaps three stories and contained a total of thirty ground floor rooms. Oppelt, *Guide to Prehistoric Ruins*, p. 90.

31. Burnham, *Burnham's Celestial Handbook*, p. 1828 and p. 1830.

32. Morgan, *Ancient Architecture of the Southwest*, p. 130.

33. Schroeder and Hastings, *Montezuma Castle*, p. 13.

34. Houk, *Sinagua*, p. 14.

35. Hodge, *Ruins Along the River*, p. 34.

36. Houk, *Tuzigoot National Monument*, p. 6.

37. For a brief description of both the major and the minor Hisatsinom/Hopi sites located along the chakra line, consult Chapter 2.

38. Fell, *Bronze Age America*, p. 261.

39. Michell, *The New View Over Atlantis*, p. 37.

40. Ibid., p. 73.

41. Ibid., p. 74.

42. Michael was the warrior of God; Gabriel the messenger of God; Raphael the helper of God; and Uriel the fire of God. These correspond to the elements of earth, air, water, and fire respectively.

43. Caesar, *The Conquest of Gaul*, , p. 33.

44. *Encyclopaedia Britannica*, 15th ed. (Chicago: Encyclopaedia Britannica, Inc., 1979), Vol. I, p. 486.

45. Lamb, *Montezuma Castle National Monument*, p. 13.

46. Peter J. Pilles, Jr., "The Southern Sinagua," *People of the Verde Valley*, p. 11.
47. Morgan, *Ancient Architecture of the Southwest*, p. 131.
48. Schroeder and Hastings, *Montezuma Castle*, pp. 25-26.
49. Pilles, *People of the Verde Valley*, p. 14.
50. This Bald Mountain is different than the location of the historic heliograph station, now known as Glassford Hill in Prescott Valley.
51. Pilles, *People of the Verde Valley*, p. 14.
52. Courlander, *The Fourth World of the Hopis*, pp. 65-66.
53. Wilcox, Robertson, and Wood, "Perry Mesa, A 14th Century Gated Community in Central Arizona," *Plateau Journal*, pp. 45-61.
54. cf. Christy Turner, *Man Corn: Cannibalism and Violence in the Prehistoric Southwest*; Steven A. LeBlanc, *Prehistoric Warfare in the American Southwest*.
55. Reid and Whittlesey, *The Archaeology of Ancient Arizona*, pp. 223-224 and p. 227.
56. Muir, "The Grand Cañon of the Colorado," *Writing the Western Landscape*, p. 94 and p. 100.
57. Duus, *The Tragic, Sacred Ground*, p. 20.
58. Noble, *Ancient Ruins of the Southwest*, pp. 97-98.
59. Reid and Whittlesey, *The Archaeology of Ancient Arizona*, pp. 191-192.
60. Smith, *When Is a Kiva and Other Questions About Southwestern Archaeology*, pp. 65-66.
61. Ferguson and Rohn, *Anasazi Ruins of the Southwest*, p. 185.
62. Located among the colorful formations of the Painted Desert, Puerco Ruin was a two-story pueblo of over one hundred rooms and several kivas. It was built in the mid-thirteenth century around the time that Tusayan to the northwest was abandoned. In the vicinity of the pueblo is a bonanza of petroglyphs, including more than a dozen solar-aligned solstice markers and the so-called Newspaper Rock, a huge boulder densely carved with perhaps a thousand images. Ekkehart Malotki has suggested that the Hopi deemed this central drainage system of the Little Colorado River *Palavayu*, a term meaning "red river." a. McCreery and Malotki, *Tapamveni*, p. 2. b. Ash, *Petrified Forest*, pp. 36-39.
63. Murdin, Allen, and Malin, *Catalogue of the Universe*, p. 84.
64. Mitton, *The Penguin Dictionary of Astronomy*, p. 369.
65. Ibid., pp. 354-356.
66. Burnham, *Burnham's Celestial Handbook*, p. 1309.
67. Todd Henry, "Target Star Selection" [online] The SETI Institute, 1994; available from World Wide Web: <http://www.seti-inst.edu/phoenix/target-selection.html>, p. 1.; accessed 3 September 1999.
68. personal e-mail communication with the author, 29 August 2002.
69. a. Oppelt, *Guide to Prehistoric Ruins of the Southwest*, pp. 44-46. b. Noble, *Ancient Ruins of the Southwest*, pp. 201-203.
70. "The Aztec Recovery 1948" [online]. Aztec UFO Web Site; available from the World Wide Web: <http://www.aztecufo.com/crash.htm>; accessed 10 November 2004.
71. Folsom and Folsom, *Ancient Treasures of the Southwest*, p. 23.
72. Jones and Euler, *A Sketch of Grand Canyon Prehistory*, pp. 1-3.
73. Circa 1800 B.C.—a few centuries after the precessional Age of Taurus had shifted to the Age of Aries (the latter possibly related to the Hopi Two Horn Society). During this period Egypt was at the end of the Middle Kingdom and Britain was experiencing the final stages of construction at Stonehenge. At the same time Mesoamerica saw the rise of the Olmec culture, which invented the dot-and-bar calendrical system of notation later inherited by the Maya. The Olmecs, we recall, are best known for a number of monumental multi-ton, helmeted heads sculpted from basalt showing decidedly Negroid facial features.
74. Schaafsma, "Shamans' Gallery: A Grand Canyon Rock Art Site," *Kiva*, pp. 213-234.

## Chapter 7: A Rainbow Fading Into the Chasm of Night

1. Senior, *Smoke Upon the Winds*, p. 31.
2. Titiev, *Old Oraibi*, p. 128.
3. Waters and Fredericks, *Book of the Hopi*, p. 200. In the year 2000 the present author witnessed a Niman dance in the village of Hotevilla on July 29th—very late indeed.
4. Gabriel, *Roads to Center Place*, p. 161.
5. Titiev, *Old Oraibi*, pp. 140-141.
6. In terms of sidereal significance, July 11th, a possible date for the conclusion of the Niman ceremony, is the time when Orion achieves its complete heliacal rising one hour before sunrise, with the right leg or foot of the constellation (Saiph) just touching the horizon.
7. Stephen, *Hopi Journal*, p. 216.
8. Only men are allowed to participate in *katsina* dances, even when female *katsinam* are being impersonated.
9. Fewkes, *Tusayan Katcinas and Hopi Altars*, p. 263.
10. Fergusson, *Dancing Gods*, p. 120.
11. Titiev, *Old Oraibi*, p. 129.
12. e.g., Barton Wright, *Hopi Kachinas: The Complete Guide to Collecting Kachina Dolls*; Alph H. Secakuku, *Following the Sun and Moon: Hopi Kachina Tradition*.
13. Colton, *Hopi Kachina Dolls with a Key to their Identification*, pp. 5-6.
14. Wright, *Hopi Kachinas*, p. 2.
15. Fewkes, *Tusayan Katcinas*, p. 265.
16. Dockstader, *The Kachina and the White Man*, p. 9.
17. Mindeleff, *A Study of Pueblo Architecture in Tusayan and Cibola*, p. 136.
18. Geertz and Lomatuway'ma, *Children of the Cottonwood*, p. 64.
19. Adams, *The Origin and Development of the Pueblo Katsina Cult*, p. 4.
20. Talayesva, *Sun Chief*, p. 86.
21. Parsons, *Pueblo Indian Religion*, Vol. 1, p. 175.
22. Adams, *Origin and Development of the Pueblo Katsina Cult*, p. 15.
23. For instance, the paucity of petroglyphic or ceramic evidence of *katsina* icons below the Mogollon Rim (Adams, *Origin and Development of the Pueblo Katsina Cult*, p. 77) suggests that the phenomenon was restricted in Arizona to the body of the terrestrial Orion, though some activity occurred in the Mimbres area of the east-central part of the state.
24. Adams, *Origin and Development of the Pueblo Katsina Cult*, p. 22.
25. Ibid., p. 25.
26. Cole, *Katsina Iconography in Homol'ovi Rock Art, Central Little Colorado River Valley, Arizona*, p. 151.
27. Ibid., p. 152.
28. Malotki and Lomatuway'ma, *Earth Fire*, p. 58 and p. 61.
29. Hieb, "The Meaning of *Katsina*: Toward a Cultural Definition of 'Person' in Hopi Religion, *Kachinas in the Pueblo World*, p. 31.
30. Malotki, *Hopi Dictionary.*.
31. Farmer, "Iconographic Evidence of Basketmaker Warfare and Human Sacrifice: A Contextual Approach to Early Anasazi Art," *Kiva*, p. 404.
32. Wright, *Hopi Kachinas*, p. 30.
33. Wright, *Kachinas: a Hopi Artist's Documentary*, p. 13.
34. Colton, *Hopi Kachina Dolls*, pp. 21-22.
35. Ibid., p. 22.
36. Secakuku, *Following the Sun and Moon*, p. 6.
37. Stephen, *Hopi Journal*, p. 165.
38. a. Colton, *Hopi Kachina Dolls*, p. 20.  b. Fewkes, *Hopi Katchinas*, pp. 67-68.
39. Ibid, p. 122.

40. Fewkes, "Sky-God Personifications in Hopi Worship, " *Journal of American Folk-lore*, p. 31.
41. Ibid., p. 24.
42. Tyler, *Pueblo Gods and Myths*, p. 99.
43. Secakuku, *Following the Sun and Moon*, p. 20.
44. Colton, *Hopi Kachina Dolls*, p. 78.
45. Fewkes, *Hopi Katchinas*, p. 120.
46. Fewkes, "Sky-God Personifications in Hopi Worship," *Journal of American Folk-lore*, p. 30.
47. Geertz and Lomatuway'ma, *Children of Cottonwood*, pp. 63-64.
48. a. Wright, *Kachinas*, p. 125. b. Colton, *Hopi Kachina Dolls*, 54.
49. Wright, *Kachinas*, p. 125.
50. Fewkes, *Hopi Katchinas*, p. 89.
51. Colton, *Hopi Kachina Dolls*, p. 55.
52. Chamberlain, *When Stars Came Down to Earth*, p. 109.
53. Hibben, *Kiva Art of the Anasazi at Pottery Mound*, p. 134.
54. Oppelt, *Guide to Prehistoric Ruins of the Southwest*, pp. 46-47.
55. Geertz and Lomatuway'ma, *Children of the Cottonwood*, p. 64.
56. Paula O'Keefe, "Leviathan Chained: The Legend of the Nephilim and the Cthulhu Mythos" [online]. Fields of the Nephilim, 1999; available from the World Wide Web: <http://www.spookhouse.net/angelynx/nephilim/tiamat.html>, p. 1; accessed 1 September, 2001.
57. Laurence, *The Book of Enoch the Prophet*, p. 150.
58. Voth, *The Traditions of the Hopi*, p. 72.
59. Laurence, *The Book of Enoch the Prophet*, pp. 7-8.
60. O'Keefe, "Leviathan Chained," p. 2.
61. Sitchin, *The Lost Realms*, p. 40.
62. "The Book of Jubilees" [online]. Bible 2000, The Forgotten Books of Eden; available from the World Wide Web: <http://www.bible2000.org/lostbooks/jubilees.htm>; accessed 1 September 2001.
63. Yava, *Big Snow Falling*, p. 97.
64. Adler, *The Prehistoric Pueblo World, A.D. 1150-1350*, p. 259.
65. Bradfield, *An Interpretation of Hopi Culture*, p. 207.
66. Geertz and Lomatuway'ma, *Children of the Cottonwood*, p. 102.
67. Mitton, *The Penguin Dictionary of Astronomy*, pp. 284-285.
68. Zeilik, *Astronomy*, p. 276.
69. Burnham, *Burnham's Celestial Handbook*, Vol. 2, p. 1317.
70. Mitton, *The Penguin Dictionary of Astronomy*, p. 284.
71. Burnham, *Burnham's Celestial Handbook*, p. 1306.

## Chapter 8: If We Could See With Eyes Made of Dust

1. Saner, *Reaching Keet Seel*, p. 32.
2. Lopez, "Searching for Ancestors," *Crossing Open Ground*.
3. Schaaf, *Ancient Ancestors of the Southwest*, p. 39.
4. Waters and Fredericks, *Book of the Hopi*, p. 139.
5. Malotki and Lomatuway'ma, *Stories of Maasaw, A Hopi God*, p. 303 and p. 305.
6. Geertz and Lomatuway'ma, *Children of Cottonwood*, p. 138 n. 81 and p. 149 n. 4.
7. Fewkes, "The New-Fire Ceremony At Walpi," *American Anthropologist*, pp. 135-136.
8. Staal, *The New Patterns in the Sky*, p. 76.
9. Allen, *Star Names*, pp. 387-388.
10. Howard A. Sheldon, "Grand Canyon Caverns: One of Arizona's Natural Wonders," Reel-One.com [online]; available from the World Wide Web, <http://www.reel-one.com/gccaverns.html>; accessed 1 January 2002.

11. David Whitehouse, "Ice Age star map discovered," 9 August 2000, BBC News, [online]; available from the World Wide Web, <http://news.bbc.co.uk/hi/english/sci/tech/newsid_871000/871930.stm>; accessed 5 January 2002.

12. Stephen, *Hopi Journal*, p. 860.

13. One Egyptian connection to Aldebaran surprisingly contains all the elements of the Hopi *mongko*: "In the Egyptian zodiacs of the late period, such as the rectangular one in Denderah, Aldebaran seems to be identified with the Egyptian god Anhur. Crowned with the double plume, he is seen holding erect a rigid snake, which is not unlike a caduceus, the Greek symbol for a herald, but may have an unsuspected phallic meaning." Fagan, *Astrological Origins*, p. 31. Hence, in this Egyptian manifestation are bird, snake, and phallic motifs, as well as the dualistic feather, which could be construed as V-shaped (also concordant with the snake's bifurcated tongue?). The name of the god Anhur means "he who leads what has gone away," (perhaps referring both to spirits and to zodiacal constellations which have departed for the Underworld) but is also translated as "sky-bearer." *New Larousse Encyclopedia of Mythology*, pp. 13-14. His aspect as leader also confirms Fagan's contention that Taurus was the fiducial point of the vernal equinox in April of 4152 B.C. when the astrological Age of Taurus began. Fagan, *Astrological Origins*, p. 23. Known as "the Saviour" or the "Good Warrior," Anhur is sometimes depicted holding a cord that leads to the sun (the ecliptic?).

14. Martineau, *The Rocks Begin To Speak*, p. 112.

15. Patterson, *Hopi Pottery Symbols*, p. 136.

16. Stephen, *Hopi Journal*, p. 860.

17. Mallery, *Picture-Writing of the American Indians*, p. 662.

18. Eggan, "The Hopi Cosmology or World-View," *Kachinas in the Pueblo World*, p. 15.

19. Titiev, *Old Oraibi*, p. 64.

20. Hewett, *Ancient Life in the American Southwest*, p. 292.

21. Ferguson and Rohn, *Anasazi Ruins of the Southwest*, p. 194.

22. Mails, *The Pueblo Children of the Earth Mother*, Vol. I, p. 190.

23. Cordell, *Prehistory of the Southwest*, p. 248.

24. Frazier, *People of Chaco*, pp. 179-180.

25. Ibid., p. 65.

26. Ibid., p. 69.

27. Anderson and Anderson, *Chaco Canyon*, unpaginated.

28. Ferguson and Rohn, *Anasazi Ruins*, p. 198.

29. *Kin Ya'a*: Diné for "House in the Sky," which included a four-story tower kiva. Another outlier to the south is Casmero (end-noted in Chapter 2).

30. Gabriel, *Roads to Center Place*, p. 131.

31. Schaaf, *Ancient Ancestors*, p. 57.

32. Ferguson and Rohn, *Anasazi Ruins of the Southwest*, p. 194 and p. 196.

33. Anderson and Anderson, *Chaco Canyon*, unpaginated.

34. Frazier, *People of Chaco*, pp. 153-159.

35. Anderson and Anderson, *Chaco Canyon*, unpaginated.

36. Stein and Lekson, "Anasazi Ritual Landscapes," *Chaco Canyon*.

37. Marshall, "The Chacoan Roads: A Cosmological Interpretation," *Anasazi Architecture and American Design*, p. 62.

38. Ibid., pp. 70-71.

39. Gabriel, *Roads to Center Place*, p. 114.

40. In addition to the longitudinal importance of Paquimé, another "coincidence" puts this ancient village on the same latitude as the Great Pyramid on the Giza Plateau in Egypt, i.e., 30 degrees. "The 30th parallel north appears to have been of particular —'sacred'— significance. Holy cities from antiquity on, from Egypt to Tibet, have been located on it." Sitchin, *The Wars of Gods and Men*, p. 135.

41. Lekson, *The Chaco Meridian*, p. 48.

42. Ibid., p. 50.
43. Ibid., p. 169.
44. Eddy, "Astronomical Alignment of the Big Horn Medicine Wheel," *Science*, pp. 1035-1043.
45. Allen, *Star Names*, pp. 117-129.
46. Hancock, *Fingerprints of the Gods*, p. 376.
47. Staal, *The New Patterns in the Sky*, pp. 86-88.
48. Allen, *Star Names*, pp. 122-123.
49. Santillana and Dechend, *Hamlet's Mill*, p. 357.
50. For a thorough discussion of the Anunnaki, consult the voluminous works of Zecharia Sitchin. Most scholars regard this sidereal point to be Sirius. Temple, *The Sirius Mystery*, p. 94.
51. Allen, *Star Names*, pp. 117-129.
52. Staal, *The New Patterns in the Sky*, p. 88.
53. Burnham, *Burnham's Celestial Handbook*, Vol. 2, p. 389, p. 395.
54. Temple, *The Sirius Mystery*, pp. 207-210.
55. Malotki, *Hopi Dictionary.*
56. Goodman, *Lakota Star Knowledge*, p. 39.
57. Weltfish, *The Lost Universe*, p. 328.
58. Chamberlain, *When the Stars Came Down to Earth*, p. 252.
59. Ibid., p. 128.
60. Waters and Fredericks, *Book of the Hopi*, p. 150.
61. Wolf, *Sons of the Shaking Earth*, p. 119.
62. Séjourné, *Burning Water*, p. 18.
63. Waters, *Mexico Mystique*, p. 62.
64. Bernal, *Mexico Before Cortez*, p. 84.
65. Ibid., p. 61, p. 66.
66. Westheim, *The Art of Ancient Mexico*, p. 104.
67. Leonard, *Ancient America*, p. 62.
68. Westheim, *The Art of Ancient Mexico*, pp. 16-17.
69. Bernal, *Mexico Before Cortez*, p. 77.
70. Ibid., p. 81.
71. Waters, *Mexico Mystique*, p. 62.
72. Malotki, *Hopi Dictionary.*
73. Lister and Lister, *Those Who Came Before*, pp. 125-126.
74. Stephen, *Hopi Journal*, p. 1221.
75. Malotki, *Hopi Dictionary.*
76. Titiev, *Old Oraibi*, p. 53.
77. Bradfield, *An Interpretation of Hopi Culture*, p. 289.
78. Ibid., p. 268.
79. Courlander, *The Fourth World of the Hopis*, p. 238.
80. Bradfield, *An Interpretation of Hopi Culture*, p. 259.
81. Waters and Fredericks, *Book of the Hopi*, p. 90.
82. Kaiser, *The Voice of the Great Spirit*, p. 41.
83. Courlander, *The Fourth World of the Hops*, p. 37.
84. Adams, *The Origin and Development of the Pueblo Katsina Cult*, p. 72.
85. For a full account, see Harry C. James, *Pages From Hopi History*, pp. 61-64.
86. Bradfield, *An Interpretation of Hopi Culture*, p. 266.
87. Waters and Fredericks, *Book of the Hopi*, p. 244.
88. Stephen, *Hopi Journal*, p. 1007.
89. Lomatuway'ma, Lomatuway'ma, and Namingha, *Hopi Ruin Legends*, p. 157.
90. Grant, *Canyon de Chelly*, p. 196, p. 247.
91. Turner and Turner, *Man Corn*, p. 484.
92. Silko, *Storyteller*, p. 131.

93. It is interesting to note that the winner of this "contest" was a conjurer who simply had a story about the coming of the White Man, the telling of which actually made it come to pass with all its genocidal consequences for the Indian. Paradoxically, this imputes to the likes of Turner and other representatives of the scientific, materialist culture that invaded this continent a lower moral standard than that of the cannibals whose victims' bones he analyses.
94. Gabriel, *Roads to Center Place*, pp. 266-267.
95. McPherson, *Sacred Land, Sacred View*, p. 87.
96. Roberts, *In Search of the Old Ones*, p. 216.
97. Gabriel, *Roads to Center Place*, pp. 94-95.
98. Anna Sofaer, "The Primary Architecture of the Chacoan Culture: A Cosmological Expression," *Anasazi Architecture and American Design*, pp. 88-132.
99. Whiting, "Hopi Kachinas," *Plateau*, p. 2.
100. Schaafsma, *Indian Rock Art of the Southwest*, p. 237.
101. Whitley, *A Guide to Rock Art in Southern California and Southern Nevada*, pp. 128-132.
102. Ibid., pp. 49-52.
103. Heizer and Clewlow, *Prehistoric Rock Art of California*, Vol. 1, p. 21.
104. Whitley, *A Guide to Rock Art*, p. 50.
105. Ibid., p. 49.
106. Ibid., p. 9.
107. Hunt, *Death Valley*, p. 173.
108. Whitley, *A Guide to Rock Art*, p. 85.
109. Cunkle and Jacquemain, *Stone Magic of the Ancients*, p. 111.
110. Bradfield, *An Interpretation of Hopi Culture*, pp. 390-391.
111. Wright, *Hopi Kachinas*, p. 102.
112. Budge, *Egyptian Language*, p. 60, p. 63.
113. *New Larousse Encyclopedia of Mythology*, pp. 29-32.
114. Budge, *Osiris & the Egyptian Resurrection*, Vol. I, p. 374.
115. Lee, *Death Valley Men*, p. 302.
116. Mike Weeks, "Ancient Civilization Beneath Death Valley?", Unknown Histories: Archaeological Anomalies of North America [online]; available from the World Wide Web, <http://www.geocities.com/TheTropics/Lagoon/1345/valley.html>; accessed 11 November, 2001.

## Chapter 9: To Calibrate the March of Time

1. Malmström, *Cycles of the Sun, Mysteries of the Moon*, p. 10.
2. Coe, *The Maya*, p. 107.
3. Freidel, Schele, and Parker, *Maya Cosmos*, pp. 76-77.
4. Stephens, *Incidents of Travel in Yucatan*, p. 63 and p. 64.
5. Bradfield, "Rock-cut Cisterns and Pollen 'Rain' in the Vicinity of Old Oraibi, Arizona," *Plateau*, p. 68.
6. Men, *Secrets of Mayan Science/Religion*, pp. 60-61.
7. Donnelly, *Atlantis*, pp. 317-322.
8. Knight and Lomas, *The Hiram Key*, p. 157.
9. Ibid., p. 241.
10. Men, *Secrets of Mayan Science/Religion*, p. 52.
11. Baldwin, *The Ancient Ones*, Fig. 46, p. 149.
12. Carlson, *The Great Migration*, p. 30.
13. Colton, "Hopi Number Systems," *Hopi Customs, Folklore and Ceremonies*, pp. 5-7.
14. Waters and Fredericks, *Book of the Hopi*, p. 149.
15. Landa, *Yucatan*, pp. 74-75.
16. Gilbert and Cotterell, *The Mayan Prophecies*, pp. 128-136.

17. Malmström, *Cycles of the Sun, Mysteries of the Moon*, p. 207.
18. Jenkins, *Maya Cosmogenesis 2012*, p. 58.
19. Bradfield, *An Interpretation of Hopi Culture*, pp. 406-407.
20. James, *Pages From Hopi History*, pp. 22-25.
21. Waters and Fredericks, *Book of the Hopi*, pp. 222-223.
22. Gilbert and Cotterell, *The Mayan Prophecies*, pp. 116-117.
23. Ibid., pp. 129-130.
24. Thompson, *The Rise and Fall of Maya Civilization*, p. 118.
25. Freidel, Schele, and Parker, *Maya Cosmos*, pp. 272-274.
26. Luckert, *Olmec Religion*, pp. 149-150.
27. Tedlock, *Popol Vuh*, p. 261.
28. Curtis, *The North American Indian: Hopi*, Vol. 12, p. 20.
29. Mindeleff, *A Study of Pueblo Architecture in Tusuyan and Cibola*, pp. 118-130, p. 222.
30. Ibid., p. 122.
31. Milbrath, *Star Gods of the Maya*, p. 266.
32. Tedlock, *Popol Vuh*, p. 341.
33. Young, "The Interconnection Between Western Puebloan and Mesoamerican Ideology and Cosmology," *Kachinas in the Pueblo World*, p. 115.
34. Schaafsma, "The Prehistoric Kachina Cult and Its Origins as Suggested by Southwestern Rock Art," *Kachinas in the Pueblo World*, pp. 65-66.
35. Tedlock, *Popol Vuh*, p. 341.
36. Ibid., pp. 63-64.
37. Malmström, *Cycles of the Sun, Mysteries of the Moon*, pp. 72-73.
38. Ibid., p. 61.
39. Ibid., pp. 152-153.
40. Ibid., p. 81.
41. Ibid., p. 78.
42. The reader shall see in the beginning of Chapter 11 that the major pyramids of Teotihuacán form the shape of Orion's belt.
43. Malmström, *Cycles of the Sun, Mysteries of the Moon*, p. 90-91.
44. Ibid., pp. 165-166.
45. Table based on McCluskey, "Historical Archaeoastronomy: The Hopi Example," *Archaeoastronomy in the New World*.
46. Mullett, *Spider Woman Stories*, p. 59.
47. McCluskey, "Calendars and Symbolism: Functions of Observation in Hopi Astronomy," *Archaeoastronomy*, p. S13.
48. Ibid., p. S2.
49. Bradfield, *An Interpretation of Hopi Culture*, p. 244.
50. Stephen, *Hopi Journal*, p. 307.
51. Ibid., p. 829.
52. Freidel, Schele, & Parker, *Maya Cosmos*, p. 82.
53. Milbrath, *Star Gods of the Maya*, p. 268.
54. This parallel is continued in Lakota (Sioux) cosmology, where Alnitak is perceived as *Keyapiya*, the soft-shelled turtle, whose terrestrial correspondence is Gillette Prairie, a grassy area located within the ponderosa pine forests of the Black Hills. Charlotte A. Black Elk, "Black Hills Sacred Ceremonies of Spring," in Goodman, *Lakota Stellar Knowledge*), p. 51.
55. Gillette, *The Shaman's Secret*, p. 72.
56. Thompson, *The Rise and Fall of Maya Civilization*, p. 218.
57. O'Kane, *The Hopis*, pp. 121-126.
58. Snyder, *Turtle Island*, from unpaginated Introductory Note.
59. Brotherston and Dorn, *Image of the New World*, p. 177.
60. Malmström, *Cycles of the Sun, Mysteries of the Moon*, p. 136.
61. For a full discussion of this complex subject, see Hoagland, *The Monuments of Mars*,

pp. 351-363.
62. James, *Pages From Hopi History*, p. 52.
63. Waters and Fredericks, *Book of the Hopi*, pp. 254-255.
64. Freidel, Schele, & Parker, *Maya Cosmos*, pp. 95-97.

# Chapter 10: They Came from Across the Ocean

1. Courlander, *Hopi Voices*, p. 37.
2. Nequatewa, *Truth of a Hopi*, p. 126.
3. Lowe, *Arizona's Natural Environment*, p. 30.
4. Courlander, *Hopi Voices*, p. 97.
5. Ibid., p. 12.
6. Curtis, *The North American Indian: Hopi*, Vol. 12, p. 99.
7. Voth, *The Traditions of the Hopi*, p. 47.
8. Stephen, *Hopi Journal*, p. 849.
9. Bradfield, *An Interpretation of Hopi Culture*, p. 248.
10. Stephen, *Hopi Journal*, p. 54.
11. Ibid., p. 311.
12. Yava, *Big Snow Falling*, p. 62.
13. Malotki, *Hopi Dictionary*, p. 383.
14. Houk, *Tuzigoot National Monument*, p. 5, p. 7. In the late nineteenth century the United Verde Copper Company opened a mine which created the boom town of Jerome, Arizona. Slag and tailings piles from the smelter operation still rest at the base of Tuzigoot National Monument.
15. Stephen, *Hopi Journal*, p. 1162.
16. Folsom and Folsom, *Ancient Treasures of the Southwest*, p. 35.
17. James, *Pages From Hopi History*, p. 23.
18. Cordell, *Prehistory of the Southwest*, pp. 275-276.
19. Waters and Fredericks, *Book of the Hopi*, footnote, p. 68.
20. Voth, *The Traditions of the Hopi*, p. 53.
21. Ricinos, *Popol Vuh.*.
22. Stephen, "Hopi Tales," *The Journal of American Folklore*, p. 60.
23. "The Mesoamericans" [map], Allen Carroll, Director of Cartography (Washington, D.C.: National Geographic Society, December 1997).
24. Schele and Mathews, *The Code of Kings*, p. 95.
25. Donnelly, *Atlantis*, p. 167.
26. Jim Allen, "Atlantis: The Andes Solution," Historic Atlantis in Bolivia [online]; available from the World Wide Web, <http://www.geocites.com/webatlantis>; accessed 9 November 2001.
27. Zapp and Erikson, *Atlantis In America*, p. 44.
28. Brunhouse, *In Search of the Maya*, p. 151.
29. Churchward, *The Lost Continent of Mu*, p. 45.
30. Ibid., pp. 226-227.
31. Prabhavananda and Manchester, *The Upanishads*, p. 53.
32. Collins, *Gateway to Atlantis*, p. 222.
33. Churchward, *The Children of Mu*, p. 28.
34. Stephen, "Hopi Tales," *The Journal of American Folklore*, pp. 35-36. From the description of these people, who made garments, shoes, and ropes from yucca as well as axes and hoes from stone, we may assume that they are a very early group of Anasazi, perhaps the Basketmakers.
35. Courlander, *The Fourth World of the Hopis*, p. 85. One account calls it the "Far-Far-Below River," which implies that it flows to the Underworld, where, as mentioned previously, the great ocean lies—thus, the reference is to the Third World, or the era prior to the present one. Mullett, *Spider Woman Stories*, p. 11.

36. "The Hopi regard Spider Woman as a major deity of their mythology, second in importance to Masau'u.... Jesse Walter Fewkes writes, 'She is the goddess of wisdom; she can change her form at will.'" Patterson-Rudolph, *On the Trail of Spider Woman*, p. 42.

37. Voth, *The Traditions of the Hopi*, p. 31.

38. Courlander, *The Fourth World of the Hopis*, p. 88.

39. "Hurúing Wuhti owned the moon, the stars, and all the hard substances, such as beads, corals, shells, etc." Voth, *The Traditions of the Hopi*, p. 5. This statement demonstrates that the western goddess is related not only to marine shells and coral but to lunar and sidereal "hard substances" as well. Hopi scholar Harold Courlander believes that Hard Beings Woman and Spider Grandmother are merely variations of the same archetype, viz., Mother Earth. Patterson-Rudolph, *On the Trail of Spider Woman*, p. 78. He goes on, however, to identify the special role of the former deity in the early maritime history of the Hopi: "Huruing Wuhti is associated with the myth that the Hopis came to their present world by a voyage across the sea rather than through the sipapuni." Courlander, *The Fourth World of the Hopis*, p. 204. The disparity between this notion and the "children's myth" was discussed at the beginning of Chapter 10.

40. Voth, *The Traditions of the Hopi*, p. 34.

41. James, *Pages From Hopi History*, pp. 18-22.

42. Bradfield, *An Interpretation of Hopi Culture*, p. 248.

43. Fewkes, *Hopi Katchinas*, pp. 50-51.

44. Childress, *Ancient Tonga & the Lost City of Mu'a*, p. 15.

45. Ibid., p. 38.

46. Fell, *Saga America*, p. 262-3, p. 294.

47. Childress, *Ancient Tonga*, pp. 26-33.

48. Ibid., p. 28.

49. Fale *Tongan Astronomy*, p. 78.

50. Childress, *Ancient Tonga*, p. 37.

51. Ibid., map on p. 41.

52. Lewis, *We, the Navigators*, p. 236.

53. Craig, *Dictionary of Polynesian Mythology*, p. 57.

54. Camp and Camp, *Citadels of Mystery*, p. 256.

55. Lewis, *We, the Navigators*, p. 247.

56. Ibid., p. 256.

57. Childress, *Ancient Tonga*, p. 14.

58. Hancock and Faiia, *Heaven's Mirror*, p. 224.

59. Ibid., p. 247.

60. Childress, *Ancient Tonga*, 125.

61. Ibid., p. 135.

62. Pinkham, *Return of the Serpents of Wisdom*, pp. 110-111.

63. Malotki, *Hopi Dictionary*, pp. 287-288.

64. Fewkes, *Hopi Katchinas*, p. 31.

65. Childress, *Ancient Tonga*, p. 158.

66. Heyerdahl, *Aku-Aku*, p. 340.

67. Bailey, *The God-King & the Titans*, pp. 196-198.

68. Heyerdahl, *Aku-Aku*, pp. 106-108.

69. Bailey, *The God-King & the Titans*, p. 186.

70. Barnett, *Dictionary of Prehistoric Indian Artifacts of the American Southwest* , p. 51.

71. Gordon, *Before Columbus*, pp. 54-67. The type of Egyptian craft mentioned in the legend measured an average of 180 feet long and 60 feet wide.

72. Zeilik, *Astronomy*, pp. 401-402.

73. Mitton, *The Penguin Dictionary of Astronomy*, p. 375-376.

74. "The Milky Way Galaxy," The Munich Astro Archive, Christine Kronberg [website online]; available from the World Wide Web, <http://www.obspm.fr/messier/more/mw.html>; accessed 9 March 2002.

75. Jenkins, *Maya Cosmogenesis 2012*, pp. 229-230.
76. Argüelles, *The Mayan Factor*, p. 52.
77. Ibid., p. 61.
78. Hunt, *Gods and Myths of the Aztecs*, p. 24.
79. Schele and Mathews, *The Code of Kings*, p. 40.
80. Ibid., p. 273, p. 134, p. 295.
81. Caroli, "When was Atlantis *really* Destroyed?", *Ancient American*, pp. 28-30.
82. Pike, *Morals and Dogma*, p. 413.

## Chapter 11: Ancient and Mysterious Monuments

1. Hancock, *Fingerprints of the Gods*, facing caption, p. 54.
2. Eliade, *Cosmos and History*, p. 9.
3. Hadingham, *Lines to the Mountain Gods*, pp. 102-103.
4. Hancock and Faiia, *Heaven's Mirror*, p. 35.
5. Freidel, Schele, and Parker, *Maya Cosmos*, p. 103.
6. "Land of the Maya: A Traveler's Map," editor, Wilbur E. Garrett, chief cartographer, John B. Garver (Washington, D.C.: *National Geographic*, October 1989).
7. Hancock, *Fingerprints of the Gods*, p. 169.
8. Bryant, *Starwalking*, pp. 228-229.
9. a. Nisbet, "The Pyramids of Scotland," *Atlantis Rising*, p. 34, p. 37, pp. 67-68.
b. Jeff Nisbet, "The Pyramids of Scotland," The Lost Secrets of the Templars and the Holy Grail [online]; available from the World Wide Web, <http://www.mythomorph.com/mm/content/2004/0215the_pyramids_of_scotland.phpl>; accessed 10 September 2004. See Jeff's excellent Web site <http://www.mythomorph.com>.
10. a. "Montevecchia: Italy's Giza," posted 17 June 2003, Farshores [online]; available from the World Wide Web, <http://www.100megsfree4.com/farshores/a03ipyr2.htm>; accessed 3 October 2003.
b. "Three Pyramids Discovered in Montevecchia, Italy," posted 9 June 2003, Farshores [online]; available from the World Wide Web, <http://www.100megsfree4.com/farshores/a03ipyr.htm>; accessed 3 October 2003.
11. Brophy, *The Origin Map*, p. 104.
12. a. Mark and Richard Wells, "The Theory of The Chinese Pyramids," Earth Quest [online]; available from the World Wide Web, <http://www.earthquest.co.uk/articales/theory.html>; accessed 26 October 2003.
b. "Eclipse brings claim of medieval African observatory," 12:53 04 December 02, NewScientist.com [online]; available from the World Wide Web, <http://www.newscientist.com/news/news.jsp?id=ns99993137>; accessed 26 October 2003.
c. The Neolithic Monument Complex of Thornborough, North Yorkshire, 2003 [online]; available from the World Wide Web, <http://thornborough.ncl.ac.uk/index.htm>; accessed 13 November 2003.
d. Rami Sajdi, "The Man Made Acu-Points That Correlate With The Belt Of Orion At The Cities of Petra, Masada, and Jerusalem," Acacia Desert-Land [online]; available from the World Wide Web, <http://www.acacialand.com/orion.html>; accessed 3 October 2003.
e. For an Irish Orion Correlation, see Patrick Conlan, "My discovery of the oldest stone star map of Orion's Belt," [online]; available from the World Wide Web, <http://www.conlanabu.com>; accessed 26 October 2004.
13. Bauval and Gilbert, *The Orion Mystery*, p. 125 ff.
14. Gilbert, *Signs in the Sky*, p. 65. The Egyptian master plan discussed by Bauval and Gilbert along with Graham Hancock is a great deal more complex than what is merely sketched out in this chapter. Their opus involves various facets such as precession of the equinoxes, star-targeted shafts in the Great Pyramid, and other topics that are not directly

relevant to our discussion. Overall, their compelling work has challenged many orthodox ideas in Egyptology and has spawned heated debates both on the amateur and the professional levels.

15. "The Orion Pyramid Theory" in the Research/Articles section, Team Atlantis [online]; available from the World Wide Web, <http://www.teamatlantis.com>; accessed 8 October 2003.
16. Reid and Whittlesey, *The Archaeology of Ancient Arizona*, p. 112.
17. Bauval and Gilbert, *The Orion Mystery*, p. 139.
18. James, *Ancient Egypt*, p. 41.
19. Krupp, *Skywatchers, Shamans, & Kings*, pp. 290-291.
20. Arnold, "Royal Cult Complexes of the Old and Middle Kingdoms," *Temples of Ancient Egypt*, p. 74.
21. Ferguson and Rohn, *Anasazi Ruins of the Southwest*, pp. 177-178.
22. Plog, *Ancient Peoples of the American Southwest*, p. 120.
23. Hancock and Bauval, *The Message of the Sphinx*, p. 175.
24. Talayesva, *Sun Chief*, pp. 121-128.
25. Loftin, *Religion and Hopi Life In the Twentieth Century*, p. 69.
26. Curtis, *The North American Indian*, Vol. 12, p. 101.
27. Wright, *Kachinas*, p. 125.
28. Budge, *An Egyptian Hieroglyphic Dictionary*, Vol. II, p. 638.
29. Fell, *America B.C.*, pp. 174-177.
30. Budge, *An Egyptian Hieroglyphic Dictionary*, Vol. I, p. cxxix.
31. Ibid., Vol. II, p. 640.
32. Ibid., Vol. II, p. 589.
33. Budge, *Osiris & the Egyptian Resurrection*, Vol. II, pp. 117-118.
34. Titiev, *Old Oraibi*, p. 135.
35. Rossini, *Egyptian Hieroglyphs*, p. 86.
36. Cunkle and Jacquemain, *Stone Magic of the Ancients*, p. 34.
37. Budge, *An Egyptian Hieroglyphic Dictionary*, Vol. I, p. 270.
38. Malotki and Lomatuway'ma, *Maasaw*, pp. 248-249.
39. Ibid., p. 253.
40. Williamson, *Road In the Sky*, p. 166.
41. Budge, *An Egyptian Hieroglyphic Dictionary*, Vol. I, p. 291.
42. Tyler, *Pueblo Gods and Myths*, pp. 21-22.
43. Titiev, *Old Oraibi*, p. 110.
44. *New Larousse Encyclopedia of Mythology*, pp. 18-19.
45. Donnelly, *Atlantis*, p. 407.
46. Courlander, *Hopi Voices*, p. 14.
47. Curtis, *The North American Indian*, Vol. 12, p. 134.
48. Williamson, *Road In the Sky*, p. 196.
49. Knight and Lomas, *The Hiram Key*, p. 93.
50. White, *A World Elsewhere*, p. 64.
51. Fell, *America B.C.*, pp. 174-177.
52. Fell, *Saga America*, p. 245.
53. Ibid., p. 246.
54. Roberts, "Below the Cliffs of Tombs: Mali's Dogon," *National Geographic*, October 1990, p. 106.
55. Temple, *The Sirius Mystery*, pp. 206-207.
56. Miller, "Hidden Mystery of the Celtic Cross," *Ancient American*, p. 2.
57. Miller, *The Golden Thread of Time*, p. 183.
See Crichton's excellent Web site <http://www.crichtonmiller.com>.
58. Ibid., p. 145.
59. personal e-mail communication with the author, 3 April 2001.
60. Bauval and Gilbert, *The Orion Mystery*, p. 198.

61. Herodotus, *The History of Herodotus*, Book 2.73, p. 162.
62. Budge, *An Egyptian Hieroglyphic Dictionary*, Vol. I, p. 218.
63. Budge, *The Gods of the Egyptians*, Vol. II, p. 371.
64. Clark, *Myth and Symbol in Ancient Egypt*, pp. 245-246.
65. Fewkes, "Two Summers' Work In Pueblo Ruins," *Twenty-Second Annual Report to the Bureau of American Ethnology*, pp. 104-106 and Pl. XLVI.
66. Smith, *When Is a Kiva and Other Questions About Southwestern Archaeology*, p. 150.
67. Fewkes, *Twenty-Second Annual Report*, p. 106.
68. The word *benpi* denotes "iron," and since we are dealing with the pre-Iron Age, this probably refers to the iron of a meteorite. Budge, *An Egyptian Hieroglyphic Dictionary*, Vol. I, p. 218.
69. Bauval and Gilbert, *The Orion Mystery*, pp. 16-19, pp. 197-204.
70. Budge, *An Egyptian Hieroglyphic Dictionary*, Vol. I, p. 217.
71. Allen, *Star Names*, p. 314.
72. Budge, *An Egyptian Hieroglyphic Dictionary*, Vol. I, p. 216 and p. 217.
73. Aldred, *The Egyptians*, p. 100.
74. Malotki, *Hopi Dictionary*, p. 693.
75. Courlander, *The Fourth World of the Hopis*, p. 236.

## Chapter 12: Beyond That Fiery Day

1. Powell, *Arizona*, p. 83.
2. Bauval, *Secret Chamber*, pp. 126-127.
3. Filmore, *Metaphysical Bible Dictionary*, p. 496.
4. Brady, *Brady's Book of Fixed Stars*), pp. 169-173.
5. Ibid., pp. 173-175.
6. Ibid., pp. 166-169.
7. Anne Wright, "Fixed Star: Mintaka," The Fixed Stars, [Web site online]; available from the World Wide Web, <http://www.winshop.com.au/annew/Mintaka.html>; accessed 10 February 2002.
8. Barnes, *Arizona Place Names*,p. 27.
9. Allen, *Star Names*, p. 304.
10. Waters and Fredericks, *Book of the Hopi*, p. 343.
11. Courlander, *The Fourth World of the Hopis*, p. 236.
12. Timms, *Beyond Prophecies and Predictions*, p. 220.
13. Day Williams, "Masons and Mystery at the 33rd Parallel," [online]; available from the World Wide Web, <http://www.daywilliams.com/masons_mystery_33rd_parallel.html>; accessed 7 January 2002.
14. Cirlot, *A Dictionary of Symbols*, p. 222.
15. West, *Serpent In the Sky*, p. 46.
16. Houk, *Hohokam*, p. 2.
17. Noble, *Ancient Ruins of the Southwest*, p. 15.
18. Cordell, *Prehistory of the Southwest*, p. 280.
19. Houk, *Hohokam*, pp. 7-8.
20. Childress, *Lost Cities of North & Central America*, p. 295-297.
21. Wormington, *Prehistoric Indians of the Southwest*, p. 125.
22. Snyder, *Prehistoric Arizona*, p. 54.
23. Plog, *Ancient Peoples of the American Southwest*, p. 136.
24. Ibid., p. 73.
25. Reid and Whittlesey, *The Archaeology of Ancient Arizona*, pp. 92-93.
26. McGregor, *Southwestern Archaeology*, p. 152.
27. Houk, *Hohokam*, p. 12.
28. Ibid., p. 13.
29. Reid and Whittlesey, *The Archaeology of Ancient Arizona*, p. 92.

30. Wilcox, "Hohokam Social Complexity," *Chaco & Hohokam*, p. 266.
31. Ibid., p. 262.
32. Gregory, "Form and Variation in Hohokam Settlement Patterns," *Chaco & Hohokam*, pp. 165-169.
33. Reid and Whittlesey, *The Archaeology of Ancient Arizona*, p. 97.
34. McGregor, *Southwestern Archaeology*, p. 428.
35. Reid and Whittlesey, *The Archaeology of Ancient Arizona*, p. 103.
36. Plog, *Ancient Peoples of the American Southwest*, p. 179.
37. Noble, *Ancient Ruins of the Southwest*, p. 24.
38. Ibid., p. 19.
39. Mathews and Evans, "The Father of Phoenix," *The Journal of Arizona History*, p. 236.
40. *The Taming of the Salt*, pp. 25-28.
41. "What is the meaning of the word Aztlan?" The Azteca Web Page [online]; available from the World Wide Web, <http://www.azteca.net/aztec/aztlan.html>; accessed 10 January 2002.
42. Hunt, *Gods and Myths of the Aztecs*, p. 85.
43. Soustelle, *The Daily Life of the Aztecs On the Eve of the Spanish Conquest*, pp. 218-219.
44. Gene D. Matlock, B.A., M.A., "Why Not Look for A-Tlan-Tis in Mexico?", ViewZone, [online]; available from the World Wide Web, <http://www.viewzone.com/atlantis2.html>; accessed 11 January 2002.
45. Greg McNamee, "How the City Got Its Name," Mondo Arizona, The newtimes.com Traveler's Guide to Unusual Arizona [journal online]; available from the World Wide Web, 1997; <http://www.phoenixnewtimes.com/extra/mondo/mondo20.html>; accessed 10 January 2002.
46. Cirlot, *A Dictionary of Symbols*, p. 242.
47. Pike, *Morals and Dogma*, p. 774.
48. Cirlot, *A Dictionary of Symbols*, p. 141.
49. Budge, *An Egyptian Hieroglyphic Dictionary*, Vol. I, p. 218.
50. Budge, *Osiris & the Egyptian Resurrection*, Vol. II, p. 139.
51. Prescott, *The Conquest of Mexico*, p. 498.
52. Wagoner, *Arizona Territory 1863-1912*, p. 280.
53. "ODD FELLOW SERVICE JEWELS," Phoenixmasonry, [online]; available from the World Wide Web, <http://www.phoenixmasonry.org/masonicmuseum/fraternalism/ioof_jewels.htm>; accessed 11 January 2002.
54. Doug Stewart, "Tale of the Lost Dutchman — bibliography, notes and chronology, 1995-2000," [online]; available from the World Wide Web, <http://www.lost-dutchman.com/dutchman/entries/high.html>; accessed 11 January 2002.
55. Goff, *George W.P. Hunt and His Arizona*, p. 266.
56. One example typical of these men of insidious power and wealth was Prescott Sheldon Bush (1895-1972), the father of forty-first U.S. president George Herbert Walker Bush and grandfather of forty-third president George W. Bush.* All three of these men had been members of the notorious Skull and Bones Society, an elite, quasi-Masonic fraternity at Yale University. Possibly the eldest Bush was named after his distant relative William Hickling Prescott.** In 1918 this Bush allegedly disinterred the skull of the famous Chiricahua Apache warrior Geronimo from its resting place at Fort Sill, Oklahoma and took it back to the secret society's meeting hall to be displayed in a glass case.*** The motive for this savage act is unclear, but it may have involved retribution for the 1869 killing of settler James G. Sheldon from Maine by Apaches at Willow Grove, Arizona.**** Sheldon, after whom a major street in Prescott was named, is perhaps an actual relative of Prescott Sheldon Bush, or he may merely be a namesake whom Bush was trying to avenge. Bush was later elected as a Republican U.S. senator from

Connecticut. The son and the grandson, of course, each became president. The Bush vacation home is located in Kennebunkport, Maine. Geronimo's skull has never been recovered.

\* "Index to Politician: Bush," The Political Graveyard [online]; available from the World Wide Web, <http://politicalgraveyard.com/bio/bush.html#R9M0IRCEC>; accessed 16 March 2002.

\*\* "Ancestry of George W. Bush," compiled by William Addams Reitwiesner [online]; available from the World Wide Web, <http://members.aol.com/wreitwiesn/candidates2000/bush.html>; accessed 16 March 2002.

\*\*\* "Where Are They Hiding Geronimo's Skull?", Notes From Indian Country, Tim Giago (Nanwica Kciji) [online]; available from the World Wide Web, <http://www.theramp.net/kohr4/geronimo_skull.html>; accessed 16 March 2002.

\*\*\*\* Hayden Arizona Pioneer Biographies (archive), Arizona State University [online]; available from the World Wide Web, <http://www.asu.edu/lib/archives/azbio/azbio.htm>; accessed 16 March 2002.

57. Haury, *The Hohokam*, p. 230.

58. Ibid., p. 374.

59. a. Barnett, *Dictionary of Prehistoric Indian Artifacts of the American Southwest*, p. 88. b. McGregor, *Southwestern Archaeology*, p. 351.

60. Séjourné, *Burning Water*, pp. 107-108.

61. "Phoenix Or Eagle, Which?", Philosophical Research Society, 1996; [online], available from the World Wide Web, <http://www.prs.org/books/book345.htm>; accessed 17 January 2001.

62. Pinkham, *The Return of the Serpents of Wisdom*, pp. 290-291.

63. Matlock, *Yishvara 2000*, p. 6.

64. West, *Serpent In the Sky,* p. 55.

65. Campbell and Moyers, *The Power of Myth*, p. 27.

66. Miller, *The Golden Thread of Time*, pp. 131-132.

67. Pike, *Morals and Dogma*, p. 291.

68. Anne Wright, "The Phoenix or mythical Bird.", The Fixed Stars, [online]; available from the World Wide Web, <http://www.winshop.com.au/annew/Phoenix.html>; accessed 16 January 2002.

69. Pike, *Morals and Dogma*, p. 276.

70. Ibid., p. 287.

71. Ibid., p. 291.

## Chapter 13: Rapidly Into the Far Future

1. Sagan, *Cosmos*, p. 197.

2. William R. Corliss, "Bubonic Plague As An Indicator of Diffusion?" Science Frontiers Online, No. 45, May-June 1986 [journal online]; available from the World Wide Web, <http://www.science-frontiers.com/sf045/sf045p02.htm>; accessed 21 October 2003.

3. Knight and Lomas, *The Second Messiah*, pp. 184-185.

4. Bourke, *Snake-Dance of the Moquis*, p. 279.

5. Zinsser, *Rats, Lice and History*, pp. 257-260.

6. Séjourné, *Burning Water*, pp. 149-150, p. 155.

7. Marrs, *Rule By Secrecy*, pp. 274-280.

8. Baigent, Leigh, and Lincoln, *Holy Blood, Holy Grail*, p. 65.

9. Ibid., 71.

10. Ibid., p. 72.

11. Gardiner, *Bloodline of the Holy Grail*, p. 272.

12. Miller, *The Golden Thread of Time*, p. 247, p. 258.

13. Miller, "Hidden Mystery of the Celtic Cross," *Ancient American*, p. 3.

14. Baigent, Leigh, and Lincoln, *Holy Blood, Holy Grail*, p. 81.
15. Knight and Lomas, *The Hiram Key*, pp. 78-79.
16. Ibid., pp. 288-289.
17. Pennick, *Sacred Geometry*, pp. 86-90.
18. Stephen, "Hopi Tales," *The Journal of American Folklore*, p. 42.
19. Collins, *From the Ashes of Angels*, p. 48.
20. Smith, *Smith's Bible Dictionary*, p. 77.
21. Stephen, "Hopi Tales," *The Journal of American Folklore*, pp. 42-43.
22. Collins, *From the Ashes of Angels*, p. 64.
23. Irwin, *Fair Gods and Stone Faces*, pp. 100-101.
24. Smith, *Smith's Bible Dictionary*, p. 34-35.
25. Pinkham, *Return of the Serpents of Wisdom*, p. 289.
26. Fell, *Saga America*, p. 367.
27. Knight and Lomas, *The Hiram Key*, pp. 302-303.
28. Ibid., p. 290.
29. Ibid., p. 54, p. 71, p. 189.
30. Bauval, *Secret Chamber*, p. 328.
31. Edwards, *The Pyramids of Egypt*, p. 293.
32. Burnham, *Burnham's Celestial Handbook,* Vol. I, p. 392.
33. Bauval, *Secret Chamber*, p. 240.
34. Johnson, *Earth Figures of the Lower Colorado and Gila River Deserts*, p. 107.
35. Haury, *The Hohokam*, p. 320.
36. Oppelt, *Guide to Prehistoric Ruins of the Southwest*, p. 47.
37. Schaafsma, *Rock Art In New Mexico*, p. 77.
38. Thomas V. Keam cited in Mallery, *Picture-Writing of the American Indians*, Vol. II, p. 729.
39. Bourke, *Snake-Dance of the Moquis,* Pl. XX.
40. Bailey, *The God-King & the Titans*, p. 113.
41. Fewkes, *Prehistoric Pottery Designs*, PL. CXXVIII facing p. 44.
42. Ibid., p. 79.
43. Hancock, *Fingerprints of the Gods*, p. 154.
44. Luckert, *Olmec Religion*, pp. 154-155.
45. Fewkes, *Prehistoric Hopi Pottery Designs*, pp. 155-156.
46. Temple, *The Sirius Mystery*, p. 45.
47. Jung, *Psychology and Alchemy*, pp. 398-399.
48. Mails, *The Hopi Survival Kit*, pp. 184-187.
49. Waters and Fredericks, *Book of the Hopi*, p. 31.
50. Dan Katchongva, Danaqyumtewa, trans., Thomas Francis, ed. "From the Beginning of Life to the Day of Purification: Teachings, History & Prophecies of the Hopi People" [online], The Hopi Information Network, 1996; available from World Wide Web, <http://www.recycles.org/hopi/messages/prophecy/katch-1.htm>; accessed 26 June 1998; originally published by the Committee for Traditional Indian Land and Life, Los Angeles, 1972, p. 5.
51. Ibid., p. 8.
52. Kaiser, *The Voice of the Great Spirit*, pp. 42-43.
53. Mails and Evehema, *Hotevilla*, p. 491.
54. Paul White, "The Secrets of Thoth," New Age On-Line Australia, [online]; available from the World Wide Web, <http://www.newage.com.au/library/thoth.html>; accessed 25 February 2002.
55. Gene D. Matlock, B.A., M.A., "Is the Hopi Deity Kokopelli an Ancient Hindu God?", ViewZone, 2001 [journal online]; available from the World Wide Web, <http://www.viewzone.com/kokopelli.html>; accessed 2 October, 2001.
56. Kaiser, *The Voice of the Great Spirit*, p. 44.
57. Katchongva, "From the Beginning of Life..." [Web site online], op. cit., p. 9.

58. Malotki and Lomatuway'ma, *Maasaw*, p. 259.
59. Shipley, *The Origins of English Words*, pp. 256-258.
60. Waters and Fredericks, *Book of the Hopi*, pp. 13-16.
61. Parsons, *Pueblo Indian Region*, Vol. I, p. 236. This notion of primeval ant-like people is reminiscent of a passage in the Greek play "Prometheus Bound" by Aeschylus (525-456 B.C.): "...They dwelt / In hollowed holes, like swarms of tiny ants, / In sunless depths of caverns; and they had / no certain signs of winter, nor of spring / Flower-laden, nor of summer with her fruits; / But without counsel fared their whole life long, / Until I showed the risings of the stars, / And settings hard to recognize..." In addition to teaching these ant creatures astronomy, the culture hero Prometheus imparted writing, mathematics, domestication of animals, and marine navigation. "Aeschylus (525-456 B.C.). Prometheus Bound. The Harvard Classics. 1909-14. Lines 400-799," Bartelby.com: Great Books Online [journal online]; available from the World Wide Web, <http://www.bartelby.com/8/4/2.html#txt7>; accessed 2 December, 2001.
62. Voth, *The Traditions of the Hopi*, p. 239.
63. Bradfield, *An Interpretation of Hopi Culture*, pp. 290-296.
64. Young, *Signs From the Ancestors*, p. 162.
65. Schaafsma, *Warrior, Shield, and Star*, p. 179.
66. Curtis, *The North American Indian*, Vol. 12, p. 143.
67. Young, *Signs From the Ancestors*, pp. 133-134.
68. Capinera, "Insects in Art and Religion: The American Southwest," *American Ethnologist*, p. 225.
69. Weltfish, *The Lost Universe*, p. 225.
70. Thompson, *Maya History and Religion*, pp. 340-341.
71. Wormington, *Prehistoric Indians of the Southwest*, p. 133.
72. "Pottery Collections," Arizona State Museum, the University of Arizona, Tucson; [online]; available from the World Wide Web, 2 January 2002, <http://www.statemuseum.arizona.edu/coll/pots5.shtml>; accessed 15 January 2002. Note: this photograph is apparently reversed because the dancers appear to be looking to their right.
73. Curtis, *The Indians' Book*, p. 315.
74. Noble, *Ancient Ruins of the Southwest*, p. 22.
75. Gladwin, *Excavations At Snaketown*, pp. 163-164.
76. McGregor, *Southwestern Archaeology*, pp. 276-277.
77. In Sanskrit the syllable *Ki* means "ant hill" and *Va* means "dwelling." Gene D. Matlock, B.A., M.A., "Is the Hopi Deity Kokopelli an Ancient Hindu God?", ViewZone, 2001 [journal online]; available from the World Wide Web, <http://www.viewzone.com/kokopelli.html>; accessed 2 October, 2001.
78. White, "Underworld Cult of the Pueblo People," *Ancient American*, p. 12.
79. Dollar, "Discover the Lava River Cave in Flagstaff Country," *Arizona Highways*, p. 11-12.
80. a. Jack Andrews, Lost Civilizations and Hidden Mysteries [online]; available from the World Wide Web, <http://mysteriousarizona.com>; accessed 25 September 2006.
b. Barry McEwen, "Ancient Egyptian Treasures In The Grand Canyon? Suppressed Archaeological Information and Metaphysical Paradox?" Farshores [online]; available from the World Wide Web, <http://farshores.org/aettgc07.htm>; accessed 25 September 2006.
81. Childress, *Lost Cities of North & Central America*, pp. 316-325.
82. Frank Joseph suggests that this robed stone figure represents instead Bes, the Nile Valley god of war. Joseph, "Underground City of the Grand Canyon, Fact or Fable?", *Ancient American*, p. 23.
83. Däniken, translated by Michael Heron, *In Search of Ancient Gods*, color photos no. 27 and no. 28.
84. Mills, *The Truth*, p. 15.

85. Ibid., p. 29.
86. Clow, *Catastrophobia*, p. 161.
87. Collins, *From the Ashes of Angels*, pp. 281-288.
88. Ibid., p. 290.
89. *New Larousse Encyclopedia of Mythology*, p. 320.
90. Santillana and Dechend, *Hamlet's Mill*, pp. 146-147.
91. Collins, *From the Ashes of Angels*, p. 290.
92. Ibid., p. 210.
93. Gene D. Matlock, personal e-mail communication with the author, 3 January 2002.
94. Tyler, *Pueblo Gods and Myths*, pp. 129-130.
95. Titiev, *Old Oraibi*, p. 116.
96. Knight and Lomas, *Uriel's Machine*, p. 137.
97. Sitchin, *The 12th Planet*, p. 171.
98. Smith, *Smith's Bible Dictionary*, p. 38.
99. Collins, *From the Ashes of Angels*, p. 27.
100. Knight and Lomas, *Uriel's Machine*, p. 103.
101. Budge, *An Egyptian Hieroglyphic Dictionary*, Vol. I, p. 56.
102. Young, *Signs From the Ancestors*, p. 162.

# BIBLIOGRAPHY

Adams, E. Charles, *The Origin and Development of the Pueblo Katsina Cult* (Tucson, Arizona: The University of Arizona Press, 1991).

Adler, Michael A., editor, *The Prehistoric Pueblo World, A.D. 1150-1350* (Tucson, Arizona: The University of Arizona Press, 1996).

Aldred, Cyril, *The Egyptians* (London: Thames and Hudson Ltd., 1988, 1961).

Allen, Richard Hinckley, *Star Names: Their Lore and Meaning* (New York: Dover Publications, Inc., 1963, reprint 1899).

Anderson, Bruce A., "Wupatki National Monument: Exploring into Prehistory," edited by David Grant Noble, *Wupatki and Walnut Canyon*, (Santa Fe: Ancient City Press).

Anderson, Douglas and Barbara, *Chaco Canyon: Center of a Culture* (Tucson, Arizona: Southwest Parks and Monument Association, 1981).

Argüelles, José, Ph.D., *The Mayan Factor: Path Beyond Technology* (Santa Fe, New Mexico: Bear & Company, 1987).

Arnold, Dieter, "Royal Cult Complexes of the Old and Middle Kingdoms," *Temples of Ancient Egypt* (Ithaca, New York: Cornell University Press, 1997).

Arroyo, Stephen, *Astrology, Karma & Transformation: The Inner Dimensions of the Birth Chart* (Sebastopol, California: CRCS Publications, 1978).

Ash, Sidney, *Petrified Forest: The Story behind the Scenery* (Petrified forest, Arizona: Petrified Forest Museum Association, 1985).

Aveni, Anthony F., *Skywatchers of Ancient Mexico* (Austin, Texas: University of Texas Press, 1980).

Baigent, Michael, Richard Leigh, and Henry Lincoln, *Holy Blood, Holy Grail* (New York Dell Publishing Co., Inc., 1985, 1983, 1982).

Bailey, James, *The God-King & the Titans: The New World Ascendancy in Ancient Times* (New York: St. Martin's Press, 1973).

Baldwin, Anne R., and J. Michael Bremer, *Walnut Canyon National Monument: An Archaeological Survey* (Tucson, Arizona: Western Archaeological and Conservation Center, 1986).

Baldwin, Gordon C., *The Ancient Ones: Basketmakers and Cliff Dwellers of the Southwest* (New York: W.W. Norton & Company, Inc. 1963).

Barlow, Bernyce, *Sacred Sites of the West* (St. Paul, Minnesota: Llewellyn Publications, 1996).

Barnes, F.A., and Michaelene Pendleton, *Canyon Country Prehistoric Indians: Their Cultures, Ruins, Artifacts and Rock Art* (Salt Lake, Utah: Wasatch Publishers, 1995 reprint 1979).

Barnes, Will C., *Arizona Place Names*, Introduction by Bernard L. Fontana (Tucson: The University of Arizona Press, 1997, reprint 1988).

Barnett, Franklin, *Dictionary of Prehistoric Indian Artifacts of the American Southwest* (Flagstaff, Arizona: Northland Press, 1974, 1973).

Barnett, Franklin, *Excavation of Main Pueblo At Fitzmaurice Ruin: Prescott Culture in Yavapai County, Arizona* (Flagstaff, Arizona: Museum of Northern    Arizona, 1974).

Bauval, Robert, and Adrian Gilbert, *The Orion Mystery: Unlocking the Secrets of the Pyramids* (New York: Crown Publishers, Inc., 1994).

Bauval, Robert, *Secret Chamber: The Quest for the Hall of Records* (London: Century/Random House, 1999).

Benedict, Ruth, *Patterns of Culture* (New York: New American Library—Mentor Books, 1953, reprint 1934).

Bernal, Ignacio, *Mexico Before Cortez: Art, History, Legend* (Garden City, New York: Anchor Press/Doubleday, 1973, 1963).

Boissière, Robert, *The Return of Pahana: A Hopi Myth* (Santa Fe, New Mexico: Bear &

Company, 1990).

Bourke, John G., *Snake-Dance of the Moquis: Being a Narrative of a Journey from Santa Fe, New Mexico to the Villages of the Moqui Indians of Arizona* (Tucson: The University of Arizona Press, 1984, 1884).

Bradfield, Maitland, "Rock-cut Cisterns and Pollen 'Rain' in the Vicinity of Old Oraibi, Arizona," *Plateau*, Vol. 46 No. 2, Fall 1973.

Bradfield, Richard Maitland, *An Interpretation of Hopi Culture* (Derby, England: privately published, 1995).

Brady, Bernadette, *Brady's Book of Fixed Stars* (York Beach, Maine: Samuel Weiser, Inc., 1998).

Brandt, John C., edited by Anthony F. Aveni, *Archaeoastronomy in Pre-Columbian America* (Austin, Texas: University of Texas Press, 1977, reprint 1975).

Brandt, John C., and Ray A. Williamson, edited by Anthony F. Aveni, *Native American Astronomy* (Austin, Texas: University of Texas Press, 1979).

Brandt, John C., "Pictographs and Petroglyphs of the Southwest Indians," edited by Kenneth Brecher and Michael Feirtag, *Astronomy of the Ancients* (Cambridge, Massachusetts: The MIT Press, 1980).

Bremer, J. Michael, *Walnut Canyon: Settlement and Land Use* (Flagstaff, Arizona: Arizona Archaeological Society, 1989).

Brophy, Thomas G., Ph.D., *The Origin Map: Discovery of a Prehistoric, Megalithic Astrophysical Map and Sculpture of the Universe* (New York/Lincoln, Nebraska: Writers Club Press/iUniverse, 2002).

Brotherston, Gordon, with Ed Dorn, *Image of the New World: The American Continent Portrayed in Native Texts* (London: Thames and Hudson, Ltd., 1979).

Brunhouse, Robert L., *In Search of the Maya: the First Archaeologists* (New York: Ballantine Books, 1976, 1973).

Bruyere, Rosalyn L., edited by Jeanne Farrens, *Wheels of Light: A Study of Chakras*, Vol. I (Sierra Madre, California: Bon Productions, 1989).

Bryant, Page, *Starwalking: Shamanic Practices For Traveling into the Night Sky* (Santa Fe, New Mexico: Bear & Company Publishing, 1997).

Budge, Sir E.A. Wallis, *Egyptian Language: Easy Lessons in Egyptian Hieroglyphics* (New York: Dover Publications, Inc., 1983, 1966, 1910, 1889).

Budge, E.A. Wallis, *The Gods of the Egyptians*, Vol. II (New York: Dover Publications, Inc., 1969, reprint 1904).

Budge, E. A. Wallis, *Osiris & the Egyptian Resurrection*, Vol. II (New York: Dover Publications, Inc., 1973, 1911).

Budge, E. A. Wallis, *An Egyptian Hieroglyphic Dictionary*, Vol. I & Vol. II (New York: Dover Publications, Inc., 1978, 1920).

Burnham, Robert, Jr., *Burnham's Celestial Handbook: An Observer's Guide to the Universe Beyond the Solar System*, Vol. 1 & 2 (New York: Dover Publications, Inc., 1978, reprint, 1966).

Byrkit, James W., *The Palatkwapi Trail* (Flagstaff, Arizona: Museum of Northern Arizona, *Plateau*, Vol. 59 No. 4, 1988).

Caesar, *The Conquest of Gaul*, translated by S.A. Handford (Harmondsworth, Middlesex, England: Penguin Books, 1979, reprint, 1951).

Calvin, William H., *The River That Flows Uphill: A Journey from the Big Bang to the Big Brain* (San Francisco: Sierra Club Books, 1986).

Calvin, William H., *How the Shaman Stole the Moon: In Search of Ancient Prophet-Scientists from Stonehenge to the Grand Canyon* (New York: Bantam Books, 1992, 1991).

Camp, Sprague de, and Catherine C. de Camp, *Citadels of Mystery* (New York: Ballantine Books, 1974, 1964).

Campbell, Joseph, *Hero With a Thousand Faces* (Princeton, New Jersey: Princeton University Press, Bollingen Series XVII, 1973, reprint, 1949).

Campbell, Joseph, with Bill Moyers, *The Power of Myth* (New York: Doubleday, 1988).

Capinera, J.L., "Insects in Art and Religion: The American Southwest," *American Ethnologist*, Vol. 39 No. 4 (Lanham, Maryland: Entomological Society of America, Winter 1993).

Carlson, Vada F.. *The Great Migration: Emergence of the Americas* (Virginia Beach, Virginia: A.R.E. Press, 1970).

Caroli, Kenneth, "When was Atlantis *really* Destroyed?", *Ancient American: The Voice of Alternative Viewpoints* (Colfax, Wisconsin, January/February 2002, Volume 7, Issue Number 43).

Cassirer, Ernst, translated by Susanne K. Langer, *Language and Myth* (New York: Dover Publications, Inc., 1946).

Chamberlain, Von del, *When Stars Came Down to Earth: Cosmology of the Skidi Pawnee Indians of North America* (Los Altos, California: Ballena Press/Center for Archeoastronomy Cooperative Publication, 1982).

Childress, David Hatcher, *Lost Cities of North & Central America* (Stelle, Illinois: Adventures Unlimited Press, 1993, 1992).

Childress, David Hatcher, *Ancient Tonga & the Lost City of Mu'a* (Stelle, Illinois: Adventures Unlimited Press, 1996).

Churchward, James, *The Lost Continent of Mu* (London: Neville Spearman, 1976, 1959).

Churchward, James. *The Children of Mu* (Albuquerque: Be Books/The C.W. Daniel Company Ltd., 1988, 1959).

Cirlot, J.E., *A Dictionary of Symbols* (New York: Philosophical Library, 1962).

Claiborne, Robert, *The Summer Stargazer: Astronomy For Absolute Beginners* (United States: Nature Library, 1975).

Clark, R.T. Rundle, *Myth and Symbol in Ancient Egypt* (New York: Thames and Hudson, 1991, 1978, 1959).

Clow, Barbara Hand, *Catastrophobia: The Truth Behind Earth Changes in the Coming Age of Light* (Rochester, Vermont: Bear & Company, 2001).

Coe, Michael D., *The Maya* (New York: Praeger Publishers, 1971, reprint, 1966).

Cole, Sally J., *Katsina Iconography in Homol'ovi Rock Art, Central Little Colorado River Valley, Arizona* (Phoenix: Arizona Archaeological Society, March 1992).

Collins, Andrew, *From the Ashes of Angels: the Forbidden Legacy of a Fallen Race* (Rochester, Vermont: Bear & Company, 2001, 1996).

Collins, Andrew, introduction by David Rohl, *Gateway to Atlantis* (New York: Graf Publishers, Inc., 2000).

Colton, Harold S., *Hopi Kachina Dolls with a Key to their Identification* (Albuquerque: University of New Mexico Press, 1990, 1949).

Colton, Harold S., "Hopi Number Systems," *Hopi Customs, Folklore and Ceremonies* (Flagstaff, Arizona: Northern Arizona Society of Science and Art/Museum of Northern Arizona, Reprint Series No. 4, 1954).

Cordell, Linda S., *Prehistory of the Southwest* (San Diego, California: Academic Press, Inc., Harcourt Brace Jovanovich, Publishers, 1984).

Courlander, Harold, *The Fourth World of the Hopis: the Epic Story of the Hopi Indians As Preserved In Their Legends and Traditions* (Albuquerque, New Mexico: University of New Mexico Press, 1991, reprint 1971).

Courlander, Harold, *Hopi Voices: Recollections, Traditions, and Narratives of the Hopi Indians* (Albuquerque: University of New Mexico Press, 1982).

Craig, Robert D., *Dictionary of Polynesian Mythology* (New York: Greenwood Press, Inc. 1989).

Cunkle, James R., *Talking Pots: Deciphering the Symbols of a Prehistoric People* (Phoenix, Arizona: Golden West Publishers, 1996, reprint 1993).

Cunkle, James R., and Markus A. Jacquemain, *Stone Magic of the Ancients: Petroglyphs, Shamanic Shine Sites, Ancient Rituals* (Phoenix: Golden West Publishers, Inc. 1996, 1995).

Cunkle, James R., *Raven Site Ruin: Interpretive Guide* (St. Johns, Arizona: White Mountain Archaeological Center, no publication date).

Curtis, Edward S., Frederick Webb Hodge, editor, *The North American Indian: Hopi*, Vol. 12 (Norwood, Mass.: The Plimpton Press, 1922).

Curtis, Natalie, *The Indians' Book: Songs and Legends of the American Indians* (New York: Dover Publications, 1968, 1923).

Däniken, Erich von, translated by Michael Heron, *In Search of Ancient Gods: My Pictorial Evidence for the Impossible* (New York: G.P. Putnam's Sons, 1973).

Dockstader, Frederick J., *The Kachina and the White Man: The Influences of White Culture on the Hopi Kachina Religion* (Albuquerque, New Mexico: University of New Mexico Press, 1985, 1954).

Dollar, Tom, "Discover the Lava River Cave in Flagstaff Country," *Arizona Highways*, May 1995, Vol. 71 No. 5.

Donnelly, Ignatius, *Atlantis: The Antediluvian World* (New York: Dover Publications, Inc., 1976, reprint 1882).

Downum, Christian E., *The Sinagua* (Flagstaff, Arizona: Museum of Northern Arizona, *Plateau*, Vol. 63, No. 1, 1992).

Duus, Erling, *The Tragic, Sacred Ground* (Freeman, South Dakota: Pine Hill Press, 1989).

Eddy, John A., "Astronomical Alignment of the Big Horn Medicine Wheel," *Science*, June 7, 1974 Vol. 184 No. 4141.

Edwards, I.E.S., *The Pyramids of Egypt* (Baltimore: Penguin Books, 1961, 1947).

Eggan, Fred, "The Hopi Cosmology or World-View," *Kachinas in the Pueblo World*, edit ed by Polly Schaafsma (Albuquerque, New Mexico: University of New Mexico Press, 1994).

Eliade, Mircea, *Cosmos and History: The Myth of the Eternal Return* (New York: Harper & Brothers, 1959, 1954).

Eliade, Mircea, *The Sacred and the Profane: The Nature of Religion* (New York: Harcourt, Brace & World, Inc.—A Harvest Book, 1959, reprint 1957).

Ellis, Florence Hawley, "Pueblo Sun-Moon-Star Calendar," edited by Anthony F. Aveni, *Archaeoastronomy In Pre-Columbian America* (Austin, Texas: University of Texas Press, 1977, reprint 1975).

Fagan, Cyril, *Astrological Origins* (St. Paul, Minnesota: Llewellyn Publications, 1971).

Fale, T.H., *Tongan Astronomy* (Nuku'alofa, Tonga: Taulua Press/Polynesian Eyes Foundation, 1999, 1990).

Farmer, James D., "Iconographic Evidence of Basketmaker Warfare and Human Sacrifice: A Contextual Approach to Early Anasazi Art," *Kiva*, Vol. 62 No. 4 (Tucson: The Arizona Archaeological and Historical Society, 1997).

Fell, Barry, *America B.C.* (New York: Demeter Press Book, Quadrangle/The New York Times Book Co., 1977, 1976).

Fell, Barry, *Saga America* (New York: Times Books, 1980).

Fell, Barry, *Bronze Age America* (Boston: Little, Brown and Co., 1982).

Ferguson, William M., and Arthur H. Rohn, *Anasazi Ruins of the Southwest In Color* (Albuquerque, New Mexico: University of New Mexico Press, 1987).

Fergusson, Erna, *Dancing Gods: Indian Ceremonials of New Mexico & Arizona* (Albuquerque: University of New Mexico Press, 1966, 1931).

Feuerstein, Georg, *Tantra: The Path of Ecstasy* (Boston: Shambala Publications, Inc., 1998).

Fewkes, Jesse Walter, *Tusayan Katcinas and Hopi Altars* (Albuquerque, New Mexico: Awanyu Publishing, Inc., 1990, reprint 1892).

Fewkes, J. Walter, "Two Ruins Recently Discovered In the Red Rock Country, Arizona," *The American Anthropologist* (Washington, D.C.: Anthropological Society, Vol. IX, No. 8, August, 1896).

Fewkes, J. Walter, "The New-Fire Ceremony At Walpi," *American Anthropologist*, Vol. 2 (new series), 1900 (New York: Kraus Reprint Corp., 1963).

Fewkes, J. Walter, "Sky-God Personifications in Hopi Worship, " *Journal of American Folk-lore*, Vol. XV, (Boston: American Folklore Society, 1902).

Fewkes, Jesse Walter, *Hopi Katcinas* (New York: Dover Publications, Inc., 1985, reprint of *Twenty-First Annual Report to the Bureau of American Ethnology*, 1903).

Fewkes, Jesse Walter, "Two Summers' Work In Pueblo Ruins," *Twenty-Second Annual Report to the Bureau of American Ethnology, 1900-1901* (Washington, D.C.: Smithsonian Institute/Government Printing Office, 1904).

Fewkes, Jesse Walter, *Prehistoric Pottery Designs* (New York: Dover Publications, Inc. 1973, reprint of *Seventeenth Annual Report to the Bureau of American Ethnology*, 1898; and *Thirty-Third Annual Report to the Bureau of American Ethnology*, 1919).

Filmore, Charles, *Metaphysical Bible Dictionary* (Unity Village, Missouri: Unity School of Christianity, 1931).

Folsom, Franklin, and Mary Elting Folsom, *Ancient Treasures of the Southwest: A Guide To Archeological Sites and Museums In Arizona, Southern Colorado, New Mexico and Utah* (Albuquerque, New Mexico: University of New Mexico Press, 1994).

Frazier, Kendrick, *People of Chaco: A Canyon and Its Culture* (New York: W.W. Norton & Co., 1986).

Frazier, Sir James, *The New Golden Bough: A New Abridgment of the Classic Work* (New York: New American Library, Mentor Book, 1964, reprint 1959).

Freidel, David, Linda Schele, and Joy Parker, *Maya Cosmos: Three Thousand Years on the Shaman's Path* (New York: William Morrow and Company, Inc., 1993).

Gabriel, Kathryn, *Roads to Center Place: A Cultural Atlas of Chaco Canyon and the Anasazi* (Boulder, Colorado: Johnson Publishing Company, 1991).

Gardiner, Laurence, *Bloodline of the Holy Grail: The Hidden Lineage of Jesus Revealed* (New York: Barnes & Noble Books, 1997, 1996).

Geertz, Armin W., and Michael Lomatuway'ma, *Children of the Cottonwood: Piety and Ceremonialism in Hopi Indian Puppetry* (Lincoln: University of Nebraska, 1987).

Gilbert, Adrian G., and Maurice M. Cotterell, *The Mayan Prophecies: Unlocking the Secrets of a Lost Civilization* (Shaftesbury, Dorset: Element Books Limited, 1995).

Gilbert, Adrian, *Signs in the Sky* (London: Bantam Books, 2000).

Gillette, Douglas, M.A., M.Div., *The Shaman's Secret: The Lost Resurrection Teachings of the Ancient Maya* (New York: Bantam Books, 1997).

Gladwin, Harold S., *Excavations At Snaketown: Material Culture* (Tucson: The University of Arizona Press, 1965, 1938).

Goff, John S., Ph.D., *George W.P. Hunt and His Arizona* (Pasadena, California: Socio Technical Publications, 1973).

Goodman, Ronald, *Lakota Star Knowledge: Studies In Lakota Stellar Theology* (Rosebud, South Dakota: Sinte Gleska College, 1990).

Gordon, Cyrus H., *Before Columbus: Links Between the Old World and Ancient America* (New York: Crown Publishers, Inc., 1971).

Grant, Campbell, *Canyon de Chelly: Its People and Rock Art* (Tucson, Arizona: The University of Arizona Press, 1984, 1978).

Gregory, David A., "Form and Variation in Hohokam Settlement Patterns," *Chaco & Hohokam: Prehistoric Regional Systems in the American Southwest*, edited by Patricia L. Crown and W. James Judge (Santa Fe, New Mexico: School of American Research Press, 1991).

Griffin-Pierce, Trudy, *Earth Is My Mother, Sky Is My Father: Space, Time, and Astronomy in Navajo Sand Painting* (Albuquerque, New Mexico: University of New Mexico Press, 1995, reprint 1992).

Grossinger, Richard, *The Night Sky* (Los Angeles: Jeremy P. Tarcher, Inc. 1988).

Hadingham, Evan, *Lines to the Mountain Gods: Nazca and the Mysteries of Peru* (New York: Random House, 1987).

Hall, Edward T., *West of the Thirties: Discoveries Among the Navajo and Hopi* (New York: Anchor Books/Doubleday, 1995, reprint 1994).

Hancock, Graham, *Fingerprints of the Gods: the Evidence of Earth's Lost Civilization*

(New York: Crown Trade Paperbacks, 1995).

Hancock, Graham, and Robert Bauval, *The Message of the Sphinx: A Quest For the Hidden Legacy of Mankind* (New York: Three Rivers Press, 1996).

Hancock, Graham, and Santha Faiia, *Heaven's Mirror: Quest For the Lost Civilization* (New York: Crown Publishers, Inc. 1998).

Hancock, Graham, *The Mars Mystery: The Secret Connection Between the Earth and the Red Planet* (New York: Crown Publishers, Inc., 1998).

Haney, Mark A., *Skyglobe 2.04 for Windows* [floppy disk] (Ann Arbor, Michigan: KlassM Software, 1997).

Haury, Emil W., *The Hohokam: Desert Farmers & Craftsmen—Excavations At Snaketown, 1964-1965* (Tucson: The University of Arizona Press, 1978, 1976).

Heizer, Robert F., and C.W. Clewlow, Jr., *Prehistoric Rock Art of California*, Vol. 1 (Ramona, California: Ballena Press, 1973).

Herodotus, *The History of Herodotus*, translated by David Grene, (Chicago: The University of Chicago Press, 1987).

Hewett, Edgar Lee, *Ancient Life in the American Southwest* (Indianapolis, Indiana: The Bobbs-Merrill Company, 1930).

Heyerdahl, Thor, *Aku-Aku: The Secret of Easter Island* (New York: Pocket Books, 1966, 1958).

Hibben, Frank C., *Kiva Art of the Anasazi at Pottery Mound* (Las Vegas, Nevada: KC Publications, Inc., 1975).

Hieb, Louis A., "The Meaning of *Katsina*: Toward a Cultural Definition of 'Person' in Hopi Religion, *Kachinas in the Pueblo World*, edited by Polly Schaafsma (Albuquerque, New Mexico: University of New Mexico Press, 1994).

Hoagland, Richard C., *The Monuments of Mars: A City on the Edge of Forever* (Berkeley, California: North Atlantic Books, 1996, 1987).

Hodge, Carle, photography by George H.H. Huey, *Ruins Along the River: Montezuma Castle, Tuzigoot, and Montezuma Well National Monuments* (Tucson, Arizona: Southwest Parks and Monuments Association, 1986).

Houk, Rose, *Hohokam* (Tucson, Arizona: Southwest Park and Monument Association, 1992).

Houk, Rose, *Sinagua: Prehistoric Cultures of the Southwest* (Tucson, Arizona: Southwest Parks and Monuments Association, 1992).

Houk, Rose, *Tuzigoot National Monument* (Tucson, Arizona: Southwest Parks and Monuments Association, 1995).

Hunt, Charles B., *Death Valley: Geology, Ecology, and Archaeology* (Berkeley: University of California Press, 1975).

Hunt, Norman Bancroft, *Gods and Myths of the Aztecs: The History and Development of the Mexican Culture* (New York: Smithmark Publishers, Inc., 1996).

Huxley, Francis, *The Way of the Sacred: The Rites and Symbols, Beliefs and Tabus, That Men Have Held in Awe and Wonder Through the Ages* (New York: Dell Publishing Co., Inc., Laurel Edition, 1976, reprint 1974).

Irwin, Constance, *Fair Gods and Stone Faces: Ancient Seafarers and the New World's Most Intriguing Riddle* (New York: St. Martin's Press, 1963).

James, Harry C., *Pages From Hopi History* (Tucson, Arizona: The University of Arizona Press, 1974).

James, T.G.H., *Ancient Egypt: The Land and Its Legacy* (Austin: University of Texas Press, 1989, 1988).

Jenkins, John Major, *Maya Cosmogenesis 2012: The True Meaning of the Maya Calendar End-Date* (Santa Fe, New Mexico: Bear & Company Publishing, 1998).

Johari, Harish, *Chakras: Energy Centers of Transformation* (Rochester, Vermont: Destiny Books, 1987).

Johnson, Boma, *Earth Figures of the Lower Colorado and Gila River Deserts: A Functional Analysis* (Phoenix, Arizona: Arizona Archaeological Society, 1986).

Johnson, Ginger, *A View of Prehistory in the Prescott Region* (Prescott, Arizona: privately published, 1995).

Jones, Anne Trinkle, and Robert C. Euler, *A Sketch of Grand Canyon Prehistory* (Grand Canyon, Arizona: Grand Canyon Natural History Association, 1979).

Jones, Marc Edmund, *Astrology: How and Why It Works* (New York: Penguins Books, Inc., 1975, reprint 1945).

Joseph, Frank, "Underground City of the Grand Canyon, Fact or Fable?", *Ancient American*, Vol. 5 No. 36, December 2000, Colfax, Wisconsin.

Jung, C.G., translated by R.F.C. Hull, *Aion: Researches Into the Phenomenology of the Self* (Princeton, New Jersey: Princeton University Press, Bollingen Paperback, 1979, reprint 1959).

Jung, C.G., *Psychology and Alchemy*, translated by R.F.C. Hull, *The Collected Works of C.G. Jung*, Vol. 12 (Princeton, New Jersey: Princeton University Press/Bollingen Paperback, 1980, 1968).

Jung, C.G., *The Portable Jung*, translated by R.F.C. Hull, edited by Joseph Campbell (New York: Penguin Books, 1977, reprint 1971).

Kaiser, Rudolf, *The Voice of the Great Spirit: Prophecies of the Hopi Indians*, (Boston: Shambala Publications, Inc., 1989, 1991).

Knight, Christopher, and Robert Lomas, *The Hiram Key: Pharaohs, Freemasons and the Discovery of the Secret Scrolls of Jesus* (Shaftesbury, Dorset: Element Books, Inc., 1998, 1996).

Knight, Christopher, and Robert Lomas, *The Second Messiah: Templars, the Turin Shroud and the Great Secret of Freemasonry* (New York: Barnes & Noble Books, 2000, 1997).

Knight, Christopher, and Robert Lomas, *Uriel's Machine: Uncovering the Secrets of Stonehenge, Noah's Flood, and the Dawn of Civilization* (Gloucester, Massachusetts: Fair Winds Press, 2001, 1999).

Krupp, E.C., *Beyond the Blue Horizon: Myths and Legends of the Sun, Moon, Stars and Planets* (New York: Harper Collins, 1991).

Krupp, E.C., "Engraved in Stone," *Sky & Telescope*, April 1995.

Krupp, E.C., *Skywatchers, Shamans, & Kings: Astronomy and the Archaeology of Power* (New York: John Wiley & Sons, Inc., 1997).

Lamb, Susan, *Montezuma Castle National Monument* (Tucson, Arizona: Southwest Parks and Monument Association, 1993).

Landa, Friar Diego de, *Yucatan: Before and After the Conquest*, translated by William Gates (New York: Dover Publications, Inc., 1978).

Laurence, Richard, translator, *The Book of Enoch the Prophet*, (San Diego: Wizards Bookshelf, 1983, reprint 1883).

Lawrence, D. H., *Mornings In Mexico* (Salt Lake City, Utah: Gibbs M. Smith, Inc., 1982, 1927).

Lee, Bourke, *Death Valley Men* (New York: MacMillan Co., 1932).

Leonard, Jonathan Norton, *Ancient America* (New York: Time Inc., 1967).

Lekson, Stephen H., *The Chaco Meridian: Centers of Political Power in the Ancient Southwest* (Walnut Creek, California: Altamira Press, 1999).

Lewis, David, *We, the Navigators: The Ancient Art of Landfinding in the Pacific* (Honolulu: The University Press of Hawaii, 1979, 1972).

Ley, Willy, *Watchers of the Skies: An Informal History of Astronomy From Babylon To the Space Age* (New York: The Viking Press, 1969, 1963).

Lister, Robert H., and Florence C. Lister, *Those Who Came Before: Southwestern Archeology in the National Park System* (Tucson, Arizona: Southwestern Parks and Monuments Association, 1994, reprint 1993).

Loftin, John D., *Religion and Hopi Life In the Twentieth Century* (Bloomington, Indiana: Indiana University Press, 1994, reprint 1991).

Lomatuway'ma, Michael, Lorena Lomatuway'ma, and Sidney Namingha, Jr., *Hopi Ruin Legends*, collected by Ekkehart Malotki (Lincoln, Nebraska: University of Nebraska, 1993).

Lopez, Barry, "Searching for Ancestors," *Crossing Open Ground* (New York: Charles Scribner's Sons, 1988).

Lowe, Charles H., *Arizona's Natural Environment: Landscapes and Habitats* (Tucson, Arizona: The University of Arizona Press), 1985).

Luckert, Karl W., *Olmec Religion: Key to Middle America and Beyond* (Norman: University of Oklahoma Press, 1976).

MacGregor, John C., *Southwestern Archaeology* (Urbana, Illinois: University of Illinois, 1977, reprint 1941).

Mails, Thomas E., *The Pueblo Children of the Earth Mother*, Vol. II (New York: Doubleday & Company, Inc., 1983).

Mails, Thomas E., and Dan Evehema, *Hotevilla: Hopi Shrine of the Convenant— Microcosm of the World* (New York: Marlowe & Company, 1995).

Mails, Thomas E., *The Hopi Survival Kit* (New York: Penguin Book USA Inc./Arkana, 1997).

Mallery, Garrick, *Picture Writing of the American Indian*, Vol. I and Vol II (New York: Dover Publications, Inc., 1972, reprint of *Tenth Annual Report to the Bureau of American Ethnology,1888-1889,* 1893).

Malmström, Vincent H., *Cycles of the Sun, Mysteries of the Moon* (Austin: University of Texas Press, 1997).

Malotki, Ekkehart, *Earth Fire: A Hopi Legend of the Sunset Crater Eruption* (Flagstaff, Arizona: Northland Press, 1987).

Malotki, Ekkehart, and Michael Lomatuway'ma, drawings by Petra Roeckerath, *Maasaw: Profile of a Hopi God* (Lincoln, Nebraska: University of Nebraska Press, 1987).

Malotki, Ekkehart, and Michael Lomatuway'ma, drawings by Petra Roeckerath, *Stories of Maasaw, A Hopi God* (Lincoln, Nebraska: University of Nebraska Press, 1987).

Malotki, Ekkehart, editor, *Hopi Dictionary: A Hopi-English Dictionary of the Third Mesa Dialect* (Tucson, Arizona: The University of Arizona Press, 1998).

Malville, J. McKim, and Claudia Putnam, *Prehistoric Astronomy in the Southwest* (Boulder, Colorado: Johnson Books, 1993, 1989).

Marrs, Jim, *Rule By Secrecy: The Hidden History That Connects the Trilateral Commission, the Freemasons, and the Great Pyramids* (New York: Perennial/Harper-Collins Publishers, 2001, 2000).

Marshall, Michael P., "The Chacoan Roads: A Cosmological Interpretation," *Anasazi Architecture and American Design,* edited by Baker H. Morrow and V.B. Price (Albuquerque, New Mexico: University of New Mexico Press, 1997).

Martineau, LaVan, *The Rocks Begin To Speak* (Las Vegas, Nevada: KC Publications, 1994, 1973).

Mathews, Stanley R., and Elwyn Ll. Evans, "The Father of Phoenix," *The Journal of Arizona History* (Arizona Historical Society: Autumn, 1988, Vol. 29 No. 3).

Matlock, Gene D., B.A., M.A., *Yishvara 2000: The Hindu Ancestor of Judaism Speaks to This Millennium!* (San Jose, California: Writer's Showcase, an imprint of iUniverse.com, Inc., 2000).

Mays, Buddy, *Ancient Cities of the Southwest: A Practical Guide to Major Prehistoric Ruins of Arizona, New Mexico, Utah, and Colorado* (San Francisco: Chronicle Books, 1982).

McCluskey, Stephen C., "Historical Archaeoastronomy: The Hopi Example," edited by A.F. Aveni, *Archaeoastronomy In the New World* (Cambridge, Massachusetts: Cambridge University Press, 1982).

McCluskey, "Calendars and Symbolism: Functions of Observation in Hopi Astronomy," *Archaeoastronomy*, no. 15 (Journal for the History of Astronomy, 1990).

McCoy, Ron, *Archaeoastronomy: Skywatching in the Native Southwest* (Flagstaff, Arizona: Museum of Northern Arizona, *Plateau*, Vol. 63 No. 2, 1992).

McCreery, Patricia, and Ekkehart Malotki, *Tapamveni: The Rock Art Galleries of*

*Petrified Forest and Beyond* (Petrified Forest, Arizona: Petrified Forest Museum Association, 1994).

McPherson, Robert S., *Sacred Land, Sacred View: Navajo Perceptions of the Four Corners Region* (Salt Lake City: Brigham Young University, 1995, 1992).

Men, Hunbatz, *Secrets of Mayan Science/Religion*, translated by Diana Gubiseh Ayala and James Jennings Dunlap II (Santa Fe, New Mexico, Bear & Company Publishing, 1990).

Michell, John, *The New View Over Atlantis* (San Francisco: Harper & Row, Publishers, 1983).

Michell, John, *Secrets of the Stones: New Revelations of Astro-archaeology and the Mystical Sciences of Antiquity* (Rochester, Vermont: Inner Traditions International, 1989).

Milbrath, Susan, *Star Gods of the Maya: Astronomy in Art, Folklore, and Calendars* (Austin: University of Texas Press, 1999).

Miller, Crichton E M, *The Golden Thread of Time: A Quest for the Truth and Hidden Knowledge of the Ancients* (Rugby, Warwickshire, United Kingdom: Pendulum Publishing, 2001).

Miller, Crichton E M, "Hidden Mystery of the Celtic Cross," *Ancient American*, Vol. 7 Issue No. 43 (Colfax, Wisconsin).

Miller, Dorcas S., *Stars of the First People: Native American Star Myths and Constellations* (Boulder, Colorado: Pruett Publishing Company, 1997).

Miller, William C., "Two Possible Astronomical Pictographs Found In Northern Arizona," *Plateau: A Quarterly*, Vol. 27 No. 4, 1955.

Mills, Thomas O., *The Truth* (privately published, 1998).

Mindeleff, Victor, *A Study of Pueblo Architecture in Tusayan and Cibola* (Washington: Smithsonian Institution Press, 1989, reprint 1891).

Mitton, Jacqueline, *The Penguin Dictionary of Astronomy* (London: Penguin Books Ltd., 1993, 1991).

Morgan, William N., *Ancient Architecture of the Southwest* (Austin, Texas: University of Texas, 1994).

Muir, John, "The Grand Cañon of the Colorado," *Writing the Western Landscape*, edited by Ann H. Zwinger, (Boston: Beacon Press, 1994).

Mullett, G.M., *Spider Woman Stories: Legends of the Hopi Indians* (Tucson, Arizona: The University of Arizona Press, 1991, reprint 1979).

Murdin, Paul, David Allen, and David Malin, *Catalogue of the Universe* (New York: Crown Publishers, Inc., 1979).

Nequatewa, Edmund, *Truth of a Hopi: Stories Relating To the Origin, Myths and Clan Histories of the Hopi* (Flagstaff, Arizona: Museum of Northern Arizona, 1967, reprint 1936).

*New Larousse Encyclopedia of Mythology* (London: The Hamlyn Publishing Group Limited, 1972, reprint 1959).

Nisbet, Jeff, "The Pyramids of Scotland," *Atlantis Rising*, Number 35 September/October 2002.

Noble, David Grant, *Ancient Ruins of the Southwest: An Archaeological Guide* (Flagstaff, Arizona: Northland Publishing, 1981).

O'Kane, Walter Collins, *The Hopis: Portrait of a Desert People* (Norman: University of Oklahoma Press, 1973, 1953).

Oppelt, Norman T., *Guide to Prehistoric Ruins of the Southwest* (Boulder, Colorado: Pruett Publishing Company, 1989, reprint 1981).

Page, Susanne and Jake, *Hopi* (New York: Abradale Press, Harry N. Abrams, Inc., 1994, reprint 1982).

Parsons, Elsie Clews, *Pueblo Indian Religion*, Vol. 1 (Lincoln, Nebraska: University of Nebraska Press, 1996, 1939).

Patterson, Alex, *A Field Guide To Rock Art Symbols of the Greater Southwest* (Boulder, Colorado: Johnson Books, 1992).

Patterson, Alex, *Hopi Pottery Symbols* (Boulder Colorado: Johnson Books, 1994).

Patterson-Rudolph, Carol, *On the Trail of Spider Woman: Petroglyphs, Pictographs, and Myths of the Southwest* (Santa Fe, New Mexico: Ancient City Press, 1997).

Pennick, Nigel, *Sacred Geometry: Symbolism and Purpose in Religious Structures* (San Francisco: Harper & Row, Publishers, 1982, 1980).

Pike, Albert, *Morals and Dogma of the Ancient and Accepted Scottish Rite of Freemasonry* (Charleston, South Carolina: A. .M. . 5632, 1928, 1906, 1871).

Pike, Donald G., foreword by Frank Waters, photographs by David Muench, *Anasazi: Ancient People of the Rock* (New York: Harmony Books, 1974).

Pilles, Peter J., Jr., "The Southern Sinagua," *People of the Verde Valley* (Flagstaff, Arizona: Museum of Northern Arizona, *Plateau*, Vol. 53 No. 1, 1984, reprint 1981).

Pilles, Peter J., Jr. "The Sinagua: Ancient People of the Flagstaff Region," *Wupatki and Walnut Canyon: New Perspectives on History, Prehistory, and Rock Art*, edited by David Grant Noble (Santa Fe, New Mexico: Ancient City Press, 1993).

Pinkham, Mark Amaru, *Return of the Serpents of Wisdom* (Kempton, Illinois: Adventures Unlimited Press, 1997).

Plog, Stephen, *Ancient Peoples of the American Southwest* (Thames and Hudson, Ltd., 1997).

Powell, J.W., *The Exploration of the Colorado River and its Canyons* (New York: Dover Publications, Inc., 1961, published in 1895 as *Canyons of the Colorado*).

Powell, Major J.W., *The Hopi Villages: The Ancient Province of Tusayan* (Palmer Lake, Colorado: Filter Press, 1972).

Powell, Lawrence Clark, *Arizona: A History* (New York: W.W. Norton & Company, Inc. 1976).

Prabhavananda, Swami, and Frederick Manchester, translators, *The Upanishads: The Breath of the Eternal*, (New York: The New American Library, Inc., 1957).

Prescott, William H., *The Conquest of Mexico* (New York: The Junior Literary Guild, 1934, 1843).

Reid, Jefferson, and Stephanie Whittlesey, *The Archaeology of Ancient Arizona* (Tucson, Arizona: The University of Arizona Press, 1997).

Ricinos, Adrian, *Popol Vuh: Sacred Book of the Ancient Quiché*, Spanish version of the original Maya translated by S.G. Morley and D. Goetz (Norman, Oklahoma: University of Oklahoma Press, 1950).

Roberts, David, "Below the Cliffs of Tombs: Mali's Dogon," *National Geographic*, October 1990.

Roberts, David, *In Search of the Old Ones: Exploring the Anasazi World of the Southwest* (New York: Touchstone Books, Simon & Schuster, 1996).

Rossini, Stéphane, *Egyptian Hieroglyphs: How to Read and Write Them* (New York: Dover Publications, Inc., 1989).

Sagan, Carl, *Cosmos*, (New York: Random House, 1980).

Saner, Reg, *Reaching Keet Seel: Ruin's Echo and the Anasazi* (Salt Lake City: The University of Utah Press, 1998).

Santillana, Giorgio de, and Hertha von Deschend, *Hamlet's Mill: An Essay Investigating the Origins of Human Knowledge and Its Transmission Through Myth* (Boston: David R. Godine, Publisher, Inc., 1998, 1969).

Sartor, J.D., "Meteorological Investigation of the Wupatki Blowhole System," *Plateau*, Vol. 37 No. 1 Summer, 1964.

Schaaf, Gregory, photography by Lewis Kemper, *Ancient Ancestors of the Southwest* (Graphic Arts Center Publishing, 1996).

Schaafsma, Polly, *Indian Rock Art of the Southwest* (Santa Fe and Albuquerque, New Mexico: School of American Research and University of New Mexico Press, 1995, 1980).

Schaafsma, Polly, "Rock Art at Wupatki—Pots, Textile, Glyphs," *Wupatki and Walnut Canyon*, edited by David Grant Noble (Santa Fe, New Mexico: Ancient City Press,

1993, 1987).

Schaafsma, Polly, "Shamans' Gallery: A Grand Canyon Rock Art Site," *Kiva*, Vol. 55 No. 3 (Tucson, Arizona: Arizona Archaeological Society, Inc., 1990).

Schaafsma, Polly, *Rock Art In New Mexico* (Santa Fe: Museum of New Mexico Press, 1992).

Schaafsma, Polly, "The Prehistoric Kachina Cult and Its Origins as Suggested by Southwestern Rock Art," *Kachinas in the Pueblo World*, Polly Schaafsma, editor (Albuquerque: University of New Mexico Press, 1994).

Schaafsma, Polly, *Warrior, Shield, and Star: Imagery and Ideology of Pueblo Warfare* (Santa Fe: Western Edge Press, 2000).

Schele, Linda, and Peter Mathews, *The Code of Kings: The Language of Seven Sacred Maya Temples and Tombs* (New York: Scribner/Simon and Schuster, Inc., 1998).

Schroeder, Albert H., and Homer F. Hastings, *Montezuma Castle* (Washington D.C.: National Park Service, U.S. Dept. of Interior, 1985, reprint 1954).

Scully, Vincent, *Pueblo: Mountain, Village, Dance* (Chicago: University of Chicago Press, 1989, reprint 1975).

Seaman, P. David, *Hopi Dictionary* (Flagstaff, Arizona: Northern Arizona University Anthropological Paper No. 2, 1996, reprint 1985).

Secakuku, Alph H., *Following the Sun and Moon: Hopi Kachina Tradition* (Flagstaff, Arizona: Northland Publishing in cooperation with the Heard Museum, 1998, reprint 1995).

Séjourné, Laurette, *Burning Water: Thought and Religion in Ancient Mexico* (New York: Grove Press, Inc., Evergreen Paperbacks, 1960).

Senior, Willoughby F., *Smoke Upon the Winds* (Denver, Colorado: Sage Books, 1961).

Shipley, Joseph T., *The Origins of English Words: A Discursive Dictionary of Indo-European Roots* (Baltimore: Johns Hopkins University Press, 1984).

Silko, Leslie Marmon, *Storyteller* (New York: Seaver Books, 1981).

Silko, Leslie Marmon, *Yellow Woman and a Beauty of the Spirit: Essays On Native American Life Today* (New York: Simon & Schuster, A Touchstone Book, 1997, reprint 1996).

Sitchin, Zecharia, *The 12th Planet* (New York: Avon Books, 1978, 1976).

Sitchin, Zecharia, *The Wars of Gods and Men* (New York: Avon Books, 1985).

Sitchin, Zecharia, *The Lost Realms* (New York: Avon Books, 1990).

Smith, LL.D., William, *Smith's Bible Dictionary* (New York: Family Library, 1973).

Smith, Stan, "House of the Badlands," *Arizona Highways*, August, 1993.

Smith, Watson, edited by Raymond H. Thompson, *When Is a Kiva and Other Questions About Southwestern Archaeology* (Tucson, Arizona: The University of Arizona Press, 1990).

Snyder, Ernest E., *Prehistoric Arizona* (Phoenix: Golden West Publishers, 1987).

Snyder, Gary, *Turtle Island* (New York: New Directions Books, 1974).

Sofaer, Anna P., and Rolf M. Sinclair, *Astronomy and Ceremony in the Prehistoric Southwest*, edited by John B. Carlson and W. James Judge (Maxwell Museum of Anthropology, Anthropological Papers, No. 2, 1983).

Sofaer, Anna, "The Primary Architecture of the Chacoan Culture: A Cosmological Expression," *Anasazi Architecture and American Design*, edited by Baker H. Morrow and V.B. Price (Albuquerque, New Mexico: University of New Mexico Press, 1997).

Soustelle, Jacques, *The Daily Life of the Aztecs On the Eve of the Spanish Conquest* (New York: MacMillan Company, 1962).

Staal, Julius D.W., *The New Patterns in the Sky: Myths and Legends of the Stars* (Blacksburg, Virginia: The McDonald and Woodward Publishing Company, 1988).

Stein, John R., and Stephen H. Lekson, "Anasazi Ritual Landscapes," *Chaco Canyon: A Center and Its World* (Santa Fe: Museum of New Mexico Press, 1994, 1992).

Stephen, Alexander M., "Hopi Tales," *The Journal of American Folklore*, Vol. 42, No. 163, January/March, 1929.

Stephen, Alexander M., and Elsie Clew Parsons, editor, *Hopi Journal*, Vol. I & Vol. II

(New York: AMS Press, Inc., 1969, reprint 1936).

Stephens, John Lloyd, *Incidents of Travel in Yucatan*, edited by Karl Ackerman (Washington: Smithsonian Institution Press, 1996).

Sturluson, Snorri, *The Prose Edda: Tales From Norse Mythology* (Berkeley: University of California Press, 1954).

Talayesva, Don, edited by Leo W. Simmons, *Sun Chief: An Autobiography of a Hopi Indian* (New Haven: Yale University Press, 1974, 1942).

*The Taming of the Salt: a collection of biographies of pioneers who contributed significantly to water development in the Salt River Valley* (Phoenix: Communications & Public Affairs Department of the Salt River Project, 1979).

Tedlock, Dennis, translator and commentator, *Popol Vuh: The Mayan Book of the Dawn of Life* (New York: Touchstone Books, Simon & Schuster, Inc., 1986, 1985).

Temple, Robert K.G., *The Sirius Mystery* (Rochester, Vermont: Destiny Books, 1987, 1976).

Thompson, J. Eric S., *The Rise and Fall of Maya Civilization* (Norman: University of Oklahoma Press, 1970, 1954).

Thompson, J. Eric S., *Maya History and Religion* (Norman: University of Oklahoma Press, 1990, 1970).

Thybony, Scott, *A Guide to Sunset Crater and Wupatki* (Tucson, Arizona: Southwest Parks and Monuments Association, 1987).

Thybony, Scott, *Walnut Canyon National Monument* (Tucson, Arizona: Southwest Parks and Monuments Association, 1988).

Thybony, Scott, *Canyon de Chelly National Monument* (Tucson, Arizona: Southwest Parks and Monument Association, 1997).

Timms, Moira, *Beyond Prophecies and Predictions: Everyone's Guide to the Coming Changes* (New York: Ballantine Books, 1994, 1980).

Titiev, Mischa, *Old Oraibi: A Study of the Hopi Indians of Third Mesa* (Albuquerque, New Mexico: University of New Mexico Press, 1992, reprint 1944).

Turner, Christy G., II, and Jacqueline A. Turner, *Man Corn: Cannibalism and Violence in the Prehistoric American Southwest* (Salt Lake City: The University of Utah Press, 1999).

Tyler, Hamilton A., *Pueblo Gods and Myths* (Norman, Oklahoma: University of Oklahoma Press, 1964).

Van Toen, Donna, "Alice Bailey Revisited," edited by Joan McEvers, *Spiritual, Metaphysical & New Trends In Modern Astrology* (St. Paul, Minnesota: Llewellyn Publications, 1988).

Velikovsky, Immanuel, *Worlds In Collision* (New York: Simon & Schuster, Inc.—Pocket Books, 1977, reprint 1950).

Voth, H.R., *The Traditions of the Hopi* (Chicago: Field Columbian Museum, Pub. 96, Anthropological Series, Vol. VIII, March, 1905).

Wagoner, Jay J., *Arizona Territory 1863-1912: A Political History* (Tucson: The University of Arizona Press, 1980, 1970).

Walker, William H., *Homol'ovi: A Cultural Crossroads* (Tucson, Arizona: Arizona Archaeological Society, Homol'ovi Chapter, 1996).

Waters, Frank, and Oswald White Bear Fredericks, *Book of the Hopi* (New York: Penguin Books, 1987, reprint 1963).

Waters, Frank, *Mexico Mystique: the Coming Sixth World of Consciousness* (Chicago: The Swallow Press, Inc., 1975).

Weltfish, Gene, *The Lost Universe: Pawnee Life and Culture* (Lincoln: University of Nebraska Press, 1977, reprint 1965).

West, John Anthony, *Serpent In the Sky: The High Wisdom of Ancient Egypt* (Wheaton, Illinois: Quest Books, The Theosophical Publishing House, 1993, reprint, 1979).

Westheim, Paul, *The Art of Ancient Mexico* (Garden City, New York: Anchor Books/Doubleday & Co., 1965).

White, Brian, "Underworld Cult of the Pueblo People," *Ancient American*, Vol. 6 No. 42, November/December 2001, Colfax, Wisconsin.

White, Jon Manchip, *A World Elsewhere: Life In the American Southwest* (College Station, Texas: Texas A&M University Press, 1989, reprint 1975).

Whiteley, Peter, *Bacavi: Journey To Reed Springs* (Flagstaff, Arizona: Northland Press, 1988).

Whiteley, Peter, *Rethinking Hopi Ethnography* (Washington: Smithsonian Institute Press, 1998).

Whiting, Alfred F., "Hopi Kachinas," *Plateau*. Vol. 37 No. 1, Summer, 1964 (Flagstaff, Arizona: Northern Arizona Society of Science and Art, Inc.).

Whitley, David S., *A Guide to Rock Art in Southern California and Southern Nevada* (Missoula, Montana: Mountain Press Publishing Company, 1996).

Whitman, Walt, *An American Primer*, edited by Horace Traubel, (San Francisco: City Lights Books, 1970, reprint 1904).

Whorf, Benjamin Lee, edited by John B. Carroll, *Language, Thought, and Reality: Selected Writings of Benjamin Lee Whorf* (Cambridge, Massachusetts: The M.I.T. Press, 1971, reprint 1956).

Widdison, Jerold G., editor., *The Anasazi: Why Did They Leave? Where Did They Go? (An Informal Discussion)* (Albuquerque, New Mexico: Southwest Natural and Cultural Heritage Association, 1991).

Wilcox, David R., "Hohokam Social Complexity," *Chaco & Hohokam: Prehistoric Regional Systems in the American Southwest*, edited by Patricia L. Crown and W. James Judge (Santa Fe, New Mexico: School of American Research Press, 1991).

Wilcox, David R., Gerald Robertson, Jr., and J. Scott Wood, "Perry Mesa, A 14th Century Gated Community in Central Arizona," *Plateau Journal*, Vol. 3 No. 1, Summer, 1999, pp. 45-61.

Williamson, George Hunt, *Road In the Sky* (London: Neville Spearman, 1959).

Williamson, Ray A., *Living the Sky: The Cosmos of the American Indian* (Norman, Oklahoma: University of Oklahoma Press, 1989, reprint 1984).

Wolf, Eric R., *Sons of the Shaking Earth: The People of Mexico and Guatemala—Their Land, History, and Culture* (Chicago: University of Chicago Press, 1959).

Wormington, H.M., *Prehistoric Indians of the Southwest* (Denver, Colorado: The Denver Museum of Natural History, 1973, reprint 1947).

Wright, Barton, *Hopi Kachinas: the Complete Guide to Collecting Kachina Dolls* (Flagstaff, Arizona: Northland Publishing, 1993, 1977).

Wright, Barton, paintings by Cliff Bahnimptewa, *Kachinas: a Hopi Artist's Documentary* (Flagstaff, Arizona: Northland Publishing, 1990, 1973).

Yava, Albert, *Big Snow Falling: A Tewa-Hopi Indian's Life and Times and the History and Traditions of His People* (Albuquerque: University of New Mexico Press, 1982, 1978).

Young, M. Jane, *Signs From the Ancestors: Zuni Cultural Symbolism and Perceptions of Rock Art* (Albuquerque: University of New Mexico Press, 1988).

Young, M. Jane, "The Interconnection Between Western Puebloan and Mesoamerican Ideology and Cosmology," *Kachinas in the Pueblo World*, edited by Polly Schaafsma (Albuquerque, New Mexico: University of New Mexico Press, 1994).

Zapp, Ivar, and George Erikson, *Atlantis In America: Navigators of the Ancient World* (Kempton, Illinois: Adventures Unlimited Press, 1998).

Zeilik, Michael, *Astronomy: The Evolving Universe* (New York: Harper & Row, Publishers, 1985).

Zinsser, Hans, *Rats, Lice and History: Being a Study in Biography, Which, after Twelve Preliminary Chapters Indispensable for the Preparation of the Lay Reader, Deals With the Life History of TYPHUS FEVER* (Boston: The Atlantic Monthly Press/Little Brown & Co.), 1963, 1934).

# INDEX

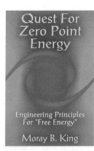

## QUEST FOR ZERO-POINT ENERGY
### Engineering Principles for "Free Energy"
### by Moray B. King

King expands, with diagrams, on how free energy and anti-gravity are possible. The theories of zero point energy maintain there are tremendous fluctuations of electrical field energy embedded within the fabric of space. King explains the following topics: Tapping the Zero-Point Energy as an Energy Source; Fundamentals of a Zero-Point Energy Technology; Vacuum Energy Vortices; The Super Tube; Charge Clusters: The Basis of Zero-Point Energy Inventions; Vortex Filaments, Torsion Fields and the Zero-Point Energy; Transforming the Planet with a Zero-Point Energy Experiment; Dual Vortex Forms: The Key to a Large Zero-Point Energy Coherence. Packed with diagrams, patents and photos. With power shortages now a daily reality in many parts of the world, this book offers a fresh approach very rarely mentioned in the mainstream media.
**224 PAGES. 6x9 PAPERBACK. ILLUSTRATED. $14.95. CODE: QZPE**

## TAPPING THE ZERO POINT ENERGY
### Free Energy & Anti-Gravity in Today's Physics
### by Moray B. King

King explains how free energy and anti-gravity are possible. The theories of the zero point energy maintain there are tremendous fluctuations of electrical field energy imbedded within the fabric of space. This book tells how, in the 1930s, inventor T. Henry Moray could produce a fifty kilowatt "free energy" machine; how an electrified plasma vortex creates anti-gravity; how the Pons/Fleischmann "cold fusion" experiment could produce tremendous heat without fusion; and how certain experiments might produce a gravitational anomaly.
**180 PAGES. 5x8 PAPERBACK. ILLUSTRATED. $12.95. CODE: TAP**

## THE FREE-ENERGY DEVICE HANDBOOK
### A Compilation of Patents and Reports
### by David Hatcher Childress

A large-format compilation of various patents, papers, descriptions and diagrams concerning free-energy devices and systems. *The Free-Energy Device Handbook* is a visual tool for experimenters and researchers into magnetic motors and other "over-unity" devices. With chapters on the Adams Motor, the Hans Coler Generator, cold fusion, superconductors, "N" machines, space-energy generators, Nikola Tesla, T. Townsend Brown, and the latest in free-energy devices. Packed with photos, technical diagrams, patents and fascinating information, this book belongs on every science shelf. With energy and profit being a major political reason for fighting various wars, free-energy devices, if ever allowed to be mass distributed to consumers, could change the world! Get your copy now before the Department of Energy bans this book!
**292 PAGES. 8x10 PAPERBACK. ILLUSTRATED. BIBLIOGRAPHY. $16.95. CODE: FEH**

## ETHER TECHNOLOGY
### A Rational Approach to Gravity Control
### by Rho Sigma

This classic book on anti-gravity and free energy is back in print and back in stock. Written by a well-known American scientist under the pseudonym of "Rho Sigma," this book delves into international efforts at gravity control and discoid craft propulsion. Before the Quantum Field, there was "Ether." This small, but informative book has chapters on John Searle and "Searle discs;" T. Townsend Brown and his work on anti-gravity and ether-vortex turbines. Includes a forward by former NASA astronaut Edgar Mitchell.
**108 PAGES. 6x9 PAPERBACK. ILLUSTRATED. $12.95. CODE: ETT**

## THE TIME TRAVEL HANDBOOK
### A Manual of Practical Teleportation & Time Travel
### edited by David Hatcher Childress

In the tradition of *The Anti-Gravity Handbook* and *The Free-Energy Device Handbook*, science and UFO author David Hatcher Childress takes us into the weird world of time travel and teleportation. Not just a whacked-out look at science fiction, this book is an authoritative chronicling of real-life time travel experiments, teleportation devices and more. *The Time Travel Handbook* takes the reader beyond the government experiments and deep into the uncharted territory of early time travellers such as Nikola Tesla and Guglielmo Marconi and their alleged time travel experiments, as well as the Wilson Brothers of EMI and their connection to the Philadelphia Experiment—the U.S. Navy's forays into invisibility, time travel, and teleportation. Childress looks into the claims of time travelling individuals, and investigates the unusual claim that the pyramids on Mars were built in the future and sent back in time. A highly visual, large format book, with patents, photos and schematics. Be the first on your block to build your own time travel device!
**316 PAGES. 7x10 PAPERBACK. ILLUSTRATED. $16.95. CODE: TTH**

## MAN-MADE UFOS 1944—1994
### Fifty Years of Suppression
### by Renato Vesco & David Hatcher Childress

A comprehensive look at the early "flying saucer" technology of Nazi Germany and the genesis of man-made UFOs. This book takes us from the work of captured German scientists to escaped battalions of Germans, secret communities in South America and Antarctica to todays state-of-the-art "Dreamland" flying machines. Heavily illustrated, this astonishing book blows the lid off the "government UFO conspiracy" and explains with technical diagrams the technology involved. Examined in detail are secret underground airfields and factories; German secret weapons; "suction" aircraft; the origin of NASA; gyroscopic stabilizers and engines; the secret Marconi aircraft factory in South America; and more. Introduction by W.A. Harbinson, author of the Dell novels *GENESIS* and *REVELATION*.
**318 PAGES. 6x9 PAPERBACK. ILLUSTRATED. INDEX & FOOTNOTES. $18.95. CODE: MMU**

# THE A.T. FACTOR
### A Scientists Encounter with UFOs: Piece For A Jigsaw Part 3
### by Leonard Cramp

British aerospace engineer Cramp began much of the scientific anti-gravity and UFO propulsion analysis back in 1955 with his landmark book *Space, Gravity & the Flying Saucer* (out-of-print and rare). His next books (available from Adventures Unlimited) *UFOs & Anti-Gravity: Piece for a Jig-Saw* and *The Cosmic Matrix: Piece for a Jig-Saw Part 2* began Cramp's in depth look into gravity control, free-energy, and the interlocking web of energy that pervades the universe. In this final book, Cramp brings to a close his detailed and controversial study of UFOs and Anti-Gravity.
**324 PAGES. 6x9 PAPERBACK. ILLUSTRATED. BIBLIOGRAPHY. INDEX. $16.95. CODE: ATF**

# COSMIC MATRIX
### Piece for a Jig-Saw, Part Two
### by Leonard G. Cramp

Leonard G. Cramp, a British aerospace engineer, wrote his first book *Space Gravity and the Flying Saucer* in 1954. Cosmic Matrix is the long-awaited sequel to his 1966 book *UFOs & Anti-Gravity: Piece for a Jig-Saw.* Cramp has had a long history of examining UFO phenomena and has concluded that UFOs use the highest possible aeronautic science to move in the way they do. Cramp examines anti-gravity effects and theorizes that this super-science used by the craft—described in detail in the book—can lift mankind into a new level of technology, transportation and understanding of the universe. The book takes a close look at gravity control, time travel, and the interlocking web of energy between all planets in our solar system with Leonard's unique technical diagrams. A fantastic voyage into the present and future!
**364 PAGES. 6x9 PAPERBACK. ILLUSTRATED. BIBLIOGRAPHY. $16.00. CODE: CMX**

# UFOS AND ANTI-GRAVITY
### Piece For A Jig-Saw
### by Leonard G. Cramp

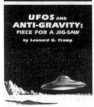

Leonard G. Cramp's 1966 classic book on flying saucer propulsion and suppressed technology is a highly technical look at the UFO phenomena by a trained scientist. Cramp first introduces the idea of 'anti-gravity' and introduces us to the various theories of gravitation. He then examines the technology necessary to build a flying saucer and examines in great detail the technical aspects of such a craft. Cramp's book is a wealth of material and diagrams on flying saucers, anti-gravity, suppressed technology, G-fields and UFOs. Chapters include Crossroads of Aerodymanics, Aerodynamic Saucers, Limitations of Rocketry, Gravitation and the Ether, Gravitational Spaceships, G-Field Lift Effects, The Bi-Field Theory, VTOL and Hovercraft, Analysis of UFO photos, more.
**388 PAGES. 6x9 PAPERBACK. ILLUSTRATED. $16.95. CODE: UAG**

# THE TESLA PAPERS
### Nikola Tesla on Free Energy & Wireless Transmission of Power
### by Nikola Tesla, edited by David Hatcher Childress

David Hatcher Childress takes us into the incredible world of Nikola Tesla and his amazing inventions. Tesla's rare article "The Problem of Increasing Human Energy with Special Reference to the Harnessing of the Sun's Energy" is included. This lengthy article was originally published in the June 1900 issue of *The Century Illustrated Monthly Magazine* and it was the outline for Tesla's master blueprint for the world. Tesla's fantastic vision of the future, including wireless power, anti-gravity, free energy and highly advanced solar power. Also included are some of the papers, patents and material collected on Tesla at the Colorado Springs Tesla Symposiums, including papers on: •The Secret History of Wireless Transmission •Tesla and the Magnifying Transmitter •Design and Construction of a Half-Wave Tesla Coil •Electrostatics: A Key to Free Energy •Progress in Zero-Point Energy Research •Electromagnetic Energy from Antennas to Atoms •Tesla's Particle Beam Technology •Fundamental Excitatory Modes of the Earth-Ionosphere Cavity
**325 PAGES. 8x10 PAPERBACK. ILLUSTRATED. $16.95. CODE: TTP**

# THE FANTASTIC INVENTIONS OF NIKOLA TESLA
### by Nikola Tesla with additional material by David Hatcher Childress

This book is a readable compendium of patents, diagrams, photos and explanations of the many incredible inventions of the originator of the modern era of electrification. In Tesla's own words are such topics as wireless transmission of power, death rays, and radio-controlled airships. In addition, rare material on German bases in Antarctica and South America, and a secret city built at a remote jungle site in South America by one of Tesla's students, Guglielmo Marconi. Marconi's secret group claims to have built flying saucers in the 1940s and to have gone to Mars in the early 1950s! Incredible photos of these Tesla craft are included. The Ancient Atlantean system of broadcasting energy through a grid system of obelisks and pyramids is discussed, and a fascinating concept comes out of one chapter: that Egyptian engineers had to wear protective metal head-shields while in these power plants, hence the Egyptian Pharoah's head covering as well as the Face on Mars! •His plan to transmit free electricity into the atmosphere. •How electrical devices would work using only small antennas. •Why unlimited power could be utilized anywhere on earth. •How radio and radar technology can be used as death-ray weapons in Star Wars.
**342 PAGES. 6x9 PAPERBACK. ILLUSTRATED. $16.95. CODE: FINT**

## REICH OF THE BLACK SUN
### Nazi Secret Weapons and the Cold War Allied Legend
### by Joseph P. Farrell

Why were the Allies worried about an atom bomb attack by the Germans in 1944? Why did the Soviets threaten to use poison gas against the Germans? Why did Hitler in 1945 insist that holding Prague could win the war for the Third Reich? Why did US General George Patton's Third Army race for the Skoda works at Pilsen in Czechoslovakia instead of Berlin? Why did the US Army not test the uranium atom bomb it dropped on Hiroshima? Why did the Luftwaffe fly a non-stop round trip mission to within twenty miles of New York City in 1944? *Reich of the Black Sun* takes the reader on a scientific-historical journey in order to answer these questions. Arguing that Nazi Germany actually won the race for the atom bomb in late 1944, and then goes on to explore the even more secretive research the Nazis were conducting into the occult, alternative physics and new energy sources.

**352 PAGES. 6X9 PAPERBACK. ILLUSTRATED. BIBLIOGRAPHY. $16.95. CODE: ROBS**

## SAUCERS OF THE ILLUMINATI
### by Jim Keith, Foreword by Kenn Thomas

Seeking the truth behind stories of alien invasion, secret underground bases, and the secret plans of the New World Order, *Saucers of the Illuminati* offers ground breaking research, uncovering clues to the nature of UFOs and to forces even more sinister: the secret cabal behind planetary control! Includes mind control, saucer abductions, the MJ-12 documents, cattle mutilations, government anti-gravity testing, the Sirius Connection, science fiction author Philip K. Dick and his efforts to expose the Illuminati, plus more from veteran conspiracy and UFO author Keith. Conspiracy expert Keith's final book on UFOs and the highly secret group that manufactures them and uses them for their own purposes: the control and manipulation of the population of planet Earth.

**148 PAGES. 6X9 PAPERBACK. ILLUSTRATED. $12.95. CODE: SOIL**

## THE ENERGY MACHINE OF T. HENRY MORAY
### by Moray B. King

In the 1920s T. Henry Moray invented a "free energy" device that reportedly output 50 kilowatts of electricity. It could not be explained by standard science at that time. The electricity exhibited a strange "cold current" characteristic where thin wires could conduct appreciable power without heating. Moray suffered ruthless suppression, and in 1939 the device was destroyed. Frontier science lecturer and author Moray B. King explains the invention with today's science. Modern physics recognizes that the vacuum contains tremendous energy called the zero-point energy. A way to coherently activate it appears surprisingly simple: first create a glow plasma or corona, then abruptly pulse it. Other inventors have discovered this approach (sometimes unwittingly) to create novel energy devices, and they too were suppressed. The common pattern of their technologies clarified the fundamental operating principle. King hopes to inspire engineers and inventors so that a new energy source can become available to mankind.

**192 PAGES. 6X8 PAPERBACK. ILLUSTRATED. $14.95. CODE: EMHM**

## THE ENERGY GRID
### Harmonic 695, The Pulse of the Universe
### by Captain Bruce Cathie.

This is the breakthrough book that explores the incredible potential of the Energy Grid and the Earth's Unified Field all around us. Cathie's first book, *Harmonic 33*, was published in 1968 when he was a commercial pilot in New Zealand. Since then, Captain Bruce Cathie has been the premier investigator into the amazing potential of the infinite energy that surrounds our planet every microsecond. Cathie investigates the Harmonics of Light and how the Energy Grid is created. In this amazing book are chapters on UFO Propulsion, Nikola Tesla, Unified Equations, the Mysterious Aerials, Pythagoras & the Grid, Nuclear Detonation and the Grid, Maps of the Ancients, an Australian Stonehenge examined, more.

**255 PAGES. 6X9 TRADEPAPER. ILLUSTRATED. $15.95. CODE: TEG**

## THE BRIDGE TO INFINITY
### Harmonic 371244
### by Captain Bruce Cathie

Cathie has popularized the concept that the earth is crisscrossed by an electromagnetic grid system that can be used for anti-gravity, free energy, levitation and more. The book includes a new analysis of the harmonic nature of reality, acoustic levitation, pyramid power, harmonic receiver towers and UFO propulsion. It concludes that today's scientists have at their command a fantastic store of knowledge with which to advance the welfare of the human race.

**204 PAGES. 6X9 TRADEPAPER. ILLUSTRATED. $14.95. CODE: BTF**

## THE HARMONIC CONQUEST OF SPACE
### by Captain Bruce Cathie

Chapters include: Mathematics of the World Grid; the Harmonics of Hiroshima and Nagasaki; Harmonic Transmission and Receiving; the Link Between Human Brain Waves; the Cavity Resonance between the Earth; the Ionosphere and Gravity; Edgar Cayce—the Harmonics of the Subconscious; Stonehenge; the Harmonics of the Moon; the Pyramids of Mars; Nikola Tesla's Electric Car; the Robert Adams Pulsed Electric Motor Generator; Harmonic Clues to the Unified Field; and more. Also included are tables showing the harmonic relations between the earth's magnetic field, the speed of light, and anti-gravity/gravity acceleration at different points on the earth's surface. New chapters in this edition on the giant stone spheres of Costa Rica, Atomic Tests and Volcanic Activity, and a chapter on Ayers Rock analysed with Stone Mountain, Georgia.

**248 PAGES. 6X9. PAPERBACK. ILLUSTRATED. BIBLIOGRAPHY. $16.95. CODE: HCS**

# THE ANTI-GRAVITY HANDBOOK
### edited by David Hatcher Childress, with Nikola Tesla, T.B. Paulicki, Bruce Cathie, Albert Einstein and others

The new expanded compilation of material on Anti-Gravity, Free Energy, Flying Saucer Propulsion, UFOs, Suppressed Technology, NASA Cover-ups and more. Highly illustrated with patents, technical illustrations and photos. This revised and expanded edition has more material, including photos of Area 51, Nevada, the government's secret testing facility. This classic on weird science is back in a 90s format!
• **How to build a flying saucer.**
• **Arthur C. Clarke on Anti-Gravity.**
• **Crystals and their role in levitation.**
• **Secret government research and development.**
• **Nikola Tesla on how anti-gravity airships could draw power from the atmosphere.**
• **Bruce Cathie's Anti-Gravity Equation.**
• **NASA, the Moon and Anti-Gravity.**
230 PAGES. 7X10 PAPERBACK. ILLUSTRATED. $14.95. CODE: **AGH**

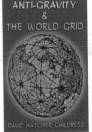

# ANTI–GRAVITY & THE WORLD GRID

Is the earth surrounded by an intricate electromagnetic grid network offering free energy? This compilation of material on ley lines and world power points contains chapters on the geography, mathematics, and light harmonics of the earth grid. Learn the purpose of ley lines and ancient megalithic structures located on the grid. Discover how the grid made the Philadelphia Experiment possible. Explore the Coral Castle and many other mysteries, including acoustic levitation, Tesla Shields and scalar wave weaponry. Browse through the section on anti-gravity patents, and research resources.
274 PAGES. 7X10 PAPERBACK. ILLUSTRATED. $14.95. CODE: **AGW**

# ANTI–GRAVITY & THE UNIFIED FIELD
### edited by David Hatcher Childress

Is Einstein's Unified Field Theory the answer to all of our energy problems? Explored in this compilation of material is how gravity, electricity and magnetism manifest from a unified field around us. Why artificial gravity is possible; secrets of UFO propulsion; free energy; Nikola Tesla and anti-gravity airships of the 20s and 30s; flying saucers as superconducting whirls of plasma; anti-mass generators; vortex propulsion; suppressed technology; government cover-ups; gravitational pulse drive; spacecraft & more.
240 PAGES. 7X10 PAPERBACK. ILLUSTRATED. $14.95. CODE: **AGU**

# THE GIZA DEATH STAR
### The Paleophysics of the Great Pyramid & the Military Complex at Giza
### by Joseph P. Farrell

Physicist Joseph Farrell's amazing book on the secrets of Great Pyramid of Giza. *The Giza Death Star* starts where British engineer Christopher Dunn leaves off in his 1998 book, *The Giza Power Plant*. Was the Giza complex part of a military installation over 10,000 years ago? Chapters include: An Archaeology of Mass Destruction, Thoth and Theories; The Machine Hypothesis; Pythagoras, Plato, Planck, and the Pyramid; The Weapon Hypothesis; Encoded Harmonics of the Planck Units in the Great Pyramid; High Fregquency Direct Current "Impulse" Technology; The Grand Gallery and its Crystals: Gravito-acoustic Resonators; The Other Two Large Pyramids; the "Causeways," and the "Temples"; A Phase Conjugate Howitzer; Evidence of the Use of Weapons of Mass Destruction in Ancient Times; more.
290 PAGES. 6X9 PAPERBACK. ILLUSTRATED. $16.95. CODE: **GDS**

# DARK MOON
### Apollo and the Whistleblowers
### by Mary Bennett and David Percy

•Was Neil Armstrong really the first man on the Moon?
•Did you know a second craft was going to the Moon at the same time as Apollo 11?
•Do you know that potentially lethal radiation is prevalent throughout deep space?
•Do you know there are serious discrepancies in the account of the Apollo 13 'accident'?
•Did you know that 'live' color TV from the Moon was not actually live at all?
•Do you know that the Lunar Surface Camera had no viewfinder?
•Do you know that lighting was used in the Apollo photographs—yet no lighting equipment was taken to the Moon?
All these questions, and more, are discussed in great detail by British researchers Bennett and Percy in *Dark Moon*, the definitive book (nearly 600 pages) on the possible faking of the Apollo Moon missions. Bennett and Percy delve into every possible aspect of this beguiling theory, one that rocks the very foundation of our beliefs concerning NASA and the space program. Tons of NASA photos analyzed for possible deceptions.
568 PAGES. 6X9 PAPERBACK. ILLUSTRATED. BIBLIOGRAPHY. INDEX. $25.00. CODE: **DMO**

## TECHNOLOGY OF THE GODS
### The Incredible Sciences of the Ancients
### by David Hatcher Childress

Popular *Lost Cities* author David Hatcher Childress takes us into the amazing world of ancient technology, from computers in antiquity to the "flying machines of the gods." Childress looks at the technology that was allegedly used in Atlantis and the theory that the Great Pyramid of Egypt was originally a gigantic power station. He examines tales of ancient flight and the technology that it involved; how the ancients used electricity; megalithic building techniques; the use of crystal lenses and the fire from the gods; evidence of various high tech weapons in the past, including atomic weapons; ancient metallurgy and heavy machinery; the role of modern inventors such as Nikola Tesla in bringing ancient technology back into modern use; impossible artifacts; and more.
**356 PAGES. 6x9 PAPERBACK. ILLUSTRATED. BIBLIOGRAPHY. $16.95. CODE: TGOD**

## VIMANA AIRCRAFT OF ANCIENT INDIA & ATLANTIS
### by David Hatcher Childress, introduction by Ivan T. Sanderson

Did the ancients have the technology of flight? In this incredible volume on ancient India, authentic Indian texts such as the *Ramayana* and the *Mahabharata* are used to prove that ancient aircraft were in use more than four thousand years ago. Included in this book is the entire Fourth Century BC manuscript *Vimaanika Shastra* by the ancient author Maharishi Bharadwaaja, translated into English by the Mysore Sanskrit professor G.R. Josyer. Also included are chapters on Atlantean technology, the incredible Rama Empire of India and the devastating wars that destroyed it. Also an entire chapter on mercury vortex propulsion and mercury gyros, the power source described in the ancient Indian texts. Not to be missed by those interested in ancient civilizations or the UFO enigma.
**334 PAGES. 6x9 PAPERBACK. ILLUSTRATED. $15.95. CODE: VAA**

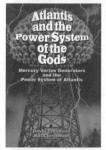

## LOST CONTINENTS & THE HOLLOW EARTH
### I Remember Lemuria and the Shaver Mystery
### by David Hatcher Childress & Richard Shaver

*Lost Continents & the Hollow Earth* is Childress' thorough examination of the early hollow earth stories of Richard Shaver and the fascination that fringe fantasy subjects such as lost continents and the hollow earth have had for the American public. Shaver's rare 1948 book *I Remember Lemuria* is reprinted in its entirety, and the book is packed with illustrations from Ray Palmer's *Amazing Stories* magazine of the 1940s. Palmer and Shaver told of tunnels running through the earth—tunnels inhabited by the Deros and Teros, humanoids from an ancient spacefaring race that had inhabited the earth, eventually going underground, hundreds of thousands of years ago. Childress discusses the famous hollow earth books and delves deep into whatever reality may be behind the stories of tunnels in the earth. Operation High Jump to Antarctica in 1947 and Admiral Byrd's bizarre statements, tunnel systems in South America and Tibet, the underground world of Agartha, the belief of UFOs coming from the South Pole, more.
**344 PAGES. 6x9 PAPERBACK. ILLUSTRATED. $16.95. CODE: LCHE**

## ATLANTIS & THE POWER SYSTEM OF THE GODS
### Mercury Vortex Generators & the Power System of Atlantis
### by David Hatcher Childress and Bill Clendenon

*Atlantis and the Power System of the Gods* starts with a reprinting of the rare 1990 book *Mercury: UFO Messenger of the Gods* by Bill Clendenon. Clendenon takes on an unusual voyage into the world of ancient flying vehicles, strange personal UFO sightings, a meeting with a "Man In Black" and then to a centuries-old library in India where he got his ideas for the diagrams of mercury vortex engines. The second part of the book is Childress' fascinating analysis of Nikola Tesla's broadcast system in light of Edgar Cayce's "Terrible Crystal" and the obelisks of ancient Egypt and Ethiopia. Includes: Atlantis and its crystal power towers that broadcast energy; how these incredible power stations may still exist today; inventor Nikola Tesla's nearly identical system of power transmission; Mercury Proton Gyros and mercury vortex propulsion; more. Richly illustrated, and packed with evidence that Atlantis not only existed—it had a world-wide energy system more sophisticated than ours today.
**246 PAGES. 6x9 PAPERBACK. ILLUSTRATED. $15.95. CODE: APSG**

## A HITCHHIKER'S GUIDE TO ARMAGEDDON
### by David Hatcher Childress

With wit and humor, popular Lost Cities author David Hatcher Childress takes us around the world and back in his trippy finalé to the Lost Cities series. He's off on an adventure in search of the apocalypse and end times. Childress hits the road from the fortress of Megiddo, the legendary citadel in northern Israel where Armageddon is prophesied to start. Hitchhiking around the world, Childress takes us from one adventure to another, to ancient cities in the deserts and the legends of worlds before our own. Childress muses on the rise and fall of civilizations, and the forces that have shaped mankind over the millennia, including wars, invasions and cataclysms. He discusses the ancient Armageddons of the past, and chronicles recent Middle East developments and their ominous undertones. In the meantime, he becomes a cargo cult god on a remote island off New Guinea, gets dragged into the Kennedy Assassination by one of the "conspirators," investigates a strange power operating out of the Altai Mountains of Mongolia, and discovers how the Knights Templar and their off-shoots have driven the world toward an epic battle centered around Jerusalem and the Middle East.

**320 PAGES. 6x9 PAPERBACK. ILLUSTRATED. BIBLIOGRAPHY. INDEX. $16.95. CODE: HGA**

**One Adventure Place**
**P.O. Box 74**
**Kempton, Illinois 60946**
**United States of America**
**Tel.: 815-253-6390 • Fax: 815-253-6300**
**Email: auphq@frontiernet.net**
**http://www.adventuresunlimitedpress.com**
**or www.adventuresunlimited.nl**

## ORDERING INSTRUCTIONS

➤➤ Remit by USD$ Check, Money Order or Credit Card

➤➤ Visa, Master Card, Discover & AmEx Accepted

➤➤ Prices May Change Without Notice

➤➤ 10% Discount for 3 or more Items

## SHIPPING CHARGES

### United States

➤➤ Postal Book Rate { $3.00 First Item
                      50¢ Each Additional Item

➤➤ Priority Mail { $4.50 First Item
                   $2.00 Each Additional Item

➤➤ UPS { $5.00 First Item
          $1.50 Each Additional Item

NOTE: UPS Delivery Available to Mainland USA Only

### Canada

➤➤ Postal Book Rate { $6.00 First Item
                       $2.00 Each Additional Item

➤➤ Postal Air Mail { $8.00 First Item
                      $2.50 Each Additional Item

➤➤ Personal Checks or Bank Drafts MUST BE

   USD$ and Drawn on a US Bank

➤➤ Canadian Postal Money Orders OK

➤➤ Payment MUST BE USD$

### All Other Countries

➤➤ Surface Delivery { $10.00 First Item
                       $4.00 Each Additional Item

➤➤ Postal Air Mail { $14.00 First Item
                      $5.00 Each Additional Item

➤➤ Payment MUST BE USD$

➤➤ Checks and Money Orders MUST BE USD$
    and Drawn on a US Bank or branch.

➤➤ Add $5.00 for Air Mail Subscription to
    Future *Adventures Unlimited* Catalogs

## SPECIAL NOTES

➤➤ RETAILERS: Standard Discounts Available

➤➤ BACKORDERS: We Backorder all Out-of-

   Stock Items Unless Otherwise Requested

➤➤ PRO FORMA INVOICES: Available on Request

➤➤ VIDEOS: NTSC Mode Only. Replacement only.

➤➤ For PAL mode videos contact our other offices:

---

*Please check:* ☑

☐ This is my first order   ☐ I have ordered before

| | |
|---|---|
| Name | |
| Address | |
| City | |
| State/Province | Postal Code |
| Country | |
| Phone day | Evening |
| Fax | |

| Item Code | Item Description | Qty | Tota |
|---|---|---|---|
| | | | |
| | | | |
| | | | |
| | | | |
| | | | |
| | | | |
| | | | |
| | | | |
| | | | |
| | | | |
| | | | |
| | | | |

*Please check:* ☑

Subtotal ➡ _____
Less Discount-10% for 3 or more items ➡ _____

☐ Postal-Surface                          Balance ➡ _____

☐ Postal-Air Mail Illinois Residents 6.25% Sales Tax ➡ _____
   (Priority in USA)                Previous Credit ➡ _____

☐ UPS                                    Shipping ➡ _____
   (Mainland USA only) Total (check/MO in USD$ only) ➡ _____

☐ Visa/MasterCard/Discover/Amex

Card Number

Expiration Date

**10% Discount When You Order 3 or More Items!**